T0275199

"Getting down to brass tacks, *Pandora's Toolbox* provides a balanced and sophisticated examination of climate interventions. The reader will take away a rigorous understanding of the engineering, economic, ethical, social, political, and international relations dimensions of climate engineering tools and an informed appreciation for how deployment of a broad range of tools can most effectively reduce the human misery caused by climate change."

Joseph Aldy, Professor of the Practice of Public Policy, Harvard Kennedy School, Cambridge, MA

"A well written, accurate and entertaining guide to climate change and climate intervention techniques that gives readers all the keys to make up their own minds on the topic."

Olivier Boucher, Climatologist, Sorbonne Université, Paris

"With careful explanations of the technologies, policies, governance issues, and ethical dilemmas involved, *Pandora's Toolbox* emerges as 'must reading' for all who seek to understand the pathways to a successful global response to climate change."

Daniel Esty, Hillhouse Professor of Environmental Law and Policy, Yale University, New Haven, CT

"Smith's book is the first-of-its-kind textbook introduction to Carbon Dioxide Removal, embedding the topic in the full spectrum of currently discussed responses, reaching from mitigation and adaptation all the way to Solar Radiation Management. It paves the way for the societal discourse we so urgently need to have now."

Sabine Fuss, Group Leader, Mercator Research Institute on Global Commons and Climate Change, Berlin

"In the Greek myth Pandora was curious and she opened a box thus releasing evils into the world. Here we explore the contents of the box more carefully. In it we find tools useful for climate repair. This great book gives us a ray of hope in a situation where everything looks rather bleak."

Hugh Hunt, Fellow of Trinity College, University of Cambridge, Cambridge, UK

"*Pandora's Toolbox* introduces the reader to climate intervention – if you haven't heard of this yet, you will, because the author makes a compelling case that managing a future world with climate change will need a bigger toolbox. Wake Smith has a remarkable gift for making his subject accessible."

"At last, a realistic and unflinching view of the hard reality of climate choices that are coming. Smith's treatise is that avoiding a dystopian nightmare future requires levels of political courage in our scientific convictions not seen since the Second World War."

"An overview of climate change and the array of possible responses that manages to be simultaneously comprehensive, detailed, and accessible. It's jam-packed with the sort of specific, practical detail that is usually missing in such overviews. A valuable contribution and an impressive achievement."

# Pandora's Toolbox

Reaching net zero emissions will not be the end of the climate struggle, but only the end of the beginning. For centuries thereafter, temperatures will remain elevated; climate damages will continue to accrue; and sea levels will continue to rise. Even the urgent and utterly essential task of reaching net zero cannot be achieved rapidly by emissions reductions alone. To hasten net zero and minimize climate damages thereafter, we will also need massive carbon removal and storage. We may even need to reduce incoming solar radiation in order to lower unacceptably high temperatures. Such unproven and potentially risky climate interventions raise mind-blowing questions of governance and ethics. *Pandora's Toolbox* offers readers an accessible and authoritative introduction to both the hopes and hazards of some of humanity's most controversial technologies, which may nevertheless provide the key to saving our world.

As a lecturer at Yale University, Wake Smith teaches a world-leading undergraduate course on climate intervention, which forms the basis for this book. Smith is also a Senior Fellow at the Mossavar-Rahmani Center for Business and Government at the Harvard Kennedy School, writing scholarly articles on costs, aeronautics, and governance of solar geoengineering. Prior to his academic career, Smith had several executive roles in the aeronautical industry, including the presidency of a division of Boeing.

# Pandora's Toolbox

## The Hopes and Hazards of Climate Intervention

Wake Smith

CAMBRIDGE
UNIVERSITY PRESS

# CAMBRIDGE
## UNIVERSITY PRESS

University Printing House, Cambridge CB2 8BS, United Kingdom

One Liberty Plaza, 20th Floor, New York, NY 10006, USA

477 Williamstown Road, Port Melbourne, VIC 3207, Australia

314–321, 3rd Floor, Plot 3, Splendor Forum, Jasola District Centre,
New Delhi – 110025, India

103 Penang Road, #05–06/07, Visioncrest Commercial, Singapore 238467

Cambridge University Press is part of the University of Cambridge.

It furthers the University's mission by disseminating knowledge in the pursuit of
education, learning, and research at the highest international levels of excellence.

www.cambridge.org
Information on this title: www.cambridge.org/9781316518434
DOI: 10.1017/9781009008877

First published 2022

Printed in the United Kingdom by TJ Books Limited, Padstow, Cornwall

A catalogue record for this publication is available from the British Library.

ISBN 978-1-316-51843-4 Hardback

For Shugs

(of course)

# CONTENTS

# FIGURES

# TABLES

# PROLOGUE

I commence this book shortly after dawn on a rainy London morning in mid-March 2020. Two days ago, the WHO declared the accelerating Coronavirus outbreak a global pandemic, which has dashed my intended agenda for the immediately foreseeable future but has simultaneously hollowed out a window during which to focus on this project.

As I strain to peer through the leaden clouds and over the horizon to foresee where the pandemic will lead, it is tempting to compare that imminent crisis to the much larger arc of climate change – tempting, but specious. At this juncture, I can little foresee whether COVID-19 will inundate graveyards as the "Spanish flu" did 100 years ago or sputter out rather harmlessly like SARS a decade ago, but I expect that I and most of humanity will survive, albeit with scrambled schedules and stories for grandchildren. If you are reading this, it is proof that in both of our cases, that prediction proved true.

Though blind to the status of COVID-19 in a month, I feel much more confident in predicting the trajectory of climate change over the remainder of the century. This may be hubristic but is at minimum reflective of one paradox that besets climate studies, summed up in variations of the recurring question "How can you idiots predict the global climate in 2100 when you can't even predict the local weather in three days?" Fair question.

The answer – unconvincing though this may sound on page one – is that at a very local level in both time and space, air flow turbulence is chaotic and difficult to predict. At that scale, infinitesimal uncertainties can produce greatly divergent manifestations. However, at a global scale and over the span of decades, trends that have been long underway are highly likely to continue for reasons that are well understood, forming at least the fat middle of the bell curve of probable outcomes. As pandemics and financial crises emphasize, the world can and regularly does surprise us, but over the course of this book, I hope to convince you of a few things that have become quite apparent to me. These are that climate change will prove dangerous and more difficult to avoid than most people realize, and that the toolbox of potential therapies broadly referred to as climate intervention or "geoengineering" (I will use those two terms somewhat interchangeably in this book) will prove essential in managing the impacts of that change.

That conviction and this book more generally grow out of a course I teach at Yale, which is, insofar as I am aware, the world's first undergraduate survey course on climate intervention. The maiden voyage of what is now a recurring course followed the trajectory I had planned but led to a conclusion that I had not. I guided a diverse group of bright students with varying degrees of prerequisite knowledge through the basics of climate science, international treaties, technology options, and policy debates to produce by the semester's end a salon of highly informed participants with whom I could debate the most vexing issues of geoengineering governance and climate ethics. By our final session, that process brought me to the conclusion that massive climate intervention is inevitable, and that we therefore need as quickly as possible to investigate all the scientific, engineering, and policy questions that flow from that.

Climate intervention is not the "solution to climate change" – at least not in the sense and to the degree that climate skeptics and fossil fuel lobbyists may wish to portray. We still need primarily and urgently to not only reduce greenhouse gas emissions, but to drive them all the way to zero as soon as possible. The prospect of climate intervention technologies doesn't change that. But the future will also confound perhaps better intentioned but equally misguided evangelists of solar power, afforestation, and fossil fuel divestiture. Photogenic tree-plantings aside, the real work of achieving net zero and then negative emissions will require substantial economic sacrifice by virtually every current and future human for many generations. This is bigger than most people appreciate.

Given that, there likely is no single thing that *will* prove to be the solution to climate change – it will require a portfolio of solutions, and climate intervention will be indispensably crucial to that portfolio. As used herein, climate intervention/geoengineering refer to two distinctly different families of interventions. We are evolving to more discriminating language that distinguishes between the two, but for now, these terms still generally refer to both branches of the field, and to a grab bag of technologies of varying degrees of maturity within those branches. Greenhouse gas removal refers to the branch that seeks via various natural and industrial approaches to remove greenhouse gases (but primarily carbon dioxide) from the climate system and/or the emissions stream. Solar radiation management refers to the alternative branch by which we may seek to reduce the amount of energy from the Sun that is absorbed into the climate system. The technological, economic, and policy challenges associated with all these possible interventions will constitute the heart of this book.

While meaningful climate science is older than most people realize, serious study of geoengineering is remarkably new. If our field were to define a fulcrum date similar to the Anno Domini of the Christian calendar, the beginning of time for climate intervention would be July 25, 2006. On that date, a paper by the late Nobel prize winning Dutch chemist Paul Crutzen argued for lifting the taboo which had previously inhibited open discussion of and research funding for climate intervention. Prior to then, the "moral hazard" concern that knowledge of a possible "Plan B" would reduce the urgency of pursuing "Plan A" (emissions reductions) forced early apostles such as Ken Caldeira and David Keith to explore geoengineering mostly in the shadows. In the post-Crutzen era however, both have received highly prestigious tenured appointments at Stanford and Harvard respectively, and the previous trickle of academic literature has turned into a rushing stream.

However, most of the central scientific and policy questions posed in Crutzen's paper remain unanswered, in part because despite its enormous future importance in preserving the world more-or-less as we know it, most people have never heard of "geoengineering," let alone "climate intervention." The latter term is increasingly favored because it refers to climate specifically rather than the Earth (geo) more generally, and because it doesn't seem to promise the precision that "engineering" does. The field is growing, but the academic community researching it could likely still fit in a basketball arena if not a mid-sized concert hall. For the greenhouse gas removal branch, the key challenge is economic, how to induce the world to pay trillions of dollars annually to fund an industry approximately the size of the fossil fuel industry it is meant to remediate, but which produces a product (negative greenhouse gas emissions) for which there is no traditional market. For the solar radiation management branch, the economics may prove trifling. The challenges there involve guarding against potentially devastating unintended physical consequences and, perhaps more dauntingly, assembling a governance structure that could garner the informed consent of approximately the entire human race to intentionally mess with mother nature in a big way, and for a long time. If those perils cause you to question whether any of this sounds like a good idea, you get full marks for paying attention. Geoengineering in any form sounds like a terrible concept, until you peer carefully into the future and realize that not geoengineering would likely prove worse.

That glance over the horizon is the first part of the journey I propose we take together. We will then get our hands dirty in the climate intervention toolbox and turn thereafter to the even grimier social and philosophical questions that flow from that. We will close by considering where we go from here.

Funding, governing, and implementing these unprecedented climate interventions are problems for tomorrow. Today's problem is that few people know anything about geoengineering. This book and the college course from which it emerged are my modest effort to add to the sum of light and help introduce this topic to a wider audience. Like virtually every other climate intervention researcher I know, I would rather that we live in a future that does not require geoengineering. I would prefer we find a cost-free, risk-free miraculous technique by which not only to bring greenhouse gas emissions to zero in the near future but to draw down carbon stocks from the climate system and preserve the climate in which we live today. I would also prefer that my beloved (accursed) New York Jets football club wins the Superbowl every year, but I have learned via repeated heartbreaks not to count on such miracles.

Instead, the way to bet (and therefore to plan) is that there is a lot of climate change in our future, and that we will need a variety of tools with which to deal with it. Emissions reductions? Urgently. Adaptation to extreme weather and sea level rise? Certainly. But in order to preserve the ecosystems and natural environments that have enabled the human population to burgeon over the last few centuries, we will also need climate intervention. For reasons I hope to make clear, I think it is inevitable.

# ACKNOWLEDGMENTS

This book would not have been realizable without the talent and tireless efforts of my research assistants at Harvard and Yale: Mary McMahon, Claire Henly, and most particularly Umang Bhattarai. I would never have started down this path without the inspiration I received from Peter Davies, who was also my most dedicated manuscript reader. Dillon Smith was a close second.

Had it not been for David Keith's generosity and patience at several junctures, I would have undoubtedly run into various dead ends instead of green lights. Gernot Wagner was an indispensable early collaborator. Joseph Aldy continues helpfully to shape my path. Donald Bingaman and Chris Rice along with Mark Holly and Jim Mace have been essential partners in my aeronautical research.

I thank each of my chapter readers for their expertise and insights: Colleen Golja, Ben Kravitz, Detlef Sprinz, Christof Ruehl, Feisal Rahman, Greg Nemet, Howard Herzog, Stephen Salter, Jesse Reynolds, Josh Horton, Lizzie Burns, and Cody Floerchinger.

Other mentors and colleagues to whom I am grateful for their valuable guidance include Trude Storelvmo, Daniel Smith, Daniel Schrag, John Holdren, Richard Zeckhauser, William Hogan, John Haigh, Frank Keutsch, Andy Parker, Susan Biniaz, John Dykema, Zhen Dai, Oliver Morton, Peter Irvine, Mariia Belaia, Eli Tziperman, Sebastian Eastham, and Robert Mendelsohn.

I am indebted to the colleagues who generously gave early reads and endorsements to this book: Joseph Aldy, Olivier Boucher, Daniel Esty, Sabine Fuss, Hugh Hunt, Douglas MacMartin, John Moore, and

Edward Parson. And nothing in my life is possible without the support
and partnership of my wife, Mary Anne Citrino, with whom I am
privileged to share every step of every journey.

I am grateful that Chris Harrison and his colleagues at the
Cambridge University Press took up this project as the world was
coming apart in early 2020.

# Section I
# CLIMATE INTRODUCTION

# 1 WHERE DO WE STAND ON CLIMATE CHANGE?

Let's start with a climate change status check to clarify where matters stand today.

## Real, Anthropogenic, and Dangerous

The first three things to understand about climate change are that it is real, anthropogenic, and dangerous. I will review briefly why we are confident that those statements are true, but if you have serious doubts about any of them, this is not (yet) the book for you. I suggest you stop browsing here and consider instead a book that delves more deeply into the basics of climate change, such as *The Climate Crisis* by Archer and Rahmstorf.

For those of you still with me, let's start with "real." There is virtually no remaining scientific debate in peer-reviewed journals on the question of whether climate change is happening, and there has not been for at least a decade. Outside the US, this may seem too obvious a point to belabor, but particularly with the White House so recently occupied by a brazen climate denier, there remain lingering pockets of doubt in America. The lack of continuing debate in the scientific community as to whether this phenomenon is real is not because climate scientists are closed-minded or colluding in a global conspiracy to destroy capitalism and justify their research grants. Instead, it is because, as that debate has run on for decades, the evidence on one side has become overwhelming, while on the other side, it has collapsed. Former climate skeptics have either changed their minds or retired. As is the way with most emerging scientific consensus, graduate students newly entering the field without a dog in the fight listen to both sides and vote overwhelmingly with their research topic choices for one or the other. What was a raging debate in one generation becomes a rout in the next as – paraphrasing Max Planck – "science advances one funeral at a time." That is where we stand on the basic question of whether climate change is real.

"But wait," you may think. "I just saw a well-coifed and very excitable talking head on cable news say the opposite." Generally, that person is not a scientist, or if they are, not with recent peer-reviewed publications on this topic. They are often paid indirectly by fossil fuel interests to cultivate confusion that justifies inaction and are therefore more nearly climate lobbyists than climate researchers. Surveys of relevant peer-reviewed literature regularly conclude that the percent of academic consensus on the man-made climate change phenomenon is in the mid-to-high 90s, which is to say nearly unanimous (more on this in Chapter 19). Not only has the rise in global average surface temperature been measured directly and extensively all over the world by generations of scientists from every inhabited continent, but as we will see in Chapter 2, given the increased concentration of greenhouse gases in the climate system, it would be difficult to explain how it could *fail* to be happening. Since the beginning of robust and global direct temperature measurements in 1880, the increase has been roughly 1.2°C, with more to come.[1] That is also roughly the temperature increase since the more commonly referenced "preindustrial baseline," so we will consider these two baselines to be the same baseline, in line with data from the US National Oceanic and Atmospheric Administration.[2]

As for "anthropogenic," it is equally clear that the cause of this 1.2°C increase (we will deal mostly in metric units herein, but that's about 2.16°F) has been human activity. This is due mostly to the combustion of fossil fuels to produce energy, but owes also to increased emissions of methane deriving from fossil fuel extraction, animal husbandry, cement production, rice farming, and other economic activity necessary both to accommodate modern industrial life and feed a human population that has increased almost eight-fold since 1800.[3] Greenhouse gas (GHG) emissions also occur naturally, but before industrialization natural sources and natural sinks (the opposite of sources, where GHGs are removed from the climate system) had struck a rough balance that contributed to general climate equilibrium. It is the addition of myriad human GHG sources with virtually no new human generated sinks that has thrown the Earth's climate out of equilibrium and precipitated the general warming.

"Dangerous" is not the same as "definitely really horrible." Despite all the reasons why I believe we should fear the impacts of climate change, it may turn out all right. We may find low-cost, low-risk solutions. Economic growth may outpace climate damages such that we can adapt easily to a warmer world. Disastrous tipping points may not materialize. Think about it this way – it's possible that driving at double the speed limit on a foggy night while drunk will turn out just fine. But the whisky, haste, and low visibility greatly enhance risks that would otherwise be quite manageable. Accommodating more than 10 billion people by 2100 on a planet that had just 1 billion 300 years earlier will prove very difficult in any circumstance. Doing so while simultaneously baking the planet with carbon dioxide levels it has not experienced for at least 800,000 to a few million years will substantially increase the risk of things going terribly wrong.[4]

## What Do We Know, and How Do We Know It?

The Intergovernmental Panel on Climate Change (IPCC) is a global group consisting of representatives from nearly 200 governments who work with hundreds of the world's leading climate researchers to assess the issue of climate change. It was established in 1988, the same year in which American climatologist James Hansen warned the US Senate about the existence and dangers of climate change. If there is a year before which climate change can be seen as accidental and after which it should be considered an act of commission, it is 1988. The IPCC's task was, and still is, to provide the world with comprehensive and objective assessments of the existence, causes, and impacts of climate change.

The IPCC's First Assessment Report (FAR) was issued in 1990 to inform the Rio Earth Summit, which was the world's first major conference bringing together world leaders (rather than merely scientists) to consider the accelerating issue of climate change. The US delegation was led by President George H. W. Bush, who as a transplanted Texan and former oil patch wildcatter was reflexively skeptical of initiatives that might undercut the fossil fuel industry, but as a former CIA Director was also respectful of analysis and open to science. The FAR stated with certainty that "there is a natural greenhouse effect that already keeps the Earth warmer than it would otherwise be" and that "emissions resulting from human activities are substantially increasing the atmospheric concentrations of the greenhouse gases."[5] It observed that global mean surface air temperature had increased by between 0.3 and 0.6°C over the previous hundred years and would keep rising substantially thereafter until and unless humanity eliminated greenhouse gas emissions. Nonetheless, the report was careful to account for uncertainties and did not stretch to infer what had not yet been proven. It noted that the indeterminacies in respect of future temperature increases derive not merely from unresolved questions of physics and chemistry but even more materially from lack of clarity about whether and how quickly humanity may respond to this problem. If humanity continued with "business as usual" emissions, temperatures could increase by 0.3°C per decade, whereas if emissions reductions were undertaken as an urgent priority, that decadal rate could be cut to 0.1°C. It further noted with scrupulous modesty that "while the size of the warming over the last century was broadly consistent with the prediction by climate models, ... it is also of the same magnitude as natural climate variability." In other words, the warming was real, but its cause was at that time uncertain. "The unequivocal detection of the enhanced greenhouse effect from observations is not likely for another decade."

Since then, the IPCC has issued additional assessments every six or so years, with each one advancing its confidence in attributing the observed warming to human causes. In 1996, the Second Assessment reported that the "balance of evidence suggests discernable human influence on climate." The Third Assessment in 2001 noted "stronger evidence that observed warming over last 50 years is due to human activities." The 2007 version stated that it is "more than 90 percent likely that warming since 1950 is due to human activity."

In the fifth and most recent assessment in 2014 (the "AR5"), the IPCC stopped mincing words on attribution. "Human influence on the climate system is clear, and recent anthropogenic emissions of greenhouse gases are the highest in history." Note the word "clear," with no qualifiers – a large departure from the intentionally equivocal First Assessment.

Broadly consistent with its predecessors, the AR5 is the work product of over 800 scientists and climate experts from 80 countries, and quite literally every word, graph, and figure in the document is the product of years of negotiation among the participants.[6] In respect of observed changes in the climate system, it states "Warming of the climate system is unequivocal, and since the 1950s, many of the observed changes are unprecedented over decades to millennia. The atmosphere and oceans have warmed, the amounts of snow and ice have diminished, and the sea level has risen."

In the preliminary discussions leading to this book, my future editor, in trying to assess the level of academic rigor that I intended, asked, "Do you expect your readers to engage with graphs?" The answer was "yes" (though mercifully, I hope, not with equations). Below from the AR5 is Figure 1.1, consisting of four line graphs. They combine to tell a compelling story, the broad strokes of which are immediately plain; the lines go up and to the right.

Figure 1.1(a) shows globally averaged land and surface temperature variations from 1850 through 2012. Note that the rise is not steady, with the overall slope essentially flat from 1850 through about 1920. Only thereafter is there a clear upward trend for about 25 years followed by a plateau from about 1945 through about 1970. Then we see another steady march upward through the mid-2000s, bracketed by what appeared to be the beginning of another plateau. Climate skeptics had a field day with that most recent mini-plateau claiming that warming had stopped, only to have that argument crumble as temperatures in the last several years have made their largest annual leaps to date.[8]

Figure 1.1(b) shows sea level rise, one of the key impacts of climate change. Unlike (a), there is little nuance in (b). Sea levels have been rising steadily since 1900. This is as one would expect, since the enormous thermal inertia of the oceans causes them to respond to longer term trends rather than annual or even decadal variability in air temperatures.

Figure 1.1(c) shows the increased concentration levels of the three most problematical greenhouse gases; from top to bottom carbon dioxide ($CO_2$), methane ($CH_4$), and nitrous oxide ($N_2O$). The concentrations of each in the atmosphere vary substantially, requiring a separate scale for each gas. All three rose slowly before 1950 and more rapidly thereafter, though methane's trajectory slowed relative to the other two after about 1990. Note that this graph measures concentrations, not emissions, not how much we are newly pumping out each year, but the total stock of these gases in the atmosphere.

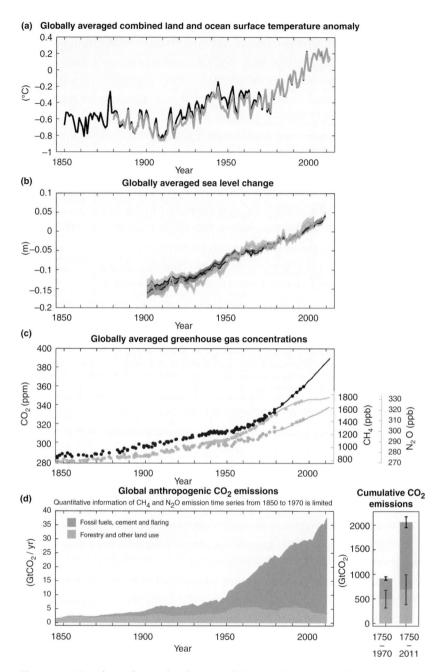

Figure 1.1 Trends in observed indicators of climate change over the past two centuries. *Source:* IPCC, Climate Change 2014: Synthesis Report[7]

Figure 1.1(d) shows the opposite – emissions rather than concentrations – segregated broadly by two sources. The mid-gray layer at the bottom shows emissions deriving from forest clearance, agriculture, and other land management practices. It experienced a modest rise and fall between 1950 and 2000, but by 2012, it is scarcely changed from 1850 levels. On the other hand, emissions from industrial activities went from near zero in 1850 to roughly equal to land management emissions by 1910 to roughly 10 times it by 2012. This is to say that land use changes matter, but the gushing spigot we have turned on since World War II is decidedly from fossil fuel combustion and other industrial processes.

Summarizing the meaning of these figures, the AR5 states

> Anthropogenic greenhouse gas emissions have increased since the pre-industrial era ... and are now higher than ever. This has led to atmospheric concentrations of carbon dioxide, methane, and nitrous oxide that are unprecedented in at least the last 800,000 years. Their effects ... have been detected throughout the climate system and are *extremely likely* [italics theirs] to have been the dominant cause of the observed warming since the mid-20th century.

"Extremely likely" in this context requires a confidence interval in excess of 95 percent, the justification of which would have required extensive documentation and analysis. Part of that justification is shown in Figure 1.2, which is a "box and whiskers" chart that quantifies the net contributions to the warming observed since 1950.

The *observed* warming (what we have actually measured irrespective of causes) shown in the topmost thick horizontal bar (a "box" in this parlance) is roughly 0.65°C, two thirds of a degree and also roughly two thirds of all the warming that has been observed since the preindustrial baseline. The remaining boxes then seek to determine whether that observed warming can be explained via the causal factors as we understand them. Note that each box is accompanied by a thin horizontal line with brackets (the "whiskers"), which clarifies the level of certainty we have in the quantity expressed by the box. In the case of observed warming, the whiskers are pretty short; we have a high degree of confidence in our data here.

The second box from the top shows the heating our models would predict given the quantity of greenhouse gases we have emitted

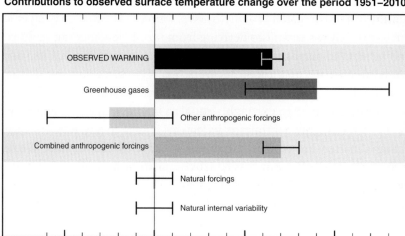

**Contributions to observed surface temperature change over the period 1951–2010**

Figure 1.2 Contributions to observed surface temperature change over the period 1951–2010. *Source:* IPCC, Climate Change 2014: Synthesis Report[9]

and notes that these should have caused warming of more nearly 0.9°C – considerably more than the observed warming. That might present a conundrum but for the third box, which illustrates that about 0.25°C of the warming we would expect is being masked by other anthropogenic forcings, primarily the veil of air pollution that shrouds many parts of the Earth and blocks some incoming sunlight. If these two countervailing forcings are netted against each other (fourth box from top), we get almost exactly the warming actually observed – a neat explanation.

However, it should be noted that the whiskers associated with the second and third boxes are quite wide, indicating substantial remaining uncertainty as to exactly how to weigh these two offsetting forcings relative to each other. The final two boxes (not the wider whiskers) are nearly invisible, meaning that the natural contribution to the observed warming is essentially zero. All the observed warming can be attributed to human causes.

The IPCC reports are the most authoritative and influential of global climate assessments, prepared as they are by as broad and diverse a swath of the international climate community as one could hope to assemble. The conclusions they express are widely echoed by national and regional climate assessments around the world. The European Commission reiterates the IPCC's assessment that the unprecedented rate of global warming is driven by humans and our consumption of fossil fuels.[10] Separately, the United Kingdom's national academy of sciences – the Royal Society – notes that "Human emissions over the last two centuries have altered the composition of the Earth's atmosphere"[11] and are expected to continue to drive further warming. In its Paris Agreement target statement, China acknowledges that human activities have significantly exacerbated climate change due to greenhouse gas generation.[12] The Government of Japan's "Long Term Strategy" under the Paris Agreement similarly recognizes and bases its planning on the assessments of the IPCC. Even two years into the Trump administration, the US Global Change Research Group's Fourth National Climate Assessment (2018) stated "Earth's climate is now changing faster than at any point in the history of modern civilization, primarily as a result of human activities." Other climate action-hesitant nations such as Australia still recognize the threat they confront, with the Australian National Climate Science Advisory Committee noting in 2019 that Australia's "prosperity and security depends on our ability to anticipate, manage and prevent the economic, social and environmental impacts of climate change and variability in Australia and our region, from the short term and through to the end of the century and beyond."[13]

The most fundamental conclusions expressed in the IPCC AR5 are virtually undisputed within the serious science community. To review, those are that the greenhouse effect is real; that human additions to the stock of greenhouse gases in the climate system will warm the planet absent countervailing factors; that warming of approximately 1.2°C has occurred since the preindustrial baseline; and that human activity is responsible for nearly all of that warming. This book will be published to roughly coincide with the release of the next IPCC Assessment Report, the AR6. This sixth assessment will deepen our understanding about a great many things, but will not contradict the consensus on any of these basic points.

## What We Don't Know

Despite the high degree of scientific confidence the world has in the IPCC's conclusions, the climate story is far from fully understood and many uncertainties remain. The climate experiment upon which we have embarked by dramatically altering the composition of our atmosphere has no analog in human history, or for a very long time before that. The brute force physics of how greenhouse gases will heat the climate system is clear, but how much the shrinking of the polar ice cap will warm the Arctic Ocean, or how much permafrost will be melted by a 2°C warming, or how European weather will change if the Gulf Stream slows – these are all factors characterized by high ranges of uncertainty. In layman's terms, unfortunately that means we are guessing. Sober and highly informed estimations, rest assured, by some of the most brilliant minds of our era – but guesses all the same. The climate system is an extremely complex mechanism governed by countless highly interdependent variables, and as we simultaneously spin so many of the dials to settings with no precedent in the human era, we simply lack the knowledge to accurately predict the outcomes.

Many of the most frightening unknowns related to our runaway climate experiment entail "tipping points." Imagine a marble rolling slowly on a perfectly flat surface, but towards a lip beyond which the slope increases to 45 degrees. If the marble is stopped anywhere before the lip, the status remains stable and the marble may remain at rest. However, if the marble passes the lip, the state changes dramatically and inexorably. The marble plunges toward the bottom of the slope to a very different state. Tipping points are most forceful in the presence of some positive feedback mechanism (vicious/virtuous cycles), whereby the more matters progress in a given direction, the more momentum there is to continue in that direction. For example, Arctic sea ice reflects sunlight back out from the Earth, helping to keep the region cool. However, as global temperatures increase and the ice cap shrinks, reflective ice is replaced by dark, heat-absorbing seawater, which results in further warming and more ice melt. Once started, the self-reinforcing trend is very difficult to stop.

What makes such tipping points particularly scary is that we may only recognize them after we have passed them and the marble is hurtling down the ramp, by which time it may be too late to reverse course. We are too new at this climate roulette to know where the thresholds may lie, which constitutes abundant reason for caution.

However, it should be noted that tipping points are also the standard stock of climate scaremongering, where perhaps well-meaning climate activists ring alarms about invisible thresholds that we cannot accurately discern. That doesn't necessarily mean they are wrong, but rather, that we need to acknowledge the continuing uncertainties. In some cases, we know there is a tipping point, but we don't know where it is. In other cases, we may not recognize the existence of such a point until we are well past it. To quote Harvard's Dr. Daniel Schrag, it is as if we are canoeing down an unexplored river on a very dark night with no paddles. "If there are waterfalls ahead, we are going over them." A profoundly scary thought.

A less dramatic but equally vexing uncertainty is "climate sensitivity," which seeks to calibrate how much the climate will respond to a given increase in greenhouse gas concentrations. This math was first worked out by one of the early pioneers of climate science before the turn of the century – the *twentieth* century! In 1896, Swedish scientist Svante Arrhenius calculated that if the concentration of greenhouse gases in the atmosphere were doubled, it would increase global average surface temperatures by 4°C.[14] He was unaware of many of the feedback loops involved, but his math wasn't far off. Furthermore, the "doubling of $CO_2$ concentrations" yardstick that Arrhenius devised by which to estimate climate sensitivity remains the primary convention to this day. By 1979, an ad hoc study group chaired by MIT meteorologist Jule Charney reported to the US National Research Council that the probable global warming for a doubling of atmospheric $CO_2$ would be near 3°C with a likely margin of error plus or minus 1.5°C.[15] Charney's 1.5°C–4.5°C range was repeated in the first IPCC Assessment Report[16] and was still unchanged by the fifth[17] – a remarkably durable estimate despite all the advances in climate modeling that have obtained over the last four decades.

The reason for trepidation in respect of this number is that while Arrhenius chose a doubling of greenhouse gases as a round but some-what arbitrary metric, we appear on track to do exactly that, in this century. The preindustrial concentration of $CO_2$ in the atmosphere was roughly 280 parts per million (ppm),[18] a number that would have changed little by Arrhenius' time. Today it stands at over 410 ppm,[19] and is increasing by an average 2.5 ppm per year.[20] At that rate, we would surpass 560 ppm (double 280) in 2070. There is of course no certainty that we will continue to increase at 2.5 ppm per year, but the arguments for a faster rate are nearly as compelling as those for a slower one.

At the bottom end of the temperature sensitivity range, a 1.5°C response to a doubling of $CO_2$ would be scandalously good news. 1.5°C is the "stretch goal" to which the Paris Agreement urges us to limit climate change, so if we can continue our emissions profligacy through at least 2070 and still adhere to that target, we would have dodged a bullet indeed (or at least arranged that a future generation be shot instead). However, if our current climate sensitivity range is to be believed, then an equally likely temperature outcome in 2070 would be 4.5°C – an amount of change that is widely seen as catastrophic. For context, at the glacial maximum of the last ice age roughly 20,000 years ago, the Earth was just 6°C cooler than the preindustrial baseline,[21] so a 4.5°C change would be a big deal indeed. Very recent research has proposed new ranges with center points above 3.0°C,[22, 23] suggesting that, if anything, the Charney range was biased low and painted too rosy a picture, but it is not yet clear whether the IPCC will change its assessment in the coming AR6 Report. Nonetheless, the fact that decades of post-Charney research on climate sensitivity have barely clarified whether the path we are on will lead to little noticeable change (1.5°C) or widespread ecosystem collapse and human calamity (4.5°C) is cause for dread indeed.

And yet, for all the scientific unknowns discussed above, the greatest cause of climate uncertainty in the latter half of this century is not tipping points or climate sensitivity, but human action. The reasons why humankind should fear dramatic climate change are numerous and awesome, and while it may turn out just fine, the consequences of the opposite eventuality are so dire that the precautionary principle screams that we should rapidly mitigate emissions and steer onto the safest possible trajectory. That could happen. However, while the collective incentives to reduce emissions are enormous, the individual incentives are nearly non existent. In a variant on the prisoner's dilemma problem, the individual interest regarding emissions reduction is opposite the collective interest. It is to each person's selfish advantage to continue to derive the benefits of cheap energy while exhorting their neighbor to mitigate. Perhaps renewable energy sources and net zero pledges will save us, but it is also easy to imagine that we continue for quite a while on the "business as usual" emissions path. The climate trajectory of the only planet we have hangs in the balance as to which path humanity chooses, and the outcome is anyone's guess.

Which brings us to where we started this chapter, with a twist. I hope you are with me that climate change is real, anthropogenic, and dangerous. But it is also coming. In a big way. More of it than most people realize. We will not entirely avoid it. The available choices on the future climate change menu will range from "a lot" to "way too much," but one entrée no longer on offer is "none." I have arrived at my conviction on this topic in part via scientific analysis and in part via social science judgment, but I am clear that substantial climate change is our future. The remainder of the first two sections of this book will be devoted to leading you to the same conclusion.

We must strenuously urge the world to opt for less climate change rather than more, or at minimum, to ensure that if mankind chooses to continue its fossil fuel binge, this is an informed choice with a clear understanding of the odds and likely consequences. But in addition, we need to prepare for such climate change as is inevitably coming. That's where climate intervention comes in.

# 2 CLIMATE SCIENCE 101

Lace up your running shoes. We're going to do a quick jog through climate science. This is intended more as a refresher than a textbook, but there are several basic concepts that you will need to have close at hand for the broader geoengineering story to make sense. If you don't consider yourself to be a "science type," don't worry – I'll trot alongside you. And if your college degree was in geophysics, feel free to sprint ahead of us.

## The Earth's Energy Budget

Let's start with the question of why the Earth's temperature is what it is. The Earth gets its heat from the Sun, which is an enormous ball of flammable gases (mostly hydrogen and helium) burning madly and blasting energy outward in the form of radiation. This radiation travels in waves of varying lengths, ranging from very short x-rays and ultraviolet waves to slightly longer visible light, and to yet longer infra-red light. These waves carry electromagnetic energy, but they do not heat the empty space through which they travel, instead conserving their energy until they encounter something, whereupon they release that energy and produce warmth.

The Sun produces unfathomable amounts of radiation, but radiation also emanates from everything in the universe with a temperature above absolute zero ($-273.15\,°C$ or zero kelvins). Trees, rocks, ocean water, the chair on which you are sitting, your body, even an ice cube – all are emitting radiation constantly, though at differing levels of intensity. Most of the solar radiation reaching the Earth arrives as high-energy "shortwave" radiation in the visible spectrum, whereas the outgoing radiation emanating from the much cooler Earth is lower-intensity infrared or "longwave" radiation.

A fundamental physics principle (the Stefan–Boltzmann relation) states that the hotter an object is, the more radiation it will emit. While you may never have crystalized that thought, you have long known it to be true. If your hands are cold, holding them up near a roaring fire will warm them, whereas holding them equally close to a snowbank will not. But the snow is in fact also emitting radiation, since, cold though it is relative to ourselves, it is much warmer than absolute zero.

If an object absorbs more radiation from its environment than it emits, it will heat up. If it sheds more radiation than it absorbs, it will cool down. When radiation absorbed equals radiation emitted, then a temperature equilibrium is reached. We have encountered here the first law of thermodynamics. Energy in must equal energy out. The object in question – a rock, say – is not "trying" to find an equilibrium, but it behaves as if it is, heating or cooling in response to the balance of radiation flows as it homes in on a stable temperature that brings it into equilibrium with its surroundings.

The Earth is a rock (more or less), and all of this applies to it as well. Our planet is groping towards a temperature that balances incoming and outgoing radiative flows. The global average surface temperature of the Earth is about 15°C (59°F).[1] This is the average temperature all over the Earth, from the poles to the equator, day and night, winter and summer, over land and sea, right at the Earth's surface (so not taking account of the cooler temperatures higher in the atmosphere). At the extremes of our solar system, Mercury and Pluto have average surface temperatures at the opposite ends of the spectrum. What makes the average surface temperature of Mercury so different than that of Pluto? The obvious answer is: Mercury is WAAAAY closer to the Sun, so it receives far more energy in the form of solar radiation than would a more distant planet of equivalent size. As radiation leaves the Sun, it emanates in all directions, such that more of it will strike a nearby target than a distant one (see Figure 2.1 below), but with a bit of math, one could figure out the expected temperature of a planet given its distance from the Sun.

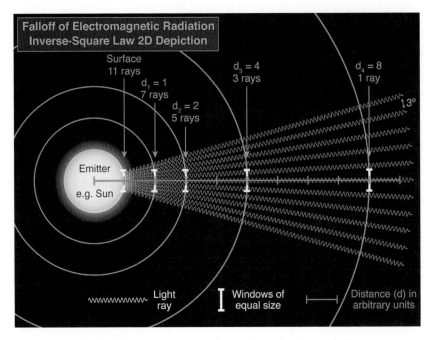

**Figure 2.1** Falloff of electromagnetic radiation from the Sun with distance.
*Source:* Dr. Wolf Read, *Electromagnetic Radiation From the Sun to the Earth*[2]

You would need to know the approximate temperature of the surface of the Sun (about 5500°C);[3] the dispersion of the Sun's rays over time and space (a function of the distance from the Sun to the planet, 150 million km for Earth);[4] and the area of the two-dimensional target the planet would comprise if it were a flat disc facing the Sun (for Earth, 128 million square km).[5] If you do it correctly, this would bring you to the conclusion that Earth's average surface temperature is −18°C (about 0°F)[6] – which clearly it isn't. This would be a snowball Earth supporting relatively few land animals. Something else must be going on.

That something else is the atmosphere – the other major factor that informs our average surface temperature. Not all planets have a substantial atmosphere and, in its early history, Earth didn't either. As it matured and stabilized, our planet outgassed certain chemicals, some of which vented to space but others of which stuck around.[7] As life arose, it produced other gases – principally oxygen – and slowly our atmosphere accumulated in approximately its present form. The significance of the atmosphere in setting the world's thermostat is that while it is generally transparent to incoming shortwave radiation, it is somewhat opaque to outgoing longwave radiation. In other words, it lets most of the radiation in, but impedes some of it on the way out; the majority of the outgoing radiation bumps into molecules in our atmosphere, interacts with them, and spills its heat. The atmosphere itself is thereby heated, and it emanates this heat (longwave radiation) in all directions, some of it out to space, but much of it back down to Earth, further heating the Earth. The now warmer Earth in turn increases its flow of outgoing radiation, causing more of it to get trapped in the atmosphere and reradiated to Earth. These energy flows are illustrated in the Trenberth diagram below. It is among the most famous diagrams in climate sciences and key among the figures in this book, so it's worth staring at for a moment if you can spare the time. The cycles it illustrates (virtuous ones from our standpoint) warm the Earth by another 33°C above that which would result from sunlight only, and rescues us from an average surface temperature of −18°C to the Goldilocks temperature of 15°C.[8] Thank you, atmosphere!

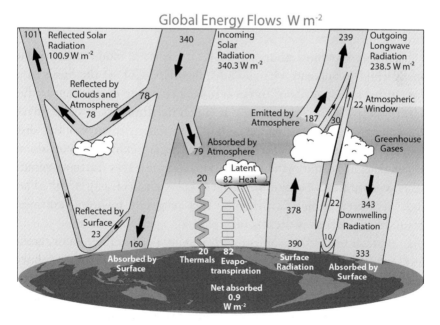

Figure 2.2 Radiation budget diagram for Earth's atmosphere showing the flow of energy in W m⁻². *Source:* Bulletin of the American Meteorological Society[9]

## The Role of Greenhouse Gases

This additional warming impact provided by our atmosphere gives rise to the well-worn "greenhouse" metaphor, and while the mechanism by which a greenhouse preserves interior heat is slightly different, it remains a potent and useful analogy. The glass roof of a greenhouse lets in solar energy (light), but slows the escape of the resulting heat, thereby creating an unusually warm space. In our atmosphere, it is by no means all constituent gases that create this greenhouse effect, but rather a very small subset of them, and those are naturally referred to as greenhouse gases (GHGs).

The most abundant and powerful GHG is water vapor. You might then immediately ask why no one seems to worry about water vapor as they do about carbon dioxide and methane. The answers are because this is naturally occurring and has been for a few billion years, and because it is self-regulating. A planet heated by climate change will evaporate more water, producing more water vapor in the atmosphere and thereby a slight further warming, but when too much water vapor builds in the atmosphere, it rains out, both limiting the buildup and producing other benefits for a society that still feeds itself primarily through agriculture.

The next most abundant GHG is carbon dioxide ($CO_2$) – the poster child for climate change-inducing gases. $CO_2$ is also naturally present in the atmosphere and everywhere else near the surface of the Earth (oceans, soils, lithosphere). It enters the atmosphere via natural causes such as volcanoes and fumaroles, vegetative decomposition, and animal respiration, and via anthropogenic causes, such as the burning of fossil fuels, deforestation, and cement making. It leaves the atmosphere via photosynthesis, dissolution into the ocean, absorption into the soils, and chemical weathering (whereby it is naturally incorporated into stone), though these processes take place on *very* different time scales. One expression of the problem with $CO_2$ is that while humans have developed myriad ways to emit it into the atmosphere, we have industrialized none by which to remove it. Rather straightforwardly, if we are creating new $CO_2$ sources but no new sinks, the concentration of $CO_2$ in our climate system is rising steadily, as the famous measurements (the Keeling curve, shown in Figure 2.3) from the top of Mount Mauna Loa in Hawaii confirm. Despite the annual seasonal variation, the increase has been steady and inexorable.

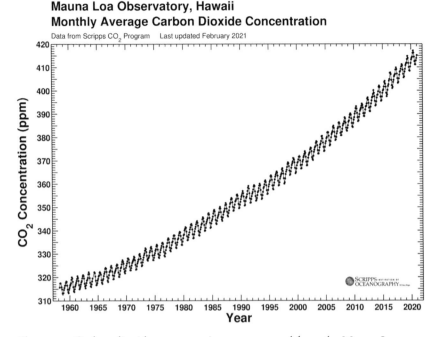

**Figure 2.3** Carbon dioxide concentrations as measured from the Mauna Loa Observatory on Hawaii. *Source*: Scripps Institute of Oceanography UC San Diego[10]

    Human endeavors have not added to the total stock of $CO_2$ on the planet. Rather, we are taking it from stable natural storehouses in the Earth's crust and redeploying it into the air. Not all of it stays in the air. Nearly 30 percent of it is integrated into plants and soils, while another quarter is dissolved in the oceans.[11] In the context of our ongoing high emissions, the fact that the atmospheric fraction is less than 50 percent is a blessing; we can emit two units of carbon and only experience the warming from one. Nonetheless, these three carbon reservoirs (atmosphere, ocean, soils/plants) are in a constant and active exchange with one another, trading carbon back and forth as they equilibrate their concentrations.

    Next up on our list of problematic GHGs is methane (CH4), which like $CO_2$ is a naturally occurring gas whose abundance in the climate system has been greatly increased by human activity. The single largest source of methane emissions into the atmosphere is natural wetlands, which produce it as plant matter decays. These are supplemented by anthropogenic agricultural wetlands, otherwise known as rice paddies. Ruminant animals such as cows and sheep may seem pastoral and innocuous, but the vastly increased stocks of these animals on the planet caused by husbandry means they produce far more methane than would be the case in the world's natural state, representing 40 percent of total methane emissions.[12] The production (as opposed to combustion) of fossil fuels also leaks substantial amounts of methane into the air from insufficient seals at wellheads and cracks in transmission pipelines.

Nitrous oxide (N2O) is another naturally occurring trace gas whose abundance has been vastly increased by the widespread production and use of nitrogen-based fertilizers. These have spawned the green revolution and enabled the world to feed an exploding human population, but at a cost of adding to the stocks of this potent GHG.

Falling in importance on the GHG list are halocarbons; purely anthropogenic GHGs (in contrast to those above) that had been widely used in refrigerants and aerosol accelerants. The majority of halocarbons fall into the category of chlorofluorocarbons (CFCs). Their ozone-destroying properties resulted in a ban under the Montreal Protocol that has led to their gradual elimination, first from the manufacturing stream and, increasingly, from the atmosphere.

Comparing the climate-warming impact of these anthropogenically increased gases is complicated for several reasons. First, their concentrations in the atmosphere are radically different, with $CO_2$ measured in parts per million whereas methane and nitrous oxide are measured in parts per billion (see Figure 1.1(c) in Chapter 1). This might suggest that the latter gases are rather irrelevant to the climate story were it not for the fact that molecule-for-molecule *while they are present*, $CH_4$ and nitrous oxide are roughly 100 and 200 times more potent respectively in trapping outgoing longwave radiation than $CO_2$.[13] Yet a further complication is introduced by the fact that while methane has an average atmospheric life of a bit more than a decade, that of nitrous oxide is over a century. However, the longevity champion is humble $CO_2$, some of which will be further absorbed by the oceans on decadal and centennial timescales, but some of which will endure for millennia. To facilitate meaningful comparisons of the warming impact of different GHGs given these differing concentrations, potencies, and endurances, the convention of global warming potential (GWP) is commonly utilized. This compares the amount of warming that would derive from like quantities of emitted

GHGs over a 100-year timeframe (another common yardstick is 20 years). $GWP_{100}$ is an imperfect yardstick that glosses over various further complications, but to reduce this to a comprehensible story, the GWPs of the most commonly considered GHGs are presented in Table 2.1. Note that over the century after their emission, a molecule of methane creates 28 times the warming of $CO_2$, with nitrous oxide roughly an order of magnitude worse yet. Vastly worse still are the various classes of CFCs which have GWPs roughly 10,000 times higher than $CO_2$.

The high GWP of other gases means that there is more near-term bang-for-buck in eliminating an emission stream of those compared to a like-sized stream of $CO_2$, but the millennial endurance of $CO_2$ combined with its much greater abundance means that it comprises roughly 80 percent of our climate problem. A large fraction of the $CO_2$ we waft into the air today will still be there as we cross into the next millennium, keeping the Earth unnaturally warm for a very long time. In this way, GHGs are very different from the air pollution to which they are sometimes naively compared. In the coronavirus-plagued season during which I have drafted this book, reduced economic activity and automobile travel have thinned urban smog in ways we had forgotten was possible, producing stunning photos of clear skies over Los Angeles, Delhi, and Beijing. I have been asked whether the same is happening in respect of GHGs and whether this economically fallow period has

Table 2.1 Sample global warming potential (GWP) values relative to $CO_2$.[14] The concentrations are given in parts per million (ppm) for $CO_2$, parts per billion (ppb) for $CH_4$ and nitrous oxide, and parts per trillion (ppt) for CFC-11, CFC-12, and CFC-13. Concentrations based on November 2020 monthly mean values for $CO_2$,[15] $CH_4$,[16] $N_2O$,[17] CFC-11,[18] and CFC-12[19] and the March 2018 monthly mean value for CFC-13.[20]

| Industrial designation or common name | Lifetime (years) | GWP value for 100-year time horizon | Atmospheric concentrations |
|---|---|---|---|
| Carbon dioxide ($CO_2$) | Decades to thousands of years | 1 | 413.11 ppm |
| Methane ($CH_4$) | 12.4 | 28 | 1891.6 ppb |
| Nitrous oxide ($N_2O$) | 121 | 265 | 333.6 ppb |
| CFC-11 ($CCl_3F$) | 45 | 4,660 | 223.3 ppt |
| CFC-12 ($CCl_2F_2$) | 100 | 10,200 | 495.7 ppt |
| CFC-13 ($CClF_3$) | 640 | 13,900 | 3.2 ppt |

enabled us to turn a corner related to climate change. The answer sadly is "no," not because we haven't temporarily staunched the flow of GHGs into the atmosphere, but because they don't quickly fall out of the air as these other air pollutants do.

This gets to another essential element of the climate issue, referred to as "tank and flow." As the discussion above indicates, in considering the source of the GHG problem, many people analogize to air pollution. They imagine say a smokestack emitting gas and conceive that our task in ameliorating the problem is to figure out how much pollution we can safely tolerate and reduce emissions to that level. However, this paradigm works in respect of air pollution because there is a pretty direct relationship between the amount we emit and the amount we breathe. Crank up pollutant emissions and our air will immediately be dirtier. Cut them in half, and we will be breathing cleaner air within a fortnight. However, the air pollution analogy is in fact misleading. Cut GHG emissions in half, and the climate problem will still *worsen*, because of the long endurance of GHGs in the atmosphere.

The more helpful analogy here is a bathtub that consists of a faucet, a tank (the tub), and a drain. In the case of air pollution, the drain functions pretty well; reduce the incoming faucet flow, and soon the drain will have vented away a significant portion of the particulates in the air and our lungs will be happier. But in the case of GHGs and particularly $CO_2$, the drain is so slow that it is essentially clogged. The long-term natural sink that removes carbon from the active exchange (atmosphere/ocean/soils) requires tens of thousands of years to slowly incorporate it into stone.[21] Therefore, if the faucet is still running, then the stock of water in the tub is rising. Cut the faucet flow in half and the water level is rising still. If the drain is clogged and we want the water level in the tub to stop rising, we can't simply reduce the faucet flow – we must stop it. Turn it off. All the way to zero. And if we want the climate to stop changing, that is what we *must* do, because it is the total stock of GHGs in the atmosphere that informs the climate, not the rate of annual emissions. It's the water level in the tank that matters, not the flow out of the faucet.

In summary, the problem created by an increased stock of airborne GHGs is that they trap more heat into the Earth's climate system. To resort to another common analogy, they thicken the atmospheric blanket swaddling the planet. The Earth's energy budget remains in a state of disequilibrium (more energy entering than exiting), so the planet will heat up in order to increase the flow of outgoing radiation and establish a new, warmer equilibrium. That's global warming in a nutshell. So long as we continue to thicken the blanket, the Earth will heat up to compensate.

A question that arises commonly in introductory climate discussions is whether the observed climate warming could be caused by variability in the Sun's output of radiation. The answer is "Yes, it could be, but that's not in fact what's happening." The Sun's output changes, but in the last centuries and decades, the changes have been minuscule. Solar irradiance fluctuates on an 11-year cycle, with a low of 1,361 W/m² and a peak a mere 0.1 percent greater.[22] In the last 300 years, that irradiance value has barely increased 0.1 percent, not enough to explain the changes we are seeing.[23]

In discussing the transparency of the atmosphere to incoming sunlight, I have deferred introducing, until now, a very important exception, which is the reflectivity (or "albedo") of the Earth. As a general matter, dark surfaces absorb sunlight and light ones reflect it. Both in its atmosphere and on the surface, the Earth displays some bright features that reflect back to space a fraction of the incoming sunlight. The most significant is clouds, which reflect about 20 percent of the sunlight that would otherwise enter the Earth's climate system. Other elements in the atmosphere, such as water and aerosols, deflect 6 percent, and bright land surfaces such as snow, ice, and sand deflect another 4 percent. Altogether then, Earth has an albedo of about 30 percent (see the deflected and upturned arrows on the left in Figure 2.2) and absorbs only 70 percent of the solar radiation that is on target to strike the planet.[24]

## Atmospheric Structure and Circulations

As the air above our heads is invisible but for clouds, it is easy to overlook all the structure that exists up there, both horizontally across the Earth's surface, but also vertically. The atmosphere is a big layer cake or, since it is spherical, a giant Baked Alaska, with layers enveloping other layers. Though our bodies have evolved not to notice it, air molecules have mass and are therefore responsive to gravity. Instead of floating out into space, they are pulled towards the Earth, and the closer they are to the planet's surface, the more strongly gravity acts upon them. Gravity compresses the air that is closest to Earth, and as one climbs in altitude, there is less air sitting above you, so the pressure decreases and the air density is reduced. At sea level, typical air pressure is roughly 14.7 pounds per square inch, or 1,013.25 millibars (a unit of atmospheric pressure).[25]

As one rises to a height of merely 5.5 km (about 3.5 miles, higher than the tallest Alp or Rocky but lower than Kilimanjaro or Everest), 50 percent of the mass of the atmosphere is below you (see Figure 2.4 below), and pressure has therefore dropped to a bit over 500 millibars.[26] At 16 km (10 miles), you are above 90 percent of the mass of the atmosphere and at roughly 100 millibars.[27] Climb to 50 km, and pressure has dropped to just 1 millibar, with 99.9 percent of the atmospheric mass below you. And yet the atmosphere extends for another 350 km above you.[28]

As anyone who has ever climbed a mountain knows, it gets cooler as you get higher. This environmental lapse rate – the rate at which temperature falls with higher altitude – averages about 6.5°C per 1,000 meters (though it is variable due to sources like convection and condensation.) This means that at 4.8 km, the top of Mont Blanc should

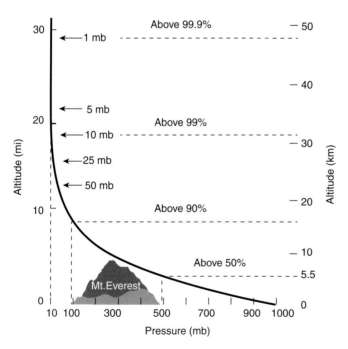

Figure 2.4 Decrease in atmospheric pressure with increasing altitude[29]

be about 31°C (56°F) cooler than the nearby sea level temperatures.[30] What mountaineering won't tell you is that there is a limit to that. At the top of the troposphere around 11 km, the lapse rate goes to zero, and then reverses at 20 km, meaning that it is *warmer* at 25 km than at 11 km (see Figure 2.5 below). This rather astonishing lapse rate reversal continues all the way up to 50 km, at which point it is nearly as warm as it is down on the surface. Amazing. Nonetheless, at 50 km the lapse rate flips once again and starts getting cooler as we further ascend. There is yet another zig back to negative lapse rates at around 85 km, and by 110 km, it is yet again nearly as warm as it was on the surface.[31]

The lowest zone in our atmospheric layer cake is the troposphere, wherein the lapse rate is positive (i.e., getting cooler as we ascend). Once the lapse rate has run to zero (an isothermal, meaning equal temperature), we have reached the tropopause, the top of the troposphere. Above that – where the lapse rate turns negative – is the stratosphere.

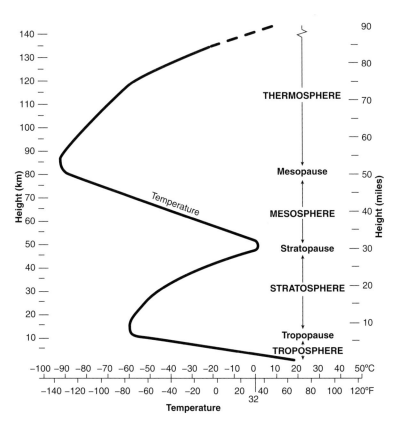

**Figure 2.5** Atmospheric temperature changes[32]

The troposphere is characterized by (among other things) huge amounts of vertical mixing for reasons that are straightforward enough. In daylight at ground level, the incoming highly energetic shortwave radiation (sunlight) hits the surface, spills its heat content, and warms the surface land or waters. That warmed surface wants to dissipate its heat (energy in = energy out), so it emits longwave radiation, which heats the air immediately above the surface. We now have a layer of hot (and therefore less dense) air at the surface, with layers of cooler, denser air above it – an unstable situation. The buoyant hot air rises, creating a vacuum which cool air rushes to fill. This might stabilize the situation, except that the air that is newly on the bottom absorbs longwave radiation emanating from the now nearby surface, repeating the cycle through the daylight hours. This bottom-up heating drives the convective "turning" of the troposphere (deriving from Greek for "turn" or "change"), during daylight hours. The endless vertical mixing drives many familiar and life-sustaining phenomena, including the hydrological cycle (rain).

Once we ascend through the tropopause and into the stratosphere, this chaotic picture becomes more stable. Due to stratospheric ozone's absorption of the Sun's UV radiation, it gets warmer as we go up, and therefore lighter warm air sits upon cooler denser air. The engine that drove vertical mixing below is now absent. More importantly for our purpose though, the direction of motion in the stratosphere changes, and is no longer primarily vertical, but horizontal, with the Brewer–Dobson circulation transporting air from the tropics towards the poles.

This poleward flow in the stratosphere is just one example of persistent global circulations that shape local weather all over the planet. Global winds all share the general flow from high pressure to low, and their different patterns are caused in turn by temperature differences and the Earth's rotation. Back down in the troposphere, near the equator, warm moist air rises. It sheds most of its water locally but is pushed aside by air newly arising beneath it, circulating from the equator toward the poles. However, what might be a straightforward story on a stationary object is complicated by the fact that the Earth is spinning beneath these poleward winds. The resulting Coriolis force deflects these winds eastward – towards the right in the northern hemisphere and left in the southern – creating the westerly winds ("westerlies") that prevail in the middle latitudes. The Coriolis effect similarly deflects the air that falls in those mid-latitudes and moves back equator-ward, creating the trade winds – or "easterlies" – that persist toward the tropics. Besides the Earth's rotation, its tilt and non-uniform landmass distribution further complicate the global pattern of winds.

In addition to these persistent wind patterns there are also seasonally reversible winds (the monsoons). The oceans have enormous thermal inertia, which from a seasonal perspective means that they warm less in the summer and cool less in the winter than does the air above them. This in turn has a moderating impact on coastal temperatures, whereas mid-continent seasonality is generally much more extreme. Therefore, in winter, the mid-continent air is much colder than the ocean air, so the ocean air rises, pulling in air from the adjacent land mass, and we get offshore winds. In summer, the mid-continent air warms dramatically whereas the ocean air warms more moderately. Now it is the mid-continent air that rises, sucking in cooler air from the sea to replace it. An onshore summer wind is full of moisture from the ocean and brings seasonal rains when the land most needs the water. Monsoons occur on all the inhabited continents, but the East Asian and Indian monsoons are the most prominent, in part due to extreme winter/summer temperature swings stemming from the large size and topography of the Asian land mass. These air circulations are one of the engines that drive ocean circulations such as the Gulf Stream, which brings warm air to a European land mass that would otherwise be much colder given its latitude.

I have intentionally glossed over lots of important detail here to come to a key point, which is that these global air and ocean circulations have enormous influence on the Earth's distribution of warmth, water, and life, helping to define where it is lush versus arid, hot versus cold, and therefore where conditions are hospitable versus hostile to life. One might expect deserts to be arrayed near the equator, where the Sun's rays are most consistent and intense, but they are not. The warm moist air at the equator tends to rise, bringing lush local rains before it is pushed poleward by the next packet of rising air. This now dry air tumbles back down to Earth in the vicinity of 30° North and South, bearing no moisture and creating the bulk of the world's deserts. Humanity has most densely propagated in the path of the Asian monsoon, where reliable annual summer rains have made agriculture most productive. Without the Gulf Stream, England's climate would resemble Newfoundland's. It is the African monsoon that supports the massive game herds of the Serengeti. The global circulations on the Earth as it exists today have informed the distribution of life on the planet, and any significant change in those circulations would therefore have enormous ramifications for living things.

## Paleoclimatology

Of course, those circulations, like many facets of the Earth, have changed over time. The field of paleoclimatology studies the climate history of the Earth and one of its primary functions is to see what the past can tell us about the likely impact of the changes we are making to the Earth's climate. Since there are of course no direct measurements of climate variables thousands or millions of years ago, the field has learned how to finagle climate data from proxy measurements such as sediment cores or air bubbles trapped in ice. Among the key findings has been the strong positive correlation between warmer climates and $CO_2$ concentrations, although which is cause and which is effect remains unclear. A spectacular spike in temperatures occurred 55 million years ago (the Paleocene–Eocene thermal maximum), when temperatures shot up by 5–8°C and airborne $CO_2$ concentrations reached around 1,600 ppm, almost four times today's levels. The historical record therefore confirms what our understanding of climate physics reveals, which is that more atmospheric $CO_2$ will bring hotter temperatures.

Over the last million years (the end of the Pleistocene era), the Earth has cycled between warm, interglacial periods and much colder glacial periods (see Figure 2.6).[33] Particularly in the latter half of that period, it is the long glacial periods and not the brief interglacial spikes that predominate. *Homo sapiens* is thought to have emerged some 200,000–300,000 years ago, a time during which Earth has usually been much cooler and has never been much warmer than it was at the beginning of the industrial era.

During the Pleistocene, glaciers grew and retreated in rhythm with Milankovitch Cycles, which are small changes in the Earth's progression in space. We may perceive the Earth to be stable in its movements, but over extended periods of time, it is not, in more ways than one might imagine.[34] The ellipse of our orbit (it's not a perfect circle) gets more and less eccentric on roughly 100,000-year time frames. Relative to the plane of our orbit, the angle of the axis on which we are spinning migrates from 22.1 to 24.5 degrees on roughly 41,000-year

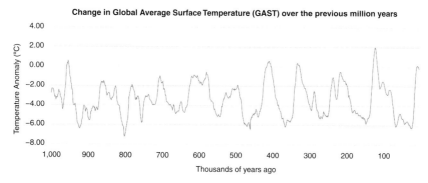

Figure 2.6 Temperature anomaly (difference from the current average temperature levels) over the last million years. *Data source*: Carolyn W. Snyder, "Evolution of global temperature over the past two million years"[35]

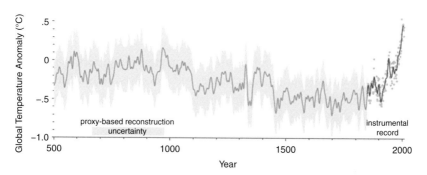

Figure 2.7 Temperature history of the last 1,500 years sourced from paleoclimate data (gray line) and modern instruments (black line). *Source*: Earth Observatory NASA built using the data from Michael E. Mann et al., 2008[36, 37]

cycles. The direction of that axis relative to fixed stars also rotates around in a circle every 26,000 years, resembling a top wobbling as it slows down. And the orientation of our ellipse relative to fixed stars also rotates on a 112,000-year cycle. (I know; it's sort of hard to envision it all, but stay with me.) None of these cycles is aligned with each other, so they sometimes amplify each other's effects and at other times offset them. However, they all cause variations in the distribution of energy around the planet and are thought to be the triggers that cause major changes in global climate such as the waxing and waning of glaciation (the "Ice Ages").

The last ice age peaked 18,000 years ago and ended roughly 12,000 years ago at the dawn of the Holocene era. Humanity had by this time spread to all the currently inhabited continents and began to evolve from cave dwellers to farmers. Narrowing our gaze to the last 1,500 years, this period witnessed natural variability in global temperatures, with the three centuries before the industrial era as well as the first century after being on the low side of the range. Then early in the twentieth century, temperatures begin to skyrocket, shooting up by mid-century to levels equaling the warmest seen since the fall of Rome, and then shooting off the top of the graph to levels not seen in 120,000 years.[38]

## The Role of Oceans and Ice

Because we are land creatures, it is easy to lose sight of the fact that we live on an ocean planet. Seventy percent of Earth's surface is covered by the sea, but even this number dwarfs the importance of the oceans in the climate story. As a matter of both physics and chemistry, the oceans are highly interactive with the atmosphere, such that it is better to see them as one integrated system rather than two, and if we aggregate the mass of that combined system, the ocean makes up over 99 percent of it.[39] Greenhouse gases that we put into the air eventually end up largely in the ocean, as the ocean is constantly absorbing from and emitting to the air above it. This is perhaps even more true from a thermal standpoint; temperatures in the atmosphere are constantly equilibrating with those in the surface ocean and vice versa. The heat storage capacity of the ocean is roughly 1,000 times that of the entire atmosphere.

As with the atmosphere, there is a vertical structure to the oceans. The bottom water is quite cold – just a few degrees above freezing – but the surface water (the topmost layer) is close in temperature to the surface air just above it – about 16°C on average.[40] Nonetheless, it takes half a century for changes in atmospheric temperatures to be fully reflected in the surface water temperatures, and several centuries for those surface water changes to then fully mix into the deep water.[41] This means that even if and when we do stop our emissions to the atmosphere, the equilibration of the oceans to the new status quo will happen on decadal to centennial time scales, which will in turn reflect impacts back to the atmosphere.

As noted above, winds drive ocean currents, but so too do many other factors, including differentials in temperature and salinity. Ocean currents flow not only horizontally, but vertically, with upwelling in some places and in others, mind-boggling waterfalls within the sea where dense cold salty water plunges from the surface to the bottom. Really cool stuff, but fragile. If we change air temperatures and therefore surface water temperatures, we can only guess at the ocean current changes that will result, and the changes to the adjacent land temperatures that will flow from that.

In addition to absorbing warmth, the oceans also absorb the $CO_2$ and other GHGs directly. $CO_2$ is native to ocean water and can dissolve within it but increasing the $CO_2$ content of seawater changes its pH. Without going too far down this rabbit hole, the pH scale indicates how acidic or basic something is. A high pH means a solution is basic and has few hydrogen ions ($H^+$), while a low pH indicates a high concentration of $H^+$. Neutral pH is 7, and the oceans are slightly basic, with a preindustrial pH of 8.2. In the last 200 years, that number has dropped to 8.1 and is dropping still. This sounds like almost nothing, but in the gallery of scary climate stories, this one is top rank. Crustaceans and mollusks form outer shells from calcium carbonate ($CaCO_3$) the building blocks of which ($Ca^{2+}$ and $CO_3^{2-}$) they extract from seawater. Fortunately for them and us, most seawater is lousy with the stuff – supersaturated. There is more $CaCO_3$ in the water than the water can hold, so it is happy to give some up to any critter that wants to take a little to build its shell. However, water that is more acidic – due to an increase in dissolved $CO_2$ – will become unbalanced in its amount of $Ca^{2+}$ and $CO_3^{2-}$, as the increased acidity means less $CO_3^{2-}$ for the organisms to use. This is because the extra $H^+$ reacts with the $CO_3^{2-}$, preventing the creatures from being able to use it to form their shells. Therefore, if we make water more acidic (it's actually dealkalinization, making it less basic, though not actually acidic), sea creatures that were previously in supersaturated water will suddenly find themselves in water that is undersaturated with $CO_3^{2-}$. At a low enough pH level, extra hydrogen ions in the surrounding seawater will steal $CO_3^{2-}$ from the critters, dissolving their shells.

Not only will oceans in a warming world come after shelled critters, but they'll also come after us – in the form of sea level rise. The water will come for two simple and inescapable reasons. The first is thermal expansion. Water (like other liquids and gases) expands as it is heated, so warmer oceans will have greater volume, meaning they will encroach on every coastline and estuary in the world. The same thermal inertia discussed earlier will mean that this process will happen slowly, but inexorably. There is nothing we can do to stop this other than cool the world and wait for generations. The other reason the water will come is – there will be more of it. Not more $H_2O$ globally, but more of it in water form because various ice sheets will shrink substantially. For instance, Mount Kilimanjaro has been snow-capped for hundreds of thousands of years,[42] but has lost most of its ice cover in the last century and is projected to be ice free before 2100. Temperate and tropical land glaciers will melt, but as these constitute a small fraction of the world's water stored in glaciers, they will contribute little to the volume in the seas.

The Arctic Ocean is capped by floating ice that covers almost all of the ocean in winter[43] but shrinks in the summer. The annual minimum extent of the ice cap is reached in September, when the long days and relative summer warmth begin to recede as the region turns back towards winter. The annual minimum size of the ice sheet has been shrinking steadily and set a record in 2012 at just 46 percent of what was observed in 1980, shrinking at an average of over 13 percent per decade.[44] Scientists had expected the cap to disappear entirely in summers before 2100,[45] but this dreary prediction has been super-seded by a more recent one that foresees a nearly ice-free summer Arctic by mid-century.[46] Nonetheless, this too will contribute little to sea level rise, since that ice is already floating. Like the ice cube that melts in a glass, its phase change won't raise the water level. However, there will be an indirect effect, in that, as discussed in Chapter 1, Arctic ice constitutes a strong positive feedback loop whereby the less Arctic ice there is, the more shortwave radiation the Arctic will absorb, resulting in yet less ice the following year. The self-reinforcing nature of the loss of Arctic Sea ice is the primary reason why the Arctic is warming faster than any other region on Earth.

One might reasonably wonder why a similar effect should not be expected for the South Pole, but the difference is that the Antarctic is covered mostly by land rather than by sea, and whereas the oceans have enormous thermal inertia that tends to moderate temperatures through the year, seasonality over land is much more extreme. The Antarctic winter is therefore much colder than the Arctic winter, and the air temperatures at the "bottom" of the world will keep Antarctica frozen for the foreseeable future. Unfortunately, the same can't be said for the water temperatures.

Still, from the standpoint of sea level rise, there are only two ice sheets that really matter – Greenland, and the ice sheets at the bottom of the world. Antarctica is garlanded by several floating ice shelves which are calving off at alarming rates and floating northward, where they eventually melt. Like the Arctic sea ice, these are already afloat, so their melting won't directly contribute to sea level rise. However, they act as dams, penning in the ice that is on the adjacent land. Once the sea dam is gone, the pace at which the ice on the land flows into the sea accelerates, speeding the loss of land ice, which does in fact raise sea levels. Moreover, if the sea ice is resting on the sea floor as is often the case for some portion of coastal ice shelves, the melting of the sea ice will cause the sea floor to subsequently rebound upwards, expelling some portion of the water above it. This recently identified "water expulsion" effect is now calculated to raise global sea levels by another 30 percent above previous forecasts.[47] To be clear, Antarctica is in no danger of becoming ice free. It is so cold in the center of the continent that even the substantial warming we are considering herein would leave most of the continent permanently blanketed with ice, but the Antarctic peninsula and other coastal regions would likely see large amounts of ice slide into the sea in a warming world.[48]

In Greenland too, coastal bays previously clogged with sea ice are now becoming open water, accelerating the slide of the adjacent land ice into the sea. However, the Greenland ice sheet is also threatened by direct melting. Antarctica is more than six times larger than Greenland and sits entirely within the Antarctic Circle, whereas a large tongue of Greenland stretches south of the Arctic Circle. The North Pole is covered by a moderating sea, while the South Pole is covered by land, permitting much more extreme temperatures. These factors conspire to mean that while all of Antarctica is ice-covered year round, much of Greenland's coastline is ice free in the warmer months, and in summer, the southern portion of the island is flecked with countless deep blue ponds of meltwater many of which tunnel down through the ice and find their way to the sea. If by magic we could immediately make the world cooler, it would be possible to regrow the waning sea ice, though even this would likely require centuries[49] since it is not merely air temperatures but also ocean temperatures to which this ice is responding.[50] The land ice however is a very different story. Antarctica is mostly a desert, receiving little snowfall year round. Such land ice as does exist there resulted from scant snowfall accumulations over the past 34 million years.[51] Once it has melted, land ice regeneration would take ages.

Our final ice melt problem concerns permafrost, frigid swamplands and marshes that have frozen at the surface and several feet down. A warming world threatens to melt permafrost all over the fringes of the world's frozen regions, principally in Siberia, Canada, and Alaska. Melting permafrost will contribute little to sea level rise, but like other marshlands, permafrost harbors substantial reserves of $CO_2$ which are semi-permanently sequestered in their current form. However, if permafrost melts, this carbon will be released into the atmosphere, threatening to replicate previous dramatic warming cycles on Earth. Moreover, the newly thawed wetlands will provide expanded habitat for anaerobic microbes, becoming a new source of methane.

As we can see from this quick jog through climate science, there is a lot to cover! I hope you have stayed with me through this chapter. There remain enormous blank spaces to fill in, but from what we already do know, it is clear that the climate system is complex and finely balanced. In altering it, we are playing with fire.

# 3 WHAT'S SO BAD ABOUT CLIMATE CHANGE?

## The Climate Apocalypse

The media can sound a bit like the book of Exodus as it describes the plagues that await us should we continue to stumble forward towards climate change. Storms, floods, droughts, fires, extinctions, wars – a gathering apocalypse. The breathlessness with which these ongoing or upcoming disasters are sometimes discussed can give wary listeners the sense that perhaps they are being played by scaremongers – and occasionally they are. There is so much (entirely valid) concern that humanity is failing to take heed of the myriad blinking warning lights on the climate dashboard that every untoward weather event is conscripted as a teachable moment and attributed to accelerating warming whether the causality is clear or not. And yet, the reflexive instinct to question such emotionally laden reporting doesn't mean the lights aren't actually blinking. They are, madly!

However, let's try a bit more systematically to separate fact from fiction. We have noted that global average surface temperatures have increased by roughly 1.2°C in the last two centuries and, despite stern admonishments to limit the rise to no more than 2°C, the pledges submitted under the Paris Agreement sketch a more nearly 3°C track,[1] with entirely credible IPCC scenarios taking us to 4°C.[2] What difference would that make? An increase of 1.2°C may seem like nearly nothing, and, you may say, even 4°C is much less than the differential between daily weather highs and lows in most places. A 4°C change may make

New York's weather resemble that of Arkansas,[3] but people in Arkansas live just fine, thank you very much, and if my air conditioning expenses go up, my heating bills are sure to go down. Warm weather seekers have been migrating to America's Sun Belt for decades. If the Sun Belt migrates to them, who's to complain?

If, instead, we view the global context rather than the local one, 4°C would change the planet's average temperature from 15°C to 19°C.[4] These numbers minimize the impact to humans, virtually all of whom live on land. Since land temperatures will warm more than ocean ones (and more quickly as well given thermal inertia), the average increase over land at mid-latitudes could be close to double that, perhaps 7°C.[5] Massachusetts could experience warmer and drier winters more akin to those currently experienced in Maryland.[6] Minneapolis could go from an average of one day per year over 100°F to ten days. Londoners would routinely need air conditioners. The UAE would become nearly uninhabitable.[7]

At the height of the last ice age, it was 6°C cooler than the pre-industrial baseline.[8] That amount of cooling built the Laurentide ice sheet that stretched down the east coast to New York City and plowed the top soil off New England to form the island on which I am sitting (Long Island is comprised of glacial moraine). It stretched over 20,000 square miles across North America and was up to 2.5 miles thick.[9] A temperature 4°C warmer would therefore also have profound consequences, though of course in the opposite direction. The point is, 2 or 3 or 4 degrees would be a really big deal. Would the Earth survive?

Of course it would. It's just a big, dumb rock with a lot of puddles on it. It doesn't care if it's a bit hotter or colder. If we go back before human history, it has been both. Would life survive? A lot of it would. But a lot of it wouldn't. Still, give it another million years or so and all sorts of new and interesting creatures would fill the niches vacated by the Darwinian losers. Would humanity survive? I expect so. Or if not, it is unlikely to be climate change that did us in. I would still put advanced artificial intelligence, designed pathogens, and most especially nuclear weapons ahead of climate change as an existential threat to the entire species. Could the global economy and human population continue to grow as they have in the recent past? I have piled too many suppositions atop one another to hazard a guess, but it's certainly unclear that the answer is "yes." We are contemplating circumstances that could be a fundamental threat to the world as we know it, not to mention the mass human suffering that would ensue from runaway warming. Too much climate change steers us into truly scary terrain.

## The Impacts of Climate Change

So how exactly would this bite us? Let's examine our most salient horsemen of the purported apocalypse.

### Sea Level Rise

As discussed in Chapter 2, if we warm the world, the water will come, due both to thermal expansion of the seas and the melting of land ice. Both of these will play out over centuries, but once started, it would take a great deal of subsequent cooling to stop them.

The impacts of sea level rise are mostly quite straightforward. Low lying coastal areas will flood – first catastrophically but temporarily à la Hurricane Katrina, and then frequently, as we realize we can't afford to rebuild in areas that endure "100-year floods" every few years. Eventually the floods will no longer recede. The sea will permanently swallow large swathes of marshlands and coastal plains, and the great cities that have been built upon them. Miami is famously threatened, built, as so much of it is, on reclaimed swamps and landfill. Dhaka seems as threatened as Rotterdam, but without the heroic Dutch water management infrastructure. Presumably, Manhattan will be defended with sea walls and storm surge barriers like London's, but will we do the same for the beach communities of Cape Cod or North Carolina's Outer Banks? Homeowners will delay the inevitable by rebuilding dunes and elevating houses, but over the medium to long term, the primary strategy for dealing with large-scale sea level rise will be retreat. It simply won't make economic sense to try to defend every inch of coastal lowlands.

Painful and costly decisions will be forced upon us, with triage calculations about which areas to reinforce and which to surrender to the waves. Perhaps tourists two or three generations hence will be able to stroll the magical canal sides of Venice. Perhaps not. Whether South Florida can survive as a contiguous landmass or become a series of archipelagos like the Florida Keys will depend on how much sea level rise we opt for. A report on climate risk from McKinsey estimates that in Florida, "losses from flooding could devalue exposed homes by

$30–$80 billion, or about 15 to 35 percent, by 2050, all else being equal."[10] Yikes! What makes that all the more scary is that this is a relatively near-term projection. The worst impacts of sea level rise are expected *after* 2100.[11]

Predicting the extent of sea level rise hinges – as most climate predictions do – on guessing what decisions humanity will make 10 and 50 and 200 years from now, but a 4°C temperature rise would raise the oceans by at least 0.5 to 1 meters vertically.[12] When considering the "rule of thumb" that one unit of vertical sea level rise means 100 times that in horizontal retreat, a 1 meter rise would push seashores inland the length of a football field, irrespective of which type of football you prefer. Coastlines all over the world would be radically altered, and trillions of dollars of property would be damaged or wiped out.[13]

While this may prove an existential threat for island nations such as the Maldives and Tuvalu, for most nations, it is not. Lives will be lost as higher and warmer seas lob cyclones onshore unpredictably, but in the main, the encroachment of the sea can be foreseen. Galveston is in serious trouble. Denver is not. Researchers estimated that between 4 percent and 10 percent of humanity lives within 10 meters of sea level, meaning that for the vast majority of humanity, sea level rise is not a direct threat.[14, 15] If the inundation comes over a century, coastal dwellers and whole cities will have a lifetime and a half to parse their options about what to defend and what to abandon. Humanity will survive this, but at a huge cost in resources and lives.

As a boy, I spent my summers on the Eastern tip of Long Island, New York. I am writing this chapter from a different house looking out onto the same bay. The Gulf Stream and related North Atlantic Current that convey warm air from the Caribbean to the British Isles lie hundreds of miles off Montauk Point (Long Island's eastern-most point), but the Gulf Stream has slowed in my lifetime and has drifted closer to Montauk (I too have done both of those things). The result is that the climate change impact on Eastern Long Island has been roughly 2°C, double the global average, warming the waters of Peconic Bay and decimating the spectacular local scallops for which the area was justly renowned. On the other hand, the milder shoulder seasons have facilitated the emergence of a robust local wine industry (Stop laughing! They're not bad.) that did not exist 50 years ago. Similar changes on land driven by changes at sea will arrive all over the world as matters progress, and like the scallops for wine trade-off, not all of them will be bad. In fact, for every locality that has changed by 2°C, there is presumably one that has not changed at all, as is the case for several counties in Alabama. For some people, this will be just fine. For the baymen of Sag Harbor, it has been devastating.

Retreat will be a necessary defensive strategy, and, in some places, it has already begun. Indonesia has recognized that the sinking of Jakarta appears inexorable and is looking to move its capital to a more elevated site in Borneo.[16] Maldives, the lowest lying country in the world, was previously considering total retreat and had been seeking lands in other countries to which its citizens could migrate. More recently, it has diverted to fight rather than flight, seeking to implement land reclamation to create new and higher islands.[17] After Hurricane Katrina, New Orleans lost 50 percent of its residents, and the city's population is still only 85 percent of what it was before the storm.[18] While many Hurricane Sandy victims applied for buyout programs to relocate, most simply rebuilt their houses on the same sites and apparently have the view that they have dodged the bullet, not yet internalizing that there are a lot more bullets coming.

At Roy Carpenter's Beach, a modest private beach resort in Rhode Island, bungalows were built 80 years ago in orderly rows arrayed parallel to the beach. Over the past 20 years the first two rows were successively swamped, surrendered, and rebuilt several hundred feet inland behind what was previously the last row. There is now a clear expectation that the third row also has a finite continued useful life. However, this perspective and the degree of coastal erosion which mandated it remain rare. Most places have only seen inches of ocean incursion and increased frequency of "100-year storms." Hopefully foreshadowing a more widespread shift, insurers have finally begun to rethink property coverage for coastal properties.[19] But this is only relevant for well-endowed landowners; many do not have the financial resources to retreat. In many parts of the world, homeowners stay put in homes they know are at risk of flooding because they have no other option. Unless we change our trajectory and better support an organized retreat for all, the advancing sea will prove unrelenting and merciless.

## Extreme Weather

The most breathlessly hyped harbingers of the coming climate catastrophe are storms and other extreme weather events. Hurricanes and tropical cyclones are a perfectly natural form of weather rowdiness that have ravaged coastal societies for the length of human history. It is unclear that climate change will increase their frequency, but it is widely predicted that it will increase their intensity.[20] Warmer oceans will possess more latent energy that can be harnessed in the right conditions into more violent and destructive storms. Moreover, population and economic growth have put more people and built structures in harm's way. The result is that when more intense storms slam into more heavily built coastal communities, ever more devastating disasters result. While the connection of any given storm to climate change may prove tenuous, the aggregate trend of increasingly destructive storms will be unmistakable.

Droughts and heat waves may also severely increase in both number and intensity. The IPCC assesses that global warming has already begun causing more frequent heat waves, and that 2°C versus 1.5°C of warming could mean a difference of 420 million more people being frequently exposed to extreme heat.[21] Additionally, areas like the Southwest US may be at risk of decades-long droughts,[22] as a combination of rainfall changes and temperature increases could result in drying and groundwater shortages. On average – though by no means a hard and fast rule – warming is expected to result in dry areas becoming drier and wet areas becoming wetter.[23]

While heat waves will become increasingly widespread, the hot spots (as it were) in their most destructive incarnations will be concentrated around the Persian Gulf, the Red Sea, and most particularly the valleys of the Ganges and Indus Rivers.[24, 25] In each of these places, the combination of elevated temperature and high humidity are projected to produce greatly increased incidences of moist heat waves, where "wet bulb" temperatures will frequently approach 35°C, a level that is life-threatening for both humans and livestock.[26] Persian Gulf nations may have the resources to deal with this,[27] and the Red Sea region is a relatively lowly populated zone,[28] but the Ganges Valley is characterized by some of the highest population densities in the world.[29] Soaked in summer by what are normally the planet's most prominent monsoonal rains,[30] the Indus and Ganges basins support hundreds of millions of predominantly agrarian rural people. Nonetheless, many of these villagers remain impoverished and food insecure, without access to the reliable electrification and air conditioning with which Emiratis might fend off a similar heat wave. A plausible but truly nightmarish vision of the future which serves as the opening scene in a recent science fiction novel[31] is one in which persistent heat waves in such regions begin to slay tens of thousands of people in their beds and fields.

Frequent and persistent droughts and heat events will prove utterly destructive, particularly to agriculture. If crop- and livestock-destroying heat waves become sufficiently frequent, land that is currently considered arable will be rendered economically untenable without irrigation, which may itself prove increasingly impractical or expensive. Desertification is accelerating in many parts of the world,[32] threatening to shrink or redistribute habitable zones.

Persistent, localized drying is also contributing to the increase in the frequency and severity of wildfires in places like the American West. To be sure, other factors also contribute, including modern forest management practices that inhibit smaller, more frequent fires as well as increased housing penetration into the wildland-urban interface. Nonetheless, a drier climate has set the stage for more destructive fire seasons with consequences for both property and life. Five of the six largest wildfires in California history occurred in 2020.[33] The increasing predictability of such losses is reflected in the fact that numerous insurance companies in California are withdrawing from these markets – a phenomenon also seen in beachfront communities. Enterprises in the business of foreseeing such disasters don't much like what they see.

## Ocean Acidification

The mechanisms behind this were also discussed in Chapter 2, and here again, the primary impacts are clear enough. If the zone of the oceans supersaturated with calcium carbonate shrinks, in the newly undersaturated zones there will be massive die-offs of everything that lives in a shell, including of course, coral reefs. The hard shell clams I learned to dig out of the bottom of Peconic Bay as a boy won't be there any longer. This fate would befall not merely mollusks, corals, and sea urchins, but the zooplankton that form the base of so much of the marine food web. This will drive not only the local disappearance of those species and everything above them in the food chain, but extinctions of countless species. A separate but related stressor is that warmer water holds less oxygen, so marine organisms will face progressively lower oxygen levels. Coral reefs and polar ecosystems will be highly vulnerable.[34] This in turn will destroy the livelihoods and threaten the survival of every person who relies upon harvesting the sea for either employment or protein. Quoting McKinsey again,

> By 2050, ocean warming is expected to reduce fish catches by about 8 percent and associated revenue by about 10 percent, affecting the livelihoods of 650 million to 800 million people globally who directly or indirectly rely on these revenues. Catch potential in many tropical regions is projected to decline by up to 50 percent, hurting fishing communities in those regions even more.[35]

## Ecosystem Collapse

Ecosystems will collapse not only at sea but on land. Just as weather will intensify and patterns will change, so too will the natural habitats of the planet be rearranged at the margins. Of course, changes or migrations of the vegetative cover, water sources, and temperature norms will define what animals can live in those areas. Some plants and animals will be able to adapt or migrate their ranges, while others will not. But countless local ecosystems will be upended and destroyed. According to the IPCC, "most plant species cannot naturally shift their geographical ranges sufficiently fast to keep up with current and high projected rates of climate change in most landscapes."[36] Future risk to plants, small mammals, and freshwater mollusks "is indicated to be high by the observation that natural global climate change at rates lower than current anthropogenic climate change caused significant ecosystem shifts and species extinctions during the past millions of years."[37]

Like so many aspects of climate impacts, the problem will be the pace of change. If these climate alterations occurred over millennia as most prior abrupt changes did, the natural world would evolve and adapt as it has for millions of years. However, the rapidity of this event, happening as it has and will over the course of a few centuries, will impact the natural world much more nearly as did the meteor strike that wiped out the dinosaurs. Not only will stranded individual plants and animals die, but whole ecosystems and countless species will be eliminated. Hundreds of thousands of years later new wondrous creatures will take their place, but our children and grandchildren will continue to witness the sixth great extinction in the planet's known history.[38]

## Water Scarcity

If one were to seek evidence of an intelligent design in our world, one promising place to look would be in the ingenious system by which freshwater is accumulated and warehoused through the winter months when it would be wasted for agricultural purposes, and is then recalled from storage and distributed during the parched summer months, when farmers desperately need it to moisten their crops. Agriculture in much of the temperate world would be impossible without meltwater from snow-packs in adjacent mountains, and when this intricate mechanism periodically fails, water stress becomes acute and famine looms. To cite one example, "In the Hindu Kush Himalayan region, where glaciers provide water for more than 240 million people, glacial mass is expected to drop by about 10 to 25 percent by 2030, and by 20 to 40 percent by 2050 in some subregions."[39] Many of the world's most important rivers originate in the mountain water towers of the Himalayas, Alps, Rockies, Andes, and other great ranges, and the world's most dense population centers have arisen on the banks of these rivers.

The simple calculation is: more warmth equals less snow, particularly in tropical and temperate regions. More of the water released by winter storms will fall as rain, and more frequent midwinter thaws will empty the snow-packs sooner. The result will be that the Rhine and the Mekong may have more water in February, but less in July when it is most needed.

By summer's end, the annual snow-pack is gone, and the sources of many rivers are permanent glaciers. If the glaciers disappear as many are now doing, that last late-season water source will dwindle as well, and many of the world's largest rivers will be affected. Of course, resourceful farmers and city water systems will turn increasingly to underwater aquifers for replacement water sources, but we are increasingly exhausting those aquifers as well. Moreover, the draining of these aquifers is another factor worsening the impact of sea level rise in that it can cause the land above them to subside. This is seen in such places as Jakarta, New Orleans, and the Mekong Delta.[40, 41]

Some areas that are productive farmland today will become untenable as these water sources disappear, with California's superabundant Central Valley being a supremely fragile example.[42] "Certain regions, for example, parts of the Mediterranean region, and parts of the United States and Mexico, are projected to see a decrease in mean annual surface water supply of more than 70 percent by 2050. Such a large decrease in water supply could cause chronic water stress and increase competition for resources across sectors."[43] These same prospective freshwater shortages also affect the future reliability of hydropower production in places like the western US and Southeast Asia.

### Altered Global Circulations

As noted in Chapter 2, local climates all over the Earth are profoundly influenced by regional and global flows of both wind and ocean water – the Gulf Stream, the polar jet stream, the trade winds, the monsoons, El Niño – are all crucial in defining where and when it is wet, dry, hot, or cold.[44] Some of these circulations are persistent, whereas others oscillate on seasonal, annual, or decadal time frames, but none of these is set in stone, so to speak.[45] Temporary alterations in the location, directionality, or intensity of these circulations cause temporary weird weather (heat waves, cold snaps, floods), but long-term changes in them would cause much larger disruptions. Western Europe is kept unexpectedly warm relative to its latitude not only by the Gulf Stream carrying warm water from the Caribbean, but also by the Atlantic Meridional Overturning Circulation, which brings a northward flow of warm salty surface water from the mid-Atlantic up past the coast of Europe to the Nordic and Labrador Seas. There it meets the magnificent waterfall in the sea south of Greenland and Iceland. The salty surface water cools and densifies, whereupon it plunges to the ocean floor and begins a southward flow in the deep ocean. This great ocean circulation appears to be slowing, perhaps because increasing ice melt from Greenland is reducing the salinity and therefore the density of this water, rendering it less prone to plunge to the ocean floor.[46] Since there is also evidence that the Gulf Stream may be weakening, it may prove that in a generally warmer world, Western Europe may get colder.[47] One could debate whether that is a harm or a benefit, but once again both the natural and the human world are adapted to the local climates that exist today, so widespread changes of those climates would be highly disruptive.

To the primary, physical threats noted above can be added coastal hypoxic events and the spread of pests and pathogens – familiar and unfamiliar – to new regions.

## Human Impacts

From the physical impacts of climate change, many human consequences will follow. Perhaps at the top of that list is concern about possible widespread food scarcity. Drawing once again from McKinsey, "in the case of a multiple breadbasket failure, a yield failure in two or more key production regions for rice, wheat, corn, and soy, we estimate that prices could spike by 100 percent or more in the short term. This would particularly hurt the poorest communities, including the 750 million people living below the international poverty line."[48] Other than perhaps war, there is nothing more destabilizing to human societies than food scarcity.

In the unequal and often xenophobic world in which we live, accelerating migration will likely be one of the more destabilizing human effects. Like the plants and animals described above, humans too could in theory migrate from the desiccated Sahel and Rajasthan to newly temperate Manitoba and Siberia, but only with enormous economic disruption and political upheaval along the way. Birds and wind-born seeds need not consider national borders, but people do – after all, controlling the movement of people is the primary purpose of borders. There are many exceptions, but as a general matter, population growth is still surging in areas that will become less habitable in a substantially warmer world, and declining (before immigration) in areas that will become more so. As an example, the Northern African countries now have a population equal to more than half of the EU and are projected to grow 50 percent by 2050.[49] If those countries are forced to support more people on less arable land, it's not difficult to imagine where their citizens will seek to go. Immigration has long been a net flow from the less developed "Global South" to the wealthier "North," but if climate change exacerbates food insecurity in the South, the barely manageable recent flows would become torrents. The outward flow of 5 million Syrians during the height of that civil war greatly destabilized Europe. Climate change could force hundreds of millions to seek new lives elsewhere, creating a refugee crisis without parallel in human history, overwhelming target destinations such as the US and Canada, but most particularly, Europe.

The degree to which the extended drought in northeast Syria a decade ago did or did not substantially precipitate the civil war and the out-migration that followed is under debate, but it is widely perceived that climate change will be a conflict multiplier.[50, 51] Anywhere threatened with food or water insecurity becomes a fertile cauldron for unrest or armed conflict. Everyone prays for peace, but history provides countless demonstrations that people will choose war over starvation. According to the UN, "Droughts in Africa and Latin America directly feed into political unrest and violence. The World Bank estimates that, in the absence of action, more than 140 million people in sub-Saharan Africa, Latin America, and South Asia will be forced to migrate within their regions by 2050."[52] Hungry states will tend to become failed states, whose conflicts can then spill into neighboring states. Too much climate change too quickly would threaten the stability of societies all over the world.

Human health will be impacted first by the exacerbation of problems that already exist but, later in the century, by new causes of ill health especially in developing countries with low income.[53] An IPPC report states that:

> In urban areas, climate change is projected to increase risks for people, assets, economies, and ecosystems, including risks from heat stress, storms and extreme precipitation, inland and coastal flooding, landslides, air pollution, drought, water scarcity, sea level rise, and storm surges. Rural areas are expected to experience major impacts on water availability and supply, food security, infrastructure and agricultural incomes.[54]

Touristic economies reliant upon natural systems such as ski or fishing vacation spots may be upended.

Another economic impact of climate change may be the income lost from a shortening of the work day because mid-day conditions will become too hostile to labor:

> The global average number of working hours that could be lost due to increasing heat and humidity in exposed regions (a measure of workability impacts) could almost double by 2050, from 10 percent to 15 to 20 percent. This is because more regions of the world are exposed, and the ones that are exposed would see higher intensity of heat and humidity effects.[55]

McKinsey estimated that the resulting loss of GDP could be $4 trillion to $6 trillion globally at risk by 2050 in an average year, which is 5–7 percent of current global GDP.[56]

The list of threats from too much climate change is long and lurid indeed. All of this may be in our future, and our descendants 100 years from now may resent us greatly. On the other hand, we may soon begin to divert sharply from the current path, in which case it may turn out all right. Per the aphorism variously attributed to physicist Niels Bohr and athlete Yogi Berra, "Predictions are hard, especially about the future." It is difficult to discern how much risk is an acceptable amount of risk, but one thing is clear. Less risk would be a safer choice. The sooner we eliminate GHG emissions, the better our range of possible outcomes will be.

# 4 CLIMATE NEGOTIATIONS

Despite our hopes to the contrary, the most significant climate accord yet devised by humanity is nonetheless unlikely to spare us from a future climate reckoning. The Paris Agreement is a magnificent piece of statecraft that tries valiantly to achieve the impossible. It seeks to beguile the living into making tangible sacrifices on behalf of the unborn and to shame the developed world into subsidizing the energy transition for the less developed. It is perhaps the best structure that can be hoped for at this time, and yet still woefully inadequate for its task. Moreover, while it appears to have evaded infant mortality via an early US exit, it will remain vulnerable to future American scuttling until such time as it is embraced by at least some sizable portion of the US Republican Party. Like the renewable energy revolution that we will review a bit further on, Paris may someday save us, but likely not soon enough.

## The Montreal Protocol Example

For our immediate purpose, the path to Paris starts in Montreal, which was the site of the negotiations that led to the extraordinarily successful agreement that served as the model for subsequent climate treaties. The Montreal Protocol was devised in order to address a different atmospheric problem, properly referred to as stratospheric ozone depletion but more commonly known as the "ozone hole." Ozone is a chemical compound consisting of three oxygen atoms bonded together ($O_3$) rather than the more common configuration of two ($O_2$) and is characterized as "good" or "bad" depending upon its location in the atmosphere. "Bad" ozone occurs down here by us in the troposphere. It is produced by humans as a secondary pollutant when sunlight reacts with two primary pollutants: oxides of nitrogen ($NO_X$) and volatile organic compounds. This "ground-level ozone" is harmful to breathe for people and animals and further damages crops and other plants. It is a major component of urban smog and is therefore the indirect subject of clean air regulations. However, the very same chemical compound is "good" ozone if it arises naturally higher up in the stratosphere where it serves a vital function in screening out most of the incoming ultraviolet (UV) radiation emitting from the Sun.

As noted in Chapter 2, the Sun emanates radiation all along the spectrum, but about 10 percent of the solar radiation reaching the top of Earth's atmosphere arrives as shortwave UV light. This radiation causes sunburn but in larger doses damages DNA and causes skin cancer, cataracts, and crop damage. In its full complement, unfiltered UV light would make life on land impossible for most creatures. Fortunately, the layer of ozone in the stratosphere screens out most of the UV light while admitting most of the visible light on which plants and therefore most animals depend.

The natural cycle by which stratospheric ozone molecules form, function as a screening mechanism, and then recombine to form normal $O_2$ was a stable one that constituted a durable protective layer of "good" ozone and allowed terrestrial life to flourish. However, this balance was disturbed in the mid-twentieth century, when newly devised chlorofluorocarbons (CFCs) began to be widely used both as refrigerants and propellants for aerosol sprays.[1] These chemicals are not directly harmful to humans, but as they leaked from cooling coils and wafted from hairspray cans, they entered the lower atmosphere and eventually mixed into the stratosphere, where they encountered the protective layer of $O_3$. CFCs in this environment are split up by UV radiation, releasing chlorine atoms. These chlorine atoms are highly reactive with $O_3$, stripping the spare oxygen atom from these unstable compounds to form chlorine monoxide (ClO). When that ClO molecule encounters a free oxygen atom, a molecule of oxygen forms and the chlorine atom is freed again to go break up other ozone molecules, leading to a general stratospheric ozone massacre. The potential for ambient CFCs to break down stratospheric ozone was first recognized by scientists at UC Irvine in the early 1970s,[2] but there was no direct proof that it was actually happening in the real world or that it constituted a threat to humans. DuPont, the world's largest manufacturer of CFCs, called the theory "a science fiction tale," "rubbish," and "utter nonsense."[3]

That changed dramatically in 1985 when the British Antarctic Survey first directly observed the "ozone hole." This is a massive area of low ozone concentrations (so in fact a "thinning" rather than an actual "hole") centered over Antarctica that appears at the beginning of the Antarctic spring in September and October. As previously discussed, due primarily to the thermal inertia of the Arctic Ocean, the North Pole never gets as cold as does the South Pole. Moreover, the South Pole sits more than a mile and a half above sea level, making it cooler still. At the depth of the southern winter, temperatures over Antarctica plunge to a level that facilitates the formation of polar stratospheric clouds. The surface of these special clouds facilitates the accumulation of chlorine molecules. When the dark of the polar winter is penetrated by the first sunlight of the southern spring, those chlorine molecules get busy seeking and destroying ozone molecules. This slaughter continues for a couple of months until the relative warmth of spring decimates the clouds themselves. The same phenomenon happens at a smaller scale and irregularly over the Arctic, but consistently and persistently in the Antarctic.

In some sense, it is fortunate that this phenomenon occurs over Antarctica, where there are few people or animals to be harmed by the intense influx of UV radiation that pours through the ozone hole. Nonetheless, the discovery of the hole and the dramatic images that resulted from mapping it (see Figure 4.1) utterly shocked and galvanized the world. What had been a sound but unproven theory suddenly became manifest and terrifying. If the hole continued to grow each year, it would enlarge to encompass populated areas in the far south such as Patagonia, New Zealand, and Tasmania, and perhaps begin to appear more consistently over the North Pole as well. This was quickly recognized as an existential threat to human civilization and most animal life on Earth and was definitively attributed to the production and release of CFCs.

The pace of the response was stunning. In 1985, the same year in which the ozone hole was definitively discovered, a convention was organized in Vienna to consider a global response. That swiftly led in 1987 to the signing of the Montreal Protocol, an agreement to phase out the production and use of CFCs and other ozone-destroying chemicals.

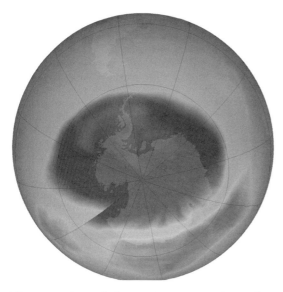

Figure 4.1 Ozone hole over Antarctica in September, 2017. *Source*: NASA/NASA Ozone Watch[4]

The Protocol entered into force in 1989, requiring phase-outs commencing in 1991 and leading to a complete cessation of the manufacture of certain classes of CFCs by 1996. Low-cost substitutes were quickly developed, often by the same companies that had previously made the CFCs. Developed countries provided financial assistance to ease the transition for less developed ones. As less harmful but still problematical chemicals were substituted for CFCs, the agreement was amended repeatedly to target and eliminate the substitutes. Today, these ozone-depleting chemicals have largely disappeared from production streams and are increasingly rare in landfills. Stratospheric ozone concentrations are increasing, and we are on pace to fully repair the ozone layer by mid-century. Crisis averted. Diplomacy can work.

## The Kyoto Protocol Failure

Sandwiched between the Vienna Convention and the signing of the Montreal Protocol came James Hansen's pivotal 1988 congressional testimony that the climate was warming due to GHG emissions. In the same year, the UN adopted a resolution declaring the prospect of climate change was a "common concern." This led in 1992 to the convening in Brazil of the United Nations Conference on Environment and Development, better known as the "Rio Earth Summit." The crowning achievement of the Summit was signing of the United Nations Framework Convention on Climate Change (UNFCCC), although this was also the birthplace of the Convention on Biological Diversity. The UNFCCC formalized the concept of "common but differentiated responsibilities", meaning "we're all in this together, but some of us are more responsible for the problem than others." More succinctly, this meant that developed countries should shoulder the mitigation burden, to the exclusion of developing countries. Pushing back against the accusatory finger pointed at the energy guzzling US in particular, President George H. W. Bush famously declared that "the American way of life is not up for negotiations."[5]

Nonetheless, given the head-spinning success of the Montreal Protocol in limiting CFC emissions, it was perhaps inevitable that the first major climate agreement to emerge from the UNFCCC process would substantially resemble the Montreal Protocol. At the 1997 third Conference of Parties to the UNFCCC (or "COP" as the annual meetings are more colloquially known) in Japan, the Kyoto Protocol was adopted (though it didn't enter into force until 2005) and took a similarly "legislative" approach. It articulated scientifically validated aggregate emissions pathways that would steer the world off its dangerous climate trajectory and attempted to cap the 2008–2012 average GHG emissions for industrialized nations at an average of 5 percent below their respective 1990 levels, recognizing that they were the ones contributing the most to the global emissions.[6] However, many parties felt aggrieved by the apportionment of responsibility. The greatest source of controversy was that Kyoto set binding emissions caps for the developed nations listed in Annex I of the agreement, while exempting developing nations from limitations on the theory that they were still emitting less than their "fair share" and bore almost no responsibility for the historical problem. Among the exempt nations were the two most populous on Earth – China and India. Nonetheless, the process established a declining annual emissions budget among the world's high per-capita emitters intended to avoid climate disaster. Like its Montreal predecessor, the top-down Kyoto targets were to be enshrined in binding international law, such that scofflaws could be penalized and brought into line.

Despite its adherence to the successful Montreal structure, the Kyoto Protocol ran aground before it even left port. The first serious blow was the Byrd-Hagel Resolution in the Senate, which stated that the US would not accept emissions restrictions if there were none for developing countries, most particularly China. It passed without a single dissenting vote and made clear that Senate ratification of such a treaty would be impossible. Rather curiously, the Clinton Administration proceeded to sign the Kyoto Protocol nonetheless, but never submitted it to the Senate for approval. The subsequent Bush (43) Administration announced that it opposed the Protocol on principle, and the prospect of US participation collapsed. With America and the entire developing world outside the agreement, Kyoto's caps applied to less than 25 percent of global GDP – too small a proportion to throttle a global emissions problem. The remaining participants tried to keep the process alive, but when no new emissions caps were agreed at the 2009 COP 19 in Copenhagen, the framework fell apart.

While, at the outset, CFC emissions and GHG emissions appeared to be similar problems that would yield to similar solutions, it became apparent that the two situations were in fact quite different. CFC emissions were a tiny part of the global economy, whereas GHG emissions affect virtually everything. There proved to be easy substitutes for CFCs, manufactured in most cases by the very same companies, so there were few reasons to lobby against it. CFCs were made by only 20 or so countries, nearly all in the developed world, so a production phaseout that applied only to developed countries could nonetheless be effective. The threat posed by the ozone hole was visible and imminent, and the world therefore proved amenable to binding targets. None of those descriptions applied to the climate problem.

## The Promise of the Paris Agreement

The autopsy of the Kyoto Protocol began well before it was officially dead. With great reluctance given their much lesser contribution to the cumulative emissions stream, developing countries came to accept that any successor agreement would need to include them as well. Ultimately, a fudge was confected where nations would voluntarily determine their own non-binding goals, acknowledging their "common but differentiated responsibilities," while ameliorating concerns by the US and others over being tied to hard targets enforceable under international law. Each country would be responsible only for its "nationally determined contribution" (NDC), which it would nominate for each five-year cycle under the Agreement. The framework announced the goal that global warming should be limited "well below 2°C," but there would be no enforced negotiation to ensure that when tallied up, all the NDCs would fit within the target. And neither would there be any enforcement mechanism beyond peer pressure to penalize countries either for setting unambitious goals or for failing to meet the goals they defined for themselves. The whole emissions reduction program would be voluntary and reliant upon good faith. If this sounds like a weak approach that may fail to adequately address the problem, you are indeed getting the gist of it. But Kyoto demonstrated that anything more ambitious was doomed to failure in the US and other climate skeptical countries. A successor agreement intended to last for perhaps a century had to be insulated from changes in governing parties in major participant countries. An agreement viable only under Democratic administrations in the US would founder sooner or later.

Nonetheless, it was hoped that a Kyoto successor would not be entirely toothless. While the NDCs of each country were neither enforceable nor required to fit under a cap, they were to be subjected to formal review, whereby each country would be queried about its NDC and perhaps asked why it could not afford to be more ambitious or whether its emissions accounting made sense. Optimists might view this review process as an opportunity for "churning and learning,"[7] whereby best practices and lessons learned might be shared among eager strivers. Pessimists might more nearly view this as a forum for "naming and shaming" that might create at least a soft incentive for laggards to catch up. Either way, the process requirements of the agreement *would* be binding and legally enforceable, meaning each country would be required to submit an NDC and would be subject to inspections by other countries to verify its total emissions profile. Nations could not be penalized for failing to meet their targets, but they could be penalized for failing to set targets at all or refusing inspections to see if they were meeting those targets.

The aspiration – scaled back to be sure – was that at least if there were an accurate monitoring and reporting mechanism for emissions, perhaps over time countries could be coaxed to step up to more ambitious targets and, conceivably in the future, more rigorous enforcement of those targets.

In that humbled spirit, the Paris Agreement was born. The groundwork for the Agreement was laid to a substantial degree in bilateral preparatory meetings between the US and China. These signaled a high-profile concurrence between Presidents Obama and Xi that the climate problem was becoming urgent and an agreement to replace Kyoto needed to be hatched. Once those twin locomotives were pulling the train, all the other cars fell in line. Obama, Xi, and over 150 heads of state were in Paris for the conference, most now chastened by the knowledge that the world had wasted nearly two decades in a failed first attempt and needed to make a go of this one. Each nation arrived with an initial NDC that applied either to the first ten-year period, which stretched from 2020 through 2029, or in the case of a few more circumspect states such as the US, for the first half of the decade. Between the signing in 2015 and the onset of the operative period for the first NDCs in 2020, the parties would continue to meet to hammer out the operational rules by which the Agreement would be run (in fact, the negotiations continue still).

The Agreement announced a goal of limiting climate change to well below 2°C by the end of the century, with efforts towards 1.5°C (the bifurcated targets were another fudge to bridge an ambitions gap among participants). However, when the NDCs were tallied, they summed to a climate outcome of more than 3°C. While that can certainly be viewed as a failure relative to the goals of the Agreement, it may well on the other hand spell success relative to unabated climate change. Among the articulated strategies of the Agreement was "broad, then deep."[8] Let's first ensure that all the nations of the world are on board and moving in the right direction. We can thereafter try to raise ambition in subsequent 5-year NDC cycles and perhaps bend the curve more nearly towards the target we intend. Given the scars of Kyoto, that seemed like admirable wisdom if more meagre ambition.

## The Path Since Paris

Given the well-established track record of the US Republican party in scuttling global agreements from Kyoto all the way back to the League of Nations, the signatories to the Paris Agreement, not least Obama himself, were keenly aware of the need to insulate it as much as possible from similar backtracking. The Agreement was signed a year before the 2016 US Presidential election and came into effect four days before the election itself, meaning that irrespective of the voting outcome, the US would initially join the Agreement. Moreover, once in effect, it required three years' notice before an intended pull-out could be announced, and a further year for it to take effect. The fact that this timing deferred the prospect of a possible withdrawal until the outcome of the 2020 election would be known was by no means a coincidence.

The modest nature of the binding provisions of the Agreement were also no accident. The US negotiating team was acutely aware of which provisions and what language (e.g., "shall" vs. "will") would trigger the need for Senate ratification and ensured the provisions fell just short of these thresholds, producing the most effective agreement that could be devised while bypassing the Senate.

Of course, all this careful planning was put to the test. As a candidate, Trump railed against the Agreement, blustering that climate change was a hoax and the Agreement would wreck the US economy. No matter that the former is flatly untrue and the latter would be an exaggeration in respect of the Kyoto Agreement but entirely inapplicable to its successor. An irony here is that from a truly US-centric and purely cynical standpoint, the clever play would have been to stay in the Agreement, fail to fulfill whatever NDC Obama may have staked out, hope that other parties naively fulfill *their* pledges, and "free ride" while others wreck *their* economies. Nonetheless, pulling out of the Paris Agreement fit well with Trump's general and reflexive distrust of multilateralism, and on the first day that a pull-out announcement was permitted, a swaggering Denier in Chief squeezed the trigger.

The US withdrawal did indeed occur on November 4, 2020, but with the contemporaneous election of Joe Biden, the world was assured that the US would quickly reverse itself and rejoin the Agreement. The failsafe mechanism built into the Paris Agreement had succeeded, but just barely. A Trump re-election in 2020 might have caused Paris to be scuttled similarly to Kyoto. A Trump or Trumpist return to the White House in 2024 would risk the same, though, by then, the Agreement may be a more robust, scampering child rather than an easily smothered infant.

The US is not the only recalcitrant party to the Agreement. Brazil too has been a foot-dragger,[9] though it remains in the Agreement, while Australia has been trying to fulfill an already weak

NDC[10] via accounting gimmickry. In addition to the US, the Climate Action Tracker[11] rates as consistent with a 4°C+ world and therefore "critically insufficient" the climate policies of Argentina, Russia, Saudi Arabia, Turkey, Ukraine, and Vietnam. In the less severe "highly insufficient" category are China, Indonesia, Japan, South Africa, and South Korea. Several of these countries are not on track to meet their NDCs.

Each of the COP meetings since Paris has hammered away at building the administrative scaffolding under the Agreement to work out such matters as the procedures by which the worldwide GHG emissions inventory exercise known as the "global stocktake" will be conducted every five years starting in 2023 and the rules by which countries can trade emissions offsets amongst themselves. One of the most contentious outstanding issues is the pledge demanded by developing countries of $100 billion per year in adaptation and mitigation financing from the developed world starting in 2020, as many developing countries have said from the outset that these financial transfers were an essential inducement to secure their participation in the Agreement. While COP 24 (2018) in Poland saw increased pledges by some countries and rules established for finance reporting, the subsequent COPs have failed to backfill the adaptation and mitigation funding shortfall, particularly in light of the peek-a-boo game being played by the US.

In summary, the Paris Agreement in many ways represents humanity at its best. It is a bid to bridge vastly different perspectives to solve one of the most intractable global problems of our age. It attempts to apply hard-won wisdom from past failures to build a durable structure that can withstand regime change as well as climate change and deliver a better world for our grandchildren and beyond. It beckons forth the "better angels of our nature" on behalf of nature, and is climate diplomacy's best hope for mankind.

It also may not work. It narrowly escaped a Trumpian rift that might have emboldened other climate deniers and foot-draggers, imperiling the adaptation and mitigation funding mechanism, and propelling the whole process towards another Kyoto-style meltdown. The NDCs pledged under the Agreement come nowhere close to achieving the 1.5 to 2°C goal and, worse yet, we are not fulfilling those commitments. The COVID-19 crisis slowed emissions in 2020 but, in the span of a several-century emissions trajectory, that will be little more than noise in the data. The bathtub is still filling.

Despite the soaring hopes the world now places on this Agreement, it is not yet clear whether Paris will save us. It is certainly not saving us yet. Perhaps it can survive, broaden, and then deepen, with participants ratcheting up their ambition as intended. The US certainly appears poised to do that, and continued European and Chinese resolve suggests that perhaps momentum towards real change is building. On the other hand, as the world recovers from the COVID economic swoon, all expectations are global emissions will resume their steady rise in the next few years. The coming five years under Paris may therefore bear an eerie resemblance to the last five, wherein we continue to talk earnestly about the need to staunch the gushing flow from our proverbial spigot but can't quite seem to grasp the handle and turn it.

Two months after the Paris Agreement was signed, the Seine overtopped its banks in the worst flooding in a century. The Floods of 2018 and 2021 were not quite as bad, but the river seems to be rinsing the adjacent sidewalks with increasing regularity. Even in the City of Light itself, the bathtub continues to fill.

# 5 CLIMATE ECONOMICS

I spent Chapter 4 paring back outsized expectations for the effectiveness and speed with which climate negotiations may spare us from the consequences of our continuing fossil fuel binge. In this chapter, we will pivot to a potential reason for optimism from an unexpected quarter. If we view climate purely through an economic lens, it might be that things turn out all right after all (maybe . . .).

## The Emissions-Economy Tug of War

The "net zero emissions" framing with which the world has lately become infatuated portrays the solution to our climate problems as a race against time, but for economic purposes it may be better to see it as a tug of war between opposing long-term trends. If we seek to predict the trajectory of the world's carbon emissions output, there are four main components which will drive it according to the Kaya Identity,[1] named after Japanese economist Yoichi Kaya, who derived this formula in the 1990s by reworking ideas earlier expressed by Paul R. Ehrlich and John Holdren of Stanford and Harvard respectively.[2] The four components are population, per capita income, watts of energy required to produce a dollar of income (energy intensity), and the carbon intensity of the energy required to produce a watt. Differently put:[3]

$$CO_2 \text{ emissions} = \text{population} \times \left(\frac{\$}{\text{person}}\right) \times \left(\frac{\text{watts}}{\$}\right) \times \left(\frac{\text{carbon}}{\text{watt}}\right)$$

(OK, I guess that's an equation, but we're not going to do any math here . . .). Let's drill down on each of those four factors.

How population might drive energy demand, and therefore carbon emissions, is straightforward – the more people there are on the Earth, the more demand there will be for energy. Global population currently stands at about 7.5 billion and is projected to peak towards the end of this century at perhaps 11 billion – a roughly 50 percent further increase from today.[4] We can try to predict these population trends, but we will not attempt to shape or manage them for the purposes of climate change. Limiting population growth would ease the global warming problem substantially, but it would seem macabre to propose that we somehow curtail births and hasten deaths for climate purposes. Demography should and will play out on its own logic. Births are to be celebrated and deaths, mourned. But if there are 50 percent more people 80 years from now, all other things being equal (and of course, all other things *won't* be equal), we should expect 50 percent more demand for energy.

Unlike population, per capita income is a variable which we *will* try to manage, but for the purposes of carbon emissions, we will try to manage it in the wrong direction – up. Everyone wants to be wealthier, and most people toil feverishly to achieve that end. In a wealthy consumerist society, comfortable sages could question the wisdom of that, but in the less developed Global South where billions of people hover in or near poverty, few do. It is the very mission of most such societies to catch up to the north in economic terms, and with a dash of good governance and luck, many of them will do exactly that in the coming century. By 2100 there will be roughly 11 billion people on Earth, all of whom will seek to live the energy-rich lifestyle enjoyed by the fortunate 2 billion today.[5] If eight of those 11 billion were to succeed in that aspiration by then, that would approximately quadruple the demand for energy. Both of these huge global forces – population and economic growth in the Global South – are working *against* our climate goals.

Pivoting to watts per dollar, if 8 billion are by the century's end living as 2 billion do today, it means that those societies will make the same economic transition the Global North has already made, from primarily manufacturing and agricultural economies to service and knowledge economies. Fortunately, the amount of energy required to produce a dollar of income in a service economy is much lower than in a heavy industry economy, so this term in our equation should move in the right direction. Equally, as more energy efficient gadgets and technologies are developed (perhaps in response to government mandates), watts per dollar of income will continue to fall. Unlike the first two variables above, energy efficiency and watts per dollar more broadly are variables that we *can* manage.

Finally, the amount of carbon emitted to produce each watt of energy can also fall. This will not necessarily nose-dive on its own – the free market may require massive nudges if not rude shoves to move at the speed we seek – but here too we have a variable we can manage. And on a net basis, we *must* manage this one all the way to zero to achieve a carbon-free stream of energy.

To win our emissions tug of war then, we don't need merely for the energy intensity (watts/$) of our economy and the carbon intensity (carbon/watt) of our energy mix to fall. Rather, we need them to fall *faster* than population and per capita income rise, and that will be a very tall order if four times as many people in 2100 expect to live the energy-rich lifestyle that we enjoy today. Several of the most reputable prognostications of energy demand and emissions in the next two or three decades do not forecast us winning much ground in that time period. In fact, the International Energy Agency predicts that energy-related $CO_2$ emissions will *increase* between now and 2040.[6] The US Energy Information Agency comes to a similar conclusion.[7]

To pull up out of the weeds a bit, the broader point here is that the main driver of GHG emissions is economic growth, which, to put it mildly, is a highly prized good. To put it less mildly, it's the world's obsession, so good luck standing in the way of that train. With no growth, temperatures would likely stay within permissible bounds – perhaps 2.5°C by 2200.[8] On the other hand, with growth continuing at historical levels, temperatures would zoom out of sight – 3.5°C by 2100 and 6°C by 2200.[9] But if growth continues at historical levels, our perspiring great grandchildren will be able to afford a lot of air conditioning. Global per capita income today is roughly $10,000. If we simply permit the world to continue on its merry growth path, it would be $55,000 by 2100 and $130,000 by 2200, all in constant dollars. Our descendants in 180 years would be 13 times richer than citizens today. And this is the average. Citizens in the slow growth Global North will merely be several times richer, whereas some societies in the high growth Global South might be 15 or 20 times richer. Unfathomable though that seems, the per capita income in China has grown roughly 100-fold over the last 50 years.[10]

With the Paris Agreement, we may imagine that we are straining mightily to save the livelihood of the destitute rice farmer in the Brahmaputra delta whose paddies are threatened with saltwater inundation. A noble aspiration indeed. But perhaps if we simply get out of the way and let the economy do its thing, by 2200 his descendants will be software engineers living in high rise apartments on the outskirts of Dhaka. The former rice paddy may indeed be underwater, but it ceased to be the family's primary source of income a few generations before it was submerged. Particularly for the world's poorest societies, a century or two of robust economic growth would bolster their climate resiliency to a degree that is scarcely comprehensible.

## The Externalities of Economic Growth

Climate change may prove highly problematical, but the economic development nurtured by all the cheap energy that precipitated it may leave the world environmentally degraded but much richer. Residents of the Global North who have already escaped poverty may opt for the luxury of perceiving that as a poor trade, but the 2 billion people who are experiencing food insecurity worldwide[11] are likely to see this differently.

Steering away from a path that promises continued growth at the cost of environmental destruction requires that we recognize the cost that continued carbon emissions confers upon future generations and enforce that cost upon the emitters today. Carbon emissions is a classic example of an economic externality, where a party is consuming a societal resource at no cost to itself. If you pour toxic industrial effluent into a river, the downstream inhabitants of that river bear costs – the fishermen can no longer catch fish, the farmers can no longer use that water to irrigate their crops, and the city needs either to clean the water or find alternative water sources. In a more primitive phase of industrialization, the sludge dumper may have insisted that he had a right to pollute the river, or at minimum hoped he would not be identified, but as the downstream costs came to be recognized, society pushed back.

The simplest and most elegant countermeasure would be to determine how much economic harm the downstream residents endure and impose a cost on the polluter equal to those damages. Once the funds are distributed downstream, then all parties are fairly incented and compensated. The polluter pays a cost for the right to dump in the river, and the downstream residents are reimbursed for their damages. If, despite the elevated cost, spoiling the river is still the cheapest disposal solution for the polluter, then the situation continues as it is. However, if these new dumping fees are unsustainable for the polluters, they may switch to some different production method that produces less sludge or may find an alternate sludge disposal method that causes less harm. Of course, another societal response to many externalities is to ban or heavily regulate them to force bad actors to find some alternative solution. But one way or another, once the polluter is forced to pay for the harms from his pollution, some better, fairer distribution of benefits and harms can be found. What we have done here is to internalize the externality – to take a valuable public good for which one party previously paid nothing (and was therefore external to the market) and place a value on it both to compensate those harmed and to incentivize the actor to find alternative solutions that cause less harm. Once the cost of polluting is higher, the polluter will opt for less of it.

Dumping GHGs into the atmosphere is the mother of all externalities. Nearly every human does it, either by driving a car or by purchasing a manufactured good – a cell phone, a shirt, a bag of potato chips – wherein fossil fuels were consumed in making it and/or transporting it to your store or door. All this will impose massive costs on others, mostly the unborn. In the sludge dumping example above, the polluter imposes harms on others while appropriating a public good for their private benefit. In the climate example, it is clear who will be harmed most – our descendants. But who is made richer?

All of us. Everyone alive today who can consume cheap energy without having to additionally pay for the harms that it will impose upon future generations. We are that polluter, upstream in time instead of in space. We are expropriating, for our benefit, public goods that we are therefore robbing from the future.

It seems likely that our descendants will see ours as a primitive incarnation of industrialism, in which this glaring externality was left to fester outside the market, but to address the climate problem, that must come to an end. There is no reason to believe that an unfettered market will lead us to a zero emissions future. In fact, we can have high confidence that it will not, or at least not soon enough. Solar and wind power will likely continue to become cheaper and more cost competitive, but carbon emitting power sources are unlikely to die a natural death in the world's energy source mix any time soon. If we want to get rid of them, we will have to murder them. We must create a market signal that charges users of this externality and incentivizes them to find less abusive practices. Indirect signals already exist in most developed economies – fuel standards for cars and efficiency standards for gadgets and buildings. These are easier to legislate and implement because voters generally imagine that their costs are borne by "big bad corporations" rather than the purchasers of the goods involved, so they serve as a stealth tax and are more popular than direct taxes. However, such indirect carbon charges are also generally inefficient, in that they impose a high economic burden relative to the amount of GHG emissions they deter.

The simpler, more efficient market signal that is favored nearly universally by economists is a direct tax on GHG emissions, or, to revert to the most widespread term, a "carbon tax" (it would presumably apply to other GHGs as well but we'll stay with the commonly used term). Such a tax would be applied to every carbon emitting form of activity and would reflect not how much energy is in the tank, but how much carbon will be emitted upon combusting that fuel or manufacturing that thing. Since coal is more carbon intensive and natural gas less so, a $25-per-tonne carbon tax would increase the price of gas by 30 percent, but coal by 130 percent.[12] Of course, more than doubling the price of coal would make it much less competitive economically and would provide a strong nudge for coal users to switch to alternative fuels – exactly as intended.

Since wind, solar, and hydropower are non-emitting, their price would increase very little, just enough to account for the carbon emitted in the manufacture and installation of the related infrastructure. The aggregate effect then would be to incentivize people to switch to "cleaner" fuels – solar over gas, gas over oil, oil over coal – and to use less fuel. Such a carbon tax would most efficiently be administered at the place where the fuel entered the country – at the wellhead for domestically produced oil and at the port for imported coal. But it would eventually be paid by consumers at the gasoline pump and in their electric rates. This would neatly internalize this glaring externality and ensure that producers and consumers made thoughtful decisions about their energy consumption and energy mix rather than continuing to binge at the expense of our descendants.

As regards what to do with the funds raised from such a tax, the fairest answer would be to set them aside to compensate our great grandchildren for their higher air conditioning bills and the loss of their seafront property. But that's a laughable policy option. Once raised, the money will be promptly spent. It could either be utilized to fund new government programs or could be given back to the people in the form of reduced income or sales taxes. Fiscal conservatives will scoff at the proposition that more taxes of one sort will be offset by less tax of another sort, but a clever proposal by which to safeguard the sanctity of carbon tax revenues had been advanced in the US by the late Ted Halstead and the Climate Leadership Council.[13] They have proposed to ensure that carbon taxes would be revenue-neutral by segregating the funds derived from them and returning them to citizens in the form of a quarterly check. This would be similar to the immensely popular (with residents, if not necessarily economists) program run by the State of Alaska that returns to its citizens the funds the state derives from oil drilling leases on the North Slope.[14] Once Americans started receiving a quarterly check from the carbon tax revenue, it would create a very powerful constituency that could at least in theory lobby to protect the program from eager bureaucrats who may seek to divert the funds elsewhere.

The other most commonly discussed mechanism by which to establish a market signal that would steer us away from carbon profligacy is a "cap-and-trade" system. This would cap the total amount of GHG emissions at some fixed amount. Rights to emit would be sold or otherwise allocated by the government, and then parties that seek to emit carbon could trade those allowances among themselves. Parties who can make easy energy substitutions or reductions would do so and sell their allowances, whereas other parties for whom substitution would be difficult or expensive (such as airlines) would buy credits and continue to emit. In this way emissions could be capped at a level acceptable to society, and those that seek to emit within the allowances pay a price for doing so. Over time, the cap could be reduced such that the price for emission allowances rises, weening society off its destructive emissions path.

Fuel standards, efficiency regulations, carbon taxes, and cap-and-trade systems would all pursue the same goal, which would be to recognize within the energy market the currently unrecognized cost of using the sky as a dump and thereby force society to make more responsible decisions about its emissions trajectory. Which is to say that they would make people poorer. They would start paying a price for something that is now free and therefore freely consumed by just about everyone. Making the world cleaner and greener is a generally popular idea. Making the world poorer is not. To be fair, fossil fuel combustion produces not only $CO_2$ but particulate air pollution, which creates health maladies not for future generations but for the current one. Reducing such pollution would therefore confer an offsetting though by no means fully countervailing economic benefit. Nonetheless, the unfortunate truth is that until some miracle dramatically changes the economics of our energy options, steering the world off our GHG trajectory will require that we increase by a little bit the price of virtually everything in the economy, meaning that people will have a little less spending power and world economic growth will slow slightly, but indefinitely.

## 2 °C is Not Free

Differently put, there would be a significant cost to constraining the global temperature increase to 2°C, and even more so for 1.5°C. If we seek to impose a climate change limit, that will cost money. If coal is the cheapest energy option for much of the world, and we take that option away via any of the mechanisms noted above, whatever substitute fuel source existing coal-fired plants switch to will be more expensive by definition. Electricity rates will have to rise to pay for that. People will therefore have a bit less to spend on groceries and will be a little poorer. Economic growth rates will be stunted.

Once we recognize that the climate targets called for by the IPCC confer a benefit but at a cost, we enter the world of cost-benefit analysis. If the cost of limiting climate change to 1.5°C is low, we will likely prefer that, but if it is high, a rational actor might actually prefer 2°C over 1.5°C, or 3°C over 2°C. Instead of "how much climate change do we want?," the question becomes "how much poorer are we willing to be today to sacrifice for a more benign climate future that many of us will not live to see?" That's a much more nuanced question. In that latter formulation, the "optimal" amount of climate change is not necessarily the lowest amount. It is the amount that strikes the best balance between our willingness to pay and our desire to bequeath to our descendants a pristine environment. It requires us to find a middle course, as Nobel prize winning Yale economist William Nordhaus mused, "between wrecking the economy and wrecking the world."[15]

This helps explain why, when the world thus far has been asked how much climate change it wants, the professed answer is "none," but the answer revealed by our actions and policy choices has consistently been "more." And more climate change might not be bad in every respect. For starters, estimates are that $CO_2$ concentrations leading to a 3°C temperature increase would be favorable to plants and thus to agriculture in many parts of the world. Therefore, according to Nordhaus, modest warming in the next few decades is likely to *decrease* food prices. More recently, the IPCC's 2019 special report on Climate Change and Land presents a more nuanced view, wherein increased crop productivity would be offset by lower nutritional quality and increased cereal prices in some scenarios. Perhaps it's fair to say then that the picture is mixed, but at modest temperature increases, it is not clear that plants and agriculture will suffer. The farming sector was roughly 10 percent of US GDP in 1929 but had declined to less than 1 percent by 2010.[16] It is still a high proportion of GDP in the developing world but will trace a similar tumble as those economies modernize. Therefore, even if the agricultural sector were to experience price shocks, this would have limited effect on the global economy. Though dependent on nature and vulnerable in particular localities, farming as a global activity doesn't appear to be threatened by limited climate change. Moreover, the incentives for adaptation in the agricultural sector are enormous – people have to eat – so particularly if the climate change is gradual (but it may not be), one should expect this sector to find a smooth way forward.

Viewed as a sector of the economy, we should expect a similar story in respect of human health. Most people witness more temperature change in a single day than we are discussing over a couple of centuries, and we have the advantage of knowing that it is coming. This is by no means to suggest that there will be no health impacts from climate change. In fact, the WHO estimates that due to stresses on social determinants of health such as clean drinking water, sufficient food, and secure shelter, climate change will cause 250,000 additional deaths per year from 2030 to 2050 from malnutrition, malaria, diarrhea, and heat stress.[17] Nonetheless, the incentives to adapt in the health arena are existential, so one should expect that in a much richer world, health care capabilities will tend to keep pace with events.[18] (I am seeking here to channel a ruthlessly economic view, so if this seems heartless in respect of individuals who may suffer the impacts of climate change, I both agree and apologize.)

Sea level rise is coming, but Nordhaus bounds its impact between best and worst case scenarios of 1 to 2 meters by 2200.[19] At one meter, Miami, New York, Venice, and Shanghai have serious problems. At 2 meters, their survival would be very much in doubt. And yet, contextualizing such looming disasters is what earned Nordhaus his Nobel. He estimates that just 4 percent of the world's population lives less than 10 meters (33 feet) above sea level, although a subsequent 2015 study placed the number near 10 percent.[20] Anyone situated higher than 10 meters is relatively invulnerable to the degree of sea level rise we might see in the next few centuries, whereas anyone fewer than 2 meters above the sea should begin to see the handwriting on the wall already.

No doubt, some countries are terribly situated for such an eventuality. Seventy-five percent of the population of the Netherlands and 60 percent of Bangladesh lie in the 10 meter zone. In terms of at-risk populations, 120 million Chinese, 92 million Bangladeshis, 80 million Indians, and 18 million Americans live below 10 meters.[21] These are enormous numbers of people. However, buildings and other structures last on average about 50 years, after which they are substantially renovated or replaced. If we foresee as much as 2 meters of sea level rise over the next 180 years, that is more than three building cycles and more than two lifetimes for the average person. That is a long time for perhaps 3–10 percent of humanity to find their way to higher ground, even if it must be acknowledged that moving whole towns and cities is a bigger proposition than simply reconstructing buildings. While for certain property holders this retreat would prove disastrous, the aggregate economic losses deriving from a 1 meter per century creep of the sea would appear modest relative to total economic output.

If rising seas bring economic disaster and large loss of life, these will arrive in the form of hurricanes and other massive storms, not slowly rising tides, but here too, as my old boss at Boeing used to say, "the data will set you free." Hurricanes are a problem mostly for the small slice of humanity that lives in the Caribbean, Central America, the Southeastern US coastline, Oceania, and East Asia. The rest of the world is barely touched. In the US, less than 3 percent of the capital stock is in the hurricane impact zone, so even for a country with high hurricane exposure, this presents a dangerous humanitarian situation but a manageable economic risk. It is true that economic damages from hurricanes are rising faster than the economic growth rate, but this is only weakly correlated to climate change.[22] There is growing confidence that warmer sea temperatures increase hurricane intensity, and the trends seem to show that the hurricanes will keep growing stronger in the future.[23] Stronger storms would logically lead to accelerating damages, but the greater factor is – we don't learn our lessons! We love to build along coastlines, despite the well-known risks (to wit, I recently bought a shore house …). Over the longer span then, hurricane risks are, to a substantial degree, assumed voluntarily, even if the tearful retirees sobbing into television cameras won't see it that way as they survey the foundations of their former beach bungalow. If storm risks are perceived to be too great, humanity can retreat from the coasts.

There is no similarly straightforward way to avoid the risks of ocean acidification. There is little debate as to whether this catastrophe is approaching. The trend is clear. Corals and mollusks will largely disappear, but large portions of the marine ecosystem will survive. Once done, there is little we can do to undo this, so fisheries and the economies that rely upon them will be devastated.

On land as well, countless species will also go extinct due to climate change. IPCC estimates place the percentage around 25, but the range of uncertainty is vast, stretching from about 10 percent to 50 percent and varying between birds, mammals, reptiles, and so on.[24] Finding ourselves most anywhere in this range would fulfill fears regarding the fabled Sixth Great Extinction and would constitute by far the worst thing that mankind has done to the natural habitat. However, viewed through the almost sinfully reductive lens of economics, species and indeed the entire natural world are judged by their "use value" – how much they contribute to the economy. Tuna are eaten. Lions in Kenya are gawked at by safari-booking tourists. Bees make honey and pollinate crops. But many creatures would seem to have little or no use value, in that they play no role in the economy. Does that mean they have no intrinsic value and that we should not mourn them if they disappear? That would seem to betray both an arrogance towards God's handiwork and a hubristic confidence in our knowledge of the interrelationships in nature, neither of which would seem justifiable.

Tallying up via Nordhaus' math this list of the economic damages of climate change, the most heavily impacted sectors are farming, fishing, and forestry, which constituted 1.2 percent of US GDP in 2011. Coastal real estate, transportation, utilities, and construction would be moderately impacted and constitute another 9 percent of the US economy. The other 90 percent of the economy would be lightly or negligibly impacted. The proportions for Western Europe and Japan would be broadly similar. The least developed countries might have as much as 10 percent of their economies in the heavily impacted sectors, but this proportion will fall substantially as the century progresses, so the entire world will modulate to less vulnerability.[25]

Counterintuitively, the first degree of warming, which has already happened, appears to have been economically neutral if not net beneficial on a global scale. Nordhaus' guess as to the economic damage by 2070 that would derive from a 2.5°C warming is just 1.5 percent of global output. However, there is high uncertainty. It could be as high as 5 percent. Nonetheless, quoting Nordhaus:

> The economic impacts from climate change will be small relative to the likely overall changes in economic activity over the next half century to century. Our estimated impacts are in the range of 1–5 percent of output for a 3°C warming. This compares to projected improvements in per capita GDP of 500 to 1,000 percent over the same period for poor and middle-income countries. The loss in income would represent approximately one year's growth for most countries spread over several decades.[26]

This surprising projection is due to the finding that our societal structures – our economy and industry – are actually quite adaptable to climate change if given the time and resources to do so. This does not mean that developing countries that lack financial resources are destined to suffer. In fact, their projected economic growth suggests their climate vulnerability will meaningfully drop by the end of this century. Many of the damaging impacts of climate change lie well outside the conventional marketplace, such as the loss of biodiversity and cultural sites. This illustrates the limitations of the economic lens we are using in this chapter – it clearly doesn't capture everything that is of importance. Costs of environmental damage are often external to the marketplace, but so are some assets.

## The Cost–Benefit of Mitigation

The economy contains many inexpensive emission reduction opportunities. Some may even have negative costs. Consider LED light-bulbs, which cost more to purchase, but earn that premium back several-fold in reduced electricity consumption (and therefore carbon emissions). While consumers economizing on grocery bills often opt for the cheaper bulb, they would be ultimately richer and less carbon profligate to spring for the more expensive one. Similar opportunities abound. Energy efficient appliances including hot water heaters, air conditioners, washers, and dryers can lead to hundreds of dollars of savings for a household. Improving insulation can also save large amounts on building heating and cooling needs. However, costs to the economy quickly rise as we exhaust the negative, neutral, and inexpensive carbon reduction opportunities and proceed to more costly strategies. This is to say that the more we seek to restrict emissions, the more costly each tenth of a degree of avoided warming will be to achieve. Letting temperatures rise to 4°C would be very cheap, whereas limiting the rise to just 1.5°C would be quite expensive. Moreover, there are no single silver bullets. Rather, the "solution" to climate change will likely prove to be small solutions, everywhere.

As we consider investments/expenditures in pursuit of emissions reductions, it is also essential to bear in mind that capital is both scarce and fungible. There are far more projects worthy of funding than there are funds to support them. The money that could be used to safeguard Venice and subsidize wind farms in California can also be used to speed the distribution of COVID-19 vaccines and promote female literacy in Mali. Climate expenditures need to compete with other societal investments and they are at a distinct disadvantage in doing so because of the time value of money. Any good is worth substantially less a year from now than it is today, for several sound reasons. First, all else being equal, people have an inherent preference for instant gratification over delayed rewards. This is in part because we have more information about the present than we do about the future, and can therefore make better resource allocation decisions about our present needs than our future ones. Moreover, money can be invested and produce a return, so a hundred dollars today is worth more than a hundred dollars a year from now, because if I have that sum today, I can buy a bond with it and have one hundred and two dollars in a year.

My use for the funds must produce more than one hundred and two dollars of benefit in a year or I would be better served spending the money today.

Increased cervical cancer screening would save lives *this year*, whereas speeding the phase-out of coal-fired power plants will yield climate benefits 50 or 100 years from now. The awesome power of discounting – even at so low a discount rate as 2 percent – would mean that if I am to divert $100 from cervical cancer screening today to reduced emissions benefits 100 years from now, those future benefits need to be worth over $700 in the future in order to be a better use of funds than the cancer screening today. At a more customary 5 percent discount rate, the value in 100 years needs to be more than $13,000. That is an extremely high hurdle that few climate projects could clear. And yet, to allocate wisely our limited public capital, we need to make exactly those sorts of cost/benefit comparisons to determine whether more benefit will accrue from increased wind farm subsidies or free COVID-19 vaccines.

Taking all the factors into account, Nordhaus' own answer is that the optimal amount of climate change that the world should prefer by 2100 is not the 1.5 °C or 2 °C touted by the IPCC, but more nearly 3 ° C. Aiming for 2 °C would be a misuse of funds that would decrease rather than increase aggregate human happiness and wellbeing. He would argue that one can't set specific climate targets without cost-benefit analysis and that the numerical targets set by others rest on weak economic and policy foundations. He would agree that perhaps 2.5 °C is optimal if you assume perfect efficiency, 100 percent participation by all citizens of the world, and no discounting for the time value of money. In other words, the 2 °C target is roughly right, if you use assumptions that everyone knows are wrong.

Nordhaus' Yale colleague Robert Mendelsohn goes one step further, stating that "the benefits of controlling greenhouse gases are quite low compared to costs. Only a moderate mitigation program is justified according to early damage estimates."[27] He goes on to suggest that succumbing to the as yet unsubstantiated arguments that we must invest heavily and soon in emissions reductions would be "one of the greatest follies mankind has ever considered." Putting it mildly, these are controversial views that are vociferously argued by other economists, but Nordhaus' glittering Nobel prize makes them hard to ignore. Maybe growth will bail us out. Maybe it's all right after all.

## The Problem of Fat Tail Risks

Among the most compelling counter-arguments is the possible existence of unacceptable catastrophes hiding in the "fat tails" of the bell curve of possible climate outcomes. The Yale economists have become world famous for bringing thoughtful numbers to the sometimes over-lathered climate debate. Analysts may sound the alarm that the Greenland ice cap may melt, inundating the world's coastlines in an existential flood. The Nordhaus school responds by saying in effect "let's run the numbers." How fast might the ice melt? How much sea level rise would that precipitate? How long would that take? How much warning would mankind have about that? What proportion of world GDP would need to be consumed to move the world's capital stock out of the way? And by the time the analysis is done, this calamity adds less than 5 percent to the social cost of carbon and therefore seems quite manageable – an enormous problem to be sure, but not one so catastrophic that the next few generations should be made substantially poorer in order to reduce its likelihood.[28]

But "likelihood" is a word we should consider for a moment, since speculating about events so far in the future is inherently risky. It is better than NOT speculating about them – running the numbers usually narrows the region of darkness – but it doesn't shed a bright and unambiguous light on the future. Rather, outcomes have to be expressed in probabilities, often forming the standard bell curve. In order to run integrated climate and economic models, Nordhaus is forced to assume some value for climate sensitivity – that a doubling of atmospheric $CO_2$ would bring say 3°C of warming. He can then determine the cost that would be required to limit warming to no more than 3°C and the benefits that would derive from holding to that limit. However, what if climate sensitivity (which we acknowledge is poorly understood) is actually much higher, producing 4.5°C of warming instead of the 3°C we had expected. That would mean the damages from a given amount of warming would be much higher than the model presumed, and we would have underestimated the ideal amount of funds that should have been spent to avoid those higher damages.

Nordhaus of course understands the limitations of his model, and is therefore evaluating how the outcomes might change if the full spectrum of possible plausible answers for climate sensitivity were to be considered. And this is just one of many uncertain variables in the model. The model therefore creates a bell curve of possible answers. The great likelihood is that correct answers will lie in the bulging middle of the curve, but what if we are surprised? After all, if you roll two die, the chances of getting "snake eyes" (two ones) are a mere 2.8 percent – tiny. Too small to worry about. But as any craps player knows, they are not zero. Snake eyes happen.

So, what if, in the context of Nordhaus' climate modeling, we come up with snake eyes and the actual outcome after 100 more years of GHG emissions does not put us in the tall middle of the probability distribution but way out in one of the tails? The left-hand tail is bounded by zero (for this reason, climate outcomes do not in fact form a symmetrical bell curve). Ending in the extreme of the left-hand tail would mean that we put a lot of carbon in the air but, for reasons we didn't predict, it had much less climate impact than we expected. That would be the best possible outcome – the all-chocolate diet that turned out to not cause a heart attack, but only some uncomfortable heartburn. We would be thrilled that Nordhaus and his colleagues talked us out of even greater expenditures on emissions reductions, because they turned out to be unnecessary. Let's hope.

But the right-hand tail has no obvious function that bounds it. It can run WAAAAY out to the right, with decreasing likelihoods of ever-more disastrous outcomes. Not only is it long, in that it doesn't run to zero for quite a way, but it is also "fat," i.e., the early bits of the tail have significant amplitude on the $y$ axis (see the left-hand graph in Figure 5.1). In other words, there is a meaningful chance that we could fall into these outcomes. But even this framing doesn't properly capture the risk in the fat tail. If the likelihood of falling into the right-hand tail is low (Figure 5.1(a)) but the impact of doing so is very high (Figure 5.1(b)), then the calibration of risk is as shown in Figure 5.1 (c). That tail looks very fat indeed – a significant chance of an utterly terrible outcome.

What if the sensitivity of permafrost to warming is much higher than we realize, and once we surpass 2°C, we get runaway melting and venting of $CO_2$ and methane into the atmosphere? Molecule for molecule, methane heats the climate 28 times greater than $CO_2$, so once the permafrost melt accelerates, it causes more warming and more permafrost melt. The sudden belch of greenhouse gases into the atmosphere heats the planet 6°C or 8°C or 10°C and makes most of the Earth uninhabitable for humans and most everything else. Likely? No. Reasonably possible? Yes,

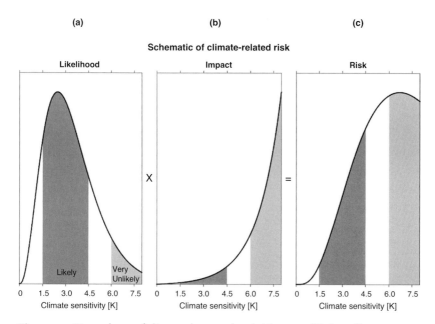

Figure 5.1 Dependence of climate-change-related risk on equilibrium climate sensitivity. The first two panels, likelihood and impact, are multiplied together to give the third panel, risk. *Source*: Earth System Dynamics. Licensed under Creative Commons CC BY 4.0 [29]

we can't rule that out. This would be a classic tipping point, where we won't know it was there until after we have crossed it, by which time there would no longer be anything we could do to stop it. All of which would have our grandchildren sprinting to Nordhaus' portrait at Yale yelling "we shouldn't have listened to you!!!" But if it could, the portrait might respond "No, I told you the tail was fat. You misunderstood and discounted the possibility of snake eyes."

As it happens, we don't need to wait for such a message from Nordhaus' future portrait (he still teaches at Yale, by the way) – we could source the message today from Weitzman's portrait. The late Martin Weitzman was an eminent climate economist at Harvard who, along with his protege Gernot Wagner, strained to ensure that the world understood the message of the "fat tail."[30] The essential question in such climate cost/benefit modeling is not where we think the outcomes are likely to fall, but whether we can stand the implications of the fat tail. Nordhaus acknowledges that the policies that he believes would result in the optimal 3°C of warming have a meaningful chance of instead delivering a disastrous 6°C. Can we accept those odds? We take out fire insurance and wear seat belts to protect against vastly lower likelihood events than snake eyes. What percent chance of "the end of the world" *can* we tolerate in the fat tail? Any?

If you are leaping out of your chair to holler "none!," remember that the fat tail is already there. Weitzman didn't create it. He just pointed out its existence and the danger of ignoring it. But we are already warming the Earth dramatically with consequences we can't predict. And neither can we estimate well what is in the fat tail – either the odds of full-on disaster or its consequences. Nonetheless we are reasonably confident that tipping points are out there somewhere as we venture into the unknown.

So where does our look through the economic lens take us? It is clear that over the long time horizons on which climate change will play out, the dynamics of economic growth will be very powerful and need to be taken into account. When we ask ourselves how much economic sacrifice we should undertake on behalf of unborn generations, it is important to recognize how much richer those future citizens are likely to be, and therefore how much more affordable climate defenses will be for them than they are for us. Our current concern for the climate welfare of the future "Global South" should be balanced against a recognition that, by the century's end, much of it will likely rival the "Global North" in living standards. From the standpoint of the very poor, economic development is likely to trump climate change as the essential concern for a few generations at least.

And yet, this doesn't get us off the hook. The Nordhaus message is that 2°C is not free, but he is not saying that no economic sacrifices should be undertaken to address climate. And Weitzman's warning that we may, at any moment, pass points of no return cannot be overlooked. There is a chance that this may not work out as badly as some alarmist observers think – but we are still sailing off the edge of the map.

# Section II
# RESPONSES TO CLIMATE CHANGE

Part II
RESPONSES TO CLIMATE CHANGE

# 6 THE ENERGY TRANSITION

I hope we have by this juncture put to rest any debate about whether we need to reduce our greenhouse gas emissions. We must do so urgently, all the way to net zero. However, to understand why this process will prove slow – much slower than many climate optimists hope – it is important to understand why it will be hard. These next two chapters will deal with the topic of "mitigation," which is the subject of most climate literature and therefore decidedly not the primary subject of this book. Nonetheless, to ensure that I do not create an impression that climate intervention is somehow a substitute for mitigation, it is important that we focus on it briefly. The bulk of greenhouse gas climate forcing derives from our energy system, so in this chapter we will focus on the energy transition necessary to wean ourselves off the fossil fuels that powered the industrial revolution and everything since. In Chapter 7, we will focus on all other mitigation.

## The Problem of Fossil Fuel Energy

While land use changes, cement manufacturing, and animal husbandry are all significant sources of GHGs, the majority of our GHG inventory derives from energy, mostly $CO_2$ that comes from burning fossil fuels, but also methane that leaks as we harvest natural gas from the ground and transport it to your stove, among other sources. Together, energy-related sources comprise two-thirds of the world's annual anthropogenic GHG output.[1] Therefore, while getting to net zero emissions is a complex and multifaceted undertaking that will affect where we live, what we eat, and how we commute, the most essential aspect of it is weaning the world off fossil fuels.

There are several reasons that this will be hard, but the most salient is that fossil fuels are awesome!! They have an energy density (the amount of energy per unit of volume) that few other economically feasible fuel sources can match (nuclear fuel, for one, has them beat).[2] Despite nearly 200 years of economic development since their initial intense adoption, the fuels themselves haven't changed much. They are magnificently abundant; in one form or another, we find them all over the Earth. To be sure, they are more easily and cheaply recoverable in some places than in others, but the Earth's crust and seabeds turn out to be full of stuff that burns.

In recent decades there had been substantial hand wringing over the prospect of "peak oil" – the idea that we might run out of "black gold" before the world had lost its appetite for the goo and that demand would begin to substantially outrun supply. That would seem to make simplistic sense if one imagines the world's oil reserves as a fixed quantity of liquid in a tank. Since the stuff takes eons to make, mother nature is not making any more of it (on a human time scale at least), so once we drain the tank, the game is over. However, this is overly simplistic.

Figure 6.1 shows how the peak oil theory that appeared plausible 50 years ago turned out over the last 15 years to prove spectacularly wrong. As it happened, fracking, horizontal drilling, offshore recovery, and other improvements in technology of finding oil have flipped the script such that many energy analysts suspect that we may run out of demand before supply, causing the world to elect to leave recoverable reserves in the ground because there may be better, cheaper alternatives. In fact, oil companies such as BP are starting to write off reserves they previously had expected to exploit.[3] The end of oil still seems a long way off, but the race between supply and demand continues to be a competitive one.

Even more than oil, improved natural gas recovery capabilities have both greatly expanded global recoverable sources, and caused the relative price of gas to plunge, accelerating its use. In the power sector particularly, gas is replacing coal at a prodigious pace, which is a benefit from a climate perspective since coal combustion emits twice as much $CO_2$ as does natural gas combustion. However, gas is not replacing coal because of governmental or societal concerns about warming. It is simply a market outcome. If some new breakthrough made coal

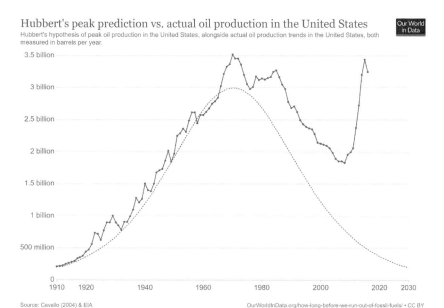

Hubbert's peak prediction vs. actual oil production in the United States
Hubbert's hypothesis of peak oil production in the United States, alongside actual oil production trends in the United States, both measured in barrels per year.

Source: Cavallo (2004) & EIA

OurWorldInData.org/how-long-before-we-run-out-of-fossil-fuels/ • CC BY

**Figure 6.1** Peak oil prediction (smooth curve) vs. actual production. *Source: OurWorldInData.org, licensed under Creative Commons CC BY*[4]

substantially cheaper, we might see it come roaring back. This doesn't change the fact that the ongoing gas-for-coal substitution is good, but it results primarily from dumb luck rather than smart policy. If environmental impacts are not priced into the market, then markets won't guide us to the right climate outcomes, and markets won't internalize these impacts on their own. It is up to those setting the ground rules in which those markets operate (i.e., governments) to do so.

For oil, global "proved reserves" (meaning the amount identified and estimated to be commercially recoverable with existing technologies) currently stand at about 50-times annual consumption,[5] but that doesn't mean we are projected to run out of oil in the next 50 years. Each year there is a spirited race between consumption and exploration, such that the reserve/production ratio has remained reasonably constant, ranging between 45 and 55 since 2000.[6] A similar picture exists with natural gas, with global reserves now standing also at about 50 years of current consumption,[7] even though consumption has been increasing markedly. If oil and gas seem quite abundant, coal is vastly more so. Global reserves stand around 130-times annual consumption,[8] meaning that we are likely never to run out of coal. In whatever way the supply/demand race with oil and gas plays out, in the case of coal, supply seems reliably the winner. There is much more coal than oil and gas put together. World coal demand is approximately flat, and coal should be the first fuel targeted for elimination from a climate perspective.

However, that climate perspective is only beginning to impinge upon the world's decision making about coal or much else in the energy sector. Price is the first consideration, and cheap fuel is desirable fuel. Again, gas has been capturing share in many places because it is cheap, not because it is green. And "green" and "clean" are words that require disaggregation, as they can be taken to mean several, sometimes contradictory things. Historically, the primary argument against coal has not been related to its $CO_2$ contributions, but its air pollution; the particulate matter, sulfur dioxide, nitrogen oxides, and heavy metals that are all part of the wheeze-inducing soot that coal puts into the sky. Emissions from coal-fired power plants inject these pollutants into the air, which can then be inhaled by downwind residents. Such pollution is a major contributor to myriad health maladies common to industrial societies, including severe respiratory and cardiovascular diseases, some cancers, and various neurological disorders. This pollution stays relatively close to the planet's surface, where it can plague respiring creatures. It generally has an endurance in the lower atmosphere ranging from a few hours up to a week or so, and exerts its primary effect on living things within a few hundred kilometers of its emission source.[9]

Almost none of that applies to $CO_2$, which is a naturally occurring substance that is essential to life on our planet (Figure 6.2). $CO_2$ derives from the combustion of fossil fuels, but it is not considered to be a classic "pollutant." It is harmless to inhale in low concentrations, although we and other respiring animals generally exhale rather than inhale it. Plants are eager that we do so, since they gobble the stuff up. Plants are made mostly of carbon, and they get most of that carbon from the air rather than from the soil. In the process of photosynthesis, they take in air-borne $CO_2$, strip the carbon from the oxygen, expire the oxygen for which they have little use, and use the carbon to build their structures. Of course, the animal respiration process does the reverse. Plants and animals therefore exist in a happy symbiosis, and to the extent that industrial life increases society's output of $CO_2$, the plant kingdom is grateful for it. $CO_2$ itself isn't a problem from an air quality standpoint. A little more of it is of no consequence whatever. Its

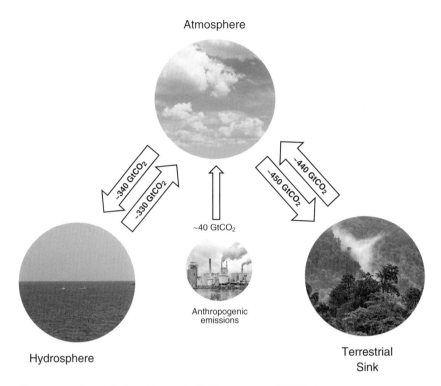

**Figure 6.2** The global carbon cycle.[10] *Data source*, NASA; *image source*, unsplash.com

problems all derive from the thermal effects of adding a lot of it – the way in which it "thickens the blanket" and warms the whole planet. Unlike particulate air pollution, $CO_2$ doesn't settle back down to Earth in a few weeks, and neither does it break down quickly in the atmosphere. Unlike soot from smokestacks, $CO_2$ is very well mixed in the global atmosphere. The carbon escaping from a power plant in Ohio will affect atmospheric concentrations over Fiji and Siberia as well.

In the pre industrial era, the carbon wafting from ancient fires would have derived almost exclusively from wood and other biomass – carbon that was already in the active ongoing exchange between the atmosphere and the biosphere. Had the trees which George Washington burned on his hearth been instead left to their natural fate, they would have toppled quite naturally a decade or century later, rotting on the ground and contributing their carbon back to the atmosphere as well as the soil. Burning the tree a few decades earlier than it would have otherwise rotted accelerated the pace of the carbon cycle only slightly and changed the total stock of carbon in the combined atmosphere/biosphere/ocean exchange not at all.

The carbon sequestered in oil is a different matter. It too was once a living thing – mostly algae – but it had most typically dropped to the bottom of an ancient sea, the floor of which is now buried within the Earth's crust due to tectonic churning. That carbon might someday have seeped or risen to the Earth's surface naturally, but on a cycle measured in millions of years rather than decades. That cycle is so slow that for human purposes we should consider it to be static – that carbon had been more or less permanently locked away from the stock of carbon cycling in the atmosphere/biosphere/oceans.

But roughly two centuries ago, modern man realized that it need not content itself merely by recycling the carbon in wood a bit more quickly. It could leverage much more energy-dense carbon stores found in coal (and later, oil and natural gas) to power the industrial world. There are plausible theories that nearly all the increase in living standards that humanity has obtained since the industrial revolution derived from this simple discovery[11, 12] – that we could harvest previously unfathomable amounts of energy from carbon buried beneath the Earth's surface. But unlike biomass fuels, this combustion of long-sequestered carbon *has* increased the total stock of carbon in the atmosphere/biosphere/oceans. We have unleashed anomalous new sources of carbon into the climate system and invented no new offsetting sinks, so the stock of carbon in the active exchange keeps rising, thus far, inexorably. It is the energy deriving from harvesting all that previously geologically sequestered carbon that has empowered the mechanized societies that have enabled the human population to swell from 1 billion at the dawn of the industrial revolution to more than 10 billion by the end of this century. And without the continued exploitation of this energy source or the development of equivalent ones, that population level would quickly become unsustainable.[13] Maintaining an abundant energy supply underpins the entire world economy. We cannot do without this riot of energy or – for the time being – without the torrent of $CO_2$ that we simultaneously vent into the atmosphere as a byproduct.

## Electrify Everything

Nonetheless, one of the early steps necessary to wean ourselves off that $CO_2$ geyser is to electrify everything that can be electrified.

There are some power uses for which electrification will prove difficult and/or very costly, such as aviation, long-distance transport, and industrial processes that require high heat. We will deal with those in turn. But in the instances where the substitution is relatively easy, we must make it – pronto. The classic (and very substantial) example is light-duty vehicles, where the world is moving rapidly towards electric models. Norway seeks to lead the way, banning the sale of new fossil-fuel-powered cars after 2025.[14] A handful of smallish European countries will follow by 2030, with Canada, France, and Spain among others joining by 2040.[15] California has announced that all new vehicles sold in the state after 2035 must be electric.[16] Among car makers, Volvo has announced a 2030 cutoff date for the sale of internal combustion engine cars,[17] with GM following by 2035.[18] By the time this book appears, the list of countries and auto manufacturers having made such announcements may well have doubled. GM's announcement on the one hand seems brave and visionary for a company that has made combustion engines for over a century, though given that tiny Tesla's market capitalization now stands at over eight times that of GM,[19] it in fact faced nearly irresistible pressure from shareholders to jump on this bandwagon. This is a theme seen repeatedly across the energy economy. The most rapid corporate transformations are generally not being driven by regulatory sticks, but by financial carrots. Shareholders are voting with their investment accounts and are rewarding companies for moving swiftly in the direction that is increasingly seen as inevitable. All that is all positive, though it should be noted that if we stop making new gasoline-powered vehicles in 2035 and those vehicles remain on the road for 15 years, this defines a mid-century full retirement of conventional engines in the leading jurisdictions, and presumably a later date for the entire planet.

This pace is set of course in part by the car makers, but also by the rate at which the surrounding infrastructure evolves. Electric vehicles (EVs) are only practical once the web of charging stations is sufficiently dense and widespread to enable them to widely operate. Nonetheless, that too is progressing, as you are undoubtedly well aware.

What is less widely appreciated is that electric vehicles are not necessarily powered by clean energy. It is merely that they are emission-free at the point of use. The EV has no tailpipe and is therefore belching no $CO_2$, but that does not mean that the utility at which the power was produced has no smokestack. Electricity is not a primary source of energy, but rather simply an intermediate form into which energy may be converted. If the ultimate energy source from which the electricity was produced was coal, then the operation of that vehicle will contribute to global warming in amounts comparable to – or even greater than – the oil-powered automobile it replaced.[20, 21, 22] That said, most modern electric grids derive power from a mix of sources, so "all coal" is a bit of a strawman. If instead the power comes from the "average American grid," then the EV contributes half the emissions of its gasoline counterpart, a huge improvement, but not "zero emissions."[23] Electric vehicles are therefore only as clean as the electric grid that stands behind them. Nonetheless, on the spectrum of energy substitutions, electric generation is considered to be relatively low-hanging fruit, so while an all-electric auto fleet doesn't directly reduce emissions, it transforms what is now a distributed system for sourcing mobility energy (i.e., cars that burn their own gasoline) into a much more centralized one. If we then decarbonize the electrical generating plant at the center of that system, we now have what we are after – a truly clean system for light-duty transport energy.

However, even that would not be the end of the story, since an EV's carbon footprint during its production is 15 percent to 68 percent larger than that of its internal combustion cousin[24] due to complexities of making the battery. This means that on a life-cycle basis, an EV starts out at a substantial climate impact deficit relative to a traditional vehicle and only overcomes that deficit after some years of use. It often seems to be that when we are poised to turn a corner, we find another corner.

Nonetheless, while autos are the biggest opportunity to electrify end-use applications, they are by no means the only one. Electric heat pumps can replace fossil fuel appliances. Industrial processes for curing and drying lend themselves well to electrification. Once we add carbon to our calculus, there is a great deal of our existing energy uses that can convert to electricity.

## The Promise of Clean, Green, Zero-Carbon Energy

The concepts of "green" or "clean" energy must be dissected in our carbon context. These are used somewhat interchangeably to refer to energy sources either that cause less conventional air pollution or that emit less carbon. We need to be concerned about both independently, for different reasons. Air pollution makes the air dangerous to breathe, for humans and most everything else. $CO_2$ emissions do not, but warm the planet in ways that will likely become intolerable. Coal is unfavorable on both scales. Relative to the amount of energy produced, it both dirties the air and contributes an outsized portion of $CO_2$. Natural gas is at the other end of the fossil fuel spectrum, creating less of both short-term pollution and long-term warming. This is all straightforward enough.

But what of bioenergy – is that somehow "green"? From an air pollution standpoint, the answer is, not particularly. Wood contains a lot of impurities and "burns dirtily," creating a relatively high amount of air pollution, as is clear to anyone who has ever built a fire in a space with insufficient ventilation. Moreover, it releases substantial carbon as it burns, so it gets few points on that scale too – it is hardly "clean." And yet it is green from the vantage point of where the carbon comes from. Wood drew its carbon from the air, generally in the last century, before releasing it back in the combustion or decomposition process. It was a carbon sink before it was a carbon source, and therefore could be considered carbon neutral through the whole cycle if the cycle were perfect, which it is not. The energy required to harvest, process, and transport the biomass all represents "leakage" from the idealized carbon cycle that we might otherwise imagine biomass to represent. That leakage can be quite substantial, particularly if those ancillary steps utilize fossil fuel energy as is mostly the case today. Moreover, burning a tree releases all of its carbon immediately, much faster than would have been the case were it to decompose on the forest floor. And the new sapling planted beside the old stump is a minuscule carbon sink until it matures. Therefore, the accelerated $CO_2$ release from combustion is not immediately offset by regrowth. All this means that biofuels may have less life-cycle emissions impact than fossil fuels, but they are generally far from carbon neutral.

Natural gas is often touted as being "green" or carbon friendly, but only in comparison to coal or oil. Substituting a gas power plant for an oil version cuts $CO_2$ emissions by about a third, and in comparison to a coal plant, cuts them in half.[25] Much of the progress that the US has made on carbon is due to such substitutions, but gas is only a halfway house. It is still taking carbon that was permanently sequestered underground and newly contributing it to the atmosphere, representing a new source without a new sink. Until it cleans up its act, the natural gas extraction and transportation industry will continue to leak prodigious amounts of methane into the air,[26] which is of course a much more potent GHG than $CO_2$. Replacing coal-fired power plants with gas burners is a forward step, but hardly a solution.

From the standpoint of both air pollution and carbon emissions, the greenest major source in our energy arsenal at the turn of the century was nuclear, a source with the least green of reputations. But to recite for a moment its praises, it is an energy source that produces neither air pollution nor carbon emissions. What it does produce of course is low-likelihood, high-consequence safety hazards as well as radioactive waste that will last considerably longer than the long-lived $CO_2$ we are venting into the atmosphere. As the ongoing Iranian standoff also demonstrates, the spread of nuclear power carries with it the risk of nuclear weapons proliferation. Also, far from the original promise of producing power "too cheap to meter,"[27] nuclear has proven economically uncompetitive without the major public support provided by countries such as France. Small modular reactors and other advanced nuclear designs present a theoretical path forward to nuclear power, but only with a dramatic and currently unforeseen change in public attitudes towards this power sector accompanied by streamlined regulatory and licensing procedures. Absent that, as we search desperately for ways to hasten a transition to emission-free fuel sources, we will nonetheless likely turn away from the best emission-free dispatchable energy source in our historical fuel arsenal. It also demonstrates that there are other dimensions of "greenness" on which to judge fuel sources besides air pollution and carbon emissions.

And neither is "greenness" in all its dimensions the only criterion on which fuel source decisions are made. Besides cost (still the primary consideration), national energy independence or security is another major and valid objective. China and India are both relatively oil-and-gas-poor but coal-rich countries. Both for reasons of local employment and national sovereignty, they can therefore be expected to persist in coal use well beyond a time when other considerations might call for its demise.

All this is to say that the consideration of the optimal mix of energy sources is much more complex than we might prefer as we view it through a primarily GHG-emission-focused lens for the purpose of this book. And yet, with all those factors considered, we must, in this century, find a path to net zero GHG emissions, as the risks and consequences of failing to do so seem utterly intolerable. The good news in this respect is that we seem to be making impressive headway in developing emissions-free fuel sources, most particularly solar and wind power, but also to a lesser degree hydropower and geothermal. Let's look at each of those in detail.

Solar power is perhaps the most promising of these fuel sources, in that the power available from the Sun seems nearly limitless. It is, or was, the ultimate origin for nearly every other source of power on Earth, certainly true in the case of fossil and biofuels. Thus, it would seem sensible to capture the power directly without first running it through the dead plants, and we are making impressive strides in that pursuit. Global solar photovoltaic (PV) power generation – the panels you are used to seeing on roofs – has expanded more than 16-fold from 33 to 724 terawatt-hours (TWh) since 2010,[28] and is projected to grow from 2 percent to 11 percent of global electricity supply by 2040 (based on current and already announced policies).[29] The numbers may be less inspiring when you consider solar power's share in global primary energy supply (i.e., the original sources of energy before they have undergone any human-induced conversion process), of which it barely represents 1 percent, though potential advances in electrifying new sectors may well see that share increase more promisingly, too.[30] Among the virtues of solar power is that, in addition to having utility-scale solar plants, it can in many cases be produced right where it is used. Unlike say nuclear power, it need not be produced centrally and distributed through a grid but can be produced via small solar panels on streetlamps or on the roof powering a rural barbershop. This of course works better in sunny places like Phoenix than in cloudy ones like Ireland, but even perpetually overcast Lima has sufficient sunlight to justify myriad solar panels. It should be noted that, like many fuel sources, solar panels are far less green in their production than they are in their use,[31] but in an energy buffet without free lunches, solar power is a pretty positive trade.

The same can be said with nearly equal optimism about wind power, which is also making impressive forward strides, having grown from generating 346 TWh to 1,429 TWh globally over the last ten years.[32] Unlike solar, wind power is much more likely to be centrally generated and distributed via the electric grid.[33] Nonetheless, it too takes advantage of a pre-existing source of power whose fuel cost is zero and whose capture requires no combustion or emissions. This isn't to say that solar or wind power are free. In fact, given the need for land, expensive machinery, and maintenance, it is only recently that they have become as cheap as fossil fuels.[34] Wind power also has environmental drawbacks of its own. Some people consider the hulking turbines a sort of visual pollution, provoking a not-in-my-backyard response when they are proposed. Nonetheless, wind and solar have fought their way into a cost competitive position with incumbent energy sources and are here to stay.

A much older component in the portfolio of low-carbon power sources is hydropower (its "renewable" nature is often debated),[35] which makes up 6.5 percent of global primary energy consumption, and 16 percent of the world's electricity, essentially the same share it has held over the past decade.[36] Despite the growth in solar and wind, hydro still remains the king among renewables (see Figure 6.3 below). Hydropower ticks all the right GHG boxes in taking advantage of a pre-existing energy source that requires no combustion, but unlike solar, it is a highly centralized power solution, with often massive dams creating power potentially quite distant from where it is needed. Hydropower projects are environmentally controversial in other ways, as they often destroy pre-existing habitats and can be devastating for migratory fish. From a climate perspective, hydropower will continue to be an important component of the non-emitting energy portfolio, but not a transformative one. At best, hydropower may be able to

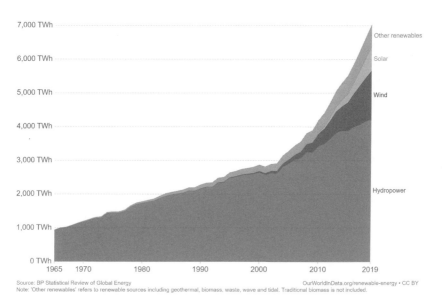

Source: BP Statistical Review of Global Energy
Note: 'Other renewables' refers to renewable sources including geothermal, biomass, waste, wave and tidal. Traditional biomass is not included.
OurWorldInData.org/renewable-energy • CC BY

**Figure 6.3** Global renewable energy generation, 1965–2019. *Source:* BP Statistical Review of Global Energy from OurWorldInData.org, licensed under Creative Commons CC BY[37]

keep pace with the growth in energy demand and maintain its current proportion of the energy pie, but it is unlikely to gain much share from fossil fuels – there are only so many profitable hydropower locations with acceptable environmental tradeoffs, and the best of those are already tapped.

Geothermal energy's position is similar to hydropower's, but vastly smaller, providing less than 1 percent of the global primary energy consumption.[38] It is highly environmentally friendly in all regards but is economically viable only in limited locales. This too is an energy source that will struggle to hold its share and will not therefore do much to slay fossil fuels. Ocean power seeks to capture and convert wave energy into low-cost clean electricity. While in theory it would be scalable to hundreds of megawatts, technical hurdles and its economic viability have been problematical, marooning it to a demonstration phase from which it has yet to escape. Hydrogen power is another extremely attractive prospect that could help decarbonize energy processes that are tricky to electrify, particularly for transportation. However, that remains sidelined by costs and logistics – producing and distributing hydrogen fuel is currently an energy-intensive process, and one that as of yet remains dependent on fossil fuels. And then there are the miracle solutions, "Hail Mary" passes that could solve all our problems. Chief among these is nuclear fusion, wherein energy is derived not from the splitting of atoms but from their merger. Scientists and industry have been chasing this holy grail since the 1950s, and in theory it would be the perfect energy source – cheap, endless, safe, and emission-free. However, harnessing the potential of fusion has eluded us for 70-odd years and may elude us for many more.

The combination of becoming Rockefeller-rich while saving the world should provide more than enough incentive for humanity to find such revolutionary energy sources in the future, and somehow, the fossil fuel era *must* give way to a post-fossil fuel era. However, it's not clear that the breakthrough is imminent, and standing idly while waiting for lightning to strike can't possibly be Plan A. We are compelled to proceed with the tools we have foreseeably at hand to devise a solution to our energy dilemma.

## Barriers to an Energy Transition

If all the above is the good news about renewable and low-carbon fuel sources, the bad news – and an essential point for this chapter – is that in the aggregate, no more of our energy mix derives from non-fossil sources than was the case when I graduated from college 40 years ago. As Figure 6.4 below demonstrates, fossil fuels comprised slightly more than 80 percent of the world's fuel sources in 1965, 2019, and every year in between. In fact, they have produced more than 80 percent of the United States' fuel mix since Henry Ford invented the Model T. Fossil fuels had conquered American energy supply mix by 1900 and have never surrendered much territory.[39]

How can we reconcile that continued fossil fuel dominance with the growth in renewable non-emitting energy sources noted above? The answer is that world energy demand is far from static. It continues to rise as the population grows and the Global South develops, such that much of the growth in renewable, non-emitting energy is necessary simply for these sources to maintain their share of the expanding energy source pie. To the extent that solar and wind have outpaced the general growth in energy demand, they have simply backfilled for nuclear, which is not growing in absolute terms and therefore losing share in the expanding pie. But the upshot is that for all the optimism about low-carbon energy sources, they are not yet reducing the planet's $CO_2$ emissions. As can be seen in Figure 6.5, global fossil fuel consumption is still growing.

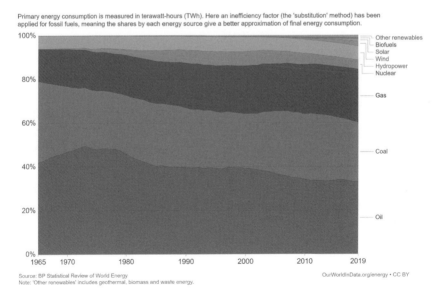

Primary energy consumption is measured in terawatt-hours (TWh). Here an inefficiency factor (the 'substitution' method) has been applied for fossil fuels, meaning the shares by each energy source give a better approximation of final energy consumption.

Source: BP Statistical Review of World Energy
Note: 'Other renewables' includes geothermal, biomass and waste energy.
OurWorldInData.org/energy • CC BY

**Figure 6.4** Energy consumption by source, world. *Source*: BP Statistical Review of World Energy (2019) from OurWorldInData.org, licensed under Creative Commons CC BY[40]

Fossil fuel consumption is given in terawatt-hour equivalents (TWh).

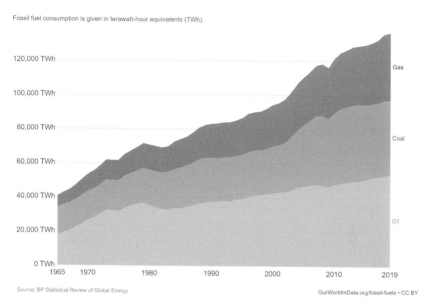

**Figure 6.5** Fossil fuel consumption trends. *Source*: BP Statistical Review of Global Energy from OurWorldInData.org, licensed under Creative Commons CC BY[41]

Arresting though the >80 percent observation is, the percentage mix isn't really what the climate "cares" about. It is informed simply by how much $CO_2$ and other GHGs we are emitting in absolute terms – how much water is coming out of the spigot – and despite what is likely to be a short-lived COVID swoon, that too is still rising.

So how can we be certain that low-carbon energies will start rapidly gobbling up shares in the coming decade despite their consistent failure to do so over the last century? The unfortunate answer is that we would be wise to curb our enthusiasm. I am optimistic in the long run, but in the short run? I would bet that we continue to muddle forward with slow incremental progress rather than start suddenly to sprint. On the plus side, the cost of solar and wind have plunged in the last decade, making them roughly competitive with fossil fuels in many places and applications. Climate scolds such as myself can be relied upon to whine even more vociferously in the coming decade about the need to make such a transition, and that ought to begin to move the needle. Nonetheless, price is still the paramount consideration, and fossil fuels remain highly abundant, very effective, and cost competitive,[42] particularly when storage and distribution costs are additionally considered. After all, the price of gas has also dropped dramatically in this century, which is why its share has grown. If oil demand begins to decline while reserves keep pace with consumption, some observers foresee price declines in that sector as well, meaning that while renewables are getting cheaper, some of their fossil fuel competitors may as well.

If climate and air quality considerations are to win out, the first fuel that must lose share is coal, but coal production has remained steady over the last several years and China has invested in building over 200 new coal-fired power plants both at home and abroad as part of The Belt and Road Initiative.[43] Coal producing regions from Kentucky to Poland are pushing back against the "war on coal" in a bid to preserve local employment. Warnings that without coal we would "freeze in the dark"[44] still resonate with many. While several projections suggest that we may have recently surpassed peak coal demand, the incentives to swiftly retire coal aren't yet winning the day, and if those incentives don't yet add up, then oil and gas will likely prove even more persistent. Until emissions become the primary basis on which the world makes energy sourcing decisions (likely some decades away still), renewables will have to engage in hand-to-hand combat with fossil fuels to grow their share, based mostly on cost. And on that basis, fossil fuels have a lot of fight left in them. This doesn't mean that low-carbon energy won't win the fight ultimately, but it does mean the transition will happen much more slowly than many people believe. Which in turn means that by the time we turn off the spigot, the water level in the bathtub will be much higher than many suppose.

All that said, the election of Joe Biden has slapped a new set of cards on the table that could change much of the above. It is still early days and therefore unclear what Biden can actually achieve in a very closely balanced Congress, but his stated intention is that by the end of his first term, he will have put the US on an irreversible path to net zero emissions and a 100 percent clean energy economy by 2050.[45] By 2035, he hopes the US will achieve carbon-free energy generation,[46] assisted in part by an intended $400 billion investment over the coming decade in clean energy research and innovation.[47] He has proposed a new Advanced Research Projects Agency to accelerate technology development and aims to upgrade the energy efficiency in millions of American buildings and homes.[48] The list goes on, a veritable blizzard of ambitious head-spinning proclamations after four years under the Climate Denier in Chief. It is tempting then to declare that the US has joined the mid-century net zero emissions club and can hereafter be a global force for good on climate issues, but it is a fair bet that the Republicans will reclaim at least one house of Congress in 2022 and perhaps more of the government in 2024. Between now and then, there are severe limits to what Biden can achieve without some bipartisan support. Until a significant portion of the Republican Party climbs aboard the climate train (inconceivable today, but also eventually inevitable), the US will remain a fickle actor on these issues.

## Intermittency and Dispatchable Power

Among the reasons why the path to a carbon-free Valhalla will be arduous and slow is that energy is not merely a technological system, but a social, economic, and political one as well.[49] You can't start from scratch to build the perfect system – rather you must start with the system you have and muddle forward incrementally without disrupting supply. There are "entrenched incumbents, sunk costs, and behavioral inertia"[50] all of which must be overcome. But there are physical challenges as well. Wind and solar are clearly a huge part of our energy future, but in addition to all their benefits, they also confront substantial drawbacks. The largest is their intermittency. They are only available when the wind is blowing and the Sun is bright. They are not "dispatchable" sources of power that can be turned on or ramped up in response to power demand. This may seem like a trivial distinction, but it is in fact a critical one. Picking on solar for a moment, on a work day, there is a small energy demand peak around 8:00 am as people get ready for work, a swale or depression during the middle of the work day, a sharp peak around 6:00 pm as people get home from work, and a trough overnight. Solar produces little power during the morning and evening peaks, since the Sun is at an oblique angle at those hours, and abundant power through the middle of the day, when relatively little is needed. Wind's contribution is a bit less predictable, but it too produces power in sync with the weather, not with demand. "No problem," you may imagine. "We'll just store the solar and wind power when it is produced, and dispatch it to demand loads when they arise." However, on the scale of an entire economy rather than say a household, the economics and technology of large-scale energy storage remain largely beyond our reach. Whereas the maximum electricity generating capacity of the US is 1,100 gigawatts (not including small-scale distributed solar),[51] our maximum utility-scale storage capacity is closer to 31 gigawatts (GW),[52] not quite even 3 percent of what we can generate.

Therefore, the concept of operations in most electrical systems is that demand must be met whenever it arises. This is extremely challenging since loads vary of course not merely based on time of day as noted above but on day of week, seasonality, temperature, and local weather. Nonetheless, at 6:00 pm on the hottest day of the year in Houston, people crank up their air conditioners and expect them to work. And on a still, frigid January night in Duluth, customers must be able to count on light and power.

Since nearly all the electricity we require at any moment must be generated at that same moment, Variable Renewable Energy sources like wind and solar are actually rather poorly or at least only randomly matched to our energy needs. They can constitute a substantial and inexpensive part of our total energy mix, but only if we don't need to count on them. Until technological breakthroughs facilitate vastly more short-term and long-term storage capacity, these should be considered "fair weather energy friends" (maybe foul weather in the case of wind). For the time being and the foreseeable future, they must be supplemented by vast quantities of highly dispatchable fossil fuel sources to meet demand peaks and fill in renewable supply valleys. Hydro and nuclear power are also well-matched to this "baseload" requirement, but as noted are not growing their share of the pie. Fast, flexible gas plants will be the preferred interim solution to balance the variability, but until more of those come on line, coal will continue to play a vital role. If we phase those out, we can get up to perhaps 60 percent decarbonization cost-effectively with such natural gas plants.[53] To decarbonize well beyond that, we will need to start phasing out the gas plants[54] and replacing those with ever more redundant layers of further renewables which we will use to lesser and lesser degrees for the reasons discussed in the next paragraph. This will render the steps beyond ~60 percent renewable increasingly expensive as we proceed.[55]

Beyond intermittency, another challenge related to wind and solar is their low capacity factors, which is a measure of actual power production relative to potential. Since nuclear plants are cumbersome to turn off once you turn them on, they score extremely high on this measure. US plants averaged over 93 percent in 2019.[56] On the other hand, utility-scale solar PV plants have an average annual capacity factor of 25 percent[57] (rooftop units are even worse). Wind farms do a bit better at 35 percent.[58] These low factors are due not only to the inconstancy of sunshine and wind, but because they are not producing power well-matched to demand, with the consequence that the grid to which they are connected often declines to accept the power. They are "curtailed" in the language of the trade, with their potential power therefore going to waste. The low capacity factors of solar and wind also mean that for every nuclear plant we wish to replace, we need to build roughly three times as much renewable capacity since they will only produce approximately one-third of the time. Even these already low capacity factors will further decline for marginal facilities as we reach high renewable penetrations, since each new facility is more likely than its predecessors to face curtailments.

While wind and Sun are present to some degree in most places, some places are better endowed than others. In the US, the Midwest is the king of wind power, while the Southwest is blessed with abundant sunshine. This creates the prospect that energy from renewable sources in these regions can be shipped east and north to regions with more load and less renewable supply. Similarly, Quebec is eager to ship more of its bountiful hydro energy supply to New England. However, such long-distance electricity transfers require massive expansions of high-voltage wholesale power transmission lines, which are extremely unpopular with residents of the transited locales, who generally do not benefit from the power. In the US, the siting requirements for such lines are made all the more difficult by the fact that they are generally regulated by individual states rather than the federal government. The consequence is that even where there are willing buyers and sellers of power (renewable or otherwise), the approval and construction process for the transmission lines can take up to a decade if they happen at all.[59]

While there is more inertia than is often generally recognized in our current systems for both generating and transmitting electricity, a bright spot in the power sector is the edge of the grid. Computing and control technology is causing the world "beyond the meter" to evolve rapidly. Not only are customers increasingly able to generate some portion of their electricity via solar panels and/or home generators, but the Internet of Things is creating vast new opportunities for customers to manage their electrical demand more intelligently. Your Nest thermostat can more finely tune your demand for heat and cooling to your usage requirements, and your electrical vehicle charging station can download power in the middle of the night, when power is abundant. As electric markets evolve further towards real-time variable pricing, demand can increasingly adjust itself to supply in contrast to the current, mostly hierarchical model. In such a grid, if renewable power supply is low, much of the demand side of the grid could shut itself off rather than command a coal-fired plant to switch on.

Nonetheless, even with improved demand management and transmission systems, we can't fully replace dispatchable generation sources with intermittent ones. Full decarbonization will require either a revolution in storage capacity or a whole new fleet of carbon-free dispatchable power plants, neither of which are foreseeable right around the corner.

## Hard Substitution Cases

Yet another reason to bet on the persistence of fossil fuels is that some sectors will simply be very difficult to decarbonize. The poster child for those is aviation, where the energy density of kerosene is simply unmatched by other similarly priced technologies. Range-payload charts are one of the fundamental bases on which aircraft are designed and evaluated. How much stuff can the plane carry, and how far can it go with that load? Within a certain spectrum, those two characteristics can be traded against each other. If you load less freight on the plane, you can load more fuel and fly farther. Increased range is also increased safety, more options to divert around inclement weather and to other airfields. Thus, a heavier, less energy-dense fuel source (like a battery) would compromise not only functionality but safety, making aviation among the last sectors to migrate away from fossil fuels. Long-haul trucking, ocean shipping, and cement making will also of necessity be late adapters. These sectors could simply delay the world's achievement of net zero emissions, but more often they are imagined to continue positive emissions after the net zero emissions date, with their emissions offset by negative emissions from other technologies. Therefore, one can envision persistent positive emissions from certain sectors after net zero emissions have been achieved.

Despite all the obstacles presented above, we know where we have to go. We must get to net zero emissions. There is simply no alternative. We can't keep baking the planet indefinitely. The question then isn't where we are headed – it's when we will get there, since the longer we keep filling the bathtub, the higher the water level will be when we finally turn the spigot off. Despite all the spectacular progress we are making on wind and solar and electrification, we still get 80 percent of our primary energy from fossil fuels, and that isn't likely to change soon enough. Weaning the world off fossil fuels will prove a more difficult and therefore more lengthy process than most people realize. Which means the tap is still running . . .

# 7 OTHER MITIGATION

An essential component of mitigation will be completing as rapidly as possible the energy transition discussed in Chapter 6. This means finding substitutes for, and weaning the world, off the fossil fuel sources that continue to comprise more than 80 percent of the world's energy supply. That seems an utterly Herculean task. Nonetheless, having just considered this, let's imagine we can wave a magic wand and it gets done. Somehow, the world finds miraculous new sources of energy, solves the storage and intermittency problems associated with wind and solar power, and convinces the Persian Gulf states, Russia, and Venezuela to wreck their economies and leave immense quantities of proven reserves in the ground. Presto! This is, by no means, the end of the mitigation story, so we will deal here with all of the other aspects necessary for comprehensive mitigation.

## Sources and Types of Emissions

Recapping from Chapter 2, if greenhouse gases are adjusted for their global warming potential (GWP), the contribution of the various gases and sources in 2019 is illustrated in Figure 7.1. Two thirds of the problem is $CO_2$ from fossil fuel use, the bit we solved with our magic wand above. However, other sources of $CO_2$ contribute a further 11 percent of total annual warming. The remaining quarter of the problem is due to other gases, principally methane and nitrous oxide, now that the other former big contributor (CFCs) has been mostly eliminated via the Montreal Protocol.[1]

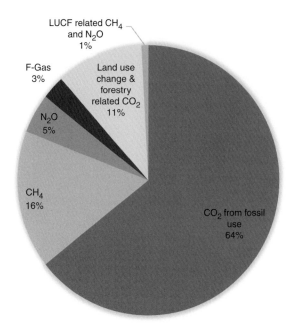

**Figure 7.1** Greenhouse gas emissions by type. *Data source*: UNEP Emissions Gap Report 2020[2]

## Fugitive Emissions and Non-fossil Fuels

However, a different way to view our emission sources is by sector of the economy. As the chart on the left in Figure 7.2 demonstrates, over 70 percent of our problem derives from the energy sector, and the vast majority of that comes from burning fossil fuels, either to produce electricity or to power vehicles. A much smaller subset produces energy used by industry and in construction. Nonetheless, the sources of the remaining fifth of our energy-related emissions lie elsewhere.

The smaller chunk of this residual wedge is fugitive emissions that derive from the process of extracting, transporting, and refining fossil fuels. Both oil and gas wells are prone to having some natural gas escape through the wellhead due to a loss of integrity of the casing. Alternatively, the gas may escape via lateral migrations along adjacent geological formations. The regulatory requirements to inspect and repair such inadvertent leaks are inconsistent. Leaks from wellheads, pipelines, and storage facilities have recently proven to be much more common and prodigious than had previously been recognized, in part

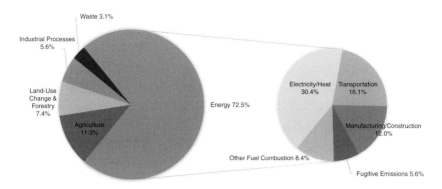

Figure 7.2 Global anthropogenic greenhouse gas emissions by sector, 2018. *Source:* LUC emissions data have been sourced from UNEP's Emissions Gap Report 2019 and other emissions data have been sourced from ClimateWatch[3, 4]

because at least in the US, the fossil fuel industry has successfully fought to defeat any requirement to monitor or regulate such leaks.[5]

Moreover, not all releases are accidental. Gas is sometimes vented occasionally to reduce well pressures, or continually if the gas is deemed uneconomical to capture and transport to market. Continual venting is often flared, such that what reaches the atmosphere is $CO_2$ rather than methane with a much higher global warming potential, but either contributes to climate change. Natural gas also commonly arises from coal mines. After all, detecting that was why we used to put the canary there. Gas escapes can also occur via undetected leaks from pipelines or accidents in the surface transportation.

Each of these emission streams seems accidental or incidental, but when multiplied by methane's powerful global warming potential, they add up to more than 5 percent of all our climate forcing. For so long as we are still producing and utilizing fossil fuels, the mitigation requirement here will be to substantially tighten reporting requirements and regulations around fugitive emissions, such that we permit far fewer escapes. As with everything else, a "carbon" price that also applied to methane (at presumably much higher rates given its GWP) would dramatically change the incentives around how important it may be to reseal leaky wells and pipelines and which emission streams it is economical to capture and bring to market after all. If we were seeking mitigation steps to substantially slow warming in the near term, slashing fugitive methane emissions would rate high on the list. Over the longer term of course, the way to get rid of fugitive emissions entirely will be to phase out fossil fuels.

The larger chunk of those residual emissions comes from burning things other than fossil fuels, or from sources that, due to the vagaries of emissions accounting by the IPCC, don't fall into other categories. Setting aside the grab bag of miscellany, one significant element of this wedge entails the methane and nitrous oxide emissions that derive from the incomplete combustion of biomass. Bioenergy is energy derived from biomass for a wide range of uses, including transport, heating, electricity production, and cooking. In the US, bioenergy production from liquid biofuel gasoline additives such as ethanol and biodiesel equals that from wood combustion, which in combination account for roughly 90 percent of our bioenergy sector.[6]

Bioenergy may contribute substantially to mitigation, but its net impact is difficult to discern. For starters, the combustion of biomass generates gross greenhouse gas emissions and particulate air pollution roughly equivalent to the combustion of fossil fuels,[7] so switching to bioenergy is not like switching to a non-emitting source such as solar power. The climate benefit derives from the fact that plant-based biomass sourced its carbon from the atmosphere rather than from geologic stores, so it recycled atmospheric carbon rather than added to it. To the extent that the biofuel substituted for a fossil fuel, then this was a net benefit. Even this, however, is not as straightforward as it seems. The assumption of one-to-one carbon neutrality through the bioenergy cycle is contested, with some researchers perceiving this to be a net negative trade.[8,9,10] Burning biomass liberates back to the atmosphere not only $CO_2$ but some methane and nitrous oxide as well.[11] My backyard firewood consumes no chemical energy in either its processing (my handsaw) or transport (my legs), but commercial grade biofuels are both processed and transported – sometimes across oceans – which of course entails substantial energy requirements that may render the bioenergy carbon-positive (i.e., bad) over its full life cycle. Dried and processed wood pellets burned in a modern power plant can combust with high efficiency, whereas heating one's rustic cabin with natural wood is very inefficient.

Even here, however, there is yet more nuance. If the biomass being used in the woodstove or power plant is either forest or agricultural residue, then combusting it in substitution for fossil fuels is likely a climate benefit. Forest residues include naturally occurring deadwood (due to windfall or beetle infestation) as well as trimmings and wood processing residues (sawdust). Agricultural residues include plant harvest residues (straw), processing residues (rice husks), and manure. All of these are environmental "freebies" that would otherwise be wastes and entail no additional environmental impact to produce. As with Russian nesting dolls, however, bioenergy entails nuance within nuance. These residues are only climate friendly if they are combusted relatively near where they were harvested. If too much energy is required to transport them, their climate benefit begins to wane. For this reason, producing bioenergy from organic wastes collected from households, restaurants, and demolition sites (wood waste) is viewed very marginally.[12] It's simply not clear that the energy expenditure justifies itself in climate terms.

Of course, what most people envision when they think of advanced bioenergy is dedicated biomass plantations that grow annuals (cereals, oil, or sugar crops), perennials (switchgrass, *Miscanthus*), or fast growing trees. As a matter of bioenergy capacity, this is where there is a real chance to move the meter and displace substantial amounts of fossil fuels, although estimates of that capacity vary by a factor of ten.[13] Part of what makes this difficult to pin down are the tradeoffs involved in large-scale bioenergy production, most particularly in terms of land, but also groundwater and fertilizer. Even if food and fiber are prioritized over bioenergy production as is generally assumed, there are substantial economic impacts in allocating agriculturally fertile land to low-value bioenergy plantations, and environmental ones in rendering infertile land suitable for such purposes. Particularly if large amounts of fertilizers are required, the increased nitrous oxide emissions from such biofuel systems can convert apparent net sinks into sources, and none of this is positive for biodiversity (more Russian dolls).

Nonetheless, despite all the nuances and tradeoffs, it is likely that sustainable bioenergy will be a significant part of the mitigation story to the extent that it can efficiently replace some portion of our fossil fuel requirements. At the same time, mitigation will also require that we *reduce* the role of traditional bioenergy, which represents 80 percent of current bioenergy use.[14] Traditional bioenergy powers several end uses, including residential water and space heating, cooking, and several small industries (brick and pottery kilns, bakeries, and others). Cooking is the dominant end use, meeting the needs of over 2.5 billon people.[15] This is mostly done in open fires and rudimentary stoves, with approximately 10–20 percent conversion efficiency, leading to very high primary energy consumption. Advanced woodburning and biogas stoves can potentially reduce biomass fuel consumption by 60 percent or more and reduce $CO_2$ emissions and black carbon emissions by up to 90 percent.[16] More complete electrification with non-emitting fuel sources would of course reduce this demand altogether. All of this would free up biomass currently being consumed in low-efficiency open fires for use in high-efficiency electric plants, further boosting our bioenergy capacity without consuming more biofuels.

The punchline with bioenergy is that it's complicated. While we need more of the advanced sort of bioenergy, we need vastly less of the traditional sort. Its climate benefit also hinges substantially on how the biomass is sourced, transported, and combusted. And there are substantial tradeoffs in its large-scale implementation that need to be balanced against other considerations.

## Agriculture and Food Production

Shifting away from energy, the biggest non-energy sector of our emissions is agriculture, which contributes over 11 percent of our climate forcing. Plants require large amounts of energy to sow, harvest, and transport, as well as lots of fertilizer. Disturbing the soil periodically renders it a much more shallow store of carbon. Much of that harvest goes not to humans but to animals, who are therefore responsible for indirect $CO_2$ and nitrous oxide emissions and in many cases copious digestive methane emissions.

As societies develop economically and incomes rise, one common result is an increase in per capita meat consumption. Animal husbandry is an inefficient way to feed humans, in that it requires 5 to 25 units of plant feed to derive one unit of meat (with chicken requiring a lower ratio and beef cows requiring the highest.)[17] Moreover, among the most common of livestock are cows, goats, and sheep, all of which are ruminants with a digestive process that ferments plant-based food in a special stomach prior to digestion with the help of anaerobic microbes. These produce prodigious methane for which cows in particular are rightly infamous. There are roughly 3.7 billion cows, sheep, and goats in the world[18] – nearly one for every two people – producing over 100 million tonnes of methane annually.[19] While recent studies have produced promising results as to how feed additives might reduce bovine methane production,[20] we could of course go about this the old-fashioned way, by eating fewer cows and less cheese. Health benefits aside, a move towards greater vegetarianism/veganism would yield substantial climate benefits. Lab-grown meat could be a game changer.

Rice is of course the staple crop that feeds the densest clusters of humanity on Earth, so as population has exploded, so has the conversion of dry land into rice paddies, which contribute methane to the atmosphere for the same reason that natural swamps do, which is that they harbor anaerobic microbes that break down the decomposing plant matter. Less rice consumption would be another dietary change that would be a hard sell despite its climate benefits.

Beyond $CO_2$ and methane, agriculture is also responsible for substantial nitrous oxide emissions, which derive substantially from the nitrogen-based fertilizer that has been the basis of the green revolution and our planet's remarkable ability to feed its skyrocketing human population. The natural nitrogen cycle is much too slow for our modern agricultural purpose, so it has been supplemented by man-made nitrogen that is used the world over to boost yields. For the most part this has been a miraculously good thing without which our current food infrastructure could not survive, but it has the downside of providing soil-dwelling microbes with more nitrogen compounds to "eat." These microbes then produce nitrous oxide that enters the atmosphere. This goes for both synthetic fertilizers and those organically made of animal waste matter. Additionally, nitrous oxide is formed when nitrogen and oxygen react with each other in very high temperature environments, like in internal combustion engines and boilers and in the burning of biomass.

Nitrous oxide is fairly inert and stable, with a mean endurance in the atmosphere of about 121 years.[21] Worse news is that while there, it has enormous global warming potential, with roughly 265 times the potency of a molecule of $CO_2$.[22] Therefore, a little of it goes a long way in exacerbating our climate problem.

We can't stop using nitrogen fertilizers. Agricultural yields would crash, risking widespread famine. What we can do, however, is seek to be much more thoughtful in our application of it, such that we increase the proportion of fertilizer actually incorporated into the plants and decrease the proportion that is lost to the atmosphere. Precision farming would enable the adjustment of fertilizer application rates based on rigorous estimates of crop needs, using slow and controlled-release fertilizer forms.[23] It would also lead to improved timing of fertilizer application when it is least susceptible to loss, often just prior to plant uptake, which is to say a few weeks after planting rather than at or before planting.[24] New methods for crop sensing, field mapping, and fertilizer delivery can similarly increase fertilizer assimilation and thereby decrease fertilizer use,[25] all of which would go a long way in reducing nitrous oxide emissions from the agricultural sector.

## Land Use Change and Forestry

Land sequesters substantial amounts of carbon. The trees and vegetation in a forest store large amounts of carbon above the ground, and decomposed plant material buries some of that carbon in the soil. Unlike the carbon that is essentially permanently trapped in underground coal or oil deposits, carbon resident in soil is already in the active biosphere exchange among the land, atmosphere, and ocean. Nonetheless, if we remove it from the land and emit it into the atmosphere, we are increasing that atmospheric fraction and thickening the proverbial blanket. All of this makes land unique among the mitigation strategies we will consider herein, in that it can be both a sink for carbon when it is allowed to return to its natural state, or a source of carbon if we disturb that natural state.

Human land management practices tend to do the latter. Clearing a forest to pave a parking lot removes all the carbon that was stored in the trees and removes that plot from the inventory of land available to replant and reabsorb carbon from the atmosphere. Tilling soil to prepare it for planting releases much of the carbon resident in the soil. Planting crops on that tilled land reabsorbs a fraction of the carbon the forest had stored there, but that carbon bank will be mostly emptied when the crops are harvested. Even when we may imagine we are disturbing the land for a climate-friendly purpose such as biomass cultivation for energy, we nonetheless start by disturbing the land as we rip out or burn whatever was previously growing there to plant our trees or switchgrass. It can take many years for the new growth to overcome the carbon deficit that this initial replanting entails.[26] In fact, in tropical forests, it can take a half century.

Marshes, mangroves, and coastal wetlands are also capacious carbon stores, so draining and filling a marsh to build a house or harbor similarly transfers carbon from the land to the atmosphere and destroys a carbon sink. Even if a forest is simply harvested for lumber and replanted, its carbon storage capacity is reduced until the forest is fully regrown and allowed to mature, at which time it might be felled again. Almost every active use to which humans put land reduces its carbon storage capacity and has negative impacts for climate. A properly functioning carbon tax scheme then would also tax land use changes with negative impacts on carbon stores and reward via a carbon bonus any changes that restored them as carbon sinks, such as reforesting a former farm.

Altogether, agriculture, forestry, and other land use ("AFOLU" in IPCC-speak) changes contribute somewhere between a sixth and a quarter of our greenhouse gas emissions[27] (they are hard to accurately measure), once again adjusted for global warming potential. As discussed above, at least half of this is from the agriculture sector, animal husbandry as well as plant cultivation. The other half of AFOLU emissions derive primarily from deforestation, but also forest degradation and land use changes, be those paving a field or replanting it.

In surveying opportunities to reduce our AFOLU emissions, the IPCC speaks of both supply side and demand side opportunities. On the supply side, as we will discuss in a few chapters, land can be utilized particularly by agriculture in ways that are much more cognizant and respectful of its role as either a carbon source or sink. Encouraging (once again, with financial taxes and incentives) land uses and management practices that not only reduce emissions but enhance sequestrations will be essential. Most particularly, deforestation (mostly a developing world phenomenon) and afforestation/ reforestation (mostly a developed world opportunity) will need to take on real urgency. And with all its potential pitfalls, thoughtful bioenergy can reduce the demand for fossil fuels.

On the demand side, reducing food loss and waste would enable the world to consume the same amount of nutrition with less agriculture, yielding a meaningful climate benefit. Continuing the advance of the green revolution and increasing crop yields would have the same effect. Easier yet (at least technologically) would be changing our diets, particularly by consuming less meat.

Unlike energy emissions, which are still rising, there is evidence that emissions from the AFOLU sector may be leveling off.[28] Moreover, there is optimism that as the world population crests later in this century (widely projected but by no means certain), land conversions for agriculture (which is what most deforestation is actually about) may also decline.[29] Nonetheless, the barriers to slowing emissions from AFOLU are formidable. The personal and national incentives to continually improve the economic productivity of land are nearly irresistible, irrespective of the GHG implications. If a rancher wants to clear brush and trees to enhance forage, or a growing population expands the village into the surrounding farmland, those are hard to prevent. If Sri Lanka wants to pave wetlands to build a new port, who has the standing to say no? If we make substantial progress on AFOLU, good policy will need to be supplemented by good luck on some very large global trends.

## Industrial Processes

In considering industrial emissions, we must be careful to distinguish them from energy emissions, but even if we were to electrify everything that can be efficiently electrified and to fully decarbonize our electrical grid, industrial emissions would still remain. Not all industrial processes are well-suited to electrification – the degree of heat required for most metallurgy would be impractical to achieve without combustion. Other industrial processes produce $CO_2$ in chemical reactions rather than via combustion for energy purposes. And industry produces the whole range of greenhouse gases rather than merely $CO_2$. The largest sectoral sources are the production of iron, steel, and cement, which account for almost half of industrial $CO_2$ emissions.[30] Other emission-intensive sectors include chemicals (including plastics), fertilizers, pulp and paper, non-ferrous metals such as aluminum, food processing, and textiles.[31] Beyond manufacturing, emission-intensive sectors can include extractive industries, construction, and various services. Despite the declining share of industry in the global economy, industry-related GHG emissions have continued to increase.[32] These emissions are now dominated by Asia, which has experienced the fastest emissions growth in this century.[33]

Given the variety of activities comprised by this sector, turning the corner and reducing industrial emissions will require a broad set of mitigation options. The IPCC estimates that a 20 percent reduction would be possible by reducing energy intensity in some particularly energy-intensive sectors, while a further 25 percent reduction could be achieved simply by widespread upgrading, replacement, and deployment of the best available technologies, particularly in developing countries.[34] These steps require new capital to be deployed for existing technologies, but thereafter, new, step-change technologies and radical product innovations would be required. Extending product lives and using products more intensively via innovations such as the sharing economy would reduce product demand without reducing the services those products enable. On the other hand, production of mitigation technologies such as enhanced building insulation as well as upgraded infrastructure for adaptation may drive increased industrial demand and therefore emissions. Free lunches remain hard to come by.

A particularly troublesome source of anthropogenic $CO_2$ emissions is the manufacture of cement, which is mixed with sand, gravel, and water to produce concrete, the most common building material on Earth.[35] If cement were a country, it would be the world's fifth largest emitter after China, the US, India, and Indonesia.[36] The fundamental ingredient in cement is limestone, which is "calcinated" at high temperatures in the manufacturing process into lime and $CO_2$, the latter of which is emitted as a waste product. While the energy-related $CO_2$ arising in the manufacturing process might conceivably be decarbonized, the portion (roughly half)[37] of cement-making $CO_2$ that derives from the calcination chemical reaction can't be addressed in the same fashion. It would instead require substituting a different material for Portland cement, and while substitutes are being considered, there is not yet a suitable alternative at a competitive price and the world still relies almost entirely on the traditional material.[38]

## Waste and Landfills

Greenhouse gas emissions from landfills and wastewater comprise a small sliver of our total warming output, about 3 percent. Nonetheless, in our "all of the above" approach, these too need to be mitigated to the greatest possible degree. The two primary waste streams considered in a climate context are municipal solid waste and wastewater, including sanitary wastewater (i.e., sewage). While in combination, these produce small amounts of nitrous oxide; roughly 90 percent of the global warming potential contributed from the waste sector is methane, which packs an outsized climate wallop. This methane derives from the anaerobic breakdown of organic substances that are in both waste streams.

For the first year after municipal solid waste is deposited in a landfill, oxygen is present and aerobic decomposition occurs, but as it is progressively buried and compressed, the oxygen exits, and anaerobic processes take over. The wastes in wastewater are of course submerged, so here too, the decomposition process is anaerobic. Viewing our combined waste stream from a purely climatic perspective, the primary mitigation question is how we can reduce the amount of methane that is vented to the atmosphere.

For municipal solid waste, the best and generally lowest cost mitigation steps are the same ones we teach in elementary schools for environmentalism more generally – reduce, reuse, recycle. Anything we can do to lessen the flow of wastes into the stream also reduces the methane-producing potential of that stream. This is true both at the pre-consumer stage, where materials input reductions can have negative costs, as well as at the post-consumer stage. Once waste is in the stream, anything that can be done to mine it for useful materials that can be recycled also lessens the amount that will end up in landfills. Once again, though, this is standard environmental boilerplate, before we directly encounter climate considerations.

Once the final stream is abandoned as waste, however, then from a climate standpoint we become concerned with the greenhouse gases that will derive from the waste rather than the volume of waste itself. To the extent that organic wastes in the stream are incinerated rather than simply buried, that accelerates their decomposition but substantially reduces their climate impact since the resulting GHG will be mostly $CO_2$ rather than methane.[39] At some expense, buried waste can also be aerated so as to promote aerobic rather than anaerobic decomposition, once again substituting some $CO_2$ for methane. Nonetheless, if we keep adding to the landfill, it will become a methane source, the best practice for which is to harvest the methane to the greatest possible degree and combust it as an energy source. Not only does this once again substitute $CO_2$ emissions for what would have been methane fluxes, but it also offsets demand for energy that might otherwise have derived from fossil fuels. Wastewater can be similarly treated and harvested for methane.

None of the above is new technology but rather is how responsibly managed waste streams are already handled all over the world. Nonetheless, these best practices are far more common in the developed world than in the developing world, where large amounts of municipal solid wastes are simply piled into unmanaged waste dumps and significant portions of wastewater are neither collected nor treated. The World

Bank estimates that 93 percent of waste is openly dumped in low-income countries versus just 2 percent in their high-income counterparts.[40] From a climate perspective then, addressing the GHG contribution of our garbage and sewage primarily requires that we more comprehensively invest in cleaning up our waste streams in the ways that would also produce enormous co-benefits for the environment.

## Belt Tightening

In addition to all of the above, one further element of successful mitigation is likely to be some degree of personal sacrifice, at minimum for the 2 billion or so of the world's residents who live a particularly energy-rich lifestyle. In the US, it would mean abandoning much of what distinguishes us culturally as Americans and living a bit more like (I hate to say it . . .) Europeans!! This would mean smaller cars and vastly fewer "light" trucks; no more pickup trucks for commuting to the office or Chevy Suburbans for ferrying the kids to school; smaller houses and fewer second houses; more vacations via car instead of by air; more chicken and less steak; more sweat and less AC; shorter commutes and more public transit, leading to more clustered living and less sprawl; less air freight and two-day delivery; fewer Uber eats; the near demise of "carbon sports" such as all-terrain vehicles, hobby aircraft, and motor boating. All the ways in which we use energy that would be resented by our great-grandchildren will need to be rethought and, in most cases, reduced. Mitigation won't merely mean different energy, but more expensive energy and less profligate use of it.

# 8 ADAPTATION

Before geoengineering became taboo, adaptation was the climate response that could not be named, because it too implied that mitigation alone would be insufficient. Today, however, governments at every level are beginning to ponder how they may be compelled to adapt to climate change impacts, be they from extreme weather, sea level rise, freshwater shortages, acidic oceans, or crop failures. Possible adaptations range from personal (buy another air conditioner) to local (move the road back from the shoreline) to regional (defend the subway system from water incursion) to national (upgrade disaster response capabilities).

A paradox related to adaptation (with a nod to Scott Barrett of Columbia University) is that its incentive structure is opposite that for mitigation.[1] The voters of Miami Beach can expect a payback in their lifetimes from raising the elevation of Alton Road, and those benefits will derive mostly to residents and businesses located in Miami Beach, who must fund such a project. Therefore, there are strong incentives for the capital project. Those same residents, however, are only weakly incentivized to turn down their air conditioners and thereby reduce carbon emissions. Their electricity bill will go down, but above a certain standard of living, many people don't much care. There is also a societal benefit from the lesser emissions, but it is non-excludable, meaning it will aid the residents of Tokyo as much as those of South Beach. It is also a generational transfer, such that by the time South Beach experiences the climate benefit from reduced emissions, most of its current residents will have been cremated. Thus, the incentives to mitigate are weak. The upshot is that relative to the optimal policy response, the world will likely mitigate too little, and adapt too much. But what will adaptation mean in practice? That will be our focus below.

## The Need for Adaptation

Thoughtful consideration of adaptation begins with the recognition that we will not stop or avoid climate change. As we have previously noted, it's coming. There is still lots of latitude to affect how much of it is coming, but "no climate change" is no longer an option. We are already at 1.2°C and currently on a trajectory for roughly 3°C by 2100, perhaps with yet more after that. The temperature increase over land will be roughly twice the global average, meaning we are contemplating an increase of 6°C (or more than 10°F) over land. That's the difference in the annual average temperature of New York City versus Atlanta. Berlin versus Madrid. Tokyo versus Hong Kong. (And to answer your question directly, "Yes, now would be a perfectly appropriate time to freak out about this".) While some of the residents of the more northerly of these city pairs may consider this a positive trade, some of the southerly cities would verge on desertification.[2] Things would be markedly different in a 3°C world.

Nonetheless, if the bad news is that staggering amounts of climate change are likely in the offing, the good news is we can see it coming miles away. Decades away more precisely. We have more than an average human lifetime to prepare for this. Eighty years ago (I write this in mid-2021), World War II was in its first phases with the US still dithering on the sidelines. Think of how much global infrastructure has been built since then – nearly all the built structures that now exist. So, there is a great deal that we can do in the coming 80 years to adapt to the warmer world that we know is coming, particularly if we start now (which is a rather big "if").

The first step in assessing our adaptation requirements is clarifying what we are adapting to. Climate change will undoubtedly surprise us in various ways, but it's a good bet to assume that there will be more extreme weather, which is to say not only stronger hurricanes and cyclones, but also longer and more extreme droughts. The former will cause both coastal and inland flooding, whereas the latter risks crop failures and food insecurity. Coastal flooding will be exacerbated by substantial sea level rise, which will present itself as a storm surge that doesn't thereafter fully recede and exposes as vulnerable and flood-prone what was previously securely dry land. Coastal erosion will cede increasing amounts of land back to the sea. That sea will be substantially more acidic, rendering its fisheries far less productive. And, of course, it will be hotter, directly stressing people, animals, and plants, and contributing to more fertile conditions for the spread of both heat-related and vector-borne diseases.[3] Large quantities of permafrost will melt in the Arctic regions, not only accelerating climate change via the release of long-trapped $CO_2$ and subsequent production of methane, but destabilizing the built structures that sit on that permafrost. And this catalogs merely the human impacts of such change. Ecosystems around the world don't have the advance warning we do about the changes to come and cannot proactively adapt to them. They will surely react as the changes come, but slowly and often poorly. Many will not be capable of keeping pace with the rate of climate change occurring around them. We should therefore expect widespread ecosystem collapses and species extinctions. Setting aside the dire ethical and aesthetic implications of this, the services humanity derives from these ecosystems will be much impaired, creating further human impacts. This just doesn't sound very good.

But again, we know it's coming, and we further know that angry though our grandchildren will be with us for having put them in this bind, they will nonetheless be desperate to survive. Therefore, they will innovate, renovate, and adapt, slowly in the near future as the impacts appear to be distant in time, but feverishly late in this century as the disasters mount. I have phrased the foregoing as if humanity were a coherent and cohesive entity, which of course it is not. Therefore, as with other matters both within and outside the climate context, wealthy and well governed countries will fare well, whereas poor and rashly governed ones will suffer unmitigated catastrophes. Within societies, those least responsible for climate change will prove least protected from its impacts. Nonetheless, unevenly and imprecisely as it may unfold, there is a great deal that humanity can do to protect itself from the worst of those impacts.

## The Cost of Adaptation

The Global Commission on Adaptation, a pan-national body launched by former United Nations (UN) Secretary General Ban

Ki-moon, released a comprehensive report in 2019 on the state of adaptation to climate change. It urged the imperatives and benefits of acting now. While most discussions of climate change remediation return with depressing consistency to the question of money, adaptation is in fact full of "freebies" – if we have foresight. The vast majority of the built structures that will exist in 2100 will either have been newly built or substantially renovated and repaired between now and then. Therefore, to get most of the built environment – bridges, roads, buildings, ports, electrical lines, sewers – ready for the altered world of 2100, we don't need to undertake and fund a massive campaign to rebuild everything. We simply need the wisdom to understand that the engineering, planning, zoning, and approval process for all the rest of the construction we will do in this century needs to be informed by a recognition that the world will be different in 2100. We need to conform to tomorrow's predicted circumstances, not those of today and yesteryear. Such modifications would add to costs very marginally (about 3 percent), but would produce fourfold benefits (see Figure 8.1) in terms of future damages avoided.[4] However, the world is still for the most part building for the environment and climate of today. Minimizing the price tag of adaptation requires changing that perspective quickly and ensuring that the planning, design, approval, and construction processes internalize this climate perspective.

## Protecting Agriculture and Food Systems

The Global Commission report reviews a handful of activity sectors that will require substantial and distinctive adaptation strategies, the first of which is food. Agriculture, livestock management, and fisheries all rely upon the natural world to supply environments in which we can nurture and capture the food we eat, and therefore these are among the areas most vulnerable to climate change. The challenge is exacerbated by the fact that food demand is predicted to grow by 50 percent between 2010 and 2050, but by even more in the most food insecure regions – 200 percent in South Asia and 300 percent in Sub-Saharan Africa.[5] Unfortunately, these are precisely the areas that are predicted to experience the greatest loss of fertile agricultural conditions due to drying, shorter growing seasons, or increased climate variability.[6] Two-thirds of adults working in poverty make a living in part through agriculture, and people in rural areas somewhat ironically

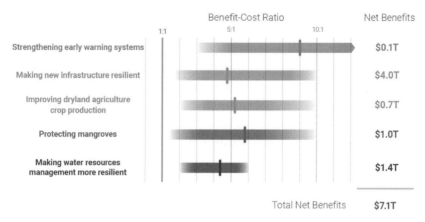

Figure 8.1 Benefits and costs of illustrative investments in adaptation. *Source:* The Global Center on Adaptation, licensed under Creative Commons CC BY 4.0.[7] This diagram is meant to illustrate the broad economic case for investment in a range of adaptation approaches. The net benefits illustrate the approximate global net benefits to be gained by 2030 from an illustrative investment of US$1.8 trillion in five areas (the total does not equal the sum of the rows due to rounding). Actual returns depend on many factors, such as economic growth and demand, policy context, institutional capacities, and condition of assets. Also, these investments neither address all that may be needed within sectors (for example, adaptation in the agricultural sector will consist of much more than dryland crop production) nor include all sectors (as health, education, and industry sectors are not included). Due to data and methodological limitations, the diagram does not imply full comparability of investments across sectors or countries

have higher rates of food insecurity and extreme poverty.[8] The steady historical growth in crop yields due to the "green revolution" is estimated to decline by 30 percent by mid-century unless we can intervene with effective adaptation.[9] While increased atmospheric $CO_2$ concentrations may enhance agricultural productivity, this likely will be more than offset by the reduced soil moisture that more frequent and more severe droughts will engender.

To adapt to this, the first step would be to do with increased vigor what we are already doing half-heartedly, which is to help small farmers in food insecure regions to improve their productivity in line with the UN's Sustainable Development Goals. These call for an increased pace of research and development into drought-resistant and heat-tolerant varieties of such heat-sensitive staples as maize, wheat, and rice. Plant and animal breeding as well as "last mile" adoption of improved techniques from the laboratory into the field remain essential. The use of digital communications and farmer-to-farmer education can amplify traditional agricultural extension and enable smallholders to make better planting and harvesting decisions.[10] The stunning penetration of cellphone technology even among the rural poor means that now data and analytics can be used to improve disease surveillance and to monitor soil health. At the same time, income diversification programs and stronger social security systems will be necessary to help farmers and pastoralists to manage increased variability and climate shocks. None of this is revolutionary or particular to climate change, but if we seek to ensure that a rapidly changing natural environment does not set off widespread famine and destabilizing waves of mass climate migration, we need to ensure that the most vulnerable among the world's populations are better able to protect their food security.

## Protecting and Building on Natural Systems

A related but distinct sector for adaptation is the natural environment. Myriad natural systems are at the breaking point for reasons that are only partly related to climate change, such as human sprawl, pollution, overexploitation, and deforestation. However, forests store and regulate water, which a warmer and drier climate will make all the more precious. Wetlands absorb floods. Mangroves blunt storm surge. All of these ecosystems absorb and store carbon when they are healthy and release it to the atmosphere when disturbed or destroyed. Thus, apart from their beauty and importance in maintaining biodiversity, these natural systems provide essential services to mankind. Already strained, climate change will push many of them to collapse. The adaptive solutions here are ones that seek to repair these systems in ways that are not necessarily particular to climate change, but which will better enable them to survive this further stressor. Those include preservation and re-establishment of forests, wetlands, and mangroves such that they serve as carbon sinks rather than sources. The restoration of upland forests preserves healthy watersheds, while urban tree planting can dramatically reduce the urban heat island effect and therefore the ambient temperatures in which billions of people spend their day. We can also go beyond simply restoring what once was and instead assist nature in surviving the ordeal we are fashioning for it. "Assisted evolution" describes an emerging field that seeks to provide Darwin a helping hand in speeding the adaptation of species and ecosystems to the changed environments we can foresee that they will confront. For example, marine biologists are selectively breeding corals that incorporate heat-resistant algae and then planting those on reefs threatened by warmer seas.[11]

As with agriculture, key steps in protecting natural systems entail accelerating progress on already extant initiatives. These include commitments under the UN Convention on Biological Diversity, the UN Convention to Combat Desertification, the Bonn Challenge of restoring 350 million hectares of degraded land by 2030, the Tropical Forest Alliance which seeks to reach net zero deforestation, and the Global Mangrove Alliance's goal to increase mangrove habitat by 20 percent by 2030. Each of these programs was articulated primarily for other benefits, but their importance is heightened by the extent to which each would slow climate change or protect against its impacts. While these and similar programs require implementation at a hyper-local level, the most impactful among them are conceived on national or international scales. China's Ecological Redlining Policy has used a science-based approach to identify nearly a quarter of the country that will be put under a high degree of protection in order to build resilience. Mexico has identified and protected water reserves in more than one third of its river basins. Twenty-one African countries including all those in Sahel region have proposed the Great Green Wall initiative to improve sustainable land and water management and combat the desertification with which the region is so notably threatened.[12] Each of these are ambitious initiatives by which to work with nature to build climate resilience.

Supplies of freshwater are another natural system that was being degraded before the onset of climate change but will be further depleted by it. The effect of droughts and desertification on local water supplies is clear, but paradoxically, increased flooding also contaminates freshwater with pollution and/or sea water. Usable water in lakes and aquifers is being overexploited and polluted, and competition for scarce water resources in the developing world is growing ever fiercer. The way forward here is quite simply to manage water better. This will require increased investment in water infrastructure at every stage, from healthier watersheds and enhanced reservoirs to repaired water mains and expanded drainage capacity. New water sources such as desalinization and wastewater reclamation must be further developed, and better flood control and protection infrastructure is required to prevent contamination of the water supply. However, beyond improved infra-structure, the world also needs improved water governance. Water pricing that is unreflective of its true cost encourages inefficiency and overuse. Dynamic pricing would enable much better allocation during droughts. Water allocation rights based on frontier history rather than modern reality as is so common in the American West encourage gross misuses of this increasingly scarce resource. The lack of recourse by downstream users against the actions of upstream users particularly when rivers cross national boundaries is a source of potential conflict in many parts of the world. A world with better water governance and therefore more efficient water use would be much more capable of dealing with the water management challenges that climate change will exacerbate.

## Making Cities Resilient

Increasingly large, dense, and numerous mega-cities create acute climate adaptation difficulties. Cities are home to more than half the world's population and produce in excess of 80 percent of its GDP.[13] Nonetheless, nearly 1 billion people live in informal urban settlements such as the infamous favelas of Rio de Janeiro, with little or no secure access to such services as water, electricity, sanitation, education, or health care.[14] These are precarious powder kegs into which to toss climate shock matches. Droughts threatened to run dry the water taps in Mexico City and Cape Town. Floods and cyclones have killed thousands and displaced countless more in Bangladesh over the years. Heat waves have imperiled cities in Europe and India, while landslides driven by torrential rains brought disaster to La Paz and Durban.[15] Extreme weather, storm surge, sea level rise, and climate variability will present acute challenges to the precarious balance that enables so many people to live in such dense proximity. To diminish and manage these risks, cities will need to become more resilient and equitable.

An essential first step is information – clarifying acute climate risks via accurate floodplain maps that can inform both individual decisions and urban planning. Ensuring that cities evolve away from rather than into known hazards can dramatically reduce the impact of calamities when they do strike and ensure that affected populations can prepare and evacuate if need be. Early warning systems and emergency preparedness are also essential to ensuring that natural disasters don't precipitate human catastrophes. As cities build and retrofit themselves over the coming decades, they need to require that projects take account of climate risks to reduce their vulnerability. In addition to greatly expanded urban tree cover, cities can pursue nature-based solutions such as green roofs and community gardens to slow stormwater runoff. Restoring or constructing urban wetlands will also build flood resistance. China has pioneered the development of "sponge cities" replete with permeable surfaces to both control runoff and recharge the underlying aquifer. Informal urban settlements also need to be incorporated into the city infrastructure and service network. In the same cynical way that tornados seem to willfully seek out trailer parks to obliterate, the ravaged urban neighborhoods shown on cable news after a storm surge or landslide devastates a portion of a city are inevitably these informal settlements. They are built on the most marginal land in ways that conform to no building code – favelas in Brazil, townships in South Africa, homeless encampments in American cities. It is longstanding inequality that creates such conditions, but climate catastrophes will thrive in them. Enhanced climate resilience would in part mean addressing these vulnerabilities.

Another way to reduce vulnerability is via more thoughtful and proactive disaster risk management. Preparedness can yield enormous benefits. After the city of Ahmedabad in Western India suffered 1,300 deaths during a heat wave in 2010, local officials analyzed their response shortcomings and developed a proactive plan. They trained local health care workers in diagnosing and treating heat stress, and mandated white roofs to reduce the heat island effect. When a similarly infernal spell struck in 2015, they communicated with the populace, distributed water by truck, and limited deaths to less than 20. The plan has since been replicated in dozens of other Indian cities.[16]

To spur the widespread adoption of similarly thoughtful risk reduction strategies, the Sendai Framework for Disaster Risk Reduction was adopted by UN member states and endorsed by the General Assembly in 2015.[17] The Framework has several priorities: better understand disaster risk; strengthen risk governance to reduce risk; invest in disaster resilience; enhance response preparedness; and ensure that societies build back better to reduce subsequent vulnerability. The goals are to reduce mortality, numbers of affected people, economic losses, infrastructure damage, and service interruptions. At the same time, the intent is to increase the number of countries that have risk reduction strategies, assist developing countries in implementing such strategies, and ensure the implementation of multi-hazard systems that can provide crucial prior warning of impending hazards. These capabilities can increase societal capacities to predict, absorb, and recover from events that cannot be prevented.

## Resisting the Sea

In the US, coastlines are six times as dense as inland counties,[18] a demographic pattern common throughout the world.[19] A climate change impact that will therefore affect an enormous proportion of world population is sea level rise. Humans have been dealing with the capricious oceans since before the commencement of recorded history, but coastlines that have changed little in centuries will begin to be substantially reshaped. Most if not all of our seaport cities were built on an unacknowledged assumption that sea level was stable and predictable in all but infrequent freak storms, and that buildings and infrastructure built a few feet above sea level were durable assets. A time-honored technique for creating something out of nothing has been to drain and fill marshlands and shallow bays to thereafter build on the landfill, and large sections of Boston, New York, and Miami sit barely above sea level on such reclaimed land. The same applies for Mumbai, Macau, and Shanghai. Such regions will prove extremely vulnerable to incursion as the seas rise.

While sea level rise will present itself with unprecedented intensity and speed in the coming decades, living with rising water is not a new phenomenon. London is also substantially built on former wetlands, and 26 percent of the Netherlands would be under the North Sea[20] today were it not for the ingenuity of centuries of Dutch farmers and engineers. It is positively mind-bending to stand in a Dutch tulip field and look *up* at barges floating in the adjacent canals, but the reason Holland needed all of its fabled windmills was to continuously pump water uphill from sub-sea level polders (fields reclaimed from the sea) to elevated canals, which evacuate it to the sea. While the Dutch are perhaps the world masters of the art of managing water, sea walls are a ubiquitous feature of coastal cities and towns around the globe. They are used to fix the land/sea boundary and prevent incursion of the sea and erosion of the land.

Common though they are, we will need a lot more of them if we are to keep the coastline where it is despite rapidly rising seas. As noted in Chapter 3, for every centimeter of vertical sea level rise, the coast would naturally retreat by 100 centimeters, so left to its own devices, a half meter[21] rise in sea levels in this century would mean a 50 meter coastal retreat. The retreat is less in places where hills or cliffs meet the sea, but much more on shallow plains like my native Long Island. That is a lot of sea to hold back.

And sea walls have many drawbacks. First, they are expensive. One estimate is that defending the US coastline with walls would require nearly a half-trillion dollars of investment by 2040.[22] And the expense is ongoing – they require substantial periodic maintenance to withstand the pounding of the waves. Second, when they fail, they can do so catastrophically, as Hurricane Katrina demonstrated in New Orleans. The tsunami triggered by the 2011 earthquake in northeastern Japan similarly resulted in the overtopping of the sea wall at the Fukushima Daiichi nuclear station. Sea walls create environmental damage in that they impede the natural process by which sediments flow from land to sea and laterally along the shore.[23] They also increase the scouring action of the sea, which tends to undermine the walls themselves.[24] We cannot possibly defend every mile of seashore with walls, but wherever the walls end, the damage to the immediately adjacent areas is amplified, resulting in further coastal erosion and sea incursion at those spots.[25]

The world's most prominent contemporary coastal defenses against the sea were prompted not by anthropogenic sea level rise but by the beastly North Sea Flood of January 1953. The combination of a severe windstorm, a low pressure system, and a high spring tide caused the North Sea to surge nearly 5 meters or 16 feet above mean sea level,[26] inundating low lying areas of the Netherlands, Belgium, England, and Scotland. Worst hit were the southwestern provinces of the Netherlands, where three mighty rivers – the Rhine, Meuse, and Scheldt – all converge as they reach the sea. Each river flows into a long, narrow estuary somewhat like the Chesapeake or Narragansett bays, where a constricted mouth to the open sea exposes an extensive inland coast to ocean waters. As the storm surge plowed up these narrowing channels, its impact was magnified and it devastated the surrounding dikes, inundating the adjacent polders and killing over 1,800 people.[27] Also hard hit was the Thames estuary near London and several other counties on England's east coast, where over 250 square miles of land was flooded.[28]

In the aftermath of the floods, the Netherlands and the UK resolved to prevent such future disasters. Decades and billions of guilders/pounds later, the mighty Dutch Delta Works and the eery-looking Thames Barrier emerged to protect these regions. The Delta Works (see Figure 8.2) is a series of dams, sluices, locks, dikes, levees, and storm surge barriers which protect coastlines from flooding and the estuaries from storm surge, all while preserving the flow of the rivers and the vital ports of Rotterdam and Antwerp. The mouths of the estuaries are capped with sluice-dams and surge barriers that can be closed if a storm surge approaches. It was deemed by the American Society of Civil Engineers as one of the Seven Wonders of the Modern World[29] and (with a few hiccups) has succeeded in protecting the Dutch coast ever since. The Delta Works has demonstrated that massive hydraulic engineering projects can prevent calamities along vulnerable coastlines, and that everything along our coasts must be rethought in an era of rising seas. It has been estimated that to keep pace with climate-change-related sea level rise, a reinforcement project requiring ten times the budget spent heretofore will be required by 2100.

**Figure 8.2** Delta Works in the Netherlands. Image taken by Rolf Kranz and licensed under the Creative Commons CC BY-SA 4.0[30]

While the Delta Works stretches intermittently for over 100 km, the Thames Barrier, east of London (see Figure 8.3), is little more than 500 meters across, but similarly defends the capital against occasional storms while remaining open at most times to preserve shipping traffic. It consists of ten sector gates that stretch across the river between artificial piers. The main mid-stream gates rest on the river bottom and can be rotated up from a horizontal to a vertical position, thereby blocking the upstream estuary from an inrushing storm surge. Completed in 1984, it was expected to be used two to three times a year, but as sea level rise has accelerated, it was used 50 times in a recent season.[31]

A comparable barrier is under construction for the purpose of shielding Venice's matchless architecture from the Adriatic. The ancient city now floods regularly (sometimes daily), with wooden walkways stretching across St Mark's Square to keep the feet of tourists dry as they queue to enter the basilica. The MOSE Barrier lies on the seafloor at the three inlets through which the Adriatic flows into the lagoon in which Venice is situated and would be raised in the event of threatening tides. Infamously delayed, over-budget, and scandal ridden, the barrier is currently planned to become fully operational in 2021. Nonetheless, it too was engineered before the extent of the twenty-first-century sea level

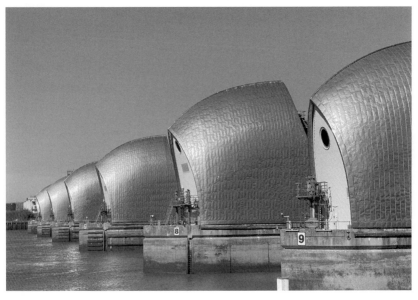

Figure 8.3 Thames Barrier in the east of London. *Image source*: Unsplash.com[32]

rise was properly accounted for, and will need to be re-engineered almost as soon as it is completed, since the 2019 IPCC report projects sea levels by 2100 rising by nearly twice the amount against which MOSE was intended to protect.[33] Similar barriers are being contemplated at the mouths of the harbors of New York,[34] Miami,[35] Charleston,[36] Jakarta,[37] and Shanghai[38] among many others.

## Retreat

And yet not every coastal city, village, and villa will merit heroic and costly sea defenses. Spectacular though projects like the Delta Works are, they will prove to be the exception rather than the rule. The rule is that over the longer run, the sea will win in most instances. The defenses that we mount will in most cases prove to be insufficient and temporary, frustrating the sea's intent for a generation or two perhaps before yielding to its inevitability.

Broadly, there are three possible approaches to adapting to sea level rise. The subject of the foregoing paragraphs represents the first – resistance, or keeping the water out. A compromise position would be to accommodate the water as envisioned in the "room for the river" design concept made famous in Holland, whereby structures are modified to be able to channel and accommodate occasional flooding in such features as urban water parks. Seaside structures could be similarly engineered to anticipate and survive occasional flooding by elevating houses several feet above expected flood levels and reinforcing roads to resist washouts. Reviving or establishing salt marshes and mangroves to blunt the force of the sea would also provide resilience against periodic flooding.

However, if sea level rise accelerates in tandem with the more extreme but plausible warming scenarios, the reluctant but eventual answer along many – if not most – coastlines will be retreat, moving structures, towns, and cities inland to higher ground. If that seems like an enormous and nearly impossible feat to achieve in economic, engineering, and political terms, that's because it is. Miami's downtown and South Beach may be sufficiently dense to protect, but most of the Florida coast would not be. Nearly the entire coast of Louisiana would surrender to the waves, as would large portions of the coastline from Texas to Maine. And of course, this is not restricted to the United States, but more nearly the opposite. The US will likely be more capable of defending its coast than most of the developing world.

In an idealized society, it would be possible to imagine a well-managed retreat, where maps would be prepared well in advance that would delineate vulnerable zones, guiding well-informed decisions about where to build defenses and where to surrender. In the latter areas, relocation assistance and buyout programs would be instituted to ease the transition for shore front homeowners who need to abandon their beachside houses and move inland. Preparations for this eventuality could be taken decades in advance, such that building codes would require that any new construction or substantial retrofits render structures more resistant to and resilient from interim storm impacts, and easier to relocate when the time comes. Neighborhoods would ultimately be condemned and whole towns would be relocated. Former beach front property would be reconfigured into protective salt marshes and other soft, natural aquatic landforms.

It is possible to imagine all this – in China and other authoritarian jurisdictions, where technocrats can make decisions that overpower the will of the local citizenry. It is much harder to imagine in a democracy, particularly one such as the US where substantial power over such decisions is devolved to state and local political interests and decision making is hamstrung by internal division. Like China, the US will be compelled by events to manage through such issues, but likely not until all other alternatives become intolerable. Given how costly and painful such retreat would be – particularly among the wealthy and powerful elites whose villas occupy large swathes of our shorelines – it may prove that in this arena, only loss will instruct. We may need lots more Sandys and Katrinas before such measures could prove politically palatable.

Nonetheless, in small and isolated instances, planning for retreat has begun. Perhaps no major city in the world is sinking as quickly as Jakarta, bits of which are already submerged, with large swathes projected to follow by 2050.[39] Indonesia is therefore scouting potential new sites for its capital. Japan is spending the equivalent of several hundred billion dollars relocating to new towns on higher ground the half million people displaced by the 2011 tsunami that destroyed 400,000 structures.[40] Kiribati, a low-lying Pacific island nation faced with the prospect of total inundation, has purchased land in Fiji so that its people may migrate "with dignity" should the time come.[41] In Louisiana, a federal grant is enabling the relocation 40 miles inland of the entire population of tiny Isle de Jean Charles, 98 percent of which has vanished under the onrushing Gulf of Mexico.[42] Since 1989, the US Federal Emergency Management Agency (FEMA) has quietly acquired more than 40,000 damaged or vulnerable properties.[43] Nonetheless, this is less than one-tenth of 1 percent of the structures in shoreline counties in the US. Acquiring just 10 percent of those would cost 30 times as much as the FEMA has spent on managed retreat to date.[44]

Adaptation to climate change will be an enormous and costly undertaking. It will entail some huge shifts in both infrastructure and thinking, but will also require a long list of small-ball actions that may be articulated at the national or pan-national level, but which must be implemented locally. All of them are steps that would reduce the impacts on humans of heat waves, droughts, hurricanes, sea level rise, and other shocks that climate change may induce or increase. And many of them are in the category of "eat your vegetables and exercise more," things we should do for other sound reasons but which climate change will make more urgent. The sooner we start in on them, the less costly and disruptive they will be to achieve.

# 9 OUR DESCENDANTS WILL DEMAND CLIMATE INTERVENTION

We have reached a juncture in this book where we should survey the territory we have covered. If we pull back and look at the bigger picture, what does that tell us?

As we noted at the outset, climate change is real, anthropogenic, dangerous, and coming. A lot of it. Almost certainly north of 2°C, and more likely 3°C or beyond in this century, with no certainty that it will stop there. Climate change in any of these amounts will be very dangerous and likely highly destructive to both the natural world and human society. The Paris Agreement is the best we seem to be able to muster at this point, but it will fall well short of riveting humanity to the stringent mitigation trajectory that climate scientists would urge upon us. Until technology renders mitigation inexpensive and relatively painless, the incentives to pursue it aggressively (local cost for global benefit) remain depressingly weak.

Given that, hats off to brave Britain, Japan, South Korea, and the EU, all of whom have announced net zero goals by 2050. Under Biden, the US has now rejoined the party with gusto, doubling its initial climate commitment under Paris to as much as a 52 percent emissions reduction by 2030 relative to 2005 levels.[1] That would be remarkable speed for so large an emitter, and yet the outside world could be forgiven for wondering how durable this commitment will prove in what remains a very polarized nation. China dismissed new US boasts of climate leadership by characterizing the American reentry into Paris "as a truant getting back to class."[2] China is giving itself an additional decade (2060) by which to reach net zero, but as by far the world's largest emitter (double the US)[3] with an electricity system that is roughly 60 percent derived from coal,[4] its pledge is in many ways even more radical than many others. This is difficult to reconcile, however, with the fact that China has hundreds new coal-fired power plants in construction or in the planning process both at home and elsewhere as part of its Belt and Road initiative.[5] China also made clear that its climate pledges are neither inviolate nor decoupled from other considerations, warning that "Chinese cooperation would depend on how the US responded to Beijing's policies regarding Hong Kong, Taiwan, and Xinjiang Province."[6]

There also are no clear blueprints for how to achieve so massive a transition for energy, transportation, industry, and agriculture. In fact, the UN Environmental Programme in its most recent (December 2020) "Emissions Gap Report," notes that none of these bold net zero pledge nations has as yet incorporated any policy changes into their NDCs under the Paris Agreement[7] (that may have changed by the time you are reading this) and there now exists a vast discrepancy between these lofty longer-term goals and the NDCs covering the coming decade.[8] Therefore, even with the best of intentions, our climate vanguard may fail or falter. Moreover, much of the world has made no such pledges, including most of those states in the developing world who tend to have high emissions growth trajectories. Many of these countries propose to hinge their future climate cooperation on debt relief from the World Bank or climate financing from the developed world,[9] portending potentially rough seas ahead as humanity tries to lash itself into a single climate boat. With that context, it is time to try to compare our intended destination with what appears to be our actual course.

## What Do Emissions Need to Look Like?

The Paris Agreement set two climate targets for the year 2100 – holding the warming well below 2°C above the preindustrial levels, with best efforts towards limiting it to 1.5°C. To bolster the credibility of the 1.5°C target, the 2018 SR15 report[10] illustrated a variety of pathways by which that goal could be achieved (see the large graph on the left in Figure 9.1). The report highlights four such paths with differing assumptions about the timing of their emissions declines, the policy mixes that facilitate them, and the degree to which they stay forever under 1.5°C or "overshoot" (i.e., temporarily reach higher temperatures) and then return. All four scenarios require a significant portion of *negative* emissions both to reach and to subsequently maintain net zero. That point is sufficiently critical to our topic that I am going to repeat it (bear with me …). None of the mid-century SR15 net zero pathways and end-of-century 1.5°C temperature outcomes are achievable via emissions reductions alone. All of them require negative emissions *just to get to net zero.* This is because of the "net" in "net zero," meaning that before, during, and long after the year when we hit net zero, there will still be ongoing positive emissions from the most difficult to decarbonize sectors such as aviation, long-distance trucking, ocean shipping, and cement manufacturing. As the three smaller graphs on the right in Figure 9.1 also illustrate, these scenarios suggest that we fail to reach zero emissions of any of methane, nitrous oxide, or black carbon either by mid-century or even by 2100 (we come close with black carbon). All those ongoing emissions from non-$CO_2$ sources need to be offset by negative carbon emissions somewhere else in the economy or we fail to get to net zero.

The amount of negative emissions that each pathway requires is inversely proportional to the aggressiveness of emissions cuts in *this* decade. Those that take a hatchet to emissions in the 2020s require less negative emissions in the 2030s and beyond. On the other hand, the slow-start P4 scenario that is relatively permissive in this decade requires massive negative emissions in subsequent decades, firstly to achieve net zero as above, but thereafter, to further reduce carbon concentrations in the atmosphere. This is because this slow-start scenario causes temperatures to exceed the 1.5°C target in the latter half of the century, so to meet the temperature increase target of 1.5°C by 2100 (the definition of success for these scenarios), we have to bring them back down via negative emissions. The magnitude of negative emissions contemplated in this scenario towards the end of this century is utterly massive – 20 Gt of $CO_2$ removal annually. That is roughly half of current global annual $CO_2$ emissions!

And ponder for a moment what this scenario is suggesting. It says there is a 1.5°C-compliant scenario that doesn't require massive emissions cuts in this decade, but it involves enduring several decades in the latter half of this century wherein temperatures will substantially overshoot that target. Well, if allowing temperatures to exceed this target is as dangerous as the IPCC gurus suggest, then how is it acceptable that we exceed that target for a half-century or so during the lifetime of many of the people reading this book? That would seem

## Global emissions pathway characteristics

General characteristics of the evolution of anthropogenic net emissions of $CO_2$, and total emissions of methane, black carbon, and nitrous oxide in model pathways that limit global warming to 1.5°C with no or limited overshoot. Net emissions are defined as anthropogenic emissions reduced by anthropogenic removals. Reductions in net emissions can be achieved through different portfolios of mitigation measures illustrated in Figure SPM.3b.

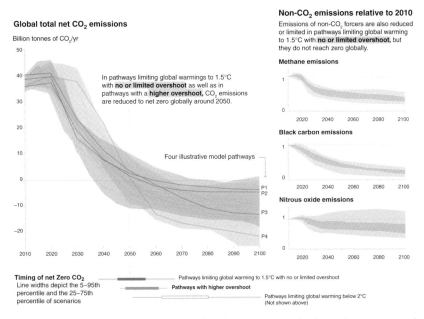

**Global total net $CO_2$ emissions**

Billion tonnes of $CO_2$/yr

**Non-$CO_2$ emissions relative to 2010**

Emissions of non-$CO_2$ forcers are also reduced or limited in pathways limiting global warming to 1.5°C with **no or limited overshoot,** but they do not reach zero globally.

In pathways limiting global warmings to 1.5°C with **no or limited overshoot** as well as in pathways with a **higher overshoot,** $CO_2$ emissions are reduced to net zero globally around 2050.

Four illustrative model pathways

**Methane emissions**

**Black carbon emissions**

**Nitrous oxide emissions**

Timing of net Zero $CO_2$
Line widths depict the 5–95th percentile and the 25–75th percentile of scenarios

Pathways limiting global warming to 1.5°C with no or limited overshoot
Pathways with higher overshoot
Pathways limiting global warming below 2°C
(Not shown above)

**Figure 9.1** IPCC lllustration of how global warming can be limited to 1.5 °C with global net anthropogenic $CO_2$ emissions under different pathways. *Source:* IPCC Special Report: Global Warming of 1.5°C[11]

unconscionably cavalier. Moreover, we are asking our as yet unborn grand- and great-grandchildren to take our word for it that the unacceptable climate impacts they will experience will be rendered merely temporary via a massive future scale-up of technologies that barely exist today. Oh, . . . and that *they* will have to pay for all this.

I suspect they will not feel very reassured.

As the source of this Figure 9.1 is the lofty IPCC, it is tempting to be lulled into perceiving these scenarios to be *predictions*, but they are decidedly not so. Instead, all of them start with a conclusion (+1.5°C in 2100) and work backwards from that. They are a response to the question "What would you have to believe to conclude that we could limit the temperature increase in 2100 to 1.5°C above the preindustrial baseline?" The IPCC assumes breathtaking ~7 percent year over year declines commencing this year (2021) and continuing without interruption for a decade,[12] after which the pace slows as we tackle the tougher-to-decarbonize sectors on our way to net zero. They are also purely technical or perhaps "techno-economic" pathways that do not attempt to factor in political viability. They illustrate what our emissions might look like if the world were run by unelected, well-intentioned technocrats – a sort of globalized Singapore. That is of course not the world in which we actually live, which is among the reasons why humanity has so consistently failed to adopt the emissions pathways previously recommended by the IPCC.

## Will COVID be a Gamechanger?

Nonetheless, exactly the sort of ~7 percent $CO_2$ emissions decline that we would need to commence down the recommended pathway did in fact happen in 2020, but only due to the "black swan" intercession of COVID. Might this be the start of just the trend we need?

Not likely. Irrespective of whether the post-COVID economic recovery is fast or slow (it looks to be both in different parts of the world), most economists imagine there *will* be a recovery and that the world will return to an economic growth track just as it did after the last pandemic 100 years ago and the last global economic shock a dozen years ago. The IEA's latest Global Energy Review predicts that energy demand in 2021 will more than offset the decline in 2020, rendering it 0.5 percent above the record 2019 level.[13] It foresees energy-related $CO_2$ emissions heading for their second highest annual increase ever, making up nearly all of the COVID swoon.[14] If that proves true, then COVID won't trigger the inflection point illustrated in the figures above, and neither will it put a perceptible dent in the buildup of GHG concentrations that ultimately define climate outcomes. In fact, UNEP has estimated that if the economic recovery commences in 2021, then the impact of the pandemic on temperatures in 2050 will be an imperceptible 0.01°C.[15] A temporary emissions hiatus achieves nothing. We need 2020-sized meat cleaver cuts to our emissions EVERY year in this decade,[16] followed by more surgical cuts of the harder-to-remediate sectors of the economy for the following 23 years in order to get to net zero on the average glide path proposed in the SR15.

While COVID did produce a one-year dip in $CO_2$ emissions, it appears not to have exerted a similar downward impact on the other

GHGs that contribute to warming. Moreover, as the International Energy Agency (IEA) points out in its 2020 World Energy Outlook, "low economic growth is not a low emissions strategy."[17] To shift rapidly to the sort of low emissions trajectory required to meet the Paris goals, the world needs huge immediate investments to spur R&D, incentivize the adoption of low carbon energy sources, electrify the transport system, and upgrade the electrical grid. At this juncture, it remains an open question whether from a climate standpoint the pandemic will prove to be a step forward or a step back, in that while the recession suppressed emissions, it also retarded economic growth and diverted funds to emergency COVID relief that might otherwise have been available to finance the energy transition. The fervent hope of the IEA is that the remaining global gusher of once-in-a-generation recovery spending that will flow in the coming year or two will be directed to climate friendly purposes like subsidizing solar panels rather than climate regressive purposes like bailing out struggling coal mines.[18] However, the global spending pattern thus far is quite mixed on that score, with countries such as France, Germany, South Korea, and the UK funding cutting-edge green initiatives while Russia and Mexico are backfilling in very brown economic sectors.[19] The US had been on the brown list under Trump, but has promptly switched to the green team under Biden. Nonetheless, this unique opening to jump-start the 30-ish year emissions plunge may well not be fully seized.

## What Will Emissions Actually Look Like?

This gets at a problem that commonly arises as one tries to consult the most prominent global prognostications of future emissions. Few of the flagship reports from the UNEP, the IEA, McKinsey, Bloomberg, BP, Equinor, or the International Renewable Energy Agency produce an unambiguous statement to the effect of "here is where we see emissions coming out mid-century." Instead, they generally produce at least two and often three scenarios illustrating possible futures along a spectrum ranging from: market-driven "business as usual"; through half-hearted slow transition; to full-on Paris-compliant. They then implicitly invite the reader to review the assumptions that underlie each and try to puzzle out some answer as to where we are headed. In some sense this is a cop out, but an understandable one in that we are asking modelers to guess at outcomes for which there are no current answers. How fast will populations and incomes grow? How quickly will technology enable transitions away from heavy industry and carbon-based energy sources? How much personal sacrifice will governments be willing to enforce upon their citizens? How will we weigh the trade-off between economic growth and environmental well-being? How quickly will dire, unacceptable climate impacts pile up? How much will future energy sourcing decisions be driven by security-of -supply considerations rather than carbon content? How inclined will the superpowers of tomorrow be to subsume some portion of their precious sovereignty to the sort of binding international commitments that will likely be necessary to reach global net zero?

Of course, no one can predict the answers to these myriad questions, so the forecasters produce alternative scenarios that generally look like the one below from BP's 2020 Energy Outlook. This is built from very carefully sourced analyses of how energy demand growth, fuel source transition, and policy changes will interact to produce different emission futures, but what it rather unhelpfully adds up to is

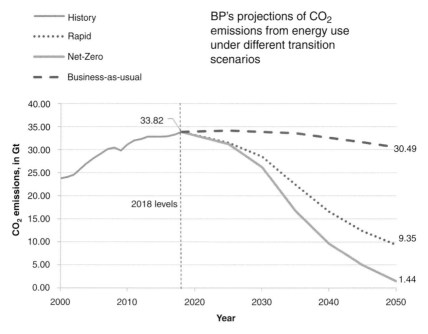

Figure 9.2 $CO_2$ emissions from energy use. *Data source:* Data regarding the $CO_2$ emissions from energy use between 2000 and 2018 were sourced from Equinor's Energy Perspectives 2020 and data for the emission scenarios are based on BP's Energy Outlook: 2020 Edition[20, 21]

a statement to the effect of "In 2050, emissions may end up somewhere between virtually unchanged and zero. We're not sure."

Figure 9.2 models only $CO_2$ emissions rather than all GHG emissions, and only those emissions from energy use rather than from other sources such as land-use changes, so it is an incomplete illustration of possible emissions futures, but adding those other sources and gases would alter the scale on the left but not so much the image itself. It would still portray a climate future hovering somewhere between probably fine and utterly disastrous.

Equinor, the Norwegian state-owned multinational energy company (formerly knowns as Statoil) produces a similarly ambiguous chart for $CO_2$ emissions through mid-century (Figure 9.3), accompanied by very helpful descriptions of the worlds the differing curves portray.

The top-most "Rivalry" scenario describes a world characterized by volatility and uncertainty in which superpower competition and energy security trump climate concerns, such that emissions in 2050 are slightly higher than those of today. The middle "Reform" scenario assumes that market outcomes and technological pacing are what drives the required energy transition and that economic growth is prioritized, leading to a mere 20 percent decline in emissions by 2050. Finally, the

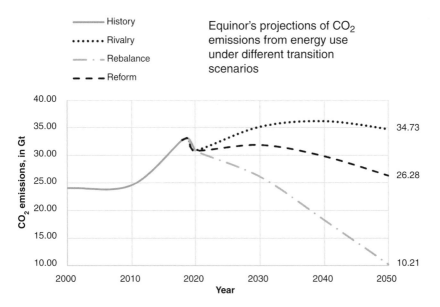

**Figure 9.3** Global energy-related $CO_2$ emissions by scenario. *Data source*: Equinor, Energy Perspectives 2020[22]

"Rebalance" pathway illustrated by the bottom line portrays an abrupt downward turn early in this decade that reduces emissions by 70 percent in 2050 and implies a net zero destination by roughly 2070[23] – late but much better than never.

However, the society this third scenario describes is one in which the developed world shifts its focus to well-being rather than wealth creation, while the developing world tempers a headlong rush towards GDP growth with a harmonization of "social inclusion, and environmental protection."[24] The developed world would pay the "full price for goods, covering negative externalities" (i.e., the carbon tax), while "emerging countries benefit [from the implicit wealth transfer] and invest in sustainable development."[25] Radical changes in consumer behavior, work practices, and lifestyle choices would be required to develop a sustainable way of life.[26] At the risk of excessive cynicism, this does not sound like the world in which we live. If these are the sorts of assumptions required to get to net zero by 2070, we are in deep trouble.

Other forecasters define their scenario alternatives differently. The IEA compares a Paris-compliant scenario with one based upon an assumption that governments continue to pursue whatever policies they have previously announced. That "Stated Policies" scenario in the IEA's latest forecast suggests the world will quickly recover from the pandemic and end this decade 7 percent above 2018 levels, a far cry from the roughly 40 percent decline below 2010 levels required for a 1.5°C target.[27] The latest projections from both Bloomberg and McKinsey each present an aspirational case along with one more consistent with recent trends. Bloomberg puts 2050 fossil fuel combustion-related emissions at 16 percent below 2019 levels, while McKinsey projects a slightly more optimistic fall of 25 percent.[28,29] This would represent forward progress of course, but in McKinsey's verbiage, these are not merely straying "far from the 1.5°C Pathway," but "implying a 3.5°C Pathway."[30]

Even the UN Environment Programme in its 2020 "Emissions Gap" report notes that the mid-century gap between "where we are likely to be and where we need to be" is vast.[31] "Are we on track to bridge that gap? Absolutely not."[32] Doing so would require the emissions reductions currently embodied in the Paris NDCs to be tripled, and for those NDCs to be subsequently honored, despite the fact that nearly half the G20 participants are either definitively off track relative to their NDCs or uncertain.[33] The current NDCs would bring the world to 3°C by 2100,[34] whereas today's stated government policies would produce 3.5°C.[35] Most dauntingly, if we were to keep to the more stringent 1.5°C target while allowing the world's poor to catch up to the global average carbon footprint of just over 2 tonnes of $CO_2e$ in 2030, the world's richest 1 percent of earners would have to cut their emissions by 30 times.[36] Not 30 percent. One-thirtieth!

## When Will We Actually Turn the Corner?

And yet someday, somehow, we *must* turn such a corner. We can't just keep filling the bathtub. At some point, the impacts of climate change will likely become intolerable to ignore. It is hard to convince people struggling to pay health care costs and college tuition, if not simply rent, to sacrifice mightily for an obscure future – to "plant trees under the shade of which they will never sit." But whenever it is finally our own bacon on the line rather than our grandchildren's – once my beach house actually washes into the sea – then I expect we will act. Fuzzy climate models about a distant sweaty tomorrow may not sufficiently instruct, but contemporary loss will. The day must come when the whole world is finally ready to make real sacrifices to stop climate change.

But when? The answer to that question matters a great deal, because it informs how full the tub might be when we finally turn the spigot off. Start shutting the tap now as the SR15 urges, and we could preserve the 1.5°C–2°C range. Start turning it off at the end of the century and we are guaranteed double that amount.[37] So "when" matters. And "when" can be broken down into two subcomponents – "when" as the Peak Emission Year, and "when" as the Net Zero Emissions Year. That oversimplifies of course. The shapes and slopes of the curves between the key dates matter too, but let's just focus on those two key junctures.

Of course, I have no crystal ball by which to divine these dates, but let's work with what we have. Some would argue that the IEA on one end of the spectrum and the IPCC on the other have "skin in the game" and a motivation to nudge emissions projections in a particular direction, but not so for McKinsey or Bloomberg. Each of them produces a "consistent with current policies" scenario that suggests that we may be near peak emissions currently, but that the decline between now and 2050 is a slow and shallow one, resulting in mid-century emission levels about 20 percent below today's. These projections pertain only to $CO_2$ emissions from energy, but let's extrapolate that the curve would be shaped the same were it instead to relate to all anthropogenic GHG emissions from all sources (note: this may be an unreasonably optimistic assumption). A blend of these two curves is presented in Figure 9.4.

McKinsey and Bloomberg don't go beyond 2050, but we must, since once again we need to know how full the bathtub will ultimately be – not just in 2050 – but in the Net Zero Emissions Year. So how might we guess at the trajectory after 2050? Hmmm.

Well let's do the more or less most optimistic thing we could *reasonably* do thereafter. Of course, the *most* optimistic thing would be to imagine that we invent cheap, safe, universal magic energy in 2050 and emissions (all GHGs) immediately drop to zero, but that evades my "reasonably" constraint. So, let's instead imagine that through 2050 the world is on the path suggested by McKinsey/Bloomberg, but in that year we finally find the willpower that the IPCC is urging upon us as of 2020. The coastal flooding, intensified hurricanes, rampant wildfires, stronger/longer droughts, and other horsemen of the clime-pocalypse become intolerable and a new era dawns of seamless international cooperation, universal carbon taxes, and radical behavioral changes, not merely in the developed world, but in the developing world as well. The luge-like emissions plummet that was intended to commence in 2020 actually commences in 2050, and for 33 years thereafter, emissions nose-dive to zero. At last.

We will have finally grasped the resource limits of our little petri-dish planet and adjusted our societies and lifestyles to fit within

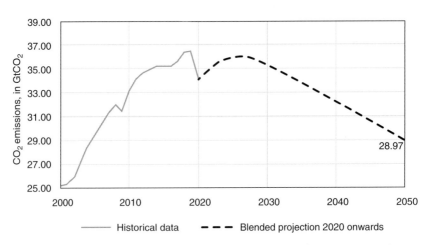

Figure 9.4 Blended McKinsey and Bloomberg projection of $CO_2$ emissions from fossil fuels and industry until 2050. *Data source*: Data for emissions from 2000 until 2019 were sourced from the Global Carbon Project database and the blended projection was created using data from Bloomberg NEF's New Energy Outlook 2020 and McKinsey's Global Energy Perspective 2021[38, 39, 40]

its finite bounds. Paris blossoms into full fruit and the nationally determined contributions are at last equal to the task. A governance and monitoring system is created that can properly keep score and enable the nice to cajole the naughty into line. The developed world comes to the financial aid of the less developed and shoulders outsized responsibility in partial account for its outsized role in fomenting the problem.

On December 31 of 2083, as the world counts down to the midnight that will ring in the Net Zero Emissions Year of 2084, huge crowds gather in city centers and town squares the world over. A sense of global anticipation builds. One hundred and eighty heads of state gather yet again in Paris, pop champagne, and toast the moment when the most extraordinary and consequential joint global project in the history of mankind is ultimately secured. Geysers of fireworks (non-carbon based of course!) explode over the Eiffel Tower, feting an event even bigger than the moon landings. Happy Net Zero Emissions New Year!!! Orderly handshakes give way to full body hugs. We have done it! Humanity has steered away from the abyss. Our grandchildren will stop resenting our embezzlement of their environmental future. Hosanna.

The global net emissions curve that charts this existential achievement would look something like Figure 9.5.

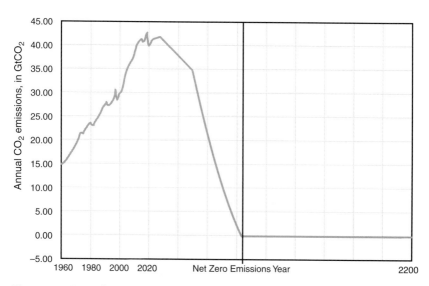

Figure 9.5 Annual $CO_2$ emissions scenario through 2200. *Data source*: Historical $CO_2$ emissions data obtained from the Global Carbon Project database.[41] Emissions between 2020 and 2050 are based on the blended projections in Figure 9.4. Annual $CO_2$ emissions beyond 2050 follow a scenario devised by the author. See Appendix

Please note that this and each of the following curves are my own creations, deriving from weeks of detailed Excel modeling performed in tandem with my trusty Masters-educated research assistant (thanks, Umang!) and grounded in the latest and best scientific literature we can find. Though they seek to account for all of the major factors at play, they are not intended to suggest specious precision on either the $x$ or the $y$ axis. (For more on our methodology, see the Appendix.) These calculations have proven to be the most difficult element of writing this book, and were I able to simply rely upon someone else's math, I would have done so. However, I haven't found such a source and was therefore compelled in the interest of illuminating a plausible future path to devise this scenario. To be clear, I don't want to sell this to you as a robust and reliable prediction. It is not that. I can't predict humanity's future decision making and the pace at which carbon-free technologies will advance any better than the next person. Nonetheless, if I start with the assumptions noted above, this is where those take us. The emissions scenario merely plateaus rather than plunges in the current decade and thereafter falls more slowly than is needed, but it finally settles to net zero late in this century.

After net zero, the surface oceans, which equilibrate their carbon load with the atmosphere on a time scale of several decades, keep diffusing carbon deeper into the surface layer, allowing them to continue to suck down some of our atmospheric carbon after we stop emitting it. Moreover, the overturning of the surface oceans with the deep oceans means that even after the surface oceans are saturated with carbon, some of this carbon-laden water will plunge to the ocean bottom, forcing relatively carbon-poor bottom water to emerge at the surface elsewhere. This upwelling water encounters the carbon-rich atmosphere and begins its equilibration process. In this fashion, the oceans keep sucking down carbon after we stop emitting it, and thus atmospheric concentrations begin to fall off after the net zero year,[42] just as we might hope. Perhaps 80 percent of the excess carbon we have put into the atmosphere will descend into the oceans over a few centuries, with the remainder dwelling in the air for millennia,[43, 44] so by no means does the $CO_2$ quickly disappear, but peak atmospheric concentrations will more or less be reached once we zero out our emissions. Good news.

## What Would it Mean for Climate Change?

That said, an emissions curve like the one above would result in a very warm world – about 2.7°C above the preindustrial baseline and way into what the IPCC identifies as a danger zone of unacceptable impacts and ominous tipping points. Nonetheless, that might make the otherwise chilly New Year's Eve of 2084 a bit more tolerable along the banks of the Seine. As you imagine enjoying your third flute of champagne with the other dignitaries gathered in the moonlight, consider that the temperature curve through 2200 might look something like the curve shown in Figure 9.6.

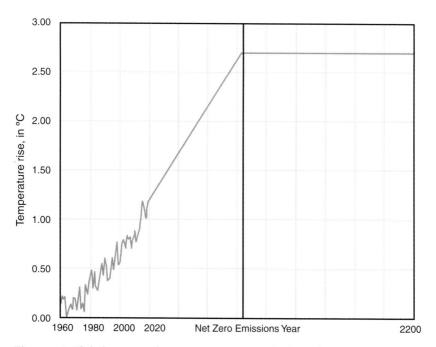

Figure 9.6 Global mean surface temperature scenario through 2200. *Data source*: Historical temperature rise data until 2020 sourced from the National Oceanic and Atmospheric Administration.[48] Temperature increase beyond 2020 is consistent with the $CO_2$ emissions scenario in Figure 9.5

The temperature curve is not going down – at least not anytime soon.[45] Not in the scale of a human lifetime, and not appreciably in the time horizon at which we are looking. None of the champagne poppers in the world's city centers as the Net Zero Emissions Year dawns are likely to see cooler temperatures in their lifetimes, at least if nature is left to take its course. "WHAT'S GOING ON???," you may want to scream! (I do every time, and I know this image is coming ...).

The problem is inertia in the climate system. The oceans are busily sucking down excess atmospheric carbon, but they are also sucking down most of the excess heat that is building up in the climate system as a result of that carbon. Once our emissions stop, this oceanic heat uptake will slow down as well.[46] Unfortunately, it appears that the cooler temperatures we might hope for once the emissions stop and the atmospheric GHG concentrations start falling are likely to be fully offset by the reduced subsequent ocean heat uptake.[47] That means that global average surface temperatures are not expected to fall substantially for a long time after net zero. If we make it hot, it will stay hot. I urge you to pause here and think about that. Look away from this page and stare at the ceiling for a moment.

All the bad stuff associated with climate impacts – the storms and droughts and floods and heat waves – will not stop when emissions stop. They won't even peak and start declining. They will simply plateau as per Figure 9.7. For generations. Maybe for centuries.

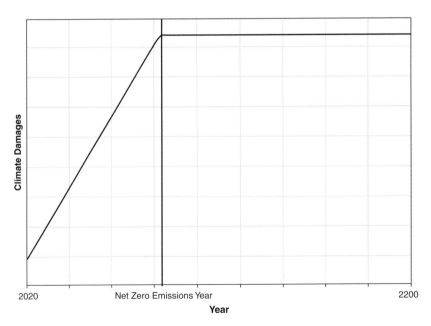

Figure 9.7 Dimensionless representation of climate damages after Net Zero

In fact, not all of them will even do that. Among the most destructive and relentless of climate impacts is sea level rise (see Figure 9.8), and it will keep rising for centuries to millennia.[49] Thermal expansion will continue. Greenland's ice cap will keep melting. Antarctica's glaciers will continue their slide into the warmer waters lapping their ice shelves. The pace of rising should slow after the emissions stop, but the waters will keep coming. This system would take a long time to reach a new equilibrium.

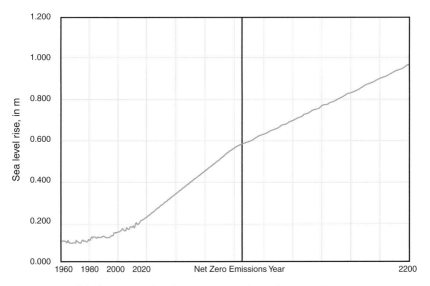

**Figure 9.8** Global mean sea level rise scenario through 2200. *Data source*: Historical sea level rise data sourced from Thomas Frederikse et al., *The Cause of Sea level Rise Since 1900*.[50] The sea level rise beyond 2019 is consistent with the $CO_2$ emissions scenario in Figure 9.5

After presenting all this awful news, I should insert here nearly every caveat I can think of. The modeling of how global average surface temperatures will respond after we reach net zero emissions remains uncertain and contested. Several of the papers I reviewed in preparing this chapter were published in the last two years,[51, 52] so the scholarship is evolving and unsettled. There had previously been a prominent view that there was substantial "committed warming" in the climate system,[53] such that temperatures might actually continue *rising* substantially for several decades after net zero, but more recent literature contradicts that,[54] so I have not represented committed warming beyond the Net Zero Year in Figure 9.6. There is believed to be some committed warming that is masked by our current air pollution,[55] particularly over industrialized Asia, and if we clean up our air as we clean up our energy system, that will become manifest (i.e., the warming will express itself) on our pathway to net zero. However, I have simply assumed that to be baked into the composite picture in Figure 9.6. How many centuries our temperature and climate damage plateaus might endure before reversing themselves is a mystery. In fact, there is a huge amount of uncertainty in all of this, so it is entirely possible that the above proves to be an unreasonably pessimistic story and that, for reasons we haven't yet predicted, things could go unexpectedly well.

Of course, they are perhaps equally likely to go unexpectedly poorly, particularly if we pass over a major tipping point such as runaway permafrost melt. It may well prove that even after net zero, the temperature line still goes up and to the right after all (committed warming) like the sea level rise chart.

At this juncture, you could accuse me of piling on – of simply spinning scary climate stories. You would be right. But perfectly plausible scary stories. They scare the heck out of me! They're why I am writing this book.

Remember our discussion of "climate sensitivity" all the way back in Chapter 1. We still have little inkling of whether a doubling of atmospheric $CO_2$ concentrations (as we will almost certainly do in this century) will warm the globe by a more manageable 1.5°C or a disastrous 4.5°C. The forthcoming AR6 climate assessment may narrow this range, but it nonetheless could turn out that we divert to a plunging emissions pathway this very year just as the IPCC recommends, reach net zero by mid-century with enormous shared sacrifice, and still blow out the 1.5°C/2°C temperature targets. The opposite also remains possible. We are simply too new at this game to have confidence in how it will play out.

But all indications are that the problem isn't over once we stop emissions. That's merely the juncture at which we stop making the problem worse. In World War II terms, reaching net zero isn't the end of the war. It's not even Stalingrad or Midway, where the tide turned. It's more nearly Dunkirk – the juncture at which the UK and the alliance which eventually coalesced around it stopped losing the war. Simply "the end of the beginning" in Churchill's memorable phrase.[56] This isn't meant to belittle the importance of eliminating emissions. While the British Expeditionary Force was encircled on the beach, getting them into boats was the ONLY thing that mattered. But once they were safely ashore in Dover, it was time to contemplate how to reverse prior losses and try to win the war. Returning to climate terms, emissions reduction is very nearly the only thing that currently matters, but the fight for an acceptable environment won't be won once we zero out emissions. We would still live in a warmed world of threatened ecosystems, dire climate impacts, and rising seas.

## The Morning After

So ask yourself – would a world that undertook the degree of global sacrifice and cooperation necessary to bring emissions to net zero thereafter be content to allow temperatures to remain unchanged for generations and live with all the resulting impacts? Would it be content to rely upon the centennial/millennial time scale that natural remediation would entail? Really?

I don't see it. I think there would be demonstrations around the globe, on a scale quite literally never seen before, to demand *further* action. I can imagine riots that may coalesce into widespread armed insurrection as tens if not hundreds of millions of people watch their homes claimed by the sea and their crops wither. The members of the new Greatest Generation that whipped greenhouse gas emissions would not then meekly return to their desiccated farms and watch their children starve. That just doesn't seem plausible. The world would demand more.

Reducing greenhouse gas concentrations to a magnitude that would start bringing down temperatures on a human timescale would require huge amounts of negative emissions – finding ways to recapture and securely bury enormous quantities of the excess $CO_2$ we had put into the air.

And arresting a further rise in sea levels and perhaps even temperatures would require finding some way to decouple surface temperatures from the ongoing high $CO_2$ concentrations. Even massive carbon removal could take lifetimes. If climate impacts become intolerable, we may need some way to stabilize or reduce temperatures to buy time.

The scenarios in the SR15 are simply not realistic predictions of the near future. The IPCC does not suggest that they are. In fact, they are quite candid that we are "absolutely not" yet on that track. The world is not yet ready to make the sacrifices required to remain within the 1.5 or 2°C targets. Reaching net zero emissions by ~2050 should be viewed as a moral imperative – but unlikely. Put a different way, if Las Vegas or the UK betting markets offered an over/under bet on net zero emissions by 2050 and you were compelled to bet your mortgage rather than a mere 100 bucks or bob, would you bet the under or the over? Stomach curdling though the realization may be, the answer is obvious.

Only time will tell whether the alternative emissions wind-down scenario I have devised herein will more closely resemble reality, but it seems to me a more likely prediction than the Paris goals. And whenever the Net Zero Emissions Year proves to occur, the subsequent century is likely to see worse climate impacts than the prior one. If that proves true, we will need climate intervention.

Our descendants will demand it.

# Section III
# CARBON DIOXIDE REMOVAL

# 10 NATURAL CLIMATE SOLUTIONS

We *must* mitigate our GHG emissions. There is no substitute for that. Not merely *reduce* our emissions, but *eliminate* them – or else the bathtub keeps filling. However, mitigation will be of only limited benefit to the mitigators. Irrespective of which future era you choose to parachute into mentally, it will still be the case that *that* generation's mitigation efforts won't solve *their* problem. It will merely stop compounding the problem that will be bequeathed to subsequent generations. Similarly, adaptation won't dial the clock backward and return the world to its earlier, presumably more attractive climate. It won't save the dying ecosystems or spare the marine food web.

If the people of 2050 or 2200 want to improve the climate and the world in *their lifetimes*, they will need additional tools beyond mitigation and adaptation. They will need ways to intervene in the near-term climate and to dial back the clock – to lower the level of water in the bathtub without having to wait a couple of millennia for nature to do the job. They will need climate intervention.

A framing for climate intervention – generally employed by those who seek to discredit it – is that it is proposed as a "plan B" by which to solve the climate problem. That's a strawman. No one actually working in this field considers climate interventions to be a substitute for emissions reductions. As is widely asserted, that would be a false solution. There is no escaping the imperative of net zero. Climate interventions are not a "plan B" by which to solve "problem A", which is climate change. They are "plan A" by which to solve "problem B", which is the persistence of widespread and likely unacceptable climate damages *after* we reach net zero. They are the tools for the next phase of our climate struggle.

It is time then to start rummaging through the geoengineering toolbox to see what's there. As earlier noted, that box has two main compartments: greenhouse gas removal and solar radiation management, with several distinct tool slots in each. We'll start first in the greenhouse gas removal compartment, and progress in later chapters to the solar radiation management compartment. On the greenhouse gas removal side, I devote this chapter to natural solutions, followed by separate chapters on each of industrial carbon capture and direct air capture.

## Natural Carbon Dioxide Removal (CDR)

Within the greenhouse gas removal compartment, we will immediately further narrow our focus to only carbon dioxide rather than greenhouse gases more generally. Dilute though it is in the atmosphere, at a mere 410 parts per million, carbon dioxide concentrations are vastly higher than those of either methane or nitrous oxide, which are two and three orders of magnitude smaller respectively. The relative rarity of methane and nitrous oxide renders them much harder to remove from the climate system post-emission, and I know of no plausibly feasible proposals by which to do so. Until and unless something very new comes along, reducing concentrations of methane and nitrous oxide will need to focus entirely on turning off their spigots rather than devising new drains. In the case of methane, at least, that is also more practical due to its relatively short dozen-year residence in the atmosphere.[1] If we eliminate new anthropogenic emissions, concentrations will start to tail off promptly, since the methane we put into the system a dozen years ago is breaking down (oxidizing more precisely), and no new anthropogenic methane is being emitted to replace it (though natural outgassing from the planet will still continue). The concentration wind-down would be much longer in the case of nitrous oxide, but there too, we will likely be compelled simply to wait. If our goal is anthropogenic removals (artificially widening the drain), then the place to focus is carbon dioxide.

I hope my "toolbox" analogy proves helpful, but like most analogies, it breaks down if pushed too far. Setting aside trees (which have other problems), there currently are hardly any handy and proven tools in the toolbox. There is more nearly a list of research-phase theories and demonstration-phase projects exploring prospective future tools. It's an R&D agenda that involves limited "R" and even less "D." But they are the ideas that seem most promising based on our existing incomplete knowledge of the situation.

Because we are merely in the ideation phase of this, all kinds of crazy ideas get tossed out as to how we might intervene in the future climate system. Some of them deserve very serious attention and urgent, well-funded research. Others are downright dumb. Yet others are perilously specious – attractive when first encountered, though impractical or inadequate upon closer examination. The simple reality is that absent an unanticipated technological miracle (always possible, but not the prudent way to plan), all of the options by which to remove carbon dioxide from the atmosphere are inadequate. They tend to be so for one of three reasons: (1) they would be expensive and therefore decrease living standards; (2) they would be unprecedented and risky; (3) or they would prove insufficiently scalable to tackle the problem we confront. When faced then with a menu of uniformly unappetizing options, people are naturally prone to grasp at specious ones – offerings that sound too good to be true, because they are. We therefore need in this chapter to clear away some of the mirages that appear to reside in the CDR side of the toolbox.

One of those is the view that the planet would heal itself if we just stopped messing with it so much. This is consistent with the Gaia hypothesis advanced most forcefully by James Lovelock, who theorized that the Earth and the life upon it coevolved in ways that influenced each other.[2] Named after the Earth goddess of Greek myth, this imagined the planet as a living thing, dancing in the embrace of all the biota which it hosts. Together, the inorganic and organic spheres of the Earth created a self-regulating homeostasis that manufactured a stable Goldilocks environment suitable for life. To be clear, this is perceived today mostly as poetry rather than science, but there remains a temptation to dream that if we simply take our thumb off the scale, the Earth would restore its natural balance and the climate problem would solve itself.

The appeal of this view is obvious, in that it would require little remedial activity from us. And in the case of methane, which again is the source of roughly 16 percent of our GHG problem,[3] it would work reasonably well. Nitrous oxide forms another 6 percent of our problem on a global warming potential basis,[4] but its atmospheric lifetime is more than a century[5] – let's call it one-and-a-half human lifetimes. Gaia would try our patience here. But the remaining almost ~80 percent of our GHG problem is $CO_2$, with an atmospheric lifetime measured in decades for the roughly half of it that will get sucked into the oceans and soils, but centuries to millennia for the remainder.[6, 7] Nonetheless, if we were to turn off the GHG spigot today – immediately and entirely – maybe this would be OK. The seas would keep rising, but the climate isn't yet intolerably out of whack. However, if we continue to emit on anything like the pathways reviewed in the prior chapter, then we may only cease emissions once we can't stand the consequences, in which case waiting for such long natural processes to play out over the span of many generations would be an unacceptable option. Gaia would need a helping hand.

All CDR concepts entail three fundamental components – capture, processing, and storage – which in concept are simple enough. Initially, the gas needs to be harvested, either directly from the atmosphere, or from a stream of GHGs that are about to enter the atmosphere from a point source such as a smokestack or tailpipe. After we have grabbed the gas, we need to process it, transform it into the form we desire, and transport it to wherever we intend to put it. Finally, we need to sequester it somewhere, so it doesn't leak back into the climate system and recreate the problem we are trying to solve.

## Reforestation/Afforestation

The prom queen of CDR concepts is trees. Everyone loves trees (including Gaia), and they would seem as natural a CDR mechanism as could be imagined. Like all plants, trees suck in $CO_2$, transform it into organic compounds with which they build their structure, and expire oxygen. To an unusual degree among plants, however, trees store a lot of that carbon, for a long time. A farm field or pasture has a lot less stored carbon biomass than a forest, and when man gets involved, a lot of forests become fields or pastures. If we reforest areas that once were forest, we both edge closer to the natural state and hoover up a lot more carbon in the process. If instead we plant a forest where none previously existed ("afforestation"), we arguably destroy a bit of nature – after all, grasslands and deserts are natural habitats too – but we once again enhance the carbon storage capacity of that land. Therefore, afforestation and reforestation rank high in any geoengineering popularity contest.

However, there is less here than meets the eye. Trees are indeed a pretty capable $CO_2$ capture mechanism, with a growing tree estimated to absorb 48 pounds of $CO_2$ a year.[8] If each tree were allocated a 10 foot by 10 foot area, an acre of land would accommodate about 440 trees. The annual per capita $CO_2$ emission of an average American is nearly 16 tonnes,[9] meaning it would require nearly 1.75 acres per American to offset our emissions. With a population of nearly 330 million, offsetting the carbon emissions of the whole country would consume 881,000 square miles of land – almost a quarter of the land area of the entire country and more than Alaska and California combined. However, large portions of those states and many others don't support dense forests – picture the Mojave Desert or the Tundra on the North Slope – so devoting the entirety of them to carbon offset forests can't be done. Moreover, much of portions of these states that *can* support forests already have forests on them. There is no purpose in cutting down the mighty coastal redwoods or dense spruce forests of the Kenai Peninsula to plant forests.

Neither can we harvest these forests after we plant them – that would be self-defeating. Logging not only removes the carbon stored in the trees, but disturbs the soils beneath them which are themselves an essential store of carbon. In fact, the soil in a healthy mature forest can store 100–200 percent of the carbon stored in the biomass above ground,[10] but after a clear cut, the soil becomes a carbon *source* for a decade or two until the forest re-establishes itself.[11] As for the lumber that came off that land, some of it may be combusted in a fireplace or a biomass power plant, in which case it is immediately returned to the atmosphere. Other portions may be turned into paper or pulp, which will likely soon be destined for an incinerator or landfill, where via combustion or decomposition that carbon too would find its way back to the atmosphere. Yet other portions may become furniture or construction materials, but most of it too will end up in the waste stream after a decade or a century. Therefore, while utilizing the lumber may delay the return to the atmosphere of the carbon it contains, most of it will find its way back there before too long and therefore isn't permanently sequestered in a way that would inform the climate. The forests we plant to address the climate problem must be left alone permanently as carbon banks.

We need to find land that can support forests but where there are no forests today. So why, one wonders, would forest-able tracts be un-forested? Ummm ... most likely because some industrious human cleared the forest decades or centuries ago to do something with that land more economically productive than growing trees. These are the places where agriculture flourishes and where most humans live – not just farms and pastures but houses and offices, roads and shopping centers, villages and cities. From a carbon standpoint, all of those land uses are suboptimal. They are mostly sources rather than sinks for carbon and we should encourage humans to stop using them in those ways and plant trees instead. Of course, in the main, that is not going to happen. In order to sustain all the people we have crammed on this planet, we need our farms to be farms and our housing lots to be housing lots. In most cases, it is human preferences expressed via economics that will govern land use choices, and more productive uses will tend to win.

However, surely there are *some* currently denuded plots of land that can support trees and which we can somehow convince humanity to replant. There must be some marginally productive agricultural lands, though converting these to forests crowds out a little food pro-duction. Perhaps we can also identify some "degraded" lands, which are commonly referred to in studies of these topics even though I don't personally recall ever seeing much of it. Surely we can accommodate additional trees in our yards and towns and cities – they all count. Undoubtedly then, putting aside the question of who will fund this, we could substantially increase the population of trees in the world if we had a will to do so. But returning to the US context, offsetting our emissions would require roughly one quarter of all the land in the country including Alaska. And the vast majority of that land is off limits for this purpose, either because it can't support trees, or because it can and already does do so, or because it is devoted to substantially more productive uses with which carbon banks can't compete. It is very difficult to imagine that we could devote a quarter of America to new permanent forests under any circumstances.

But even if we could, the carbon-sucking ability of these newly planted forests would not be evergreen, so to speak. While it is matur-ing, the forest is a sink for carbon, inhaling it from the air and fixing it in the trunk, roots, and branches. Once the forest is mature, so long as it is left undisturbed, it is thereafter a bank for carbon, locking it safely away indefinitely. However, it is a bank in which we may deposit only once.

Thereafter the bank is full (saturated), and it can accept no more deposits. Individual trees may keep respiring, and as one tree dies and decomposes, another young sapling may rise in its place, inhaling some of the carbon leaching out of the adjacent stump. But to see the forest for the trees (see what I did there?), once the woodland has reached maturity, it has done all the carbon removal it will do for us. Our task thereafter is to keep the bank locked and safe.

That's easier said than done, as the forest fires in the American West in recent years have shown. Majestic and enduring though forests may seem to a human observer, it is in fact their natural tendency to burn periodically. The more we try to prevent such fires, the more destructive the eventual conflagrations become. We are increasingly learning to better manage that dynamic via intentional controlled burns outside the traditional fire season, which clear some of the accumulated underbrush without escaping the intended restraints. However, whether we manage the fires or let them burn naturally, the fate of most forests is flame, carbon release, and subsequent regrowth.

Of course, not all burned forests rise from the ashes. Many are cleared intentionally, via flame, saw, or bulldozer. This is the primary reason for the loss of tropical forests in such places as Brazil and Indonesia. The great fires seen annually in these regions are not unintended infernos like those in the Sierras – they are set by ranchers and farmers bent on clearing the land for subsequent agricultural use. Principally by virtue of such intentional forest clearance, we are still going backwards in terms of total tree cover rather than forward.[12] While the hope implicit in the concept of trees as a carbon solution is that this trend may level off and reverse itself, there is no guarantee it remains that way. Eager would-be ranchers in the future may look at that lush thicket we dutifully planted and have the same clever value-enhancing idea their ancestors did. Due to the prospects of fire, future land use changes, or newly dominant pests such as the pine and spruce beetles currently destroying huge swathes of Colorado's woodlands,[13] newly planted forests should not be conceived as permanent carbon stores, but rather as fragile and temporary reservoirs.

The time frame on which a newly planted forest matures and reaches its carbon saturation point is a bit complex. Of course it depends on the types of trees planted and the conditions in which they grow, but broadly, there are two phases – the first, when saplings become fully grown trees, and the second, when slower growing larger tree species succeed the faster growing first growth species. Nonetheless, forests can reach carbon saturation after 10–100 years,[14] with a half century being reasonably in the range.

If then America could somehow perform the miracle of setting aside a quarter of its land – all of it currently unforested but hospitable – for newly planted permanent forests, and if we could wave a magic wand over those forests that would ensure they are never burned, cleared, or logged, they would still only offset our emissions for 50 years. After that point, the forests are mature, the bank stops accepting new deposits, and we need to find a new solution for our carbon emission problem. Having already committed all of Alaska and California to our first tranche, let's now set aside all the land from Minnesota and Iowa out to Washington and Oregon, the whole upper left hand quadrant of the lower 48. Then 50 years later . . .

The point, of course, is that forests can't be the answer to our climate problem. They could and almost certainly will be some small fraction of the answer, but nothing close to the whole answer. A comprehensive recent study estimated that by 2050, the carbon sink capacity of afforestation and reforestation might be most sensibly estimated at under 4 Gt of $CO_2$ per year,[15] which is roughly 10 percent of the 2019 global $CO_2$ emissions[16] and closer to 7 percent of all greenhouse gas emissions expressed in $CO_2$ equivalents.[17] Seven percent would be a sizable chunk, but not "the solution," and this study saw that annual sequestration capacity dropping to zero by the end of the century, as the new forests became saturated.

The capacity of afforestation/reforestation is further limited by the fact this is only a suitable climate intervention in the tropical and subtropical regions of the world.[18] In high latitude boreal forest regions (principally Siberia, Canada, Alaska, and Scandinavia), newly planted trees would be much darker in color than the seasonally snow-covered grass and scrub lands they would occlude, reducing the albedo of these areas and thereby inducing local warming rather than cooling – exactly the opposite of what we intend.

Employing trees to vacuum up all the carbon we are emitting would consume far too much land – land that a still-burgeoning human population will of course need for other things, such as growing food or siting houses. In fact, forests are among the *least* economically productive uses for land, particularly if they are not being harvested for lumber and are instead left unmolested as carbon banks. Alternative purposes are nearly always more productive economically, which is why nations in the developing world are still deforesting rather than reforesting their land. And who can blame them, given that the developed world long ago did the same? On the one hand, we should all hope that Brazil puts an end to ongoing land clearance of the majestic Amazon rain forests, often referred to as the "lungs of the world." On the other hand, one can imagine Brazilians retorting "Why don't you replant some forests in Ohio and let *those* be the lungs of the world?"

Forests *do* confer enormous carbon benefit, even if planting them in non-forest habitats may reduce biodiversity,[19] so we need to take account of them when devising climate solutions. Since they provide global benefit at local cost (or at least at local suboptimal land use), a well-ordered world would provide incentives to maintain and restore them – perhaps this would provide a use for some of the carbon taxes we will need to impose to disincentivize other behaviors. Amazonian nations might prove happy to be the lungs of the world after all were the world willing to pay them for it. That of course seems a long way off.

In the CDR compartment of our toolbox, trees are a serviceable and necessary though insufficient implement. Nonetheless, in the aggregate, we are still moving in the opposite direction, clearing forests rather than restoring them.

## Bioenergy with Carbon Capture and Sequestration (BECCS)

Given the limitations that inhibit forests as a stand-alone climate intervention, trees are often considered as one facet of a broader climate solution referred to as bioenergy with carbon capture and sequestration. BECCS utilizes the same carbon capture mechanism – trees or other biomass crops – linked to a much more permanent and secure storage mechanism. The biomass would be harvested and burned in an electric plant, creating (somewhat) renewable bioenergy. However, rather than allowing the $CO_2$ to escape up the smokestack and into the atmosphere, the flue gas would be scrubbed of it. The remaining, now more climate-friendly effluent (depending upon the efficiency of the scrubbing process, it may still contain 5–15 percent of its original $CO_2$)[20] would be vented to the atmosphere, while the captured $CO_2$ would be purified, compressed, and transported (likely via pipeline) to a disposal site, where it would be pumped down into the ground. If the site is properly chosen, the $CO_2$ would remain sequestered essentially permanently.

Suitable geological formations for BECCS include played out and disused oil and gas fields (where rather ironically the excess carbon came from in the first place) and saline aquifers, which being salty are unlikely to be tapped for human purposes such as irrigation or drinking water. While suitable storage sites may not always be directly adjacent to a given $CO_2$ source, there is lots of storage capacity.[21] This sort of "reverse oil drilling" is already being extensively used in the Permian Basin of West Texas and elsewhere in the process known as "enhanced oil recovery." The natural pressure built up in underground reservoirs drives only perhaps 10 percent of the oil in a formation to the surface. Thereafter, to get more to come up, one has to pump something down to drive it along. Since a great deal of water generally rises along with the oil, that is usually the first substance pumped back down into the formation, but as the recovery sequence progresses, other working fluids become necessary, and the most common of those is $CO_2$. One might hope that the $CO_2$ used for such enhanced oil recovery was harvested from the air or from smokestacks, but alas, mostly not. It is instead generally mined from underground caverns in Colorado and elsewhere. The US has over 4,500 miles of pipelines[22] devoted exclusively to transporting mined $CO_2$ to oil and gas fields for enhanced oil recovery. From a climate change standpoint, it seems mad that we are pulling new $CO_2$ from the ground for this purpose rather than removing it from the stream of carbon we are spewing into the air for other purposes, but in a world with minimal carbon pricing, this is the cheapest solution.

Not only would BECCS create a renewable source of energy that would remove carbon from the atmosphere, but it would greatly reduce the land allocation pressure that rendered forestation by itself a highly constrained solution. Unfortunately, it likely means that the economically sensible way to get started with a BECCS installation is not to send children into a field to plant trees, but to send lumberjacks with chain saws into a forest to cut it down. We deforest it and then reforest it – hardly the green image we likely had in mind, but consistent with the theme that the items on the climate intervention menu generally prove less appetizing the more we examine them. Nonetheless, in this scheme, a plot of forested land can accept a deposit of carbon not merely once, but repeatedly as the forest is harvested, its captured carbon is pumped underground, and a new batch of trees is planted to inhale another load of carbon. This rescues BECCS from the margins of the climate intervention discussion, but only partly.

Even a BECCS plan that harvested the forest as soon as it was mature and immediately recycled the land with another planting would require an enormous amount of land. The BECCS schemes that were incorporated into many of the scenarios considered in the IPCC SR15 report in 2018 were subsequently calculated to require arable land between one and three times the size of India, the upper bound of which would make it equal in area to the entire US including Alaska. And this BECCS program was by no means the entire portfolio of solutions necessary to limit climate change to no more than 1.5°C but rather was paired with aggressive mitigation.

Like afforestation/reforestation, BECCS on so massive a scale would begin to conflict with other laudable goals, such as ecosystem conservation, biodiversity, and food production. Most BECCS plans assume a "food first" orientation, whereby food production is recognized to be the highest priority and only land not needed for food would be diverted to bioenergy production. Feed and fiber might also be recognized as higher priority land uses. However, if we exclude from consideration for bioenergy production any land needed for food, feed, fiber, habitation, transportation, and conservation, as well as all boreal regions, we have shunted bioenergy production to very marginal lands which are likely not well suited to this purpose. This often raises the question of whether we should restrict bioenergy production to rain-fed land, or whether we should treat this low-value crop like any other agricultural good, which is to say irrigate and fertilize fields that would produce low yields without such interventions. But fertilizers produce greenhouse gas emissions in the form of nitrous oxide,[23] and irrigation diverts increasingly scarce water from other uses. BECCS programs using biomass from agricultural wastes can be seen as very green, but massive production of biomass for carbon capture purposes is much less so. Nor is biomass an ideal fuel source with which to generate electricity. Its energy content is at the lower end of the fuel sources commonly used for power generation by combustion (like methane or coal),[24] and while wood is a renewable resource, it is by no means a clean combustion fuel, creating air pollution on par with or possibly higher than the coal we are so desperately trying to eradicate from our energy mix.[25]

For all these reasons, BECCS confronts capacity limits less severe than but nonetheless somewhat similar to those noted above for afforestation/reforestation, with global capacity under reasonable constraints also capped at roughly 5 Gt annually[26] – once again in the range of 10 percent of all greenhouse gas emissions. Unlike the above propositions that conceive the forest as a carbon bank, BECCS doesn't saturate – we could keep making deposits in this bank indefinitely. Nonetheless, a BECCS proposal large enough to appreciably move the global thermostat would consume enormous amounts of land. A recent MIT study estimated that a BECCS program large enough to meet the Paris Agreement 1.5°C goal would consume 33 percent–43 percent of all the cropland that was in use in 2015.[27] This in turn would drive up food prices 5–15 percent, and still only solve a small fraction of the climate problem. Most fatally, however, the cost of BECCS is estimated to be $100–200 per tonne of $CO_2$ captured.[28] Given that carbon price proposals currently being discussed (mostly by economists rather than actual policy makers) are in the range of $40–$100 per tonne, ~$150 per tonne for BECCS is way underwater economically. As we will see, there are lots of ways to reduce emissions that are much cheaper than BECCS. Like afforestation/reforestation, it can be a very important wedge of the solution someday, but is nothing like a complete solution.

## Soil Carbon Sequestration and Regenerative Agriculture

Shifting our focus from plants to the dirt in which they thrive, soil comprises an enormous carbon reservoir, containing roughly twice as much carbon as the entire atmosphere.[29] However, most everything that humans do to the soil disturbs it and reduces its stored carbon content. Clearing forests for farming or any other purpose, tilling soil periodically to prepare it for planting, harvesting a crop, moving dirt to level a site for construction, intensively grazing cattle or sheep on pastureland – all of that causes the soil to yield some of its stored carbon back to the atmosphere. In theory then, we could coax the soil to reabsorb enormous amounts of carbon if we simply stopped messing with it, which of course we cannot do. Farmers need to farm and builders need to build. The next best thing is to at least be cognizant of those land use practices which are more carbon friendly and seek to shift our land use practice in that direction. The level of carbon in the soil is a balance between carbon inputs (leaves and plant litter, residues, roots, manure) and losses (mostly through respiration, which is increased by soil disturbance), so anything that increases inputs or decreases losses can promote soil carbon sequestration.[30] Restoring previously degraded lands and controlling/halting desertification would enable land over time to re-establish its vegetative cover and build up soil carbon. Mixing trees in with cropland ("agroforestry") also increases carbon sequestration, as does planting legumes on pastureland and engaging in less intensive grazing.

Yet another soil carbon enhancement is regenerative agriculture, which "describes farming and grazing practices that, among other benefits, reverse climate change by rebuilding soil organic matter and restoring degraded soil biodiversity – resulting in both carbon drawdown and an improved water cycle."[31] The idea behind regenerative agriculture is that because agricultural practices in the last 12,000 years have resulted in a cumulative loss of about 133 Gt of soil organic carbon from the top 2 m of soil cover,[32] we should be able to sequester some carbon back into it as well. The soil carbon loss and other GHG emissions from agriculture are results of overgrazing, excessive use of pesticides and fertilizers, monoculture cropping patterns, constant tilling of soil leading into erosion and $CO_2$ release, among other practices. So, the goal with regenerative agriculture is to improve the water retention and percolation in soil, improve topsoil generation to better capture carbon, and leverage biodiversity to maximize organic nutrition for plants and crops. All this would not only reabsorb some carbon from the atmosphere, but fix it in the soils and make them more resilient in the face of prospective future climate change.

Common practices of regenerative agriculture include:

- No or minimum tillage: tillage refers to the overwhelmingly common global practice of periodically overturning soil to prepare it for agriculture. While this churning breaks up encrusted soil and inhibits weeds and insects, it also disaggregates soil, over-oxygenating it while releasing $CO_2$. It also creates more compact soil, resulting in increased surface erosion and lower water retention and percolation. In contrast, no-till practices prevent soil erosion, increase retention of soil nutrients and organic matter, reduce the energy usage associated with heavy machinery for plowing, and improve water retention.

- Grazing management: conventional grazing practices often result in overgrazing of pastoral land, disrupting the root structure of the grasses and other forage and thereby degrading the pasture. However, if the animals are carefully rotated among pastures such that the plants are allowed enough time to recover between successive grazing, the root structure thus formed allows for more abundant forage, better sequestration of $CO_2$, and improved interaction between the microbes and the root of the plant.

- Enhanced crop rotation: planting different kinds of crops in a sequence across seasons can improve the health of the soil and optimize the nutrient cycle if the selected crops use different nutrients. Properly done, this can also result in higher sequestration of carbon.

- Use of cover crops: these are often planted seasonally between main cash crops with a primary purpose of covering the soil to reduce erosion, weeds, and diseases and to increase fertility and biodiversity. Cover crops help in better retention of residue and sequestration of carbon since "at least half of the cropland carbon is fixed aboveground in plant biomass."[33]

- Other methods of regenerative agriculture include enhanced uses of manure as an organic fertilizer and compost as source of nutrients and organic pesticide. Aquaculture involves sustainable breeding, rearing, and harvesting of aquatic plants and animals under controlled conditions. Agroforestry proposes planting crops between rows of trees, which not only increases the nutrient and carbon cycling along with enhanced protection of soil from water and wind erosion, but also promotes biodiversity and makes the land more drought resistant. Add livestock to that mix and you get "silvopasture" – a well-managed integration of trees, forage, and domesticated animals that expands the pasture acreage while optimizing farmland utilization and enhancing wildlife abundance and biodiversity.

Most of the above was for decades simply described as organic farming. The primary objectives had nothing to do with climate and instead aimed at minimizing or eliminating the use of chemicals and pesticides to remove toxic residues from our food, reducing air and water pollution, enhancing soil health, and restoring biodiversity. The extent to which many of these same practices could also provide a co-benefit by turning agricultural soils into a sink rather than a source of additional anthropogenic emissions has only gradually and recently come to be widely recognized.

However, here too, we have come to a juncture in which an externality in the global carbon economy creates a dilemma. The myriad ways in which the regenerative agricultural ideas noted above might translate into changed practices in a given location in the world might from an economic perspective sort themselves into three buckets. The first (and best) is the win/win/win bucket, wherein newly adopted regenerative agriculture practices will benefit the farmers/ranchers by increasing their profits; benefit the consumers by giving them improved products; and benefit the climate by sequestering more carbon. That would of course be great, and many evangelists for this movement present matters in such terms. Any such practices that achieve this triple win represent a forward step for the world and will presumably be rushed into service. We don't need to put our thumb on that scale – the economy will make it happen via the invisible hand of the market.

However, most of the green revolution by which the world food supply has kept pace with the still-burgeoning population has been achieved not through pioneering organic/regenerative agriculture but by the expansion of industrial farming. Nor are these regenerative ideas new. The Rodale Institute in Pennsylvania was founded shortly after WWII and has been preaching the organic farming gospel ever since. Farmers aren't stupid – they engage in modern mechanized farming practices because they increase yields and profits, securing food avail-ability for humans around the globe. This suggests that much if not most of the regenerative practices proposed above fall into other categories, where there are tradeoffs and not wins all round.

A second bucket then is one in which regenerative practices in fact increase costs or decrease yields for farmers, though they may at the same time lead to healthier and less toxic food. In that case, regenerative agriculture would co-exist as a niche in a market in which industrial farming would also continue to flourish. Consumers concerned with the toxicity of the food they eat can choose higher cost organic brands, while those most concerned with prices can choose the opposite. This is mostly where we stand today.

The real dilemma lies in a third bucket, wherein regenerative practices might raise costs for agriculturalists without improving the quality of the output, but would result in higher carbon sequestration in the soil. There is as yet little or no market appetite to pay higher costs for foods grown via practices that sequester more carbon in the soil without producing other benefits. This would be a new market niche, where the benefit for buying the regenerative produce is not that it is healthier for the consumer, but that it is healthier for the planet. That market niche doesn't yet exist in any substantial way, and it is not clear that it ever will in the absence of carbon taxes. So long as regenerative agriculture is twinned with direct consumer benefits, it can expand, but if the benefit is purely carbon-related, some value will have to be placed on that carbon in the marketplace. In this case, it would not be a tax for emitting carbon, but a credit for absorbing it back into the land. Such a practice seems a long way off.

A characteristic that both regenerative agriculture and soil carbon sequestration share with the forest-related interventions discussed above is that once again, it could form a meaningful wedge in the portfolio of climate solutions, but not a huge one. Widespread global adoption of all the soil management changes discussed here is estimated once again to countervail roughly 10 percent of current global $CO_2$ emissions, another 4 Gt slice[34] of our annual 40 Gt pie. And this too is a saturable sink – once we restore the carbon content of the soil and reduce our subsequent disturbances, it will exist more or less in equilibrium, neither shedding nor absorbing more carbon. Therefore, if we maximize soil carbon sequestration over the coming few decades, it would no longer be available as a further sink later in the century.

## Biochar and Blue Carbon

Another biomass-based proposal is "biochar," whereby wood or other plant material is turned to charcoal via pyrolysis, an ancient process of heating in the absence of oxygen. This prevents the biomass from combusting and produces a residue of nearly pure carbon, which may then be ground up and infused into the soil. Pyrolysis releases up to half the feedstock carbon as $CO_2$, but the remaining residue is a stable bank that can sequester carbon indefinitely.[35] Reinforcing soil with biochar enhances soil fertility and aids in water retention, thereby increasing agricultural productivity. Not enough, however, to make biochar an economically viable soil additive for most farmers.[36] Large scale biochar additions to agricultural soils in real-world conditions have yet to receive field trials, so its feasibility, side-effects, and costs remain poorly understood.[37] Nonetheless, the best guess is that this would be a considerably smaller wedge in our climate solution portfolio than the preceding items, more in the range of 1 Gt annually[38] or 2.5 percent of current emissions. This is also another instance in which the carbon-virtuous action is not the profit-maximizing action. Without carbon subsidies perhaps funded by carbon taxes, widespread carbon sequestration via biochar is unlikely.

Another nature-based CDR tool is referred to as "blue carbon," which denotes the fact that mangroves and coastal marshlands are particularly intensive carbon stores. When these dense carbon reservoirs are eradicated to build seaside homes, buildings, ports, and infrastructure, the carbon is released to the environment. The blue carbon aspiration is to reverse this process, restore natural coastal habitats, and allow them to reabsorb that carbon – essentially, reforestation by the sea. This similarly points to a need to be mindful of the carbon impact of building a new port where a mangrove once thrived, but is yet another instance when we are rooting for David to beat Goliath. That story is so famous precisely because it is so unlikely – in most such encounters, the "David" usually gets squashed like a bug. Similarly, the economic forces strongly favor turning mangroves into ports rather than the reverse. I don't hold out a lot of hope for widespread "remangrovization" on what is often the most valuable land for many miles.

In fact, this theme runs throughout the other land-based interventions that are referred to in the IPCC AR5 report. In myriad ways, modern society puts land to uses that increase its economic productivity but decrease its carbon storage capacity. Despite our intense focus on the atmosphere, it stores only half the carbon sequestered in soil, and when we disturb the soil by tilling it, plowing it, paving it, and most everything else we do to increase its value, we tend to reduce its carbon storage capacity and eject some of that carbon to the air. We need to take much more heed of these impacts and manage them in the right direction wherever possible, but doing so in ways large enough to materially impact our climate problem usually returns to the theme of local cost for global benefit. Until the world evolves new ways to pay for that, the incentives for such undertakings will be scant.

## Enhanced Weathering

As Holly Jean Buck aptly phrased it, "the eventual fate of carbon is stone" via a process called chemical weathering.[39]

Atmospheric $CO_2$ dissolves into rainwater, forming weak carbonic acid that in turn slightly dissolves some of the rocks (specifically silicates) on which it may happen to fall. The resulting inorganic carbonates eventually wash into the ocean "where shell-building creatures and plankton turn the calcium ions into calcium carbonate."[40] These calcifying critters eventually die, but their shells and skeletons endure, falling to the seabed to be compressed over eons into limestone. There is something more that these inorganic carbonates and bicarbonates do – they increase the alkalinity of the ocean waters by reacting with the dissolved inorganic carbon. On one hand, this reduces the concentration of $CO_2$ at the ocean-air boundary layer, increasing the $CO_2$ uptake capacity of the ocean. On the other hand, when the ocean is supersaturated with mineral carbonates and bicarbonates, they precipitate in the form of secondary minerals.[41] Such precipitates then travel towards the bottom of the ocean, just like the shells. This is the drain in our proverbial bathtub – the way nature removes $CO_2$ back out of the climate system and sequesters it deep in the Earth's crust. It takes for-flipping-ever!

The chemical weathering drain is leaching $CO_2$ out of the climate system at a rate of roughly one gigaton per year,[42] whereas we are gushing it in at 40 times that rate. Hence the mismatch between sources and sinks and the conclusion that on a human-relevant timeframe, the drain is essentially clogged – which gives rise to the question of whether we could somehow widen the drainpipe and let the natural process flow faster. The most commonly considered "enhanced weathering" technique would entail grinding up silicate rocks and spreading the resulting dust over vast portions of the Earth to increase the surface area of the exposed stone and thereby speed the process. The chemistry of this seems straightforward and it's clear that it would work. What is unclear is whether such a process would make economical or practical sense as a climate solution. One estimate concluded that in order to produce a solution approximately the size of our forestation or BECCS wedge, we would need a mining and transport operation roughly the size of the current coal industry.[43] Extracting, transporting, pulverizing, and scattering all that stone would require a tremendous amount of energy, so until that energy can be produced in a carbon-free fashion, it is unclear how much of a net carbon sink enhanced weathering would comprise. Another source suggested that in order to properly distribute all this stone powder in the tropics where it would operate most favorably, it may need to be spread via aircraft.[44] The idea that all the equivalent of all the coal now moved by trains, ships, and barges might for this purpose need to be loaded onto aircraft and lofted skyward seems clearly impractical.

Another variant of such ocean alkalinity enhancement includes direct addition of calcium hydroxide (commonly known as slaked lime) into the seawaters.[45] The lime can be sourced from the calcination of limestone, and the geochemical process involves the aforementioned boost in the alkalinity of the ocean, which would consequently increase its $CO_2$ uptake capacity. However, the energy requirement associated with the raw material preparation and ocean disposal has been estimated to lie between 6 and 10 GJ per net tonne of $CO_2$ sequestered[46] – once again, a huge new requirement. Cost estimates per tonne of $CO_2$ sequestered range from $72 to $159.[47] However, at roughly $100 per tonne, they would be broadly cost competitive with other technologies we will consider. The hesitation is that the environmental impacts of dumping so much mineral into the seas are poorly understood but potentially disastrous, particularly near the injection (i.e., dumping) sites. Since these minerals will be sourced and processed on land, the most economical injection sites would be in coastal areas, where their potential environmental impacts would be magnified.

Enhanced weathering and other ocean alkalinization processes would constitute a secure sink, but would require enormous amounts of energy and funds to source, transport, and distribute all the crushed stone, with environmental impacts not yet well understood.

## Ocean Iron Fertilization

Enhanced weathering broadened the concept of natural solutions rather far, but ocean iron fertilization stretches this concept to the breaking point. Now discredited, this idea proceeded from the concept that large sections of the open ocean are iron deficient, which inhibits the growth of algae there.[48] However, if iron were artificially added, huge blooms of algae would result. These microscopic marine photosynthesizers would suck in large quantities of $CO_2$, die at the end of their short life cycle, sink to the bottom of the sea, and safely sequester their carbon there. Armed with little scientific research but ample chutzpah, an American entrepreneur named Russ George beguiled the Haida tribe in British Columbia into sponsoring and funding such an experiment off

British Columbia in 2012 on the theory that this would enhance the productivity of the sea and restore their dwindling salmon harvest.[49] The test did nothing for the salmon harvest, but widely frightened the global environmental community, which perceived this (not without justification) as an opaque and ill-considered act of marine pollution rather than a potential climate solution. It also appeared to violate the UN's Convention of Biological Diversity and perhaps the London Convention of the Dumping of Wastes at Sea.[50]

The stunt did produce a spectacular algae bloom but proved to sequester very little carbon. It appears that upon dying, the algae yielded most of its carbon back to the sea rather than plunging it to the bottom.[51] The experiment therefore failed not merely on procedural and legitimacy grounds but scientifically as well. Little further consideration is being given to ocean iron fertilization.

Attractive though the rubric of natural climate solutions sounds, there is as yet no silver bullet among them. Many of these concepts will form substantial strands in the final tapestry of climate solutions, but nothing like the whole tableau. They generally look better from afar than they do upon closer examination and often don't scale sufficiently to make the big dents in the problem that are required. In Holly Jean Buck's brilliantly turned phrase, we shouldn't "risk placing all of our regeneratively grown eggs into one lovely, but small, regeneratively grown basket." All climate solutions have drawbacks, so these shortcomings don't eliminate natural climate solutions from consideration, but these are more likely to be sideshows than the main event.

# 11 | CARBON CAPTURE AND SEQUESTRATION

If nature will provide myriad and widespread climate solutions that will nonetheless prove woefully insufficient to solve our climate problems, then where will the primary tools be found? For better and for worse, the answer is: massive, industrial interventions that will look a lot like the fossil fuel industry that got us into this mess. Envision big metal machines doing very unnatural tasks, but in that way resembling solar panels and wind turbines – "green" climate solutions wrapped in steel and aluminum.

## Taking the CCS out of BECCS

Of the interventions discussed in Chapter 10, the one that had the most going for it was bioenergy with carbon capture and sequestration (BECCS). Many of the other interventions are merely carbon banking or delayed emissions – pulling some carbon out of the atmosphere, but placing it in temporary or fragile stores elsewhere in the biosphere or climate system, from which it may escape and yet again re-enter the atmosphere if future generations intend different uses for those resources. In the case of standalone bioenergy, putting the carbon back in the atmosphere is in fact the plan. We'll grow the trees and then burn them, so through the cycle, this is theoretically carbon neutral (in practice, there is generally lots of leakage that makes this far less than carbon neutral). On the one hand, that's better than digging carbon out of geological reservoirs (i.e., fossil fuels) and burning it, thereby adding to the stock of carbon in the active exchange, but bioenergy doesn't draw down those stocks. BECCS on the other hand does. After the biomass is combusted, the smoke wafting up the flue is scrubbed of its carbon, which is then purified and transported to a disposal site. It is thereafter pumped down underground into suitable mineral formations where it will remain safely sequestered indefinitely – permanently from a human perspective.

The problem with BECCS and all of its forestation-related cousins is the land requirements. As we saw in Chapter 10, trying to set aside enough forested land to merely offset our current levels of emissions would over a few generations consume most of the arable land on the planet – obviously both an expensive and untenable situation on a planet that may top out with 10+ billion humans. BECCS solves part of that problem by harvesting the forest as soon as it is mature, such that the designated land can be replanted and thereby reused to suck down a new load of carbon. Still, the land required is massive.

Nonetheless, if we further consider BECCS, we realize that it entails two capture processes rather than just one. The majestic trees ingest the carbon from the air, but that carbon is released in the combustion process and turned right back into the $CO_2$ gas we are trying to get rid of. That got us nowhere.

The carbon must then be *recaptured* as it tries to make its way up the smokestack and back to the atmosphere. Only after the second capture do we have a substance that we can manipulate, transport, and sequester underground. Which begs the question: if we have the technology and financing to suck the carbon out of smokestacks before it reaches the atmosphere, why don't we just start with that? After all, we have roughly 10,000 major power plant smokestacks all over the world plus thousands more in the industrial sector all belching fossil fuel effluent into the air day and night, and for that matter, hundreds of millions of cars.[1] If the purpose of mowing down the beautiful forest was simply to funnel the carbon into a smokestack so we could capture it there, why don't we leave the poor trees out of this? BECCS envisions a double carbon cycle, as shown in Figure 11.1.

So long as we are still emitting madly from flues, the middle part of that double cycle is a distraction. Let's just eliminate it, grab the fossil fuel carbon as its going up the flue the first time, and sequester it directly.

Let's dispense with the need to take huge swathes of farm and pastureland out of production and/or cannibalize natural grasslands

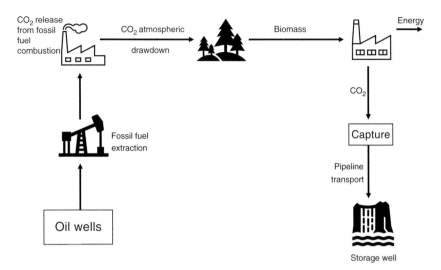

Figure 11.1 Flow of carbon dioxide in BECCS

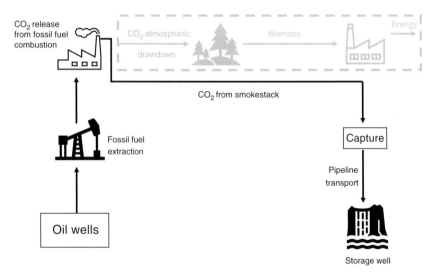

Figure 11.2 Flow of carbon dioxide in CCS

and other ecosystems, only to periodically destroy the forests we nurture.

This of course strips BECCS of its green veneer and reveals the gritty industrial process underneath, but fair enough. The more serious issue that this reconceptualization illuminates is that whereas the "BE" part of BECCS entails the production of a product (energy) that could and in some markets does offset the cost of producing that energy, there is very little market revenue to be derived from the "CCS" part of the process (see Figure 11.2). Scrubbing smokestack emission streams of their carbon effluent creates nothing the market currently values. It simply adds to cost, which is to say it will increase the price of the electricity or steel or cement that our proverbial plant is selling.

The magnitude of that additional cost is quite substantial. As noted in Chapter 10, BECCS costs are estimated to be \$100–\$200 per tonne of $CO_2$ captured,[2] and this is after accounting for the revenue that derives from selling the bioenergy. BECCS is often mischaracterized as a bioenergy process that also captures $CO_2$. It is more nearly a $CO_2$ capture process that also produces a little energy, but the economics of the energy it produces are very marginal. The revenue from the power sale merely pays for the additional capital equipment and operating costs necessary to generate it,[3] but produces no substantial surplus that reduces the cost of the carbon capture. Differently put, the economics of CCS would be roughly the same whether it produced bioenergy or not.

Few electric utilities or industrial facilities will therefore volunteer to install such technology. After all, it produces a global good (reduced carbon emissions) at a local cost, so it will be unpopular with rate payers. The lever that might plausibly induce widespread adoption of such technologies would be legislation and regulation. This would essentially be a tax levied upon the population by government decree, though the "tax" would in fact be collected by the local utility rather than the government and then used to pay the carbon capture and storage costs. Prices for manufactured goods and electricity would increase, reducing slightly the demand for them, which is problematical for economic growth but good from a carbon standpoint.

## How CCS Would Work

The first major carbon capture operation for combustion flue gases (Figure 11.2) was built in 1978 at a chemicals plant northeast of Los Angeles.[4] The intended purpose was not climate remediation but carbon utilization in their chemical manufacturing processes. In order to mine a rich source of $CO_2$, the plant was built adjacent to a coal boiler used to make process heat for an industrial application. If you want to catch fish, you fish where the fish are, and as coal is the most carbon-intensive fuel source, the flue of the boiler plant was a great place from which to harvest $CO_2$. The carbon capture operation utilized the amine process, whereby the flue gas is cycled through a separate vessel filled with packing material that is infused with an amine solution (see Figure 11.3). Amines are chemicals that remove acid gases like $CO_2$ from process streams. In the "absorber" step, about 90 percent of the $CO_2$ gets "scrubbed" out of gas as it chemically binds to amines (10 percent still escapes up the flue).[5] The amine solution is then recovered from the baffles and heated. Amines capture $CO_2$ at the relatively low ambient temperatures in a flue (still quite hot of course) but release them at higher temperatures. The amines are therefore further heated in the "stripper" step, shedding their $CO_2$. As amines are expensive, they are recycled numerous times back into the flue in a repeat of the absorber step. Also expensive is the energy required to heat the amines and the accompanying steam to a temperature sufficient to break the chemical bonds and strip out the $CO_2$.

The $CO_2$ is collected at the top of the stripper and subsequently cooled, causing it to shed some water. It is thereafter compressed, which causes it to further shed water. The high-pressure $CO_2$ exits as a liquid, ready for transportation. Pressurized liquid $CO_2$ can be transported in tanks via road, rail, or ship, but for a high-capacity operation, one would hope to move it via pipeline.

As the California chemical plant demonstrates, there are uses for $CO_2$ in such operations as chemicals and plastics manufacturing. It is notably used to carbonate soft drinks, although those tiny bubbles comprise a comparably tiny aggregate demand for $CO_2$. The largest use globally for $CO_2$ is in the production of urea by the fertilizer industry, followed by use for enhanced recovery by the oil and gas industry[6] (in the US, EOR is #1).[7, 8] In all, it is estimated that there is demand for about 1 percent of the $CO_2$ we anthropogenically produce, with 57 percent of that for fertilizer production and 33 percent for enhanced oil recovery (EOR).[9] The final 10 percent is used in a range of applications, from the food and beverage industry to the production of metal and fire suppression equipment.[10] Not all these $CO_2$ uses are long term. When a Pepsi drinker belches, that $CO_2$ is returned to the atmosphere. There are optimistic estimates that our use of carbon dioxide could triple from less than 1 percent to 2–3 percent of our production stream for uses such as the creation of new building materials or fuels, but those markets have yet to materialize.[11] Even should

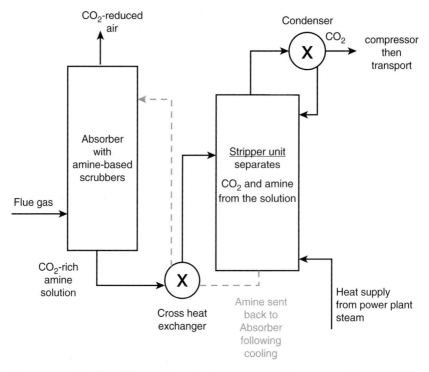

**Figure 11.3** Simplified illustration of carbon capture using amine solvents

they do so, there is very little progress we can make on the climate front via "carbon use."

One prospect that might substantially expand the utilization of recovered atmospheric carbon would be to funnel it into the front end of the fuel cycle rather than into the ground. After all, $CO_2$ of course contains carbon, the very thing we are trying to coax up from the ground so we can burn it. The problem is that this carbon is already combined with $O_2$ and therefore very stable and non-combustible. But if we combined that $CO_2$ with hydrogen under the right conditions, then we could have synthetic fuel that can be combusted in the normal fashion for energy generation. This wouldn't put any carbon back into the ground, but it could at least substitute for fossil fuels we would otherwise newly recover. Differently put, recycling our spent carbon by turning it into synthetic fuel doesn't lower the water level in the bathtub, but it at least would slow that rate at which we are filling it. In theory, we could wean ourselves off fossil fuels and endlessly recycle the carbon already in the climate system – a huge step forward from where we are now. Several ventures including Carbon Engineering of British Columbia, Global Thermostat of New York, and Carbon Recycling International in Iceland are already working on demonstration projects to prove out such a process.

The problem, as it almost always is in the CCS side of our toolbox, is cost. So long as dumping $CO_2$ into the atmosphere is free, the price of synthetic fuels from recovered atmospheric carbon is considerably higher than good old gas, oil, and coal. Carbon Engineering touts synthetic fuel prices in the range of $4 per gallon,[12] nearly twice the cost of oil. Until and unless that changes, there will be little market demand for fuel from recycled carbon.

Synthetic fuels aside, nearly all the $CO_2$ we might in the future strip out of flues would presumably be destined for sequestration rather than usage. It would travel via pipeline from capture sites (power plants and $CO_2$-intensive industrial plants) to appropriate storage sites, such as played out oil fields or saline aquifers. While only certain geological formations are appropriate storage locations, these are found all over the world and there is no issue regarding capacity – there is far more scope for sequestration than we could possibly need.[13] Once at the storage site, the carbon would be pumped down a borehole to a depth suitable for geological sequestration – exactly the opposite of the oil drilling process that may have wrenched that carbon from the subsurface in the first place. Monitoring, measurement, and verification technologies would be required to ensure that the carbon remains locked away as intended, but this sort of secure permanent storage is what is ultimately needed to solve our carbon problem.

The amine process described above is nearly 40 years old, but remains the dominant process. Better solvents and sorbents are being engineered, as is the concept of replacing the amines with absorptive membranes. As the fleet of CCS facilities grows, substantial "learning by doing" efficiencies are being discovered in machine design, construction techniques, and operational processes. This has put CCS at an earlier phase of a cost-reduction track similar to that of other new energy technologies such as wind and solar, where the cost declines open new markets and opportunities. Nonetheless, the progress remains impressive, but incremental.

## Status of CCS

Despite the urgent need for more carbon capture and sequestration, the technology is "obstinately unused" in the words of Oliver Morton.[14] According to the 2020 Annual Report of the Global Carbon Capture and Storage Institute (GCCSI), there were just 26 commercial CCS facilities in the world at the end of 2020 with a combined capture capacity of 40 million metric tonnes per annum.[15] While that may sound like a huge mass of gas, it is just one thousandth of current annual emissions[16] – symbolically important, but of no climatic impact. Another three plants were under construction in 2020 with 34 more in planning stages,[17] but if all 37 of the additional plants were fully operational, the combined fleet would still have capacity of far less than 1 percent of current emissions, and emissions are still growing. The International Energy Agency has mapped out a Sustainable Development Scenario[18] which seeks to chart a viable climate and energy future. Although it is produced by an institution closely associated with (and in the eyes of some, unduly influenced by) the global fossil fuel industry, it is in fact reasonably parallel with some scenarios produced by the IPCC. The IEA plan foresees a need for 2,000 large carbon capture plants by 2040 – one hundred-fold what we have today. Relative to such a requirement, our current pipeline of 34 – which will require most of this decade to complete – looks downright paltry.

Moreover, few of the 26 plants in existence today attack what one might imagine to be the heart of the matter, rendering our fossil fuel power plants carbon neutral. Instead of capturing post-combustion $CO_2$ from power plants, roughly half of our existing CCS capacity is devoted to siphoning off $CO_2$ from natural gas before it is burned. When it emerges from the ground, natural gas is mostly methane (the stuff we want to burn), but may also contain water vapor, other forms of hydrocarbons (ethane, propane, butane), and various extraneous gases including sulfur dioxide, helium, and carbon dioxide. To meet regulations and commercial standards, most of those impurities including the $CO_2$ must be removed before the gas can enter a pipeline and thereafter be combusted in your stove. If instead the gas is destined for liquefaction and shipment as liquefied natural gas, it needs to be much purer still. Therefore, LNG processing already requires harvesting these chemicals out of the "wet" natural gas, and the further cost required to separate the $CO_2$ from the other compounds is very marginal – roughly 25 US$ per metric tonne.[19]

Unfortunately, even this meager cost is greater than the $CO_2$'s value in most markets. Therefore, about 85 percent of $CO_2$ culled out of natural gas is simply vented into the atmosphere, with only 25 Mtpa captured of the 175 Mtpa produced from these processes.[20] Amongst the thousand-plus gas processing plants in the world, there are just 11[21] where the stream of low cost $CO_2$ emanating from the refining process has been linked to a customer, and these constitute more than half the world fleet of capture facilities and more than 60 percent of the capture capacity.[22] Today, carbon capture is mostly about finding some customer for the waste chemicals streaming out of gas processing plants.

One major use to which the world puts this small fraction of retained $CO_2$ is enhanced oil recovery (EOR). As previously noted, EOR is a recovery technique that is sometimes used once primary and secondary production has encountered diminishing returns and entails pumping $CO_2$ down injection wells to drive more oil to the surface. Recent research has also suggested that $CO_2$ could provide a better and greener alternative to water in the hydraulic fracturing ("fracking") process.

For our CCS story, these are fortunate developments. *Somebody* wants at least a small fraction of $CO_2$ the world is pumping out, and roughly three quarters of the $CO_2$ captured by the current world fleet of facilities is destined for EOR. However, this is from a climate perspective a rather ironic circumstance, in that most of the $CO_2$ being sequestered in this way simply serves as a plunger intended to flush to the surface more of the hydrocarbons that created the climate problem in the first place. The $CO_2$ pumped into the ground for EOR is mostly permanently sequestered, and the fraction that flows back up a recovery well is siphoned off and re-pumped down another injection well until it ultimately lodges in the pores of the rock formation. On the one hand then, EOR is a real and secure form of geologic storage, but on the other hand, it is a bit circular in that what goes down is roughly countervailed by what comes up as new fossil fuels, and therefore represents carbon offset rather than removal.

To summarize, we are recapturing just one thousandth of our current anthropogenic $CO_2$ emissions. Of the little bit we do recover, three quarters comes from refining natural gas, and a good deal of it is then devoted to recovering more oil. To have a sustainable energy and climate future, we need 2,000 more CCS plants in 20 years,[23] but in addition to the 26 currently operational, we have articulated plans for just 34. And rather than growing, the pipeline of new projects since 2010 has shrunk. For a CCS intervention that is essential to saving the world, that's a rather depressing scorecard. So, what's (not) happening? Why is this where we find ourselves?

## Barriers to More CCS

The one-word answer is "money." We know how to capture carbon, but beyond the somewhat self-defeating practice of EOR plus a few niche markets, the world doesn't need it and will pay nothing for it. So long as there is no economic motivation to do otherwise, all the rest of this unwanted carbon will be dumped into the atmosphere, as it ever was. Global anthropogenic $CO_2$ emissions in 2019 from energy and industry were estimated by the United Nations Environment Programme to be 38 billion tonnes.[24] Emissions from land use are a bit tougher to pin down, but a respectable recent estimate is roughly 3.5 billion tonnes,[25] bringing total annual emissions to roughly 41 billion. CCS costs (both capture and storage) vary based on the source of the emissions, but to keep our math easy, lets choose a value of $100 per tonne, which is plausibly in the range.[26, 27] The simple math then is that the cost of sequestering all our carbon each year would be roughly $ 4.1 trillion. That is roughly 5 percent of the global economy, 20 percent of the US economy, and larger than the economies of every nation on Earth save the US, China, and Japan.[28] It is almost 25 percent greater than the global oil and gas industry.[29] Granted, this is simplistic math. On the one hand, many analysts believe a carbon price necessary to get to net zero emissions will exceed $100.[30] On the other hand, as carbon prices approach and perhaps exceed $100 per tonne, that will drive massive substitutions and innovation that will reduce the "demand" for emissions, such that the world may be willing to pay higher prices-per-tonne to remediate a shrinking sum of tonnes. Nonetheless, our simple math gets us into the right ballpark as to how big the CCS industry may need to be. Really big!

Differently put, we would have to more than double the price of oil and gas to pay for all the necessary CCS – five to seven dollars for a gallon of gasoline in the US rather as opposed to two or three[31] (this has oil and gas paying for coal and cement's emissions as well, so the numbers are simply illustrative, but they get us into a sensible range). Could we convince the whole world to double its fuel costs? That would be a very heavy lift. Nonetheless, would that destroy the world economy? Many Europeans pay fuel prices roughly double those enjoyed by Americans and seem to live pretty well. It's ultimately a question of political will – and values.

Nonetheless, the above costings suggest that there is a single cost per tonne of CCS, whereas there are in fact several, and to better understand the cost problem, we need to delve down a bit. It is no coincidence that the vast majority of captured $CO_2$ derives from natural gas processing – it's the cheapest source, with capture costs as previously noted in the range of $25 per tonne.[32] Ammonia fertilizer and biomass-to-ethanol production plants yield similarly cheap gas streams, and when these CCS operations are added in, these cheap $CO_2$ sources represent 80 percent of world capture capacity and 18 of the 26 operating facilities.[33]

The remaining eight operational facilities fit into one of two other categories. Two of the existing facilities are situated in the next cost tier, roughly $90 per tonne,[34] up roughly 3.5 times versus the cheapest tier. These consist of one iron and steel production plant with CCS in Abu Dhabi that deserves kudos for blazing a path to a green future but whose financing derives from what is perhaps the world's richest petrostate per capita and therefore may not reflect replicable economics. The other plant operating in this cost tier is the Boundary Dam CCS in Canada.[35] It is the only plant in the world capturing post-combustion carbon streams from power production. Ironically, since coal is more carbon intensive than natural gas, coal-fired plants yield a more carbon-rich effluent stream that is therefore less costly to capture.

To capture the less concentrated $CO_2$ from the flue of a gas-fired power plant, we take another upward cost step to the vicinity of $120 per tonne.[36] As we clean up our power plant fleet and switch from coal to gas, the carbon capture gets more expensive. Rinsing the carbon from cement production bumps costs up to $150 per tonne,[37] six times that of the low-cost streams. Not surprisingly, there are zero large-scale CCS facilities operating in these high remediation cost tiers. Not one gas fired power plant or cement plant in the world is recapturing its carbon. So, while the world's growing fleet of CCS facilities is a reason for optimism, it is important to understand that the business case currently closes only in these low-cost streams, and seldom even then.

Three of the final six operational CCS facilities are capturing $CO_2$ from the hydrogen fuel production process, but in two distinct ways that lead to different cost structures. The Great Plains coal-to-synthetic-natural-gas plant that has operated at a large scale in North Dakota for over 20 years produces a high concentration $CO_2$ effluent that enables low-cost capture.[38] The Air Products and Quest hydrogen plants near Houston and Edmonton respectively utilize a steam methane reforming process that places them in a mid-tier cost category.[39] Another low-cost capture operation is the Sturgeon Oil Refinery in Alberta, which produces ultra-low sulfur diesel and uses the Alberta Carbon Trunk Line to transport the captured $CO_2$ to Central Alberta.[40] The list of commercial plants is rounded out by two CCS operations in China that are used in chemical production, but their cost profiles are opaque.[41]

The cost tiering above enables us to take a second, more nuanced look at CCS costs. Breaking down our previous estimate of total anthropogenic emissions into these cost tiers, and pairing each tier with an appropriate cost, a few trends become clear. Only 68 percent or so of emissions derive from sources which involve a stationary smokestack or chimney that could in theory be scrubbed, and these involve not only large power plants but home heating furnaces.[42] Even if every one of these sources were paired with capture technology and then piped to sequestration wells and buried, we have only solved about two thirds of the problem. A second group of emission sources, mostly in the transport sector, are unlikely to be directly remediable, but could instead be converted to energy sources that are non-emitting at the point of use, such as electricity or hydrogen. These sources may still involve emissions at the point of energy processing – the electricity or hydrogen production plant – but we thereby turn vehicles into an energy use whose carbon emissions can be captured at the plant. We'll call these indirectly remediable, in that they first require an energy transition before CCS is feasible, but they thereafter yield to standard CCS solutions. These indirect sectors comprise about 20 percent of current emissions.[43] Finally, there are non-remediable sources, such as agriculture and land use changes. Perhaps processes and practices can be changed in these sectors to diminish $CO_2$ emissions, but CCS is not a tool that will lend itself to eliminating such emissions. This last category accounts for around 7 percent of emissions.[44] In summary then, a fully mature CCS infrastructure could solve nearly 95 percent of our emissions problem. Yet the weighted cost of these CCS interventions would still tally more than $3 trillion annually, which is to say we still need an industry for CCS that is roughly as large as the oil and gas industry, even though such a massive system would nonetheless leave a small percentage of our emissions problem unabated.

## The Future of CCS

Noting then that CCS could at best be an expensive and partial solution, let's focus momentarily on where progress is actually being made. The clear national leader in the CCS space is the US, where almost half the facilities and nearly two thirds of the capacity is located.[45] The world's biggest CCS plant with more than 20 percent of the global capacity is the Century plant in West Texas.[46] At full capacity, it is capable of culling 8.4 million tonnes per annum (Mtpa) of $CO_2$[47] from its natural gas processing operation, all of which is piped to the bountiful oil fields of the Permian Basin for EOR. Nearly as large is the Shute Creek plant (7 Mtpa)[48] in Wyoming – another gas processing-to-EOR operation. The Great Plains plant (3 Mtpa) in North Dakota also serves the EOR market but derives its $CO_2$ from coal gasification.[49] There are nine other commercial CCS operations in the US and four more in adjacent Canada, all but two of which serve the EOR market.[50] The exceptions are the Illinois Industrial CCS project at the Archer Daniels Midland ethanol plant in Decatur, Illinois and the Quest project outside of Edmonton, both of which have capacities of about 1 Mtpa but which sequester their carbon underground purely for the purpose of storage.[51] However, both are harvesting gas streams needed to refine other fuels rather than the combustion gases deriving from burning fuels.

There are just nine commercial CCS facilities outside North America, all of which either derive their $CO_2$ from gas processing or sell it into the EOR market, or both.[52] Norway has demonstrated the inclination and resources to pioneer a path to a greener energy future and has used that financial, technological, and soft power to become a leader in CCS. Its Sleipner and Snohvit plants are Europe's major sequestration facilities, harvesting $CO_2$ from Norway's plentiful offshore natural gas fields and burying it under the North Sea.

While Europe has no commercial operational CCS plants outside of Norway, it does have what is perhaps the world's most impressive inventory of projects on the drawing boards. One of the challenges in building out CCS infrastructure is the geographical question of how one matches source locations with storage locations. Most of the world's existing projects are vertically integrated on a single site and function as self-contained projects, with the $CO_2$ source plant and the storage operation owned and operated by the same party. However, in the mature CCS infrastructure required to scale up this activity by 100 times, one should expect storage hubs linked by pipeline to clusters of $CO_2$ sources – economic ecosystems of production plants linked into major, multi-user sequestration sites. There are five such hubs and clusters being planned in Europe – two each in the Netherlands and the UK, and one in Norway.[53] The Ports of Amsterdam and Rotterdam are each planning pipeline systems that would channel emissions from a variety of plants into offshore storage systems.[54] The Net Zero Teesside and Zero Carbon Humber clusters in the English Midlands similarly envision linking major emission sources to onshore sequestration sites.[55] And the Northern Lights project envisions ship-borne transport of $CO_2$ from multiple coastal sites in Northern Europe to Norway's already developed North Sea sequestration sites.[56] These and other planned projects suggest that Europe may soon be the world leader in CCS, although the CarbonSAFE program whereby the Department of Energy is funding the search for appropriate large-scale sequestration sites is keeping the US in the game as well.

China has built its economy in substantial measure by bringing onshore many of the high-emitting industries that the West has shed and now accounts for almost one third of global emissions.[57] Relative to that, its CCS capacity is underdeveloped, with just three operating facilities and two more in construction all of which combined will have less than half the capacity of the massive Century Plant in Texas.[58] In 2019 China published an updated version of its carbon capture Roadmap that pledges impressive future endeavors most of which have yet to be commenced.[59] The leading CCS project in the Asia Pacific region is the massive Gorgon plant in Australia that sources coal from the Latrobe Valley in Victoria and processes it into hydrogen fuel for export to Japan.[60] As one of the world's highest $CO_2$ emitters per capita,[61] Australia has struggled to limit its emissions and has seen climate politics dominate the national dialogue like few other countries.

In that context, it was a condition of project approval that Gorgon sequester its $CO_2$ emissions, which has caused the facility to leap into third place in terms of mature capacity. Brazil, Saudi Arabia, and Abu Dhabi host one operational commercial CCS facility each, while India and Africa have none.[62]

In order for CCS to move beyond the fringes of the energy and climate story, there must be a value placed upon carbon that charges parties for emitting $CO_2$ and thereby creates an incentive not to. Such carbon pricing exists in the world, but only around the periphery. Norway has one of the world's most stringent carbon pricing schemes,[63] which is both a symptom and a cause of its pioneering role in the development of CCS infrastructure. The EU has implemented an Emissions Trading System in 2005 that was intended to drive a rapid reduction in emissions, but which proved too permissive in terms of emissions allowances, resulting in a carbon price in the range of €25,[64] too low to drive major changes. In an effort to address this, in 2021 the EU will accelerate the rate at which allowances are withdrawn from the market,[65] presumably leading to a scarcity premium and higher carbon prices.

The US has taken an opposite approach, issuing tax credits rather than levying taxes. The federal 45Q tax credit program was approved in 2017 and will issue credits for CCS projects that begin construction before 2024.[66] Sequestration via EOR will produce credits of $35 per tonne, whereas straight sequestration will receive $50.[67] The program has engendered substantial interest but has been bogged down by a governmental failure to produce implementation details. Its ultimate impact is therefore unclear. In keeping with its reputation as an environmental leader, the State of California has also passed a tax credit system for initiatives that reduce the carbon intensity of the fuel consumed in the California market, including CCS projects.[68]

If we are to keep straight our semantics, CCS as discussed here is mitigation, not climate intervention. Capturing combusted $CO_2$ before it escapes to the atmosphere reduces the stream of new emissions rather than the stock of carbon already in the climate system and in that sense does not fit with some definitions of the term "geoengineering." Yet I include it prominently here for several reasons. First, the technologies of which CCS is comprised will be similar in the capture step and identical in the sequestration step to those required to work down greenhouse gases stocks in the atmosphere. Second, CCS will be essential to getting us to Net Zero. Finally, we will still need loads of CCS after we reach net zero emissions, because some industrial sectors may continue to emit $CO_2$, even if the world no longer does on a net basis. In fact, given the expected persistence of fossil fuel use far into the future, ramping up CCS capability is every bit as urgent and necessary as is mitigation by other means. It is difficult to conceive a successful mitigation strategy that does not include recapturing and burying vast amounts of our emission stream.

In the entire geoengineering toolbox, the single best near-term implement is CCS. From the standpoints of policy, economics, and technology, we need to get busy with it. All good climate outcomes lie down this path.

# 12 DIRECT AIR CARBON CAPTURE AND SEQUESTRATION

If we wish to scrub carbon from the climate system, the reason to start with flues is that $CO_2$ is more plentiful there, comprising 5–20 percent of the exhaust gases emanating from fossil fuel combustion and similar if not higher proportions from natural gas processing, versus 0.04 percent (just over 400 parts per million) in ambient air. The energy, and therefore money, required to capture that $CO_2$ is correlated to its concentration within the background medium (though far from directly proportional). Rephrasing an analogy from MIT's Howard Herzog, if our task is to capture ten red balls from a mix of red and white ones, it is relatively easy if every other ball is red, because we need only to handle 20 to get ten of the ones we want. If more like one in 2,500 is red, we need to sift 25,000 balls to get ten red ones, requiring much more work. So, being cost-motivated, we will start where the concentrations of our target species are high and we are therefore getting the most bangs for our buck.

However, we will presumably work our way through the high-concentration, low-cost flues to the low-concentration, high-cost flues and will (we pray) one day run out of unremediated flues to scrub. All the smokestacks and chimneys in the world will either have been dismantled because the associated plant has decarbonized its production process or will have been fitted with carbon capture systems that whisk away the $CO_2$ before it escapes into the atmosphere and enable it to be safely spirited underground. Our work is done!

Hardly. For starters, "zero flue emissions" does not equal "zero emissions." Some industrial sectors such as aviation and long-distance surface travel may resist decarbonization for a very long time. Moreover, the agricultural sector – including livestock – as well as various land use changes will continue to release $CO_2$ and methane in ways that can't be captured at the source. There is no practical way to deploy CCS over the world's rice paddies. And it would seem unrealistic to build our climate scenarios on the expectation of universal participation – some people and societies may openly refuse to cooperate, and others may covertly cheat. Therefore, in order to get the world to net zero emissions, there will need to be a large slice of negative emissions – pulling $CO_2$ out of the climate system in order to countervail a continuing inflow of anthropogenic emissions. Unfortunately, even then, our work will not be done.

Returning to our bathtub analogy, net zero emissions is achieved when we reduce the flow from the tap by say 80 or 90 percent, and as well bore a new anthropogenic drain pipe that can evacuate the last 10 or 20 percent (our negative emissions), such that sources and sinks finally balance and the water level stops rising. To assume that we can stop there is to assume that humanity in that distant future will be happy with the level to which the water ultimately rose. But if our mitigation efforts prove too little too late as now seems likely, humanity may be distinctly *unhappy* with that water level. It may be way too high, generating a climate that is much too warm relative to the historical climate in which modern society blossomed. The future may well demand that the anthropogenic drain be further widened such that sinks are greater than sources and that after cresting, the water begins to recede. To do any of that, we will need to go beyond flue capture and distill $CO_2$ from the air – direct air carbon capture and sequestration, or DACCS.

## How DACCS Would Work

From Chapter 11, the latter stages of the DACCS process will be very familiar. Precisely the same purification, compression, transportation, sequestration, and monitoring infrastructure that was presumably pioneered for CCS from standard flues or bioenergy with CCS (BECCS) will be further employed for DACCS. In fact, this infrastructure won't differentiate between $CO_2$ captured from smokestacks or from the air. It will all need to be disposed of in the same way and likely in the same repositories.

The front end of the process won't seem very novel either. Once again, we need some way to run air past chemicals that will capture the red balls (in our analogy) and spit out the white ones. The chemicals are then treated (usually by heating them) to regurgitate their collected $CO_2$ and then recycled back to the collection step. However, relative to flue gas capture, the first major difference here is – there are a lot more white balls. The concentration of $CO_2$ in the open air is tiny, so we need to sift a lot of air to yield a little of our target. This means more energy and more money. As well, there was no need to propel the air in a flue in order to get exposure to it – it was already moving as the hot air raced up the flue towards the ambient air. However, for an efficient DAC process, we need to propel the air past our capture chemicals, which with our current technology means running big fans endlessly. The energy requirement for DAC is estimated to be 2.5 to 4 times that required to cleanse $CO_2$ from power plant exhaust streams.[1] And all this energy needs to derive from non-emitting sources if it is to ameliorate rather than exacerbate our climate problem, so lots of DAC means lots of wind turbines or solar panels (or natural gas with CCS), but if we find ourselves sufficiently motivated, all that could be done.

One way in which direct air capture diverges from flue capture is geography. With flues, we have to connect sources and sinks, and the two may be distant from one another, creating a need for transportation infrastructure (principally pipelines) that channel the $CO_2$ from the power plant where it is produced to the oil patch where it might be sequestered. But with direct air capture, the source is anywhere there is air. As $CO_2$ is well mixed in the atmosphere, there is also no regional or national beneficial effect to undertaking direct air capture in one country or region versus another. Given that, direct air capture facilities will be placed wherever the appropriate sequestration facility is, such that one may dispense with the need for long pipelines and bury the carbon where it was captured. Or, given the large energy requirements, they may be located where non-emitting energy is cheap and plentiful. But these requirements could be fulfilled in many places on the planet, which is perhaps good news, since they will be needed in huge volumes. One estimate is that capturing 1 percent of our current carbon emissions from the air would require 750,000 small-scale installations.[2] Should the world opt instead for large-scale facilities each capable of extracting $CO_2$ masses on the order of 1 million tonnes per year, the ultimate fleet size would still likely number in the thousands or tens of thousands.[3]

## Barriers to DACCS

The volume of air we would have to scrub to make an appreciable difference would be enormous. Forget about cubic miles or kilometers of air and think instead of fractions of the entire atmosphere. The preindustrial atmosphere had a $CO_2$ concentration of roughly 280 parts per million (ppm).[4] Our anthropogenic contributions are now increasing that at an average of 2.5 ppm per year, and we now have a concentration of around 410 ppm.[5] At this rate of increase, we are on track to more than double the preindustrial concentration and reach near 600 ppm before the end of this century. If we wanted to offset 1 ppm of continuing emissions via DAC, that would require capturing nearly 8 Gt[6] (billion metric tonnes) of $CO_2$ from the air. But since $CO_2$ comprises so tiny a proportion of air, one would need to scrub an enormous amount of air to capture that – roughly 20,000 Gt, and even this assumes an overly optimistic 100 percent efficient process, whereby every molecule of $CO_2$ is removed from the air we handle. If instead our goal were to offset all of our emissions, or in a future post-net-zero world, to reduce atmospheric concentrations at the same rate at which we are now increasing them, that would require removal of roughly 20 Gt annually, requiring that we launder 50,000 Gt of air. In such a scenario, however, a pesky problem would arise. As earlier noted, the oceans, along with the soils and the atmosphere, are all porous components of a single seamless climate system. As we increase the atmospheric concentration of $CO_2$, these other elements of the climate system absorb roughly half of it as they seek to equilibrate with the air, which is a benefit in our current circumstances.[7] However, were we to start reducing the atmospheric concentrations, the rest of the climate system would run in reverse, shedding some of its carbon load back into the atmosphere. Therefore, to reduce atmospheric concentrations by our targeted 20 Gt, we actually have to remove over 40 Gt and wash over 100,000 Gt of air. This is over 2 percent of *all the air in the atmosphere!!!* Year after year! If the cost of DACCS settles in the range of $200 per tonne of $CO_2$, scrubbing 2 percent of all the air in the atmosphere every year would cost more than $8 trillion or roughly 10 percent of current global GDP. At a more optimistic $100 per tonne, the aggregate cost would still be 5 percent of global economic output. Either way, offsetting our current emissions or buying down atmospheric concentrations via DACCS would entail an enormous industrial program with a crushing price tag. Nonetheless, as with CCS, we may put ourselves in a position where we have no choice.

## Status of DACCS

If we are today merely in the early stages of the roll out of CCS, we are several decades behind that in the world of DACCS. A process for capturing $CO_2$ from the air was first commercialized in the 1950s but proved of little practical significance, since there are much cheaper ways to source $CO_2$.[8] The idea of harvesting it for climate management purposes was first suggested in the 1990s by Klaus Lackner, an American scientist who now runs the Center for Negative Carbon Emissions at Arizona State University. It took another decade before the three start-ups that now lead this field were established in 2009 and 2010. Climeworks is a Swiss company founded by two former mechanical engineering students at ETH Zurich, Switzerland's "MIT" and the alma mater of Albert Einstein. After attracting outside capital to develop prototypes, the world's first commercial facility filtering $CO_2$ from ambient air was dedicated in May 2017 in the quaint alpine village of Hinwil, where it supplies $CO_2$ to enhance the productivity of a local greenhouse (see Figure 12.1). Climeworks' carbon capture units are also being used to supply carbonation to a mineral water company, manufacture synthetic fuels, and sequester carbon underground in Iceland. They even sell carbon offsets to the public at pricing of €1 per kilogram of $CO_2$, which works out to more than $1100 per tonne.[9] In August of 2020, the company closed a funding round of $110 million,[10] bringing its total capitalization since inception to roughly $160 million.[11] It intends to use the bulk of its latest funding round to build a facility capable of capturing 100,000 tonnes of $CO_2$ per year, which it hopes may be operational as soon as 2022. This is all impressive momentum, but is puny relative to the flue capture operations discussed in Chapter 11, the smallest of which were in the range of 1 million annual tonnes of capture. Nonetheless, Climeworks is thinking big, and has announced a goal of ramping up such that they are capturing 1 percent of anthropogenic emissions by 2025 – a huge scaling challenge that there is as yet little evidence the company could meet.

Also founded in 2009 was Carbon Engineering, a Canadian company based on the inspiration of David Keith. Dr. Keith is perhaps more than anyone the person most responsible for pushing forward

Figure 12.1 Climeworks plant in Hinwil, Switzerland. Courtesy of Climeworks[12]

climate intervention in all its forms. He leads Harvard's Solar Geoengineering Research Group, the world's foremost academic enterprise devoted to this field (to which I should disclose I am an ongoing minor financial contributor). He has published over 150 papers, articles, and other scholarly works relevant to geoengineering on an extraordinarily wide range of topics, the first of which appeared in 1992 – virtually pre-history in the climate intervention calendar. Keith is perhaps best known for pioneering research into solar radiation management – the other side of the geoengineering toolbox – but he is also the founder and first president of Carbon Engineering. Dr. Keith and his colleagues at Harvard also served as my own conduit into this field. With his encouragement and mentorship, I embarked on my first scholarly papers on the costs and logistics of forms of solar radiation management to which we will get in a couple of chapters. The opportunity to learn from and collaborate with the climate studies ecosystem that he helped build at Harvard is what drew me to return my graduate school alma mater as a Senior Fellow.

Carbon Engineering's headquarters sits on the bank of a Pacific fjord in Squamish, British Columbia, a fading logging town 30 miles north of Vancouver. It bills itself as a clean energy company in that one fate of the carbon that it could remove from the air would be synthetic fuels that could be used for transportation or other purposes with little or no carbon footprint. However, its direct air capture technology is equally well suited to putting carbon to other uses, such as EOR. And of course, that carbon could under different economic circumstances be instead sequestered underground in an effort to reduce atmospheric concentrations. All these downstream destinations for the carbon depend on getting the upstream bit – the capture process from direct air – cheap enough that the business cases start to close. Due in part to Keith's star power, CE has been able to attract a glitzy roster of investors, starting with Bill Gates, for whom Keith serves as a climate advisor. Gates is also the single biggest funder of Keith's research group at Harvard. Another billionaire investor is Murray Edwards, a Canadian oil sands financier and owner of the Calgary Flames hockey franchise. Corporate backers include Occidental Petroleum and Chevron, both of which have taken seats on the board, and Anglo-Australian mining giant BHP. Both the Canadian and US governments have also funded research projects. The company has been removing carbon from the atmosphere since 2015, and converting it into fuels since 2017. Unlike the amine process described in Chapter 11 and utilized by Climeworks, Carbon Engineering's capture process relies on chemicals (potassium hydroxides) that are a much stronger base than amines.[13] The strong base is more efficient at grabbing passing molecules of $CO_2$, which is a weak acid, boosting the percentage of carbon that is captured. However, the strong resulting chemical bond is substantially harder to break in the stripping process, requiring much higher process temperatures and therefore greater energy input.[14] Whether the weak base (amine) or strong base (hydroxide) process will win in the marketplace remains to be seen.

Synthetic fuels made from captured atmospheric $CO_2$ are still carbon emitting when burned, so they don't solve the climate problem in the way that non-emitting fuel sources like wind and solar do. Rather, their manufacture involves removing carbon from the atmosphere before their combustion puts it back, so it is broadly carbon neutral rather than non-emitting. In that way it is like burning a tree. The combustion process emits $CO_2$, but since the tree removed it from the atmosphere as it grew, it is really carbon recycling rather than a net new emission. Synthetic fuels from captured carbon are, and look to continue to be, more expensive than fossil fuels. Quoting Keith, "There is no way we are beating oil from the ground in a head-to-head competition without regulation." Still, whereas batteries are likely the way to decarbonize passenger cars and small vehicles, in a world with a high carbon price, such synthetic fuels could be the key to decarbonizing some of the most difficult to remediate sectors such as aviation, long-distance trucks, and ships.

Braced by a new infusion of US$ 68 million in capital in 2019, the company is now engineering the world's largest direct air capture plant, capable initially of capturing half-a-million (and eventually, one million) tonnes of $CO_2$ from the atmosphere. Preliminary engineering has begun for a similarly sized facility in the UK. At this scale, such plants would rival the capacities of many of the CCS facilities noted in Chapter 11, making it still a mere drop in the 40-ish billion tonne bucket of current global emissions, but no longer nothing. More importantly, it would prove the operational feasibility of such a facility and thereby open a path whereby the world could someday pursue direct air capture on the sort of scale that would be required to make a dent in our climate issues.

Carbon Engineering has licensed its technology to 1 PointFive, a company started by Occidental's Oxy Low Carbon Ventures unit to build, own, and operate multiple DAC plants in the United States. Engineering and design work are underway with the expectation that the facility will become operational in 2024 (see Figure 12.2). It will be located in the Permian Basin of western Texas, and when fully

Figure 12.2 Rendering of a Carbon Engineering large-scale Direct Air Capture facility. Courtesy of Carbon Engineering[15]

operational will capture 500 kilotonnes of atmospheric carbon per year. The good news is that this will be the first large-scale operation beginning to remove carbon directly from the atmosphere and sequester it back underground where it will no longer harm the world. The bad news is that this is being done for the purpose of dredging more hydrocarbons up the wells via EOR. One could then be forgiven for viewing all this rather cynically as a project steered and funded by major oil companies furthering their dirty and planet-destroying fossil fuel agenda. One could perhaps go one step further and perceive this as the hijacking of geoengineering to ensure that it does not pose a threat to their business model. But there is an alternative interpretation that is both kinder and I think more accurate, which is that we need to start somewhere, and this is a very promising start. Occidental proclaims that its ambition is to provide carbon management services well beyond what is required for EOR.[16] Currently we are recapturing very little of our emitted carbon, either from flues or from direct air. It is clear that getting ourselves out of the enormous climate bind into which we are sliding will take massive amounts of both. There are several problems preventing us from undertaking serious carbon capture but the primary one is cost – it's really expensive.

David Keith has projected that future costs of a mature DAC industry could be as low as $94–$232 per tonne of $CO_2$ captured,[17] placing the cost to capture all of our current emissions in the range of 5 percent–11 percent of the total current global economy today. However, even this huge sum casts Keith as one of the world's most optimistic prognosticators of DACCS costs. Climeworks claims current costs in the $600–700 range.[18] Howard Herzog of MIT is skeptical that costs will ever get to the $100–$300 range, and considers numbers above $600 to be much more likely.[19] This wide range of cost projections will begin to narrow later in this decade once Carbon Engineering's large Texas plant begins operating at full capacity. Nonetheless, at $600, remediating our current emissions would consume 30 percent of gross world product – a huge sum.

I should note that while I am comparing these sums to current gross world product in order to try to put them in some comprehensible context, that is somewhat misleading, both because gross world product is expected to continue to grow and because emissions are (we hope) going to shrink. Therefore, by mid-century, remediating all of our 2050 emissions may be a much smaller percentage of gross world product than the above percentages indicate. On the other hand, later in the century, the goal for DACCS may no longer be to offset a small sum of ongoing emissions, but to reduce atmospheric concentrations, in which case the annual DACCS target may not shrink even if emissions do. Whichever way one slices it, the fact that it is meaningful to characterize this as a percentage of gross world product at all indicates at least with the technology we can now envision, the cost of DACCS is likely to be utterly enormous.

To solve the climate problem, we will have to someday reckon with that cost, but the lower the cost, the easier a pill it will be to swallow. We must get ourselves down the cost decline curve somehow. As solar power demonstrates, the economies of scale and learning-by-doing cost reductions can be astonishing – since 2010, solar photovoltaic module prices have dropped over 80 percent.[20] We need to start where we can start, prove the concept, improve the technology, and figure out how to slash costs and do it cheaper. Any customer therefore who is currently willing to pay for us to remove carbon from the atmosphere and get this cycle started is a good customer, and like it or not, one of the world's largest markets for $CO_2$ is EOR. If Carbon Engineering develops a way to source $CO_2$ from the air at a cost that is reasonably competitive with the flue gas capture process that in part supplies the EOR industry, that would be an enormous achievement. But it is of course not flue gas capture that we should first seek to replace, but rather the utterly outrageous practice of mining $CO_2$ from caverns in Colorado, transporting it via pipeline to Texas, only to then rebury it in the EOR process. I make no moral judgment about this $CO_2$ mining – it obviously fulfills a market need – but the fact that we are pumping to the surface safely buried $CO_2$ rather than using the superabundance of the stuff in which we are already drowning is from a climate perspective CRAZY! If the aforementioned direct air capture plant in West Texas can begin to put an end to that, it would be a major climate contribution.

Direct air capture facilities don't need to be enormous. Many are conceived in a modular fashion, such that a large facility may consist of several modules. Small ones such as those conceived by Climeworks could fit in a back yard. That said, in a sector where dramatic cost reduction is key, Carbon Engineering has put its faith in the economies of scale that derive from massive facilities. The horse race is underway and early results should be revealing by the middle of this decade.

The third competitor generally seen as being in this race is Global Thermostat. Founded in 2010 and based in New York, it is the brainchild of two Columbia University professors who sourced their initial financing from the Seagram Company heir Edgar Bronfman Jr. Global Thermostat's patented capture process is intended to be applicable to both flue and direct air capture and aims to take advantage of waste heat generated by industrial facilities to power its carbon capture operations. It claims that not only can it turn power plants carbon neutral, it can actually make them carbon sinks, removing more carbon from both the flue and direct air than the power plant emits. In 2019, Global Thermostat signed a major agreement with ExxonMobil to evaluate the potential scalability of its technology with the hope that pilot projects at ExxonMobil facilities might follow. Perhaps even more than its competitors, Global Thermostat is focused in the near term primarily on the carbon use market, seeking customers who will pay for captured $CO_2$ in such sectors as plastics, food and beverages, greenhouses, fertilizers, building materials, synthetic fuels, and EOR.[21]

Of course, the dream is that eventually we might be taking carbon out of the air neither to prospect for more oil nor to replace oil in airliners and trucks, but rather to bury it under the ground for climate purposes – not just recycling the carbon already in the climate system but reducing our atmospheric concentrations. This is not carbon use, but carbon sequestration. Unless one is unreasonably optimistic about the mitigation that we will undertake in the coming decades, it is hard to imagine an acceptable future without huge amounts of DACCS, but it is also hard to imagine how we will pay for that. The faster and farther we get down the learning and cost curves on this technology, the easier it will be to imagine such a future.

# Section IV
# SOLAR RADIATION MANAGEMENT

# 13 SOLAR RADIATION MANAGEMENT ALTERNATIVES

In this chapter, we are going to leap over the divider in our geoengineering toolbox to the other set of instruments. We have for the last few chapters focused on how we might remove carbon first from our emissions streams and then from the atmosphere itself and bury it safely back underground. I can't foresee a world in which we *won't* need to do that, in a big way and for a long time. We will need to perfect those tools, and more crucially, we will need to organize the world to pay the trillions of dollars required to deploy them year in and year out for decades to come.

But there are other levers we can pull. Not perfect levers. They won't obviate the need for mitigation, adaptation, and carbon dioxide removal (CDR). But they could prove handy levers. Unlike CDR, some may prove eye-wateringly cheap, which could hasten their adoption. The basic concept is simple. Our problem is that our stock of greenhouse gases in the atmosphere has increased to the point that it is interfering with the Earth's ability to shed its excess energy. We have an energy imbalance, with more energy entering the climate system than leaving it, causing the planet to heat up. So yes, we should assist the planet to restore its ability to shed heat by thinning the blanket of GHGs that are trapping in that energy. But, what if at the same time, we shifted some of our attention to the other side of the energy balance equation – the incoming energy. In theory, if we could reduce the amount of energy coming in, that would offset the Earth's reduced ability to shed heat. Less energy leaving, but less arriving too. If we could in some way turn down the level of energy coming from the Sun, then we could restore the balance at a lower level and the Earth would stop heating up.

Of course, there is no practical way to turn down the Sun. It's very big and very hot and I know of no one who is thinking of trying to mess with that. The popular press sometimes gets batty with headlines that suggest solar geoengineering would "dim the Sun," but that's not an accurate description of the concept. The idea is to find ways to cause the Earth to absorb a little less of the incoming sunlight. The objective would not be to change the Sun, but instead to change how the Sun impacts us. After all, there are already lots of mechanisms in the atmosphere and on the planet's surface that deflect back out to space a portion of the incoming radiation. As we reviewed in Chapter 2, the Earth's albedo is about 30 percent, meaning that only 70 percent of the incoming solar radiation is absorbed by the Earth's climate system. The other 30 percent gets reflected back out to space without interfering with our energy equation. The principal drivers of albedo are clouds in our lower atmosphere and snow/ice on the Earth's surface. But all sorts of other features on the surface are also light in color and therefore also contribute to albedo, including sand, light-colored crops, foam on the sea, and white buildings. Anything exposed to the Sun and light in color.

A productive way to frame the problem of "dialing down sunlight" is to consider how we might increase our albedo. All we would need to do is increase that reflectivity ratio by 1 or 2 percent – from 30 percent say to 32 percent – and we would offset all the excess heat that is building up in the climate system. This is still an enormous task – the Earth is pretty huge – but it no longer seems as impossible as dimming the Sun. There must be ways that we could increase the reflectivity of the Earth and reduce the input of solar energy. This chapter reviews most of the ideas that are receiving serious attention as to how we might do that.

## Surface Modifications

For starters, why don't we just paint everything white? Everything. Roofs, buildings, cars, streets, sidewalks, every built structure and manufactured product that sits outside.

This sounds silly, but is only partly silly. Some things – like solar panels – have functional reasons why they need to be black, but most things don't. Roofs, buildings, and pavements, particularly in urban areas, would be a very promising place to start. Cities are well known to suffer from summer heat island effects whereby the urban core can be several degrees hotter than the surrounding countryside. A major reason for that is all the built structures and paved surfaces that soak up and then re-radiate solar energy. The Global Cool Cities Alliance estimates that roofs typically comprise 20–25 percent of urban surfaces, with pavements almost double that at 40 percent.[1] If those surfaces were re-engineered to reflect rather than absorb sunlight, they would exert a cooling rather than warming effect. We don't in fact need everything to be monochromatically white – shades of light gray and red would also do. And pavements could be reconstituted to include reflective materials rather than painted over. But cool roofs and pavements would result in cooler cities on the hottest days of the year, not only reducing the heat island effect, but thereby reducing smog and energy requirements as well. Some studies show that cool roofs would reduce air conditioning requirements by more than 20 percent, but the greatest impact would be felt in non-conditioned buildings, where people are therefore most heat-exposed.[2]

None of this is technologically novel. The whitewashed houses of Greece and elsewhere around the Mediterranean make clear that people have understood this for a very long time. It is for good reason that people break out their white clothes for summer. But we mostly laid aside this ancient wisdom when we built out modern cities of glass and steel buildings in a sea of blacktop. California's Title 24 Energy Efficiency Building Standard exemplifies a building code in which the benefits of lighter cities are recognized. Over half of the world's population now lives in cities, a proportion that is expected to rise to 70 percent by 2040.[3] Therefore, cooler cities on the hottest days would reduce heat stress on most people – a substantial achievement.

However, what would reduce heat stress for residents of Fresno or for that matter New Delhi on the hottest days of the summer won't save the world. Urban areas cover just 3 percent of the land surface[4] of a planet 70 percent of which is covered by water. The 2009 report on Geoengineering by the Royal Society estimated that if we painted virtually all of our built structures white – comprising a total land area 10 percent larger than India – that would remediate just 12 percent of the warming that has occurred since the preindustrial baseline.[5] That's nearly one-eighth of our warming thus far, so offsetting that would be a big deal, but this won't be the primary solution to the climate problem.

The cool roofs idea flips a relatively small amount of the Earth's surface from highly absorptive (black – albedo close to o) to highly reflective (white – albedo close to 1.0). An alternative approach to increase aggregate surface albedo would be to take large swathes of the land and make them just a little more reflective. This might be done by bioengineering crops, grasslands, and forests to be a slightly lighter shade of green, increasing their albedo from roughly 0.15 to 0.20, just 5 percent.[6] We don't want to make them much lighter – after all, we are contemplating forcing plants to reflect back some of the very sunlight which they need to absorb for photosynthesis. But perhaps a small change in the biosphere could make a substantial difference for the planet. The Royal Society estimated the potential of this to be five times that of cool roofs, capable of offsetting more than half the warming to date.

Nonetheless, the potential drawbacks here should be obvious. We are contemplating repopulating the world with Frankenplants. If they are a little lighter than what they are replacing, that may reduce their productivity and nutritional value, on which the rest of the land-based food web depends. White roofs don't breed, but lightened plants would, so if something went wrong, this could be hard to contain or reverse. This might be presented as a (light) green solution, but it would in fact be quite literally GMOs gone wild.

A different way to think big with respect to surface albedo would be to cover large parts of the Earth with giant white tarpaulins of some sort, like a Christo installation gone mad. But of course, this is mad. If we intend to reflect an additional 2 percent of incoming sunlight, we need to cover 2 percent of the planet's surface area (a bit more in fact, since the land albedo is already around 0.15, but let's not quibble). Only 30 percent of the planet is land, so that's 6.67 percent of the land area, and 12 percent of that is covered in ice, so there is no point in wrapping that – it's already white. So now we are up to 7.8 percent of the ice-free land that we have to tarpaulin, or 3.9 million square miles. That's the size of China, with Japan and both Koreas tossed in. Somehow I'm guessing China won't go for this. One could suggest that that's a straw man (of course it is) and that one would more sensibly do this in the world's most unproductive places such as deserts, but would Niger be more enthusiastic about this than China? Would Arizona voters opt to destroy their Sonoran ecosystems?

An equally dubious concept is to focus on the 70 percent rather than the 30 percent of the Earth's surface and churn the seas to create white reflective surface bubbles. But such bubbles have a lifetime measured in seconds, which can be extended to several minutes via the additional of certain chemicals.[7] Nonetheless, given the limited lifetimes, the churning must be constant during daylight hours at least, and we would still need a China-plus sized patch of ocean in which to deploy this. Our salvation won't lie in bubbles on the sea.

## Ice

The most reflective surfaces on the Earth's surface are those covered with ice, so if we want to increase the planet's overall albedo, focusing on that seems like a promising avenue. Unfortunately, however, as one might expect in a warming world, we are losing ice cover rather than gaining it. Less of the Earth is permanently covered in ice than was the case 200 hundred years ago,[8] and seasonal ice and snow cover is shrinking both spatially and temporally,[9] i.e., both in how much area is snow or ice bound, and in how many days per year it is blanketed in white. As discussed in Chapter 2, this is happening not only on land, but on the Arctic Ocean, where the ice cap continues to shrink. Where the ice retreat can be most dramatically observed is the world's glaciers in tropical and mid-latitudes. They will contribute to sea level rise since the water previously suspended in them will trickle into the oceans, but the magnitude of that will be small.[10]

In addition to being year-round ice, another distinguishing feature of glaciers is that they move. In fact, they flow like rivers, though of course comparatively quite slowly – at a "glacial pace" one might say, measured in meters and sometimes kilometers per year. The mechanism by which Antarctica is contributing to sea level rise is not via the warm weather melting of its ice cover, but by its ice sliding into the sea. When a glacier meets the sea, there is often an ice shelf that extends out into the sea. This is the ice that formed on land, slowly flowed downhill to the sea, and was then pushed by the ice behind it out onto the sea. The ice shelf (the ice in the sea) may be grounded on the sea floor, or floating in the sea, or progressively the former and then the latter. Eventually, the front lip of the shelf, which is directly in contact with the sea water, may calve off from the shelf or disintegrate along the grounding line and form an iceberg. This naturally is most common in the summer season, when the water is relatively warm and may weaken the leading edge of the ice shelf. If the iceberg is not grounded on the seabed or obstructed by islands, it may then float freely. If it floats towards the equator, which it will do in almost any direction if it started near the South Pole, it will eventually encounter warmer water, whereupon it will melt and disappear.

Nonetheless, if a floating ice shelf becomes an iceberg and then sea water, that does not contribute to rising seas, since the ice shelf was already afloat. It is the flow of land ice into the sea that adds to sea level. There is of course also a countervailing cycle, wherein water is harvested from the sea by the atmosphere. Some of that drifts over Antarctica and precipitates out as snow, replacing some of the ice that flowed to the sea. Most of Antarctica is classified as desert, since it is generally too cold to snow, but of course there must be some precipitation – that's how the ice got there after all. So the real question in respect of sea level rise is whether Antarctica is shedding ice faster than it is gaining snow. As the planet warms, most of that heat is finding its way into the oceans rather than into the atmosphere. Even the frigid waters around Antarctica are not immune to that warming, so the floating ice shelves are being bathed in ever warmer water. Quite predictably, this is speeding the rate at which ice shelves are cleaving off into the sea and floating away as icebergs. This in turn has an effect upstream (imagining once again a glacier as a river of ice), in that the ice shelves at the glacial terminus previously acted as corks in the bottle, buttressing the glacier and damming its flow. If the ice shelf disintegrates and disappears, then the landed ice of the glacier can much more easily flow into the sea. The glacial flow rate speeds up.

While this is happening in many places in Antarctica, there are two particular glaciers – the Thwaites and the Pine Island – that appear particularly vulnerable to an "uncorking" that could speed their flow rates dramatically and substantially increase sea level rise in this century.[11] Over the last decade, satellite imagery has revealed the development of damage areas in the shear zones of these glaciers.[12] The damage consists of crevasses and open fractures that will eventually lead to accelerated glacial calving and the disintegration of the leading edge, causing the glacier to retreat. It is clear that the process is both accelerating and self-reinforcing, but how quickly and substantially this will contribute to sea level rise is the subject of ongoing study.

Nonetheless, some scientists wonder whether this sort of runaway glacial slide into the sea could be amenable to engineering solutions. One concept is to either remove or refreeze the film of liquid water on which many glaciers glide.[13] The friction generated as the huge mass of ice scrapes along a rock bed melts the water at the base of the glacier, which in turn lubricates its slide. If wells were drilled into the glacier all the way to the bedrock, that liquid water could theoretically be either pumped out or refrozen, thereby removing the lubricant and impeding the flow. To the extent that the glacier flows into a narrow fjord as many do, another alternative would be to build artificial islands in the fjord that are grounded to the seabed.[14] These would jam (though not halt) the ice flow in the fjord, buttressing the ice shelf and impeding the escape of icebergs. Yet a third idea would be to build an undersea berm at the mouth of the fjord that would substantially reduce the circulation of seawater into and out of the fjord.[15] This would expose the ice shelf to a reduced volume of warm water, perhaps stabilizing it and allowing it to recover. None of these ideas has yet been field-tested, and each of them may prove to have unidentified drawbacks or environmental effects. Massive engineering projects in some of the most remote and inhospitable conditions on Earth could prove dangerous or entirely untenable, but it remains tempting to consider whether Miami and Venice could be defended in Antarctica rather than in Biscayne Bay and the Lido.

Antarctica's ice sheet is by far the largest in the world, with enough water to raise global mean sea levels by about 60 meters[16] were it all to melt (which it won't), but the other ice shelf that really matters is that of Greenland, which contains 7 meters of potential sea level rise.[17] Greenland is vulnerable to the same glacial flow dynamics as Antarctica, but it does not sit quite on the top of the world. Northerly and frigid though it is, it is actually far enough south that it experiences substantial direct melting in the summer months particularly in its southern reaches, with ponds of meltwater forming on the surface of the ice. As with the Arctic Ocean, blue meltwater where there once was white ice means more absorption of solar energy, which creates more meltwater. Much of this meltwater eventually tunnels down under the ice and finds a way to the sea, contributing directly to sea level rise.

There is little in the geoengineering toolbox that would make ice more resistant to melting, but one creative concept is pursued by the Arctic Ice Project, formerly known by the catchier name Ice911.[18] By whatever name, the idea is to make ice that is already pretty reflective yet more so by sprinkling on top of it a layer of silica glass.[19] Though "lightening ice" would seem a bit futile, it should be noted that yet another small but not insignificant source of warming is the emission of black carbon, which floats around the world before descending everywhere, including on the world's ice surfaces. That tiny fleck of black is nonetheless highly absorptive of solar radiation, commencing or enhancing ice melt. To the extent that dusting that same ice with a little glass can help it reflect more sunlight, the waning ice of Greenland, the Arctic Ocean, and Kilimanjaro might welcome the help.

Intriguing though that may seem, problems with this leap off the page. The glass's behavior in the environment and effect on plants, animals, and the hydrological cycle are all unknown.[20] Delivering any amount of glass to the entire surface of Greenland or the Arctic ice cap would be a massive industrial undertaking that might do as much harm

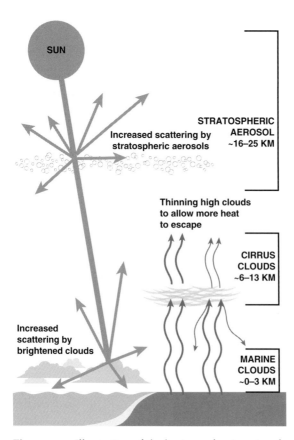

Figure 13.1 Illustration of the basic mechanisms involved in marine cloud brightening, cirrus cloud thinning, and stratospheric aerosol injection[21]

via transport emissions as this intervention would ameliorate. And were it to snow (as it tends to do in snowy places), then our reflective coating is buried beneath the freshly fallen snow and is no longer helping us. One would struggle to place much faith in this.

## Marine Cloud Brightening

If the objective is to block a bit of incoming sunlight, many prominent researchers see more promise above our heads than beneath our feet (see Figure 13.1). After all, clouds already reflect over 20 percent of the incoming sunlight that would otherwise enter the climate system, more than twice as much as does surface albedo. I am always quite struck taking off on an airliner under leaden skies only to see the brilliant sunshine once the plane breaks through the clouds. Clearly there is a lot of light and potential heat that those clouds are deflecting away from the surface below. If we could just get clouds to reflect away a percent or two more incoming sunlight, that might well do the trick.

There is a long history of attempts to seed clouds, both for agricultural benefit and for military purposes. The US famously flew over 2,000 missions over Vietnam[22] in an effort to boost rainfall and wash out the Ho Chi Minh Trail, ultimately to little effect. In the same era, Israel attempted to increase rainfall, with mixed and limited results.[23] More recently, China also ran an active Weather Modification Office which was called into action to variously seed or impede rains including a famous effort to stave off downpours that might have washed out the opening ceremony for the 2008 Olympics.[24] For the most part, these weather modification attempts have had limited success, though not quite none, so China for instance is devoting new efforts to it in Tibet via the Sky River project. We haven't yet found an effective way to harness ephemeral clouds for our purpose, and yet they are such ubiquitous and effective Sun blockers that they are too tempting to ignore, so the research continues.

The most promising idea relates to a particular type of cloud, big puffy stratocumulus clouds that appear over about a quarter of the world's oceans. The Twomey effect is a well-established bit of cloud physics positing that a cloud's reflectivity is dependent on the size distribution of the water droplets within it.[25] For the same amount of liquid water, a cloud with lots of small droplets will be more reflective than one with fewer, bigger droplets. This is commonly demonstrated

**Figure 13.2** Twomey effect demonstration. Image provided by Dr. Stephen Salter[26]

by comparing two jars of transparent glass beads (see Figure 13.2). If the beads are a bit smaller than common BB (i.e. ball bearing) pellets, the jar of beads appears gray in color, but if the beads are 100 times smaller, the jar looks white, like salt in a shaker. Left to their own devices in clean air, clouds tend to form large droplets. However, air over land is filled with aerosol particles of both natural (dust) and anthropogenic (air pollution) origin, so clouds over land have loads of small nuclei on which to condense, and tend therefore to be comprised of lots of the small-sized droplets that are ideal for reflecting sunlight. In the mid-ocean, on the other hand, the air tends to be clean and relatively aerosol free. This means there are far fewer ambient condensation nuclei available, such that marine clouds are comprised of large-sized droplets that produce lower reflectivity.

The impact of impregnating marine air with additional nuclei is plainly visible from an aerial view of the "ship tracks" that crisscross the world's oceans. Large ocean-going vessels are mostly powered by combustion engines that spew soot and aerosols above their wakes. Long after the ships have passed, their paths are etched in the sky via white reflective clouds. The ships aren't making those clouds but are instead demonstrating the Twomey effect in action (see Figure 13.3), sprinkling into existing clouds additional condensation nuclei that produce more small droplets and brighten the clouds.

**Figure 13.3** Ship tracks off the US West Coast. *Source*: NASA Earth Observatory[27]

In 1990 British physicist John Latham proposed to turn this incidental effect of marine navigation into a climate solution.[28] If we sprayed into the mid-ocean air lots of new nuclei, we could brighten marine clouds not merely in shipping lanes, but all over the oceans where conditions are favorable. And while soot from boat engines would do the trick, so too would an entirely natural aerosol source that happens to be superabundant in the mid-oceans just where we need it – salt water! If we hoover up ocean water and spray it into the air in the right droplet size range, some of that water will be dispersed through the marine boundary layer, which is a 1–2 km thick stratum of air that sits directly above the sea and is constantly exchanging energy and moisture with it. We don't have to propel the water very far into the air, according to British scientist Stephen Salter. If we just loft it above the ocean surface, the natural turbulence of rising and falling air will loft lots of it up to the height of the low clouds we are seeking to affect. Once there, much of the water will evaporate, leaving salt residues – perfect little nuclei on which water in the cloud can condense. If distributed over large portions of the oceans, our newly brightened marine clouds would in theory cool the seas and increase the Earth's overall albedo, thereby offsetting some of the warming caused by increased concentrations of GHGs.

In theory. There are small pockets of researchers around the world including at the University of Washington trying to figure out whether this is truly a viable and scalable solution, but most of the big questions remain unanswered. Clouds are fiddly. Small changes in local conditions can make clouds appear or disappear. It's not merely the presence of water vapor that affects the formation of a cloud, but temperature, atmospheric pressure, and relative humidity. It's clear that the Twomey effect is real, but if we are seeding our clouds with salt water resulting in numerous smaller cloud droplets, we might possibly be increasing their rates of evaporation and this could inhibit cloud formation to begin with.[29] Alternatively, such seeding may brighten the cloud temporarily but cause it to rain prematurely, shortening its lifetime and compromising its sun-shielding effectiveness.[30] Not only do we not yet understand the physics here – not everyone is confident even about the sign, meaning it's not yet clear whether implementing such a program would decrease or increase warming. Heavens!

On the other hand, if marine cloud brightening worked, it would have myriad advantages. The logistics of implementing it would be quite straightforward. Build a bunch of boats or floating rigs similar to oil drilling platforms, and spray salt water from them into the air. Stephen Salter's estimate is that several hundreds of such boats weighing 90 tonnes each (the size of small ferries) would suffice to cool the Earth by 1°C,[31] though that is a very preliminary estimate. But a few hundred boats would be a vanishingly inexpensive climate solution. It also would be uncontroversial relative to lots of other geoengineering solutions. If we ask the world's permission to cover China in cheesecloth or divert trillions of dollars into vacuuming up carbon from the atmosphere, those will be very short discussions ending in "no." But if we say we are going to build a fleet of ferries to spray sea water into the ocean air, I suspect most people will shrug.

It would also be highly targetable in both time and space. If we are having a particularly hot year in Africa, crank up the marine cloud brightening in the Indian Ocean and Kenya will cool in days. If a Pinatubo- or Tambora-sized volcano erupts, turn off the salt sprayers and the artificially brightened clouds will disappear with the next rainstorm, meaning we would no longer add cooling in what would be an abnormally cool year. Very few of the tools in our toolbox would allow that sort of precision response.

## Cirrus Cloud Thinning

The other significant cloud modification climate intervention idea involves a similar strategy, to produce an opposite outcome. While low, thick clouds block a lot of incoming sunlight, high wispy cirrus clouds are too thin to do much reflecting. On the other hand, they are pretty effective at trapping outgoing longwave radiation and thereby acting as a greenhouse gas (look back at Figure 13.1). Cirrus cloud thinning would artificially hollow out such clouds, reducing their lifetime and effectiveness in thickening the blanket. Our technique for doing this will sound a lot like marine cloud brightening. We would seed the clouds with condensation nuclei to change the size distribution of their particle density. However, here, we would change matters in the opposite direction, precipitating the creation of larger rather than smaller particles.

Unlike the low-level clouds that were the target of marine cloud brightening, cirrus clouds are comprised of ice crystals. As the water vapor freezes, it naturally forms small, homogeneous particles that have a long residence time in the sky. Introducing aerosols as condensation nuclei (no longer salt water but chemicals or perhaps dust) would cause ice crystals to grow rapidly and deplete water vapor, resulting in a heterogeneous distribution of particles, some small, but some large. These larger average particle sizes would increase settling velocities, speeding the sedimentation process (i.e., falling to the Earth) and reducing the lifetime of the cloud. A thinner cirrus cloud layer would mean a slightly thinner blanket, enhancing the Earth's ability to shed radiation.

We might do this by spraying aerosols from high flying aircraft into the regions of the sky where such clouds are found. Lofting the particles into the heavens would be an unusual mission but doable. On the other hand, if the physics of marine cloud brightening are unproven, those of cirrus cloud thinning are "unproven squared." Again, we are not even confident about the sign, and therefore don't know how much research funding this deserves. This is another intriguing theory, but not necessarily a handy tool, and in all events, not a near-term prospect.

I should note that I have placed this theoretical intervention in the wrong side of our toolbox. It is really another idea for thinning the blanket and enhancing the Earth's ability to shed radiation, but as it is another cloud modification that shares some characteristics with marine cloud brightening, it seemed sensible to slot it in here.

## Space-Based Solar Shields

Ascending yet farther into the heavens, another major class of prospective solar radiation management techniques involves using space-based assets to intercept some sunlight before it even gets to the top of our atmosphere. These ideas are not new. In fact, by the standards of geoengineering, they are positively ancient, dating all the way back to a proposal by Mautner and Parks in 1990.[32] However, very little work has been done to advance such ideas, with only 2 percent of climate intervention academic literature devoted to them.[33] In an attempt to return focus to this field, David Keith and associates convened a conference at Harvard in late 2019 that assembled scientists, scholars, and entrepreneurs from both the geoengineering and the space communities to consider whether space-based geoengineering seemed plausible. While considerable attention was initially given to arrays of low Earth orbit satellites similar to those being launched for communications and

Earth observation, these were set aside out of concerns about both space debris and the aesthetics of night-sky pollution and flickering sunlight. Attention flowed instead to the creation of a sunshield located at the Sun–Earth Lagrangian equilibrium point[34] (which is abbreviated as L1), where orbital mechanics would facilitate a stable shield that could be kept in place with (relatively) minimal effort. Quoting a post-conference publication,

> [An] L1 sunshield ... capable of intercepting 1 percent of the sunlight headed for Earth – an amount that might be expected to counter half the radiative force of a doubling of $CO_2$ – would need to have at least an area of nearly 1 million $km^2$, which is to say around that of Egypt, but more likely be many times that size.[35]

Such a shield might be constructed either out of highly efficient engineered scattering structures manufactured on Earth and launched into place, or out of space dust harvested from passing meteors. Either array could be kept in place via gravitational shepherding from small asteroids or via electrostatic or electromagnetic confinement.

All L1 sunshield ideas would be an "order of magnitude more ambitious than anything previously attempted in space" and would therefore be reliant upon the continued expansion of space technology.[36] The costs involved might be in the $1 trillion range which would be vastly more costly than say marine cloud brightening, but likely much cheaper than the damages deriving from unchecked climate change. The timeframe envisions commencing the construction of such a shield by mid-century, ramping into full maturity by 2100.

Advantages of space-based climate intervention over the atmospheric kind include the fact that its effects would be far more even across the globe than those of cloud modifications or surface albedo solutions, which may make it politically more palatable. It would act as a direct reduction of the solar constant, making its impacts more predictable. A more complex L1 sunshield design could block specific infrared wavelengths in the incoming sunlight rather than scattering all of it, which would have significantly less impact on the hydrological cycle than other forms of solar radiation management. This might allow a geoengineered climate quite comparable to the historical climate in terms not only of temperature but of rainfall.

Should this seem rather half-baked (quarter-baked?), the conference participants would agree, concluding that while an $L_1$ sunshield is not a plausible near-term goal or aspiration, neither should it be ruled out in the longer run. Like so much else in geoengineering, it requires much more research.

If none of the above sounds terribly likely to save our world from the impacts of climate change, you are seeing it as I do. Nonetheless, as all of these ideas pop up from time to time in the media, it was important that we systematically review them and take stock. This is a list of potentially promising ideas some of which merit further urgent exploration, and in a few cases, would constitute no-brainer small contributions to a larger solution (white roofs), but none of them sound like a near-term kill switch – a reliable "break glass in case of emergency" intervention. Fortunately, there is one tool still in this side of the toolbox that more nearly fits that description.

# 14 STRATOSPHERIC AEROSOL INJECTION

In rummaging around our toolbox, we have finally come to stratospheric aerosol injection (SAI) – what many of you may have expected this entire book to be about. This is the big, bad, scary idea of spraying chemicals into the sky to slightly reduce the incoming sunlight. Whatever controversy this book may engender will mostly center on SAI, and not without reason. SAI *is* frightening – a gigantic global experiment with the only planet we have, with consequences that we would work tirelessly to predict but that may surprise us, nonetheless. There likely are hidden, irreversible tipping points in unrestrained climate change, but there may be in SAI as well. Even after we commence implementation, it may be years (or even decades) before we properly understand its impacts. And the governance problems associated with obtaining informed consent to do this from the entire human race both living and unborn – how possibly could we achieve that? Are we really so desperate that we should even consider this?

Ah ... yup. Once you remove the rose-colored glasses and methodically work through the alternatives, you realize that we are not on a good trajectory. There are no effective, low-cost options. The effective high-cost options would require decades if not lifetimes to remediate the problem, and therefore this option needs to be on the table. Not the only option. Definitely not the first option, or a perfect option, or a sufficient option all by itself. But a tool worth evaluating? You bet. So, let's evaluate.

## The Mechanics of SAI: A Planetary Veil

SAI would have the same objective as everything else in the solar radiation management (SRM) side of our toolbox – reducing slightly the amount of solar radiation absorbed by the climate system. But, like marine cloud brightening or cirrus cloud thinning, it would operate in the atmosphere rather than either on the planet's surface or in outer space. The objective once again would be to increase Earth's albedo by 1 or 2 percent and thereby restore the balance between incoming and outgoing radiation. The basic concept should by now be quite familiar. However, instead of lofting aerosols intended to modify the properties of clouds, we would intend that the aerosols themselves do the reflecting we desire – microscopic mirrors hoisted into the atmosphere to deflect just a little bit of the incoming sunlight.

To focus on the mechanics a bit, aerosols suspended in our atmosphere scatter some of the incoming sunlight. Some of it is down-scattered or forward-scattered, bumping into the aerosol, deflecting its path a bit, but still striking the planet's surface and spilling its energy into our climate system. But some of it is up-scattered or back-scattered, ricocheting off the aerosol and shooting back out into space. We know it works this way because it happens all the time. Air is naturally full of aerosols (dust, sea salt, bits of organic matter), and human activity supplements that (soot, sulfates, nitrates, black carbon).[1] While some of these substances are more efficient than others at scattering incoming sunlight, they all do so to some degree. Rather ironically then, the air pollution that often enshrouds cities in smog has a beneficial climate effect, shielding those same cities from a bit of the solar energy and therefore heat they would otherwise absorb. However, no one seriously suggests this is a positive trade. We need to clean our air, and separately we need to deal with the climate problem.

A better proxy for how SAI might operate is volcanoes, which can vent large amounts of sulfur dioxide ($SO_2$) into the atmosphere. After a few weeks, the $SO_2$ precursor evolves into $H_2SO_4$ (sulfuric acid), in which form it is then an effective scatterer of sunlight for as long as it remains airborne. Most of the $SO_2$ that the Earth emits is not from eruptive volcanoes, but from passive outgassing[2]: fumaroles, sulfur springs, mud pots, and other openings in the Earth's crust that vent gas more or less continuously. The $SO_2$ emitting from these sources mostly stays in the lower atmosphere (the troposphere) and has a residence time measured in days,[3] after which it settles back down to Earth. However, a rare, powerful volcanic eruption can blast $SO_2$ all the way up into the stratosphere. This gets the $SO_2$ above the turbulent vertical mixing zone and into a relatively stable region of the sky where its lifetime is more nearly a year than a week. Most of it will be wafted by the slow-moving Brewer–Dobson circulation towards the pole of whatever hemisphere it started in, scattering sunlight all the way.[4] Only once it has completed its poleward journey would it descend back down to Earth in the Arctic or Antarctic.

Locally spectacular volcanic eruptions occur somewhere in the world several times annually, but the ones that blast enough $SO_2$ to the stratosphere to substantially affect global weather happen a few times per century. The last real monster was Mount Pinatubo on the island of Luzon in the Philippines. It exploded in June 1991 and erupted for four days,[5] launching a huge cloud of soot and ash miles into the sky while sending waves of lava rolling down its slopes. The soot and ash covered nearby Clark Air Force Base in several inches of muck, and was carried by the winds to mainland Asia, but for the most part, it stayed regionally confined.[6] On the other hand, the roughly 20 million tonnes of $SO_2$ that the eruption blasted all the way to the stratosphere quickly began to circulate around the globe.[7] Given that the Earth completes a full rotation on its axis every day, the east/west mixing of gases in its atmosphere is quite efficient, and the $SO_2$ that originated in Luzon was distributed around the Earth at that latitude (between 20°S and 30°N) within two weeks.[8] Over the following year or so, that circumferentially distributed $SO_2$ evolved to sulfuric acid and completed its slow poleward migration to the Arctic, thereby covering the entire hemisphere north of 15 degrees[9] with a thin reflective veil. This deflected enough sunlight to cool the affected areas by 0.7°C[10] and reduce global average surface temperatures (the southern hemisphere was barely affected)[11] by 0.5°C. This is the principle behind SAI at work.

More than 100 years earlier in 1883, Krakatoa, a small island in Indonesia's Banda Strait, erupted spectacularly, plunging global average temperatures by as much as 1.2°C in the following year.[12] The eruption in 1815 of Mount Tambora (also in what is today Indonesia) caused 1816 to be known as "the year without a summer" in Europe and North America[13]. Snow was reported in tropical Taiwan,[14] starving rioters rampaged in German cities,[15] and retired President Thomas Jefferson's ruined corn crop at Monticello drove him further into debt.[16] Yet earlier major eruptions are theorized to have helped precipitate the French Revolution,[17] the fall of Constantinople,[18] and the raiding culture of the Vikings.[19]

There is then no doubt that large masses of $SO_2$ injected into the stratosphere can, and periodically do, dramatically cool the Earth. But as our earlier consideration of clouds demonstrates, the crucial question is whether we can somehow domesticate the cooling capability of sulfur and bend it to our purpose. How might we create anthropogenic volcanoes?

At a conceptual level, the answer is simple. We don't need the heat, soot, lava, and pressure of a volcano. All we need is the $SO_2$, which we would need to deliver to a high altitude every day for as long as we want the cooling effects of SAI to last. Luckily, $SO_2$ is quite common on the Earth. Not only are there fumaroles constantly venting the stuff all over the planet, but sulfur – the basic building block of $SO_2$ – is present in all sorts of natural compounds but particularly our fossil fuels. In refining oil or processing natural gas, most of the sulfur is commonly removed, so the world produces literally millions of tonnes[20] of the stuff annually as a byproduct of the oil and gas business. It is therefore extraordinarily cheap because we manufacture it irrespective of world demand. While the cost has lately been in the range of $100/tonne, there are times in the last decade when the price has fallen below $50[21] – more or less giving it away to make room for the next batch tumbling out of the refinery. Getting sulfur is no problem.

And neither is getting it up into the sky. To be clear, we need to get it high in the sky – roughly 20 km or 65,000 feet – such that it is comfortably into the stratosphere and will endure for a year rather than a week. That's more than twice as high as Mount Everest and almost twice as high as an airliner normally cruises, so we can't waft this from a smokestack or dump it from 737 airliners on their way to Dallas. But there are lots of ways to get things as high as 20 km. Rockets of course regularly deposit satellites at altitudes of 200–500 km[22] and can go to the moon if need be, but are expensive overkill for our rather piddling 20 km. Balloons can get this high but wouldn't loft much of a payload. Modernized big guns could easily loft a shell to 20 km, though deploying a large mass of gas would require millions of shells.[23] In theory, one could build a *really* long hose, tether it to balloons that would loft it to 20 km, and pump the $SO_2$ up the hose, though material science has not evolved to a point where we could build such a thing. After brainstorming about dazzling possibilities, one returns back to the simple idea: why don't we just pile this gunk into an airplane and fly it up there? Sure, most jets don't get this high, but a few do, or nearly so. The cold war era U-2 spy plane in which Gary Powers was shot down got above 18 km, as did the roughly contemporaneous WB-57. NASA still operates a few civilianized versions of both for high-altitude research. The SR-71 Blackbird got equally high before it was retired, and the US Air Force operates over 100 unmanned Global Hawks which top out near these heights. Each of these aircraft carries just a few tonnes of payload – little more than a pilot (maybe) and a few cameras – so, as currently configured, they couldn't deploy much aerosol, but they demonstrate that we can build aircraft that get to the required altitude.

Having focused a bit on SAI's location in space, let's as well try to locate it in time. It's difficult to say of course, but the first clarifying statement would be – not soon. For starters, the fleet of high-payload, high-altitude crop duster aircraft that would be the logical and cost-effective method by which to deploy this doesn't yet exist, and under normal circumstances would take five to seven years to develop and manufacture. In fact, it wasn't even on the drawing boards so to speak until January 2020, when I and a few former Boeing engineers presented the first preliminary designs for such an aircraft (more about that in Chapter 15). But ours is not a funded effort. No financially capable government or corporation has allocated the few billion dollars that would be necessary to get this rolling. At this point, we remain in the preliminary conceptual stage of such an effort, clarifying its feasibility and costs, meaning that from a hardware standpoint alone, we are at least a decade away from being capable of such a program.

But the creation of the deployment hardware is in fact a *short* pole in this tent. It would take much more than a decade to develop the scientific understandings necessary to prudently commence such a program. Volcanoes prove that such an intervention would succeed in its fundamental goal of cooling the planet, but how best to do it, and what risks can and should be avoided? We are only at the beginning of even asking those questions. The research is nearly all still in the lab. The number of field experiments that have been done on SAI remains perilously close to zero. David Keith and my colleagues at Harvard constitute the world's leading research effort into SAI, and the group's total funding stands at $20 million (total, not per year). One would expect hundreds of millions if not billions of dollars to be spent in lab and field research around the world via major government and intergovernmental organizations before we would have the confidence to undertake this, and quite literally none of that is yet being done. We are in my opinion decades (plural) away from implementing SAI.

Nonetheless, the long pole in the tent may well prove to be governance rather than science. How would we obtain enough informed consent from approximately all of humanity to conclude we had the legitimacy to undertake such an intervention? The world is awash with environmental laws and treaties, but none that would seem appropriate forums via which to implement so consequential a program and to adjudicate the harms or unequal distribution of benefits that may derive from it. We will return to these governance challenges later, but as the Montreal to Kyoto to Paris saga demonstrates, the development of legitimate structures by which to govern such a program would likely themselves take decades. So we are not right around the corner from deploying SAI. But might we be ready in the 2040s or 2050s? Maybe. It will depend on how serious we get about research in the current decade and how desperate we become in that later decade.

In all events though, one would hope that the onset of SAI deployment – if we ever get to that – would be characterized by a slow ramp up rather than a flick of a light switch. A prudent program would progress from small, localized experiments to global low-dose experiments. If those proved promising, a cautious approach would be to commence SAI deployment at the smallest detectable scale, ramping up thereafter in prudent small increments as we monitor the impacts and ensure that we are producing the results we intended. Even after the onset of deployment, it may be decades before we would choose to build to the ultimate programmatic scale we might intend. I have been asked whether all this scientific caution and patient consensus building could render SAI too late to solve our climate problem rather than too early. Maybe . . .

## The Potential Benefits of SAI

The reason to consider any of this of course would be the benefits we would hope for from SAI. We could cool the planet. Setting aside for a moment the prudent ramp up suggested above and focusing simply on physical impacts, from what we now know, it appears that SAI could cool the planet a lot and immediately. If we built a deployment fleet of several hundred aircraft (less than the freighter fleet of Fedex), we could haul enough sulfur dioxide to the stratosphere in a year to cool the planet by 2°C the very next year. Boom! A 4°C fleet would more nearly be the size of American Airlines, but could also have an equally swift effect. There is nothing else in our toolbox that would have so dramatic and immediate an impact. Mitigation can't reduce temperatures at all, at least not in the span of a human lifetime. It merely curtails their rise. Adaptation would not stop warming at all. CCS is more mitigation. DACCS and BECCS and everything else in the GGR compartment would likely be built out at a scale that would take generations to buy down temperatures by a degree or two. But the leverage that appears possible with SAI is miraculous.

SAI's wide spectrum of possible temperature impacts also provides some flexibility as to what temperature target we should aim for. Should we simply try to slow the rate of warming to buy time for other interventions to take effect? Perhaps we cut the rate of warming in half to give mitigation, adaptation, and DACCS more time to develop. Or should we preserve temperatures at their current levels and permit no further rise? After all, people worry gravely about the future climate, but few people seem unhappy with the current climate, even though it is already 1.2°C warmer than the preindustrial baseline. Alternatively, we could reverse warming, starting say in 2050 to bring temperatures back to the levels we were happy with in 2020. In theory, any one of these is a plausible objective.

Another benefit of SAI, at least in its early years, is that it is reversible on what is a rapid timeframe in a climate context. Should we observe impacts that are unfavorable, we could halt deployment with the result that in a year or so, all the injected sulfur dioxide would sediment out of the atmosphere and the direct impacts of the program would cease. Not to oversell this point, reversal in a year is not the same as reversal in a day or week, and further, it is entirely possible that climate impacts might continue even after the direct forcing from SAI had ceased. Moreover, an abrupt halt might create problems of its own as noted below, but compared to the time scales required for $CO_2$ levels and temperatures to revert naturally to their preindustrial levels, SAI can be turned on and off rapidly.

Relatedly, there is no biological aspect of an SAI program that could escape our control the way say genetically modified crops or viruses stored in a lab could do. To put it waggishly "sulfur doesn't have sex."

For an intervention that may exert such enormous influence on every living thing on Earth, the cost of SAI is stunningly small. Such a program might have late century costs measured in tens of billions[24] rather than single digit trillions for either DACCS or mitigation,[25] a differential of two orders of magnitude. However, it should be noted that these are apple/orange comparisons, in that SAI would address merely a salient symptom of climate change rather than the underlying cause. Still, as climate interventions go, SAI is remarkably cheap.

## The Risks, Challenges, and Limitations of SAI

However, before we get too carried away with the leverage and versatility of our cheap new toy, we should note that it has limitations, as well as other potential impacts. In addition to affecting temperatures, SAI would affect other climate variables. The first one people worry about is rainfall. Critics commonly state that SAI would reduce rainfall, but the true picture is more nuanced. In a warmer world, the pace of the hydrological cycle increases: more heat, more evaporation, more airborne water vapor, more rain. If SAI then cooled the world, that would have the opposite effect, but there would not be less rain than is natural – there would be less rain than was observed in the artificially wet climate-changed world. Still, even if the currently hotter and wetter world is an anthropogenic artefact, reduced rain might still be regretted.

However, there is yet another nuance here. For the purposes of agriculture and natural ecosystems, it is not actually rain that we care about. It is water availability and soil moisture. In scientific terms, not merely precipitation, but "precipitation minus evaporation." A warmer climate will induce more rain, but also faster evaporation, such that it is not immediately clear whether plants would be more lush in a slightly warmer or slightly cooler climate. As always, more study is required.

The impacts of climate change are not homogeneous across the globe. Eastern Long Island, where I am writing this chapter, has warmed nearly 2°C – twice the global average. SAI may well prove to have similarly heterogeneous effects, although no one yet has good knowledge as to how to map that or where its greater or lesser impacts would lie. This is complicated by the fact that the regional impacts which may emerge may not be a direct result of the atmospheric sulfur load above any given patch of ground, but rather may be due to a change in wind and water circulations, which would likely prove much more difficult to model in advance. One thing that should not be expected, however, is that even a maximal SAI program intended say to return the Earth to its 2020 average temperatures would return every region of the world to its 2020 climate. A world warmed by excess $CO_2$ and then cooled via enhanced $SO_2$ would not be exactly the same as a world in which emissions had stopped in 2020. SAI would not be a perfect antidote.

Nor would it cure everything that might ail us in a warmer world. Most particularly, it would do nothing to stop ocean acidification. The world might be cooler, but the marine die-off would continue unchecked.

SAI also has a high risk of unintended consequences. If it were done at a scale that would have substantial temperature impact, then it may well have other impacts too. We may achieve the lower global average surface temperatures we intended, but with wind and water currents that don't approximate the preindustrial baseline. Or despite the nuance noted above, there may prove to be net changes to water availability after all. Perhaps the ozone recovery is delayed more than we expected. One valid charge that critics level at SAI is that its impacts can only be known with certainty after a global implementation, after which time it may be too late to undo any impacts we turned out not to like. For these and other reasons, it may well prove that SAI is simply a bad idea – a cure worse than the disease it is meant to remediate. It should be research rather than emotion that leads us to such a conclusion, but we should remain humble and open to the prospect that the bottom line may turn out simply to be – no.

If the program were in advanced stages and exerting substantial climate forcing, turning it off would not prove straightforward. SAI is not a one-time intervention wherein we haul a load of sulfates to the stratosphere and then relax. Our sunshield would only remain effective if we continue to tend it. After 12 to 18 months, our deployed aerosols will have completed their journey to the poles and then to the ground, so we would need to replenish the front end of our stratospheric conveyor belt continuously. Every day, year in and year out, for decades and perhaps centuries, until some combination of mitigation, CDR, and natural sinks got atmospheric greenhouse gas concentrations down to acceptable levels.

Given that, SAI is afflicted by a problem known as "termination shock," whereby once we really get going, an abrupt halt brings its own problems. This is not true in the early years of a slowly ramping program – if the early year deployed masses are small, so too would be the climate "snap back" that would result from stopping the program. But once the program was large enough to shield the Earth from say 1° C, then stopping it suddenly would cause that 1°C of warming to happen in roughly a year rather than over decades, which would be yet much more of a shock to everything impacted by climate. Therefore, even if the program proved to have some problematical unintended impact, if it is a large program producing substantial climate impact, it would need to be ramped down over decades rather than simply turned off, or else we wreck the world in a different way.

Making a decision to terminate an SAI program would be greatly complicated by the fact that attributing undesirable impacts to SAI might prove very difficult. If the Indian monsoon doubles in intensity causing massive flooding – or halves, bringing droughts and starvation – what lever would we pull to solve that problem? Was it caused by the SAI program? Or the underlying climate change? Or the continuing air pollution? Or by natural variability unrelated to mankind? Would the remedy be more SAI, or less SAI, or different SAI – say calcium carbonate instead of sulfates, or 18 km altitude rather than 22? In a rapidly changing climate where we may be spinning many different dials at once, it may prove very difficult to diagnose the source of the problem and thereby identify the remedy.

The severity of that attribution problem is one of many reasons why it is widely perceived that if an SAI program were implemented, a separate but adjacent monitoring program would need to be stood up alongside it. The purposes of the monitoring program would be first to provide transparency as to the deployment program and provide confidence to the world that the program that was mandated is in fact the one being implemented. If conspiracists are gyrating now about secret deployments that are in fact not happening, imagine the world's trepidation once they actually are! Transparency and accountability would be essential. A second objective would be to assess and document the impacts of SAI in all corners of the world in order to measure the changes that take place and to compare them with our models. Finally, we would hope to use this data to determine how to alter and improve the program going forward. Far from being an ancillary activity, many sources imagine the size and cost of the monitoring program to rival that of the deployment program.

The low cost of SAI has given rise to the quip by the late Martin Weitzman of Harvard that SAI flips the free-rider problem associated with mitigation on its head. SAI is so cheap that we risk having "free drivers" who simply take matters into their own hands and decide to geoengineer the world unilaterally. Perhaps this is David Victor's imagined "Greenfinger," an environmentally obsessed billionaire anti-hero, but would more likely be a coalition of small or mid-sized climate-vulnerable states. However, my own research indicates that this is better science fiction than political science. SAI may be cheap, but a program large enough to intervene meaningfully in the climate system would be very sizable and therefore entirely detectable, likely before it left the ground, but certainly immediately thereafter. If the uninvolved world can detect a rogue SAI program, then it can also deter it, via trade sanctions or cruise missiles as the circumstances and power dynamics between the parties may warrant. Therefore, implementing an unauthorized SAI program requires more than a mid-sized budget. It would ultimately require the military umbrella of a major power, meaning that the main financial resource necessary to carry out rogue SAI is not the cost of the deployment effort, but the cost of the military arsenal necessary to prevent the outside world from terminating it, which is a much bigger kettle of fish.

For those wishing for more information on the science of SAI, the current best deep-dive source is the 2021 report by the National Academy of Science titled "Reflecting Sunlight: Recommendations for Solar Geoengineering Research and Research Governance," although that will be superseded shortly by the IPCC AR6 report, which will be issued more or less contemporaneously with this book.

So where does all the above leave us in respect of SAI? Mostly with a lot of unanswered questions. Nonetheless, while a recurring theme of this book has been that there is less than meets the eye in many of our intended climate interventions, this is a tool that appears to offer a lot of climate leverage. It looks like we could cool the planet substantially and quickly via SAI. It also appears to be pretty scalable – if we wanted a one or two degree impact rather than a tenth of a degree, this appears to be a dial we could turn. Its implementation doesn't require huge technological breakthroughs. We could build the planes and deploy the material. And this won't bankrupt us – it's cheap. Maybe even too cheap.

All that said, we know vastly too little about what other impacts this might have to know whether the net effects of SAI would prove beneficial, and if so, to whom. No field engineering has been done to determine how to optimally deploy it. We are more or less at square one in terms of understanding how to monitor such a program and to attribute subsequent climate developments to causes. And we are nowhere on the governance architecture for such a program. So if I somehow magically found my finger on the button that would activate a global SAI program, would I push it?

Absolutely not!!!

But neither can we ignore what seems to be among the most promising prospective tools in our toolbox. With all due caution as we note how her curiosity played out for Pandora, we need to start examining this tool.

# 15 SAI DEPLOYMENT

Within the geoengineering toolbox, I am trying to allocate ink to the various tools in approximate proportion to the seriousness with which I believe you should consider them. This is intended to be in direct contrast to so much geoengineering literature produced by journalists, who devote equal space to the most promising tools in this trade and to utter whack-doodle ideas that they hope will serve as tempting click-bait to keep readers engaged. "Giant parasols hovering above the Earth" and "lasers shooting up into clouds." Imagine!! Such breathless chatter misinforms both by failing to distinguish wheat from chaff but as well by creating the impression that there are reams of easy solutions out there – just pick from the menu! It ain't so.

This is a "heads up" that here I will devote a second chapter to SAI and in doing so, give it disproportionate ink. SAI does not deserve more attention than say CCS or DACCS. If anything, less so. But it happens to be where my career background enables me to make a meaningful contribution to the scholarly enterprise as a primary researcher rather than a synthesizer. It is where my deeper expertise lies. So kindly give me license to devote one additional chapter to the nuts and bolts of SAI deployment, without concluding thereby that I am seeking to skew the world in this direction. Or skip this chapter, as suits you. I am entirely sympathetic to those who view SAI with a "Has it really come to this??" sort of horror. (And the answer by the way is "No, it hasn't yet. But it may … ").

## A Best Guess SAI Program

What follows is not a positive prediction of how the world *will* proceed with an SAI program. Nor is it the sort of hands-off normative prescription offered by most academics or journalists who write about this, seeking to state how some anonymous "they" *should* do it. My personal "come from" is much more practical, as befits a former businessman and entrepreneur. If God came through the door (OK, that wasn't practical, but stay with me) and said "Wake, you have 15 years to implement an SAI program. Don't worry about getting consent or permission – I just gave it to you. Get it done," then how *would* I do it? If I reconceive this as a practical rather than a theoretical problem, how would I go about it?

Well, the first thing I would do is gather all the futurists and visionaries and kick them (hard!) out of the room. If I were truly in mission-mode, I wouldn't have time to dink around with people trying to invent self-levitating particles and rain-making lasers. I would need to constrain myself to tools that are mature or reasonably foreseeable. Neither would I get bogged down in the governance questions, not because I am dismissive of them – in fact I think they are the fulcrum on which any SAI program would need to pivot – but rather because they comprise a different facet of the problem to which we will get shortly. Here, I want to focus on the nuts and bolts.

Because this degree of practical thinking about SAI is rare, many observers are confused about whether it could be done. Some still conceive such interventions as "sociotechnical imaginaries,"[1] no more immediately practicable than our space-based L1 shield. That is a mistake. Give me a legitimate mandate, a few billion dollars, and seven years, and I could have the initial veil over the Earth. Being kindly as she is, God gave me in my hypothetical plan described above twice as much time as I would need.

For the remainder of this chapter, we will set aside the facts that:

- we don't in fact have any such legitimate mandate, and no governance structure exists that could confer one
- we don't understand the physics well enough to predict in detail SAI's impacts
- we haven't done field experiments to determine how to optimize deployment

- we haven't developed our monitoring capability

All of the above is why we can't in fact charge right into deployment, but if we somehow set all those hard parts aside, getting the gunk up in the sky would be the easy part.

## Injection Locations

Like most everything associated with geoengineering, more research is needed, but it appears that 20 km is both necessary and sufficient for effective SAI deployment – high enough to be safely in the lower stratosphere anywhere in the world. The height of the tropopause (the boundary layer between the troposphere and the stratosphere) varies with latitude, peaking above 16 km near the equator but dipping below 10 near the poles.[2] Nonetheless, since at least some of the deployment would be in the tropics, one would need to plan for average tropopause heights of 15–17 km and local/seasonal/diurnal variations that reach even higher.[3] There is recent research suggesting that even higher – say 25 km – might increase scattering effectiveness by as much as 50 percent,[4] though this remains uncertain. However, there is a ceiling in the sky above which fixed-wing, self-propelled, air-breathing aircraft could no longer attain sustained level flight, and 25 km is almost certainly above it. That said, I am now working with a team to consider more exotic rocket-boosted aircraft, ballistic zoom climbers, or supersonic jets that might reach these heights. If we need to get yet higher, that would call for alternative lofting platforms with at least ten times the cost per lofted tonne. However, most SAI research assumes 20 km, in which case, for the foreseeable future at least, the vehicle of choice would be a newly designed fleet of high-altitude crop dusters.

As regards the other locational coordinates that would define the question of where to inject aerosols, latitude matters and longitude doesn't. As earlier noted, the high altitude required is necessary to deposit the aerosols in the equator-to-pole Brewer–Dobson circulation. The closer to the equator we inject the material, the longer its ride to the pole and therefore its residence time in the atmosphere. Equatorial regions are also generally characterized by hot and therefore rising air masses, which is helpful in the deployment process. Early SAI research therefore generally assumed injection at the equator. However, since the Brewer–Dobson circulation doesn't operate efficiently right at the equator, shifting a bit north and south of the "line" gets the material properly onto the conveyer belt we seek.[5]

Moreover, global warming is not uniform by latitude. The equator is warming at rates well below the global average, whereas the poles are warming at three times the world rate.[6] If we seek to offset these temperature changes, we would ideally want to cool the equator very little, the mid-latitudes some, and the poles a lot. A more thoughtful SAI program would deploy some of the material at 15°N/15°S, but an even larger proportion at 30°N/30°S.[7] That way, the concentration of aerosols in the belt between 15°N and 15°S will be small (a bit of it will drift there), but larger in the ribbons between 15°N and 30°N or 15°S and 30°S, and more than double that amount poleward of 30°N or 30°S.

We could also vary our injections hemispherically in recognition of the seasons. In the northern summer, there is a lot of sunlight in the northern hemisphere – 24 hours of it in late June within the Arctic Circle. At the same time it is entirely dark at the South Pole with short days in Australia and Argentina. If our goal is to block sunlight, we will get a lot more bang for our buck if we vary our injection masses seasonally, placing more of our aerosols in the summer hemisphere where it will encounter a lot of sunlight, and less in the winter hemisphere where it will have limited impact. While one shouldn't imagine that a deployment program dependent upon global atmospheric circulations will achieve precision, it is clear that by varying deployment masses seasonally and between tropical and subtropical deployment latitudes, a more thoughtfully targeted program can be achieved.

On the other hand, longitude seems to matter very little. As volcanoes demonstrate, aerosols deposited in the stratosphere at any longitude pretty quickly get to every longitude, and with residence times of a year or more, the higher initial concentration at the point of injection has limited overall impact. For the purpose of operational robustness, one certainly wouldn't seek to geoengineer the entire Earth from just a single quartet of bases at our four chosen latitudes, but as a matter of distributional efficiency, one wouldn't go too far wrong with such a solution. If the latitude and other local conditions are right, we could put the bases in Africa, Asia, or the Americas (again, the eventual answer would be all of the above).

What we couldn't do – or at least shouldn't do – is to put them in one hemisphere (say north) and not the other. Both the atmosphere and the oceans are characterized by persistent or periodic currents and flows

233 / SAI Deployment

such as the jet stream or the south Asian monsoon that define climate around the world. While one could perhaps imagine that other currents might serve the world as well or better than the existing ones, both natural ecosystems and human societies have evolved in harmony with *this* arrangement of currents. Europe is wetter and warmer than its location on the planet might otherwise suggest, and the Sahara is dry. One of the major features of global air flows is the Intertropical Convergence Zone or ITCZ, which one might think of as the climatic equator rather than the geographical one, where the air currents of the northern hemisphere encounter those of the southern hemisphere. The ITCZ is roughly at the equator, but varies north and south with the seasons, causing both dry and rainy seasons in the northern and southern hemispheres. If we were to implement SAI in the northern hemisphere but not the southern, we would increase the equator-to-pole temperature gradient in one hemisphere while leaving it unaltered in the other. This would shift the location of the ITCZ and therefore the distribution of seasonal rains in the tropics, which would wreak havoc on the natural world and therefore human societies. It would be essential therefore to try to geoengineer the world in thoughtful and proportional ways that would change global circulations as little as possible – which as we mess with the climate of the entire planet is easier said than done.

## Aerosols

Among the prominent implementation questions would be what aerosol we intend to utilize. Nature's own answer – $SO_2$ – seems to do the trick but isn't necessarily the ideal choice. To clarify, $SO_2$ itself is not effective in deflecting sunlight, but is the precursor of something that is. After a few weeks in the atmosphere, sulfur dioxide oxidizes to become sulfur trioxide – $SO_3$ – and then nearly instantaneously further evolves to sulfuric acid, $H_2SO_4$. This is the aerosol form that does the deflective work. Natural and common though it is, sulfuric acid is somewhat nasty stuff. It is the cause of acid rain of which neither plants nor animals are particularly fond, and is also destructive to stratospheric ozone (the "good" kind). So while even a large SAI program would make only a very modest contribution to pre-existing levels of sulfates in the atmosphere and would only slightly delay (but not reverse) the ozone recovery, both of those are negative impacts, which has researchers exploring other possible aerosol candidates. Calcium carbonate (limestone/chalk) is super abundant on the planet, though not native to the atmosphere. It is as reflective as sulfuric acid, but without the environmental downsides. Substances that would be more nearly manufactured than mined are also under consideration, such as titanium dioxide, aluminum oxide, silicon carbide, and even synthetic diamond dust. All of these would be more reflective than sulfates or calcium carbonate, but by 10 percent to 25 percent rather than hugely so. They would also be more expensive, though so long as we don't choose to dump gem stones out the back of aircraft, cost won't be the deciding factor. What likely *would* be the deciding factor is environmental impacts and risks, and despite its known downsides, sulfates are native to the atmosphere and therefore present reduced (or perhaps better understood) risks. At least at the beginning of such a program, there would be strong arguments for dancing with the devil we know.

## Deployment Platforms

The Global Hawk and other high-altitude aircraft currently in service have payloads a few tonnes at most which would render them impractical for this mission. But their payloads are not so meager because physics prevents one from hauling more to the lower stratosphere. Rather, these spy planes were designed for long endurance, say to fly over the Soviet Union from bases in Europe or to circle a battlespace in the Middle East for a day. In designing an aircraft, a key parameter through which nearly everything is viewed is weight. What is the maximum tonnage the aircraft can incorporate and still retain the ability to take off, climb, and cruise? That Maximum Take-Off Weight is further broken down into Operating Empty Weight and fuel/payload. Operating Empty Weight is the weight of all the structure on the plane – all the metal, composites, plastics, rubber and so on – but with no payload or fuel. The differential between the Operating Empty Weight – the weight of the structure – and the Maximum Take-Off Weight delineates how much stuff you can load onto the plane. Some of that weight must be reserved for fuel or the plane couldn't even power itself down the runway and take off. And some must be reserved for payload; after all, the plane is presumably intended to take something or someone somewhere. But there is a broad "trade space" wherein one can opt for more fuel and less payload, or vice versa, with more fuel meaning more range – the plane can fly longer and therefore farther. This fuel/payload trade space is illustrated in range/payload charts, which are a fundamental illustration of the capabilities of any given aircraft. Spy planes such as those noted above are generally designed as high-altitude long-endurance (HALE) aircraft, and they achieve that long dwell or cruise capability by maximizing their fuel carrying capacity, which in turn means minimizing one's capacity to carry anything else. Beyond fuel, the U-2 carried little more than a pilot and a camera. The Global Hawk leaves the pilot on the ground (it's a drone) to make room for more imagery and signals intelligence sensors, LIDAR, and other observational instruments, but is still limited to a ~1 tonne instrumentation suite.

For SAI, on the other hand, we need high-altitude, short-dwell. We need a leaping aerial dump truck capable of zipping up to 20 km, flushing its tanks, and plunging back down to get another load. It would make several sorties per day per aircraft, just like an airliner or better yet, like the specialized water bombers that are used to fight forest fires. Such an aircraft is buildable but hasn't been developed because no customer has needed such a mission. Even military bombers – which in some sense have a similar (though hostile) mission of hauling a massive load somewhere and dropping it mid-flight – have no need to achieve such high altitude. They tend to cruise at the same 10–13 km (33,000–43,000 feet) altitude that commercial airliners do. But because we need to inject our aerosols into the stratosphere in the tropics, we need to get unusually high for an unusually short cruise leg.

In order to clarify the feasibility, capability, and cost of such an aircraft, I have collaborated with several other retired Boeing alumni in developing a preliminary design for the first-generation stratospheric aerosol injection lofter, or "SAIL-01." The preliminary design was presented to the SciTech 2020 meeting of the American Institute of Aeronautics and Astronautics and was published in the conference proceedings. The length and Operating Empty Weight of the SAIL are 5 percent–10 percent smaller than those of standard narrowbody short-haul airliners such as the B737-800 or the A320, but its wings are much larger, with a wingspan of 172 feet versus 117 for the A320. This is to accommodate a total wing area that is almost three times the size of the A320's. The lift capacity of a wing is proportional to its wing area – the bigger the wing, the more air it is in contact with as it slices through the sky and therefore the more lift it can generate. The atmosphere gets less dense as one rises, and by the time one gets up to 20 km, the air density is only 7 percent what it was at sea level.[8] In order then to continue to produce lift in this very thin air, we need those enormous wings.

The thin air also requires this plane to be fortified with tremendous thrust, mandating six engines rather than the two on most modern airliners. This is because at altitude, the engines will generate merely 10 percent of the thrust they do at sea level. The high-bypass engines installed on current production airliners, with big front-end fans that route most of the air around the engine core rather than through it, operate very poorly above 15 km, so SAIL-01 would utilize medium bypass engines such as the F118 GE-101 high-altitude turbofan. The engines would be mounted on four pylon nacelles on the wings, an inboard twin pod (two engines) and a mid-span single pod.

The wings are swept at a severe angle – 37 degrees vs. 25 on the A320 – allowing the aircraft to fly higher and faster. More than any other predecessor, the SAIL will resemble the B-47, an early post-war Boeing military aircraft design that looked nothing like what Boeing had built before, yet shaped everything it and its competitors built afterwards. The SAIL-01 wing geometry would be selected to substantially reduce drag. Check out the cool renderings in Figures 15.1 to 15.3!

All the subsystems (hydraulic, fuel, pressurization, and thermal management) would utilize contemporary off-the-shelf electrical

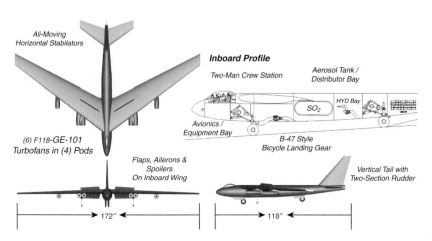

Figure 15.1 SAI lofter ("SAIL") three-view drawing. Image courtesy of: Donald A. Bingaman and Christian Rice, VPE Aerospace Consulting

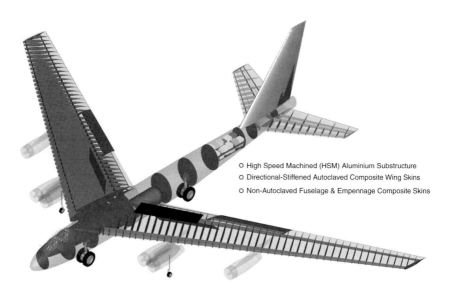

O High Speed Machined (HSM) Aluminium Substructure
O Directional-Stiffened Autoclaved Composite Wing Skins
O Non-Autoclaved Fuselage & Empennage Composite Skins

Figure 15.2 SAIL structural concept. Image courtesy of: Donald A. Bingaman and Christian Rice, VPE Aerospace Consulting

Figure 15.3 SAIL aircraft in flight. Image courtesy of: Donald A. Bingaman and Christian Rice, VPE Aerospace Consulting

components. The cockpit would incorporate a pressurized crew station under a bubble canopy, with flat panel programmable LED displays. It would have sufficient volume for flight suits, since the cruise leg would be above the Armstrong Limit (50,000 feet) beyond which a loss of pressurization would cause pilots to rapidly lose consciousness and perish. As befits a modern lightweight aircraft, the bill of materials would be at least half composites by weight, with aluminum, titanium, steel, and plastic comprising the remainder. Compared to its enormous wings, the fuselage would appear sleek and slender since it is intended to carry a dense load of chemicals rather than passengers who demand a certain amount of personal space and ample air around their heads. This is already more aircraft description than most readers will have appetite for, but for those (few) who may want more detail, the AIAA paper is available at https://doi.org/10.1088/1748-9326/aba7e7.

Despite the advancement of drone technologies, if we had to design SAIL-01 today, it would still have its pilots in the cockpit rather than on the ground. This is because the certification requirements for a large drone remain much more onerous (for good reason) than for an in situ piloted (what we used to call "manned") aircraft. Therefore, if the initial objective will be to reduce developmental cost, time, and risk, SAIL-01 would start as an in situ piloted program and likely evolve later into a remotely piloted one.

SAIL-01 would have a payload of 13.6 tonnes or 30,000 pounds, making it much more capable than its ~1 tonne spy plane predecessors. As currently conceived, it would also be very efficient in terms of "cycle time" – the time required to take off, climb, cruise and disperse its payload, descend, and land. Because its wings and engines are optimized for the cruise leg in the thin air at 20 km, they are oversized for all the other flight segments, meaning this plane would pop off the tarmac and scream up to 20 km in a mere 10 minutes. Once it had vented its load, it would descend equally rapidly.

The length of the cruise leg, however, is defined by what our payload is and what phase it is in. We have assumed that the initial payload is the devil we know – sulfates – but those could be loaded and deployed in various forms, either as sulfur dioxide ($SO_2$), or as sulfuric acid ($H_2SO_4$). The primary benefit of $H_2SO_4$ is that if we vent this form of sulfate, we can better manage the final size of the aerosol particles. For ideal sunlight scattering, we seek a Goldilocks particle size – not so small that it won't deflect much sunlight, but not so big as to reduce aggregate surface area. We would seek to release particles of roughly the same size as the sunlight they are trying to intercept, about 0.3 microns.[9] The hazard we seek to avoid is having our sulfate particles coagulate with each other and form blobs larger than 1 micron. These would still deflect some sunlight, but less of it since the aggregate surface area would be reduced if they combine into fewer, larger particles. If we release the aerosols in the ideal particle size, we can reduce their tendency to glom onto each other.

This also means we can't dump all the particles in an instant, as if we were a World War II bomber with bomb bay doors that we could just open and let the aerosols fall out. We would need to meter the flow of the aerosols out the back of the aircraft at a measured pace, with a maximum dispersal rate per kilometer flown so as to not to create too dense and "glommy" a plume. This means that the distance and therefore time of our cruise leg is defined by the size of our payload divided by this maximum venting parameter. At a cruise speed of roughly 0.8 Mach and over 13.6 tonnes of payload, this would define a cruise time of roughly 1.2 hours.

If, on the other hand, we were to haul $SO_2$ in a gaseous phase, then there is no maximum venting parameter that applies. Remember, $SO_2$ is a precursor to $H_2SO_4$, not the final product. It will take on average several weeks for the $SO_2$ to evolve into $SO_3$ and then $H_2SO_4$, by which time it will have dispersed far from the deployment location and mixed itself at low density into a very large parcel of air. The good news from a deployment standpoint is that we can vent our entire load of $SO_2$ as fast as it will flow out of the pressurized tanks – a few minutes rather than the roughly 72-minute cruise required for $H_2SO_4$. That reduces our total cycle time to 25 or 30 minutes rather than 95, which means in turn that a single aircraft can fly six cycles a day rather than four. We have cut our fleet requirement by a third.

Moreover, if the cruise leg is a few minutes rather than 72, that is perhaps 70 minutes *less* fuel we need to carry, which (back to our range/payload trade space) means an equivalent increase in the weight of the payload we can carry. More payload per sortie means fewer required sorties to loft the same payload and therefore fewer planes – we have cut our fleet requirement yet again. Furthermore, $SO_2$ weighs just two thirds of $H_2SO_4$, meaning that our 13.6 tonne $SO_2$ payload will eventually turn into over 20 tonnes of airborne $H_2SO_4$. More bang for our buck. $SO_2$ seems like the clear winner.

The problem, however, is that we have no control over the particle size that will result from the evolution of this $SO_2$ into $H_2SO_4$ several weeks later. For all the cost and weight efficiencies of hauling $SO_2$, if the aggregate scattering efficiency of the resulting $H_2SO_4$ is reduced by roughly one-third,[10] the trade-off may not be worth it.

And if the lifetime of our sulfur dioxide in the atmosphere were 52 weeks (it isn't that exact but to illustrate the point), and it takes three weeks for the $SO_2$ to become $H_2SO_4$ and start scattering sunlight, we lose 3/52 or nearly 6 percent of our effective scattering lifetime. The right answer as to which form of sulfur we should disperse remains uncertain. Nonetheless, for the fleet plan discussed below for SAIL-01, $SO_2$ was assumed to be the initial species hauled.

SAIL-01 could be flown in two configurations: a deployment mode, and a ferry mode (see Figure 15.4). Of course, the plane is optimized for its performance in deployment mode, but in order to be ferried to and from remote deployment locations, it would require a roughly 4,000 nautical mile ferry range during which it would fly at normal airliner altitudes, hauling no payload, but carrying additional fuel in auxiliary tanks.

## Developmental Program and Fleet Plan

In considering the developmental program for SAIL-01, I have drawn upon my experience as the President of the training division of Boeing, Chief Operating Officer of a global cargo airline (Atlas Air Worldwide Holdings), and CEO of an aircraft maintenance and modification company (Pemco World Air Services). I also corresponded, spoke, or met with: Airbus, Boeing, Bombardier, Gulfstream, Lockheed Martin, Northrup Grumman, GE Engines, Rolls Royce Engines, Atlas Air, Near Space Corporation, Scaled Composites, The

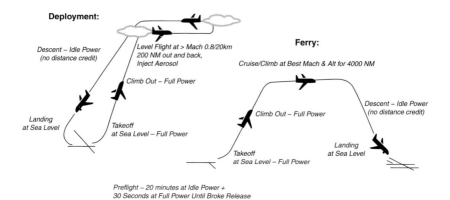

Figure 15.4 SAIL mission profiles. Image courtesy of: Donald A. Bingaman and Christian Rice, VPE Aerospace Consulting

Spaceship Company, Virgin Orbit, and NASA, the latter in respect of its high-altitude research aircraft fleet. With that background, I am confident that such an aircraft could be developed in 5–7 years for a few billion dollars if its financing were firm from the outset. That said, aircraft development programs have a long and sordid history of delays and cost overruns, so if you wish to apply an appropriate margin of error to those figures, feel free. Doubling them would not change the basic story very much.

Nonetheless, it is likely that the first-generation deployment aircraft would be developed in an uncertain political environment where the public acceptance of SAI cannot be assured. Confronting a material likelihood that the plane will never fly or may have its mandate revoked early and abruptly, the financial plan for SAIL-01 minimizes developmental cost at the expense of higher operating cost. The certification path (the process by which the aircraft design receives governmental approvals) will assure merely that the aircraft is safe and airworthy, but little money will be spent to optimize weight, fuel performance, or maintenance cost as would be done with a commercial airliner. This is one major reason why this plane would be developed far more cheaply than would a new commercial airliner, though the "down and dirty" developmental plan will also shorten both the production run of the SAIL-01 aircraft program and the useful economic life of each aircraft (20 years).

If, however, SAIL-01 proves the desirability and efficacy of SAI, then it will pave the way for further generations of deployment aircraft as the program matures. The next generation SAIL-02 will merit a much larger developmental budget ($10 billion versus less than $2.5 billion). That budget assumes SAIL-02 will be a remotely piloted craft with newly developed engines and a substantially more efficient airframe design. Engine technology, drag reduction, and lighter materials will likely advance in the coming decades as they have in the prior ones, with successive generations of aircraft leapfrogging their predecessors every couple of decades, delivering economic performance that improves at a rate of roughly 1 percent per year or 15–20 percent per aircraft generation (a design objective common in the industry). The entry into service of SAIL-02 is also a logical time to imagine that the aerosol decision made in respect of SAIL-01 might be reconsidered. By that time, the low initial risks associated with sulfates may finally be outweighed by the advantages of some other material, though there is no purpose at this time in guessing whether it may be calcium carbonate, titanium oxide, industrial diamond, or some newly engineered material. I refer to it simply as Aerosol 2.

SAIL-02 is planned to enter into service in year 16 of the SAI program, after which no additional SAIL-01s will be delivered, though each Generation 1 aircraft will continue flying to the end of its 20-year economic useful life. SAIL-02 is assumed to have a 35 percent larger Operating Empty Weight (51.6 tonnes) and a 35 percent larger payload, and will have four substantially more powerful engines, enabling it to burn 20 percent less fuel. Cycle time however will grow to 2 hours due to the change to Aerosol 2, which will be assumed to have a maximum dispersal rate parameter. SAIL-02 will be the backbone of the deployment fleet through Year 45, when SAIL-03 will enter into service, capping the production of SAIL-02 aircraft and commencing their phase out after a 30-year useful economic life.

SAIL-03 has a developmental budget equal to that of SAIL-02. It entails no Operating Empty Weight increase, but augments payload by a further 20 percent and improves fuel burn. Cycle time grows commensurate with the increased payload. By Year 66, the SAI fleet will consist entirely of SAIL-03s, with the last of the SAIL-02s having reached the end of their economic useful lives a year earlier.

As for how many aircraft would be in the fleet at any one time, that depends not only on the capabilities of the aircraft as discussed above, but also on how much continuing greenhouse gases the world is emitting, and what our objective is in respect of temperature management. If we are on a low emissions pathway and we wish merely to cut the rate of further warming in half, we might start with a handful of aircraft and ramp up to a fleet of 100 after 70 years, making the mature fleet smaller than that of Alaska Airlines today. Perhaps by that time, we are in an era of net negative emissions such that atmospheric concentrations and temperatures are declining, in which case our fleet count and annual deployed mass could ramp down as well. If on the other hand we are on a high emissions pathway and we seek an aggressive program to return temperatures to 2020 levels, we may require 1,000 aircraft 70 years in, with perhaps more thereafter if emissions continue to grow. 1,000 aircraft is a big fleet, but not an unmanageable one – American Airlines operates nearly 900 today. Both the low and the high fleet counts above assume that we slowly ramp into any SAI program rather than turn on the spigot full bore on day 1. All of these fleet counts assume that aircraft will continue to be the preferred aerosol lofting method for the foreseeable future, though it is of course quite possible that eventually, better, cheaper, and perhaps radically different lofting technologies may become available hereafter which would prompt a reformulated scenario.

Like the preliminary aircraft designs on which it is built, a fleet plan for a not-yet-extant air freight operation extending decades into the future requires substantial speculation on matters that cannot be easily predicted. Given that, the plan discussed here is intended to establish a reasonable order of magnitude for this operation rather than to imply specious precision. Nonetheless, it provides the building blocks for an illuminating cost model.

## Costs

The cost of SAI deployment scales quite linearly with the mass deployed and therefore the varying fleet counts discussed above. Early year operating costs for a small, slowly building program intended to halve the further increase of temperatures would range in the low single-digit billions of dollars. If such a program started in 2035 (it won't be that soon), then annual costs by the year 2100 would be $7 billion in the 100 aircraft (modest intervention) scenario above, and $70 billion in the 1,000 aircraft (aggressive intervention) scenario (all in 2020 dollars). To put those numbers in perspective, there are 430 public companies in the US with more than $7 billion in revenue according to the Fortune 500 listing, and 43 with over $70 billion, meaning that at either end of the scale, this would be a big but not unmanageable industrial program.

Framed another way, the aggregate cost for the above SAI programs from commencement of aircraft development in the 2020s through 2100 would range from a quarter trillion in the low case to $2.5 trillion in the high case. Gross world product today is roughly $85 trillion.[11] Since these costs vary by a factor of 10 from the low case to the high case, a final way to calibrate them is that for each degree C that we wish to remediate (and setting aside any diminishing returns phenomena), the annual cost would be roughly $18 billion.

These operational plans all entail a seven-year pre-start process to design and certify the first-generation deployment aircraft, with the last two years of that interval also used to establish and organize the "airline" necessary to fly them. The aircraft would operate initially from one quartet and eventually from several quartets of bases arrayed at latitudes of 30°N/15°N/15°S/30°S to allow latitudinal and seasonal variations in deployment mass. The expansion to additional quartets of bases represents one of several assumptions made to increase resiliency and limit the probability that operational factors would lead to an unplanned program discontinuation and therefore "termination shock." To further bolster resiliency, each aircraft is expected to be out of service for 35 days per year for planned maintenance, leading to a total fleet that is larger than the available fleet on any given day. Aircraft utilization is capped at roughly ten block hours per day, though this could be exceeded in unusual circumstances such as following a service interruption due to strikes, fires, floods, earthquakes, or local political disturbances. Each base would be provisioned with a substantial inventory of spare parts, which would grow with each aircraft added to the fleet. Aircraft can of course be redeployed to other bases in the event that their home base were to become inoperative. Each base is also assumed to have one "hot spare" available at all times to provide substitutes for unplanned maintenance or accidents. Flight crews are planned with similarly robust and flexible numbers. In combination, these measures would provide for high operational reliability and limit the prospect of unplanned, long-term program discontinuations, although none of the measures is particularly unusual. These are the kinds of robustness features that would seem very ordinary at a large, well-run airline. More on the operational and fleet plan details (but who would want more???) as well as costs for the theoretical SAI operation described here can be found at https://doi.org/10.1088/1748-9326/aba7e7.

## Organizational Structure for SAI

To pull up out of the weeds a bit (although, as you can see, I spend a lot of my time playing in the weeds), another dimension through which to view SAI deployment is organizational structure namely, what might the organogram for an SAI enterprise look like? One commonly assumed answer is that it might be undertaken by the military, or by several militaries, in which case it would look like the Air Force. However, that would be a curious fit, as there is no human enemy involved. The problem set is more similar to that confronted by FEMA (the US Federal Emergency Management Agency) than by the Air Force. Another common answer is that private corporations might take this on, though that is only conceivable as government contractors. There is no market revenue that would derive from this, so no corporation will perform this task unbidden. There would have to be a governmental or intergovernmental entity paying for it. One could imagine separate national efforts, but the uninvolved world would prove immediately and implacably hostile to that, so there will be strong incentives for countries to cooperate.

The future could certainly unfold differently, but in my view, the best-case-scenario organizationally for this worst-case-scenario climate intervention would be that it is undertaken by a single rational and legitimate global monopolist deployer operating on a not-for-profit basis and backed by substantial guarantees from one or more economically powerful governments (more on this in Chapter 17). The fleet and operational plans noted above are all undergirded by this optimistic assumption. They suppose that we wouldn't have competing aircraft programs (i.e., Boeing vs. Airbus), let alone uncoordinated or even divergent targets amongst multiple, perhaps competing actors. One program for the world – that should be the goal. And while cost likely won't be the deciding factor, this would also be the lowest cost option since it would optimize economies of scale.

Staying with this "benign global monopolist" paradigm, I seek to distinguish the governance superstructure from the deployment substructure. The governance superstructure is where all the high-rent questions lie. What are the targets? Who decides and how? Who pays? What entitlement is there to compensation for damages that may be caused? What are the stopping rules? All of that is deeply vexing, and will be the subject of Chapter 17. But beneath all that, if and when clear and legitimate decisions could be made, a substructure would need to exist that could carry out those instructions and fly the missions.

As a starting point for conceiving that substructure, I envision three layers of enterprises. The first would be a Science Directorate, whose role it would be both to advise the governance superstructure on scientific questions to facilitate its decisions, and to translate the climate and temperature goals articulated by the governance apparatus into actionable targets. Temperature goal A requires B tonnes of aerosol in this form to these places on these days, to be modified in these ways under these weather and atmospheric decisions. None of those decisions can be made by the governance superstructure, but neither should be left to the flying enterprise.

Below the Science Directorate would be at least two operational organizations – one to fly, and one to "spy" ("monitor" actually, but that doesn't rhyme). "Flyco" would be a cargo airline, though a somewhat virtual and not-for-profit one. It would direct the development and manufacture of planes, plan missions to be flown, lease bases, purchase aerosols/precursors, and ensure that the missions specified by the Science Directorate are in fact flown. However, it would be as asset light and employee light as possible. It may own lots of intellectual property including perhaps the aircraft designs, but the aircraft would be manufactured by an airframer like Airbus or Boeing, who would in turn source engines and components from the usual suspects. The aircraft would be owned by an aircraft leasing company, or likely several of them. They would be leased in by airlines around the world with the traffic rights necessary to fly the missions in their sectors. The crews, maintenance, and insurance would be provided by the airlines. Fuel, aerosols, and all other required supplies would be purchased from the private market. The bases would be owned and operated by local contractors or governments, with services leased by Flyco. Flyco would have managerial personnel, but no operational personnel. All the pilots, maintenance workers, ground staff, etc., would be employed by airlines or other private contractors whose services are purchased via open bidding. In this way, Flyco can build a global air enterprise capable of operating all over the world, but with minimal internal constituencies that could ossify the organization into continuing with technologies that become obsolete or climate interventions that are no longer useful. At the same time, however, it can take advantage of the efficiencies of the private market and employ contractors and personnel from all over the world.

"Spyco" would be the monitoring organization, whose first mission would be to inspect Flyco's activities on the ground and in the air to ensure that it is faithfully carrying out the instructions of the Science Directorate. Keeping the world united in a "single monopolist deployer" model would hinge in substantial measure on ensuring full transparency as to the activities of Flyco and assuring the world that it is faithfully carrying out its instructions. How many missions, with what deployed masses, to what locations, with what aerosols, at what particle size – all the parameters on which the world would require assurance.

Second, Spyco would seek to monitor the physical migration and evolution of the aerosols. Are they behaving in the ways we expected? Are their interactions with the environment as our models had predicted? And finally, it would monitor the impacts of SAI in the atmosphere, oceans, and on land to catalogue the benefits and possible harms that it may cause, both on a global and local level around the world. It is of course essential that Spyco work intimately with Flyco, but also that it have entirely separate management. Spyco would report only to the Science Directorate and not to Flyco. All its reporting would also be public. Like Flyco, Spyco would be as asset and personnel light as possible, so it would purchase data from satellite providers rather than own its own satellites, and so on.

This chapter has entailed extensive speculation about all manner of aspects of SAI deployment, many of which would undoubtedly unfold differently than is suggested here. My purpose in all respects is not to convince you of the accuracy of this vision, but rather of its plausibility and practicability. The plane is buildable. The missions are flyable. The costs are bearable. The organization is feasible. There are no technological breakthroughs or "unobtainium" required.

If we needed to, we could do this.

# Section V

# SOCIAL RAMIFICATIONS
# OF CLIMATE INTERVENTION

# 16 GOVERNANCE OF CARBON REMOVAL

If our wealthier but uncomfortably sweaty descendants seem likely to demand climate intervention in abundance both to secure a net zero aspiration and to thereafter reduce the atmospheric greenhouse gas (GHG) concentrations that are boosting temperatures, a fair question is "how will that be organized?" Not simply what tools will be used, but in what set of hands? If we seek to crank down the global thermostat, whose fingers are on the dials and whose preferences are they pursuing? What policies, processes, and institutions would be required to bring this into being, and how would we ensure proper control over it? How would decisions be made, and on what criteria? As we contemplate such questions, we pivot from physical science and engineering to social science, and in these next two chapters, more specifically to the domain of "governance" in respect of geoengineering.

Governance "refers to the range of actions, processes, traditions, and institutions by which authority is exercised, and decisions are taken and implemented in order to direct behavior towards a specific goal."[1] Governance certainly includes regulations, laws and treaties, but also refers to social norms, practices, and processes at local, national, and international levels, undertaken by both public and private actors. It may organize and coordinate activities, incentivize or disincentivize them, prohibit them, or channel them in desired directions. It refers to the broad suite of tactics by which societies implement policy and get things done. This first governance chapter focuses on introducing key topics in climate intervention governance in the context of carbon dioxide removal. Next, we will address the more problematic governance of solar radiation modification.

## Initial Concepts of Climate Intervention Governance

At a global level, one might well imagine that the governance of geoengineering would look very much like the governance of emissions, where overarching international agreements defining or codifying national responsibilities or pledges are translated into local laws and policies within states. Perhaps the very same instruments and institutions might be appropriate to the global task – the United Nations Framework Convention on Climate Change (UNFCCC), the Intergovernmental Panel on Climate Change (IPCC), and the Paris Agreement.

However, it only took a few short years after Paul Crutzen's explicit call for research into climate engineering in 2006 for many parties to wonder whether the institutions being assembled to govern emissions would prove sufficient to govern the full climate intervention tool set. Whereas the transboundary impact of burning coal is an unintended consequence of producing electricity, in any geoengineering program the global effects would be the direct objective. It raises the question of whether bridling and steering intentional climate interventions requires a different level of governance than does reducing harms that derive unintentionally from acts that were previously seen as harmless. Whereas the intended transboundary effects of carbon dioxide removal (CDR) might be entirely positive, those deriving from stratospheric aerosol injection (SAI) could conceivably prove damaging to some or all affected parties, yet again raising the same question. Thus, the governance architecture that may adequately transfer from emissions reductions to afforestation may prove poorly matched to the challenges posed by massive carbon dioxide removal or stratospheric aerosol injection.

A governance line might seem to be properly drawn between the two halves of our geoengineering toolbox (CDR and SRM) were it not for the fact that the most spectacular and unsettling early attempt at geoengineering deployment was in fact on the CDR side of the box. Russ George's ill-fated ocean iron fertilization experiment off the coast of British Columbia in 2012 (see Chapter 10) entailed exactly the sort of reckless unbounded intervention that stimulates fear about SAI, despite the fact that its objective was in fact to test a CDR technique.

With truly remarkable foresight as to how events might later unfold, the British Royal Society convened in 2007 to consider both the science and the governance of geoengineering.[2] The resulting 2009 report set the stage later that year for an articulation of general tenets that were intended to govern all forms of geoengineering and came subsequently to be known as the "Oxford Principles."[3] These apply more clearly and sensibly to the transgressive tools found in greater abundance on the SRM side of the toolbox, but were devised to apply to CDR governance as well.

In an order that does not signal priority among them, the five Oxford Principles are:[4]

**Table 16.1** The Oxford Principles

| Oxford Principle | Description |
| --- | --- |
| Geoengineering to be regulated as a public good | While the involvement of the private sector in deployment may prove efficient and therefore desirable, "regulation of such techniques should be undertaken in the public interest" so as to ensure that private gain is not the motivating factor behind such endeavors. Climate intervention should not be a private good or service. |
| Public participation in geoengineering decision making | Noting that different techniques present varying levels of potential risk and requirements for transparency, "those conducting geoengineering research should be required to notify, consult, and ideally obtain the prior informed consent of those affected." |
| Disclosure of geoengineering research and open publication of results | In order to "facilitate better public understanding" of the risks and benefits, it is essential that all results of all research be made publicly available. |
| Independent assessment of impacts | Impact assessments "should be conducted by a body independent of those undertaking the research" to "mitigate the risks of lock-in to particular technologies or vested interests." |
| Governance before deployment | "Any decisions with respect to deployment should only be taken with robust governance structures in place." In other words, no more rogue escapades. |

The Oxford Principles have proven very durable and are the starting point for most of the discussions of climate intervention governance that have followed. Subsequent conferences and publications have attempted to add to the list with varying degrees of success. Two important principles that also derive from the Royal Academy Report but did not make the Oxford cut are:[5]

**Table 16.1** (continued)

| Implied Principle | Description |
| --- | --- |
| The primacy of mitigation over geoengineering | Geoengineering should be viewed as a supplement to rather than a substitute for the reduction and ultimate elimination of emissions. |
| The need for climate interventions to achieve political legitimacy and public acceptance | This extends the previous concepts of public good and public participation a further step, suggesting that given its universal impact and widespread consequences, geoengineering will require political and public buy-in, difficult though that may be to achieve. |

While these Oxford and subsequent principles have proven durable in an academic context, they have not been promulgated into public policy, nor do they describe a complete picture of what would be required for climate intervention governance. To illuminate this larger picture, we turn to the current state of international climate governance mechanisms and how they apply to geoengineering.

## The Problem of Collective Action

Both emissions reductions and climate intervention require governance because they are collective action problems wherein the interests of the collective diverge from those of the individual. We are *all* better served collectively if we reduce, eliminate, and remove our GHG emissions, but I am better off personally if I do not. My best outcome is that I keep emitting while *you* conserve. All of you. That way, the collective gets most of what it wants (low emissions) and I get all of what I want, continued carbon services. The problem here of course, as with all collective action problems, is that this distribution of benefits and harms is offensive to everyone but me. No one wants the "sucker's share," where you sacrifice but I don't. It is one thing for me to give up my Honda and lug my groceries on the bus so that my grand-children can enjoy a stable and hospitable planet. If my sacrifice instead simply opens space in the planetary carbon budget for my neighbor to continue to commute to the office in his Bubba-chic pick-up truck, then screw it. I'm keeping my Honda!

To solve a collective action problem in a durable fashion, we need to find a way to align the individual incentives with the collective incentives, such that what is good for me is also good for the collective. In some small group and specialized problems, this is possible without coercion, but with carbon emissions – the mother of all collective action problems involving the entire human race now and for generations – moral suasion likely won't do it. That, unfortunately, is the lesson of our era. The required sacrifices will be substantial, and no one can stand the sucker's share. We will need to put in place laws and policies that reliably line up the incentives, which returns us yet again to some form of a carbon (GHG actually) tax or other price mechanism, as well as an international law maker who can enforce it between countries. The more carbon-intensive car, steak, or loaf of bread needs to sell at a slight premium to the other one to pay for its greater environmental impact. I am welcome to buy that one, if I am willing to pay that premium. My neighbor can keep his pick-up truck, if it is worth the hefty tax that buying it and fueling it will require. If he doesn't want to pay that premium, I can introduce him to my Honda dealer or, cheaper still, show him where the bus stops. We still have freedom of choice, but that freedom is now constrained by the carbon impact of our selections. I can still select the pick-up. What I can no longer select is the pick-up with no added carbon tax. And importantly, the tax creates incentives to innovate new means of transportation, electricity generation, and the other low-emission technologies we will require as well of lower-cost CDR methods.

## Governing Collective Action on Climate Change

The world has been attempting to address the collective action problem of climate change mitigation for decades. At a global level, the operative frameworks that govern greenhouse gas mitigation are the United Nations Framework Convention on Climate Change

(UNFCCC) and its older sibling, the Intergovernmental Panel on Climate Change (IPCC), which assesses climate science. Moreover, there is of course the UNFCCC's Paris Agreement, which attempts to establish momentum towards achieving climate goals. Paris has articulated long-term global temperature and net emissions targets, but, unlike the earlier Kyoto Protocol, it does not allocate responsibility for achieving those targets among various nations. Rather, it facilitates five-year cycles of voluntary pledges (nationally determined contributions or NDCs) among the signatories and leaves it to each of them to fulfill (or not) those pledges.

On the face of it, the Paris Agreement does not appear to include much in the way of true international governance. The Paris pledges are nationally determined and the governance of compliance does not override the sovereignty of states. However, parties to the Paris Agreement have agreed on one critical aspect of governance: accounting. The Agreement substantially bolstered the pre-existing emissions bookkeeping system that seeks to understand the carbon profile of each country and track it over time. The Agreement is non-binding in respect of pledges but binding regarding accounting and reporting. Carbon accounting may sound eye-glazingly dull, but no emissions reduction or CDR scheme – voluntary or otherwise – is possible without it. Unless we can accurately monitor both the aggregate sources and sinks within any country, we can't know whether it has fulfilled its pledges. In some sense, this hardly matters, since the pledges are non-binding and reflect widely divergent levels of true ambition and statistical chicanery. Nevertheless, it is hoped that Paris will endure for a century or more, and that over that span, the level of both ambition and accountability is presumed to ratchet up substantially, such that these minute accounting details will be critically important in the future. There is no solution to climate change that does not incorporate accurate and reliable country-level climate accounting.

What that means, in turn, is that an awesome global inspection regime will burrow deeply into every economy in the world. We will eventually need visibility of the emissions profile of every power plant, factory, building, construction site, farm, and ranch in the world, either directly, or via reliable proxies. The initial Paris Agreement was a compromise kluged together after exhaustive negotiations involving virtually every nation on Earth. However, the rules for the climate accounting framework necessary to implement it were only the half-baked remnants of the collapsed Kyoto process. Those rules have been painstakingly refashioned and honed ever since and remain very much a work in progress. The ultimate goal of this tinkering, as laid out in Article 4.13 of the Paris Agreement, is to establish tracking and accounting procedures that are TACCC:[6]

- **Transparent,** such that external parties can understand and interrogate the data
- **Accurate,** which implies procedures and permissions by which to perform extensive on-site audits
- **Consistent,** both from one time period to the next and across both sinks and sources
- **Comparable,** such that countries may be accurately compared to one another
- **Complete,** to avoid cherry picking only favorable data

TACCC procedures are also required to reveal and prevent the intentional distortions that will surface in this sea of data. Countries will have incentives to overcount sinks and undercount sources. Carbon removal contractors will have every incentive to sell the same removal many times over or to sell removals that did not in fact occur. Few will have an interest in revealing unintentional or negligent carbon escapes. This will be a system ripe with temptation for cheats and fraudsters.

Nonetheless, the initial dry run by which to put all this into action – the first global stocktake – will commence in 2021 and be completed by 2023.[7] It will produce the most detailed look at GHG emissions ever undertaken and will undoubtedly reveal myriad flaws in the accounting system: intentional cheating; inadvertent double counting; targets that were met before they were set; others whose fulfillment can't be accurately measured. But slowly, and via subsequent cycles, presumably the system can get tightened to produce increasingly meaningful results.

## Governing Carbon Dioxide Removal with the Paris Agreement

What, you might ask, does the Paris Agreement and all this emissions accounting have to do with the governance of CDR? Likely, everything. Included in the NDCs are not merely emission reductions, but certain kinds of sink enhancements, such as reforestation or soil restoration. Flue gas capture, direct air capture with carbon storage (DACCS), and enhanced weathering should be expected to be folded into future NDCs as well. The NDCs are typically net numbers relative to some baseline. For example, if a country pledged to reduce its emissions by 100 units, it could either burn 100 units less of oil, or reduce its emissions by only 80 units, but engage in DACCS that sequesters another 20. This permits flexibility and efficiency in fulfilling NDCs in the ways best suited to national circumstances and capabilities.

Under Paris, NDCs will be met with nationally specific policy structures. Each country may incentivize its greenhouse gas mitigation and removal mix through a different set of policy measures. However, the accounting rules for CDR will be determined internationally. As a result, much of the current literature on the governance of CDR concerns better codifying negative emission technologies included in the NDCs under Paris. The 2006 IPCC guidance on accounting for the types of terrestrial carbon removals including afforestation, reforestation, and BECCS is still favored by the IPCC. A separate report on land sector accounting was issued as a part of the Kyoto process. The IPCC has not however issued accounting guidance in respect of DACCS, and the pre-Paris guidance that exists is limited in its specifics and is not yet applicable to NDCs.[8]

As an example of the sorts of questions that arise in CDR accounting, imagine that as a part of my NDC, I propose to reforest one acre of what is now pasture land, which I propose will offset four metric tonnes of $CO_2$ per year.[9] The question is whether my estimated four tonne annual offset is accurate or even reasonable. Do I need to convincingly demonstrate that I was not planning on planting those trees all along? Do I need to specify what sort of trees I will plant on that land, and do different tree types deserve different carbon accounting? They should, since some will grow more quickly than others and will therefore absorb more carbon. Is my carbon accounting based simply on how much land area I reforest, or how many trees I actually plant? How much more credit do I deserve if the land is well watered and temperate rather than dry or otherwise marginal? Can I get additional credit for irrigation? I will disturb that land in the planting process, which will release some carbon initially. Must that initial emission of carbon from the soil be accounted for in my NDC, and how many years of tree growth will it take to break even on that and start being net carbon positive? Once the trees reach maturity and are no longer substantial net carbon sinks, do I have to stop claiming them as offsets? If a beetle infestation or fire (or logging) destroys the forest, must I make a one-time adjustment in the year of the disaster to reverse all the offsets I previously claimed?

Terrestrial sinks such as forests or soils are particularly fragile and impermanent, giving rise to many of these questions, but similar issues would arise with the geological sinks into which captured gases might be pumped. What sort of inspection and certification procedure should be required before a spent oil field or saline aquifer can be deemed an acceptable storage site? What verification procedures are needed to ensure the gases are properly captured from the flue and piped into the ground rather than vented into the air? What sort of monitoring procedure is required to ensure that the buried carbon is not leaking up to the surface via a fissure or adjacent well? How much should the offsets be decremented if such leaks are detected? Though leaks are a risk, geologic storage is far more reliable than biological storage in the form of trees. How much more credit, then, do I deserve for 1 unit of geological storage vs. 1 unit of biological storage?

These issues become yet more complicated once international supply chains and emissions trading are considered. If Japan pays to have trees planted in Indonesia, who can claim the resulting offsets? Japan certainly will, as the offset within its NDC was almost certainly the reason it made the payment, but Indonesia may feel equally entitled, since the carbon capture and sequestration is occurring within its territory. Without a comprehensive global reconciliation, such double counting will be tempting, if not rampant.

The risk of leakage also calls for global reconciliations. If a forest in Canada is preserved instead of logged, but the global demand for wood products remains unchanged, that implies that a forest somewhere else will likely be harvested instead, defeating our purpose.

We should wish that the need for better CDR accounting were an urgent one, but yet another governance problem in this sector is scaling. Simply put, we are moving MUCH too slowly with CDR. If these technologies are to be deployed at the levels needed to meet 1.5°C and 2°C targets then research as well as actual infrastructure roll out need to proceed at roughly 100 times the pace at which we are currently moving.[10] Since there is no private market for CDR, our woefully insufficient pace is really a governance problem. Until governments create a market where none exists now (cue the carbon taxes yet again), only halting progress will be made. (Don't hold your breath.)

## Risks of Governing CDR with the Paris Agreement

To be sure, there are dangers in the fungibility between mitigation and removal that is sanctioned in the Paris Agreement. Among the permutations of the "moral hazard" or "emissions deterrence" problem that I most fear is the degree to which large amounts of future CDR are presumed and promised as a way to make up for mitigation shortfalls today. This is exactly what occurs in several of the SR15 pathways, which not only call for massive emissions cuts beginning immediately, but also bake in huge negative emissions in the mid and late century of which the general public is only dimly aware. We are of course blithely ignoring the emissions cuts demanded, but the presumed future CDR makes the consequences of that mitigation failure appear less dire than they are. The worst of all worlds results if the public relies upon promised negative emissions that the future proves unable to deliver.

For this reason, there are many in the governance community who urge separate targets for mitigation and CDR.[11] The idea would be that we commit to a stringent emissions reduction pathway, and separately map a CDR future, but the success or failure of CDR ought not to change our mitigation ambition. This would be admirable climate discipline and therefore perhaps a better world than the one in which we now live, but that doesn't necessarily make it wise policy. In fact, the search for the least-cost option to climate stability would suggest that we should actively trade emissions cuts and removals as the costs of each evolve over time.

Motivating the world to undertake meaningful climate action at all has proven very difficult, but the most successful framing has proven to be "carbon neutrality" or "net zero." These are simple two-word concepts that establish a comprehensible long-term goal and suggest we can keep doing some of the harmful stuff we still want to do so long as we find some countervailing helpful stuff to do alongside it. We don't have to eliminate emissions entirely, but rather reduce some, and offset the others. There may be some gimmickry in that, but the public is increasingly rallying around such carbon neutrality pledges, and rallying the public is an essential step. The most salient alternative to meaningful climate targets is not greater targets, but lesser targets, or no targets at all. We therefore should not let "perfect be the enemy of good" in this sphere and support the net-zero framing despite the flaws that a merged emissions/removals target may entail. If nations can be coaxed out of their torpor to undertake sacrifices under the banner of carbon neutrality, we should encourage them to march forward.

## Governing CDR Beyond Net Zero

Another issue with governing CDR through the construct of the Paris Agreement is: what do we do after countries reach net zero? Even if the world were to reach net-zero emissions sooner than we (at least I) may expect, more climate intervention will be required. The bathtub will likely be too full, and the natural drain works too slowly to relieve the devastating impacts of the temperature increases we are prone to see. If the world is to pursue CDR to lessen its climate burden, we currently have very little concept of how to govern it and, in particular, how to pay for it.

Like reaching net zero, CDR beyond net zero will remain a collective action problem. We need to convince people all over the world to undertake local cost for global benefit, in this case the cost of sucking carbon back out of the air and burying it in the ground. The fundamental governance question will still be: how do we get people to do that? There is no longer a negative tool we can use here. We can't prohibit (or disincentivize via taxes) people from doing some harmful things like emitting carbon. We instead need a positive tool to get them to do something they are not now doing. The answer of course is obvious. We need to pay them. If we pay people to capture and sequester carbon, they will do it. If we pay them a lot, they will do a lot of it, which is just what we need.

This is where the governance of CDR beyond net zero gets thorny. Even if we tackled all the governance challenges noted above in respect of emissions – obeyed the Oxford Principles, heard from all the affected parties, followed fair and just procedures, developed a flawless accounting system, and incented the technology development – we are still left with the enormous elephant in the center of the room. Who is going to pay for the removals? Trillions of dollars every year. Likely for generations.

There is a significant climate justice contingent for whom the answer is obvious, "The rich! The Global North! The polluter!" And undeniably, they would have a principled point. This would seem the fair answer. Its application is complicated by the fact that by the time this question is being asked in earnest, many of those polluters and beneficiaries will in fact be dead, but no matter. One view is that these responsibilities should attach not to individuals, but to states, so France is responsible for its historical emissions even if many of the bad actors themselves have passed on.

Some of the most prominent and detailed literature on CDR governance suggests that payment for the required future CDR be extracted on one of two bases: either cumulative per capita emissions; or ability to pay.[12] For the former, a 1990 baseline is established on the rationale that the formation of the UNFCCC in that year demarcates a division between prior acts of omission and subsequent acts of commission. Prior to that date, emitters could credibly claim ignorance as to climate impact of their actions, whereas afterwards, no such claim would be reasonable. If the tax scheme were to commence in 2080, then the cumulative per capita emissions between 1990 and 2080 would be calculated for each country. A total budget for the CDR required in 2081 would be determined and would be allocated among countries per their historical emissions. Rinse and repeat for 2082. Under this scheme, one rationale by which countries are being urged to reduce emissions today is to reduce their relative bill for the required CDR in the future. The pitch is that you will actually *save* money in the long run by funding emissions reductions today.

The alternative approach would be to skip the historical emissions calculation and simply tax countries based upon their per capita income in that future year, a global CDR income tax. A problem prominently noted with respect to either of these schemes is that unless the world immediately and drastically cuts emissions, the magnitude of the future CDR funding requirements could become unsustainable. This is particularly true in light of the Sustainable Development Goals that the UN has repeatedly articulated as the pathways by which the Global South may catch up economically to the Global North.

This ethical allocation of payment responsibilities is portrayed as merely one among an undifferentiated laundry list of governance gaps and challenges related to CDR. The charts and graphs that illustrate the possible funding solutions are complex and exquisitely crafted,[13] and have a remarkably unselfconscious "castles in the air" quality about them reminiscent of the 1928 Kellogg–Briand Pact in which the world's powers promised not to use war to resolve disputes. The biggest funding requirement in the history of the world can simply be tackled by telling people what ethics demands of them. We have already tried this with the Kyoto Protocol, and it didn't end well.

There are loads of governance challenges awaiting us as we approach the challenge of CDR, but by far the biggest is money. Technology will evolve – perhaps quickly – and it is possible that what appears in prospect to be an impossible funding burden may prove manageable in a warmer but richer and more technically advanced world. Maybe. But it seems a good bet that the institutional frameworks that are being assembled for the governance of mitigation can evolve to encompass CDR as well. Not so as we flip over to the governance of SRM and particularly SAI.

# 17 GOVERNANCE OF SRM AND SAI

If the governance of CDR is mostly affirmative – getting people to do stuff that no one wants to do – the governance of SAI is the opposite. The primary objective will be to prevent people from doing things we don't want them to do. The salient risk with CDR is too little, too late. The salient risk with SAI is too much, too soon, or at least that is the view of many. SAI is often seen as a bogeyman, and the challenge therefore is to keep it in the cage. To be clear, SAI may in time prove to be a bogeyman, or a savior. We simply don't yet have a sufficient scientific basis by which to judge its potentially beneficial impacts or possible unintended consequences, and neither can we accurately predict the emissions pathway the world will choose and therefore what remedies the future may demand. But fears that SAI will escape its cage are in my view exaggerated, though, to be fair, the governance architecture that would be required to restrain and domesticate this technology does not yet exist. Much more so than CDR, the UNFCCC and Paris seem poorly matched for this task. Nor do existing laws or treaties squarely apply to this novel climate intervention. New governance institutions and practices would be required.

While, as earlier noted, the SRM side of our toolbox includes at least a handful of prospective tools, we will focus for the remainder of this chapter on SAI specifically. From a governance perspective, white roofs look much more like reforestation than SAI. It is an inherently local action squarely within the confines of national sovereignty and municipal regulations. Its purpose would be to ameliorate urban heat islands rather than global temperatures, and the imperceptible transboundary effects that it could have are positive rather than negative, leaving it beyond the scope of any duty to prevent transboundary harms. Bioengineering crops to increase albedo is also a local intervention. Its potential transboundary effects derive less from potential temperature impacts than from the prospect of seed dispersal and the crowding out of native crops in adjacent countries, but these sorts of issues are already well addressed in both domestic laws and international protocols related to GMOs, such as the Cartagena Protocol.[1]

Cloud modifications, on the other hand, seem more similar in character to SAI, particularly if they were done over the high seas with the intent of modifying global climate. However, these technologies are so immature that the governance of them is a much less imminent concern. Such governance structures as are developed for SAI would seem likely to set precedents for cloud modifications if not apply to them directly. The key governance questions then on the SRM side of the box and in the current decade pertain particularly to SAI, which remains very early in its development, but is no longer an utter pipe dream. And, as we will consider later, if SAI is to proceed at all, there are enormous advantages to focusing on its governance early on.

## Potentially Relevant Existing International Institutions

Turning to the matter of existing institutions well suited to the governance of SAI, the quick summary is: there are none. The UNFCCC has a mandate to stabilize atmospheric greenhouse gas concentrations, but not to actively engage in countervailing climate modifications. The goal of parties to convention agreements is "to stabilize greenhouse gas concentrations in the atmosphere at a level that will prevent dangerous human interference with the climate system, in a time frame which allows ecosystems to adapt naturally and enables sustainable development."[2] Given the consensus-oriented character of any UN body as well as the likely near-term opposition of some states to SAI, the prospect of expanding the UNFCCC's remit to include SAI seems incompatible with the concept of early governance. Many would in fact see a mandate expanded to include SAI as being precisely the opposite of the current mandate and an admission of defeat in the quest to limit climate change via emissions reductions. The IPCC has agreed in its coming Sixth Assessment Report to evaluate the science on both sides of our toolbox, but its mandate is specifically limited to observation and assessment.[3] It cannot even engage in science let alone active climate engineering. Paris is an attempt at a voluntary global emissions limitation scheme, but the concrete actions it seeks to motivate are meant to be undertaken by each state within its territory. Like its UNFCCC parent, Paris is a slow-moving consensus-oriented alliance. It is a forum for states to negotiate with and cajole each other, but it lacks the sort of strong executive function that would be required to carry out a program like SAI.

Nor are there other international treaties or agreements with clear and explicit jurisdiction over SAI. The Convention on the Prohibition of Military or any Other Hostile Use of Environmental Modification Techniques ("ENMOD") would, at first blush, seem relevant to SAI, in that its definition of "environmental modification" would encompass most, if not all, solar geoengineering proposals. ENMOD Parties agree "not to engage in military or any other hostile use of environmental modification techniques having widespread, long-lasting, or severe effects as the means of destruction, damage, or injury to any other State Party."[4] However, the agreement explicitly states that it "shall not hinder the use of environmental modification techniques for peaceful purposes,"[5] and since SAI as contemplated here would be intended to benefit rather than harm humanity, it would not seem to be constrained by ENMOD. The Convention on the Prevention of Marine Pollution by Dumping of Wastes and Other Matters, better known as the "London Convention," would potentially present problems for interventions such as ocean iron fertilization, though it could be claimed that the goal of such a program is not dumping of wastes but the supply of nutrients to benefit the cultivation of marine organisms. In all events, aircraft emissions that are not intended to dispose of wastes would fall outside the London Convention, even if some of them would eventually descend into the oceans. Aircraft emissions are separately the subject of guidelines from the International Civil Aviation Organization, but these pertain only to specific pollutants and do not address materials such as sulfates that are presently considered for solar geoengineering purposes. Moreover, the Convention on International Civil Aviation (the "Chicago Convention") codified the exclusive sovereignty which member states exercise over their airspace, so deployments within one's own territory would appear beyond the scope of aviation agreements.

The one international treaty that has had its remit stretched to encompass geoengineering is the United Nations Convention on Biological Diversity (CBD). In 2010, its parties ratified a declaration that "no climate-related geo-engineering activities that may affect biodiversity [may] take place, until there is an adequate scientific basis on which to justify such activities,"[6] though small-scale scientific research studies were specifically exempted. The anti-geoengineering activists who lobbied for this provision in the first place have subsequently insisted that this is tantamount to a "de facto moratorium on geoengineering projects and experiments,"[7] though the text makes clear that this would in fact apply only to projects that would affect biodiversity and could not be construed as small scientific experiments.[8] From a climate intervention perspective, this "moratorium" could be seen as a bit of a jurisdictional land grab, whereby the convention intruded into an issue only tangentially related to its scope or mandate. In 2016, the parties to the CBD themselves appeared to acknowledge the prior overreach, issuing a decision that explicitly calls for more research on the possible impacts of geoengineering on biodiversity.[9] There is therefore no international agreement that substantially constrains or shapes climate intervention research.

Nor are there domestic laws in the US or most anywhere else that directly apply to SAI specifically. In 2009 and 2010, the US House of Representatives Committee on Science and Technology held hearings on geoengineering which raised the need for a defined "allowed zone" for geoengineering research whereby "small-scale, low impact, short lifetime, limited ozone impact" experiments would be sanctioned.[10] The congressional service report that followed noted that while some forms of CDR may be adequately governed by existing domestic mechanisms, technologies that would be researched or deployed on the high seas, in the upper atmosphere, or otherwise beyond national jurisdictions, such as solar geoengineering, would need international governance for which no frameworks are yet operative.[11] Nonetheless, no legislative action derived from these hearings.[12]

Such governance as does apply in the US to field experiments is rather indirect and procedural. The National Environmental Policy Act states that major federal actions that significantly affect the quality of the human environment must be preceded by a publicly available Environmental Impact Statement. However, an agency is not barred from proceeding with a proposed action once it satisfies its procedural requirement, and small-scale field experiments with minimal physical effects would not trigger the requirement in the first place. There are no procedural requirements that would apply to private actors. Many states (though fewer than half) have similar regulations applicable to state agencies.

The Weather Modification Reporting Act requires any person engaging in weather modification activity in the United States to submit a report of such activity to the National Oceanic and Atmospheric Administration. As defined in the statute, "weather modification" would encompass some types of solar geoengineering experiments, but not all. Moreover, a duty to report does not prevent or even necessarily precede such an experiment. Again, several states have analogous requirements. Field experiments that harm persons or property could lead to tort law liability, but linking such harms to small experiments in the atmosphere would be very tenuous.

Given that there are few treaties or laws that specifically apply, the governance of geoengineering research that exists today is more nearly in the form of national regulations or international laws intended for other purposes but which might limit degrees of freedom in this arena. Examples would be routine environmental regulations that may require impact assessments or aeronautical rules requiring the filing of flight plans before take-off. Beyond such enforceable but perhaps tangential obligations, there are voluntary norms that may at least establish expectations. These start, as previously noted, with the Oxford Principles (geoengineering as a public good; public participation; transparency; independent assessment; governance before deployment) as well as some of the corollaries often appended to them, such as the primacy of mitigation and the requirement for legitimacy. To these, scholar Daniel Bodansky has suggested the possible addition of a requirement to prevent transboundary harm and to observe the precautionary principle, the idea that in the absence of sufficient scientific knowledge as to the impacts of environmental actions, parties ought to exercise due caution, with the potential actors assuming the burden of proof.[13]

Each of these ideas seems imminently sensible and they articulate norms that may in time solidify into something like obligations. Nonetheless, at this point, there is no formal codification or agreement on them, or even clarity as to which forum could or should debate, clarify, and adopt them. There is certainly therefore no party that could seek to enforce them.

## Current Governance Efforts and SCoPEx

Given that SAI research remains almost entirely lab- and model-based, the lack of an applicable governance regime is perhaps just as well. The only field test to date was a 2009 experiment, led by Russian researcher Yu Izrael, that examined how solar radiation passes through aerosol layers.[14] Since then, an attempted 2012 field test in the United Kingdom of a delivery system that envisioned lifting hoses to the stratosphere via balloons – the "SPICE" project – literally never got off the ground due to vehement local opposition to the acceptability of SAI.[15] In contrast, the Scripps Institute of Oceanography conducted a one-day aerial experiment in 2011 to monitor aerosol-cloud-radiation interactions for the purpose of better understanding prospective marine cloud brightening[16] that went off without a hitch. Similarly, the Australian government is currently funding marine cloud brightening experiments intended to shield the Great Barrier Reef from destruction,[17] once again with scant local opposition. It appears that the prospect of localized cloud interventions is seen quite differently than is SAI that would aspire to global impacts, even if the experiment itself were hyperlocal.

The next attempt to step outside and perform an experiment in the atmosphere is the Stratospheric Controlled Perturbation Experiment (SCoPEx) being led by Harvard's Frank Keutsch. The purpose of SCoPEx is to help tune the computer models used to portray SAI and ensure that they accurately reflect how injected particles high in the atmosphere would actually behave and interact both with the background air and each other. Despite the importance of accuracy in respect of such parameters, the current models rely upon unverified assumptions about, say, how much aerosol would be required to produce a certain degree of sunlight scattering and therefore cooling, or how substantially such material might impact the ozone layer. Reducing and ultimately resolving such uncertainties would be essential to producing accurate predictions as to how SAI would perform in the real world rather than simply in computer models.

For all its attention and potential importance, SCoPEx is a remarkably small experiment. A high-altitude balloon would loft a gondola up to 20 kilometers, not coincidentally, the same height at which we imagine SAI might occur.[18] The gondola would release roughly a kilogram of material into a linear plume perhaps 1 km long and a few hundred meters wide.[19] Onboard propellers would then allow the balloon to turn around and fly back through the plume, sampling the air as it goes and tracking the evolution of the released particles (see Figure 17.1 below).[20] The hope is that the craft could continue to traverse the plume several times over 24 hours, after which time the plume will be significantly dissipated. The initial payload is intended to be nothing more than ice to ensure that the hardware works as planned. Assuming it does, later flights would then deploy calcium carbonate, basically chalk. Releasing 1 kg of chalk high in the atmosphere would have no conceivable impact on anyone or anything back on Earth – after all, a Boeing 777-200 releases approximately 1.4 kg of considerably more toxic nitrous oxides every minute.[21] Nonetheless, SCoPEx has engendered substantial apprehension in the environmental community due to the precedent that some claim it would set in allowing geoengineering research to escape the laboratory.

To responsibly address those concerns in the absence of external governance constraints, the SCoPEx team under the auspices of

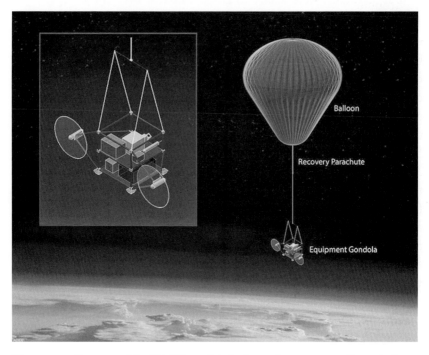

**Figure 17.1** Cartoon of the SCoPEx aerial platform. *Image source*: Keutsch Group at Harvard[22]

Harvard has imposed upon itself an extraordinarily rigorous governance structure. An external Advisory Committee was appointed to examine the ethical, environmental, and geopolitical impacts of the project. It consists of eight specialists in environmental law and policy, none of whom are affiliated with Harvard. Even the search committee appointed to choose the members of the Advisory Committee included at least one prominent geoengineering skeptic but no Harvard affiliates. The Committee is mandated to opine on the importance and related risks of the project and ensure its transparency. The SCoPEx team has agreed to be bound by the recommendations of the Committee and to delay or even abandon the project if the Committee is not satisfied. An initial platform test was announced for June 2021 in the far north of Sweden in cooperation with the Swedish Space Corporation. The balloon experiment would be an assessment of the flight hardware only, including the horizontal and vertical controls as well as the power, data, navigation, and communications systems. Not only would there be no aerosol release, but – presumably to tamp down any speculation about a covert release – the aerosol injection/release system would be left on the ground.[23]

All of that caution nonetheless proved insufficient to spare the test from controversy. In February 2021, an open letter was published by local environmental groups and indigenous people's representatives demanding the cancellation of the flight, citing the possible catastrophic consequences of SAI and noting that no consultations had taken place either with the local Saami people or Swedish society at large. Alluding to the presumed slippery slope from this pitifully small experiment to full-on deployment, the letter closes by stating that "Stratospheric Aerosol Injection research and technology development have implications for the whole world, and must not be advanced in the absence of full, global consensus on its acceptability."[24] On the one hand, who can argue against consultation? On the other, since I don't expect there will ever be "full, global consensus" on the acceptability of SAI, this is tantamount to a prohibition against outdoor research in this field, which may well be what the authors in fact have in mind. In all events, the public pressure overwhelmed the SCoPEx governance structure such that the June test has been scrubbed and no new dates have been announced.

While this may seem to be governance overkill in respect of a very small test, the project team seems to be conscious that this process has the potential to establish precedents by which future, and perhaps much larger, SAI field experiments will likely be guided. In this sense, SCoPEx is quite intentionally as much a governance experiment as a scientific one. One may in fact conceive of it as an upside-down pyramid, with an enormous governance superstructure built upon a teeny tiny 1 kg experiment. However, the Swedish imbroglio may demonstrate that even this scrupulous self-imposed governance procedure will prove insufficient to confer legitimacy on such research.

The SCoPEx advisory panel is not mandated or conceived of as an ongoing institution, but many believe that something much like it ought to be established on a permanent basis to interrogate future field experiments. However, no such organization yet seems in the offing. As governing geoengineering experiments is not consistent with the missions of any organizations tangentially related to global environmental progress, it would likely need to be a new institution. Edward Parson of UCLA, among the world's leading authorities on the governance of geoengineering, has called for the creation of a "World Commission on Climate Engineering."[25] We should not be surprised if, in this decade, a convention is organized to consider just that.

## Outdated Fears About SAI Research Governance

However, in the run-up to any such convention, one would expect many of the loudest voices to urge a boycott, echoing the perspective of the SCoPEx opponents that no such convention could be legitimate since no field experiments related to SAI should ever be conducted.[26] There are five main arguments about the risks of SAI that critics use in attempts to justify a ban on field research: covert deployment, non-state deployment, weaponization/threat multiplier, blurry line, and slippery slope/technological lock-in.

The first reservation that motivates a subset of those who seek to limit SAI research is the prospect of covert deployment wherein a rogue actor might attempt to modify the global climate without international knowledge or consent.[27] The rogue actor could be conceived as a grievously climate-damaged country that has lost patience with global dithering or a large greedy corporation, but is more colorfully envisioned as "Greenfinger," "a self-appointed protector of the planet" with access to a billionaire fortune who in classic James Bond anti-hero fashion decides to take matters into his or her own hands.[28]

While SAI would be dramatically cheaper than other climate interventions,[29] a globally substantial intervention would still be a massive industrial undertaking, involving hundreds of airliner-sized planes, thousands of employees, an extensive supply chain, and enormous financial resources.[30] Even a program intended to have merely regional or national impact would still require a substantial fleet of large aircraft. The activity required not only to fly these aircraft but to purchase, maintain, and base them would be readily detectable not only by multiple intelligence services but by civilian satellites selling observational data to the general public.[31] It would take months if not years to build to a climate-changing concentration of aerosols in the atmosphere, and the aviation activity would need to be repeated every day, around the clock and across the globe.[32] All of this is far too much industrial activity to hide.

A second reservation wrapped up in the Greenfinger scenario is non-state deployment. However, given the arguments refuting covert deployment, the non-state conjecture also quickly crumbles upon examination. Pre-start capital costs for a climate-altering SAI program would require several billion US$,[33] and the ongoing, annual cost to change global climate by 1°C is roughly US $18 billion.[34] These costs would quickly drain the fortunes of even the world's wealthiest individuals and surpass the annual military budget of all but perhaps a dozen countries. Even if non-state actors could amass the fortune required to fund a climate-altering SAI operation, they would require territorial sovereignty to carry it out[35] and the military wherewithal to defend the program from a likely hostile uninvolved world.[36]

Another oft-cited reservation about SAI research is that the end product might be weaponized,[37] although since the sort of global intervention considered herein is not readily targetable, it is hard to see how. Similarly, it has been theorized that like climate change, geoengineering should be considered a "threat multiplier"[38] because it may disrupt underlying social, political, and economic structures, but this seems to confuse SAI with the problems it is meant to ameliorate. While much research remains to be completed, at this early juncture the best available study indicates that moderate SAI would have a positive climate impact in all large regions of the world.[39] While climate change would indeed seem to be a threat multiplier, if SAI masks some of the warming associated with climate change and returns temperatures closer to the preindustrial baseline, it would seem more likely to function as a "threat divider."

Yet another common critique is the hypothesized blurry line between experimentation and deployment, the idea that planned experiments draw too clean a distinction between researching and deploying technology[40] and that testing SAI would be impossible without its full-scale deployment.[41] However, such objections were much more compelling before we had any concrete examples to consider. We would learn quite a lot from the tiny SCoPEx project, and yet the gulf between that 1 kg dispersal and the 200,000 tonnes of aerosols proposed in just the first year of one theorized deployment scenario demonstrates the absurdity of this objection.[42] The very last stages of pre-deployment experimentation would indeed need to be global in scale even if small in scope and temporary in duration, but we are hundreds of experiments and many years from there. For a decade and perhaps several, the distance between experimentation and deployment would be a vast gulf.

Finally, it is commonly proclaimed that any serious consideration of SAI creates the risk of an inexorable descent down a slippery slope to deployment.[43, 44, 45] One author, Clive Hamilton, claims that "On the slippery slope, technologies gather added political momentum because we live in societies predisposed to seek technological answers to social problems."[46] Another, Mike Hulme, adds that "Once SAI technology has reached a certain scale of development, the next stage of development is easily justified. The momentum grows until full-scale deployment eventually becomes unstoppable."[47] However, none of these authors has offered a causal chain that would render SAI more prone to having a slippery slope than any other technology.[48] And, further, a recent survey of researchers found so many barriers to SAI research progress that the authors concluded the "challenges for climate engineering should therefore today be thought of as less of a slippery slope than an 'uphill struggle'."[49] The most compelling, hypothesized causal chain is that commercial interests may drive SAI forward out of greed. While this dynamic is wholly plausible in later stages when infrastructure development is underway, in the research phase, with deployment highly uncertain even decades from now, the incentives have proven insufficient to attract investors big or small. In fact, I have been attempting for several years to entice the commercial aviation community to engage with this program, with little industry participation to show for it.

In a related argument, some SAI critics argue that the technology is prone to "technological lock-in," whereby market failures enable a weaker solution to prevail over stronger ones.[50, 51] Jack Stilgoe asserts: "The history of technology tells us that innovation is 'path dependent' and prone to 'lock in,' which can result in the triumph of bad technologies ... Geoengineering is already being scientized, creating lock-in and path dependency that may prove irreversible."[52] As with the slippery slope, the operative question related to technological lock-in should be whether SAI technology is subject to path dependency either to an unusually high degree or in an unusually harmful manner. Given the widespread perception that it is an imperfect remedy with high risks of unintended consequences, it is hard to see SAI crowding out other solutions such as mitigation, CCS, or DACCS.

I don't perceive any of the above as valid bases on which to seek to impede research into SAI. In fact, I believe we need vastly more of it, which is why I have volunteered to join this effort. I can imagine that the world would be well served by a global body not merely interrogating such research and ensuring its transparency, but in fact facilitating and accelerating it. Not merely negative governance of irresponsible or covert research, but positive governance to ensure that if and when the world demands such an intervention, we can deliver it with as much confidence as possible. We need vastly more dedicated research at universities and in government institutions than exists today. What we must affirmatively guard against is a future scenario in which the world perceives a climate emergency and plunges forward into SAI without sufficient pre-deployment research. There are those who imagine that by constraining research today, we can prevent deployment tomorrow. However, the future will make decisions about remediating prospective climate emergencies without bothering to ask the permission of the present. It seems much more likely that a lack of research in the coming decade or two would precipitate rash, risky deployment rather than non-deployment.

## Governance of Pre-Deployment Research and Preparation

In considering governance of SAI research prior to deployment, the concept of an "allowed zone" continues to arise. The idea is to acknowledge that small-scale, short-duration experiments with *de minimis* climatic impact need not be the subject of governance any more than other physics or chemistry experiments, but that beyond some threshold, different rules should apply. David Keith and Edward Parson have suggested that the threshold should be set at 0.01 watts per meter squared,[53] an extraordinarily small amount given that to change global temperatures by 1°C one would require a sustained reduction of 1.43 W/m² across the entire surface of the planet.[54] Nonetheless, this very low threshold illustrates that scientists believe they can learn a great deal via very small experiments. Research that sits below the threshold should also be required to pose no risk of material transboundary impacts.

Below the *de minimis* threshold, research could be decentralized and heterogeneous, as most other research in the physical and natural sciences is today. On the other hand, field experiments above the threshold would be the subject of review by an international panel such as Parson's World Commission, with "rules and procedures that would likely be increasingly centralized, legalized, and promulgated by states and intergovernmental institutions."[55] As envisioned by Jesse Reynolds, the author of a major new compendium of scholarship on SRM governance, such a commission would have five core functions: facilitate research; ensure research is done responsibly; prevent premature escalation or deployment; foster international trust in SRM efforts; and minimize mitigation obstruction.[56]

Such a body might also be more legitimately situated to call for a global moratorium on research above some higher threshold, irrespective of whether it has impact on biodiversity or is intended for peaceful purposes. This would then create a layer-cake of permitted research: a free for all below the *de minimis* threshold, and inspection regime above it, and a prohibited zone above that for projects that in the ENMOD framing might have impacts that would be "widespread, long-lasting, and severe."[57]

## Governance of Deployment

If ever the world crossed over the threshold to commence deployment, different governance considerations come into play, but perhaps it is necessary for a moment to pause right on the cusp of that threshold. From my current vantage point, the commencement of an intended long-term SAI deployment for the purpose of cooling the planet (rather than as a last research step) looks as if it would be among the most consequential decisions in human history. In fairness, that assessment may be overkill. Further research may prove that SAI would be far more benign and less risky than it now appears (it of course could also prove exactly the opposite). Our confidence in monitoring its impacts, attributing them to causes, and fine-tuning the implementation should and, one hopes, would increase dramatically. By the time we commence, it may not seem like so big a deal, particularly following other major climate interventions we may have undertaken by then, such as a more binding and enforced regime of emissions reductions and/or a massive global CDR program. Nonetheless, from where I sit today, the onset of SAI would seem to be a pivotal point in human history.

There are myriad permutations by which humanity could arrive at such a juncture, but most of them involve a world that has gotten pretty hot. In the absence of that, I would imagine that the entirely rational fears associated with this radical intervention would be very difficult to overcome. However, I think it more likely than not that it will get hot indeed, so future decision makers may perceive the cost/benefit calculus differently than we do.

As discussed above, SAI deployment will necessarily be the province of large states or clubs of them. Perhaps the easiest scenario to imagine is one wherein a nuclear superpower decides that it must deploy SAI for its own climate security. It adorns this decision with claims about climate sovereignty and coaxes other members into a coalition. However, it does not necessarily seek a universal coalition and, in all events, does not achieve one. Rival coalitions with differing preferences as to the manner, magnitude, or timing of climate intervention may form. This is the scenario envisioned by Jesse Reynolds in his recent book. Reynolds therefore imagines the primary role of deployment governance may be limited to be one of encouraging openness and cooperation among multiple national or multilateral coalitions of deployers.[58] Such a scenario takes a realistic view of the degree to which the preservation and assertion of sovereign rights of action among military superpowers is the default mode. If the US or China or even India concluded that climate change was an imminent threat to its agricultural sector, it might simply assert its right to vent aerosols in its own airspace and perhaps over the high seas too and assign the task to its air force.

Realistic though it may be, this is also a formula for governance outcomes somewhere between bad and disastrous. Not only might contrasting climate goals and preferences lead to conflicting and cacophonous climate interventions, but it would be nearly impossible to attribute harmful or beneficial SAI impacts to particular SAI programs. Attribution of SAI impacts will be very difficult in the best of circumstances. If the Indian monsoon doubles in intensity (or halves), it might take a decade to tease out whether that was due to SAI, to ongoing climate change, to changes in the heat uptake of the Indian Ocean, or to unrelated, natural climate variation. And while this delicate science is being undertaken by earnest climate researchers and also being negotiated among perhaps less earnest government officials, mounting deaths from catastrophic floods or droughts in the Ganges basin may have India screaming for less – or more – SAI (apologies for picking on India here. I love the place!). Ongoing attribution uncertainties may make it difficult for a deployer to fine-tune and modulate its intervention programs as they progress. Such problems would be greatly multiplied if there were not one but several potentially competing, conflicting, or uncoordinated simultaneous deployment efforts. Deployments by superpowers in the northern hemisphere risk under-deployment in the southern hemisphere, with all the disruptions to global atmospheric and oceanic circulations that could result. No doubt that, in such a scenario, governance that encourages cooperation would be much better than no such governance, but the best case would be to avoid this scenario altogether.

As noted earlier, the best-case governance framework would be to entice the world into a single global SAI program carried out by a monopolist deployer on behalf of humanity. While yoking all the states of the world (or at least all the major military powers) to a single cart would seem like an extraordinarily tall order, I am in fact more optimistic on this front than I would be in respect of equally coordinated global action on mitigation or CDR. What makes mitigation cooperation so hard is the free-rider dynamic, whereby it is in everyone's interest to delay and cheat, while hoping their neighbor does the "right" thing. SAI is instead characterized by the free-driver temptation, wherein it is cheap enough that many large national economies could fund a global program. This could lead to a race to the bottom in which the (sufficiently powerful) party desiring the lowest temperature level would prevail, were it not for the fact that an SAI program would be easily detectable by the uninvolved world, which would then be mightily motivated to object and either deter the program or demand a seat at the table. Add to this the fact that SAI is a non-excludable good, and we get circumstances in which there are in fact powerful incentives to cooperate.

The governance objective then for SAI should be that if humanity seems likely to deploy it, we should establish an entity that could act as a global monopolist deployer. An entity not merely with a mandate to coordinate and referee among deployers, but to actually plan and direct the deploying, thereby ensuring a single global program that pursues the interests of the entire planet rather than any single nation. Hopefully this would be done in a manner consistent with the Oxford Principles, such that it is acting for the public interest in a fully transparent way (you may wonder if I have started drinking early today . . .), but *acting*, which is the most positive form of governance.

It is too soon to begin putting a global monopolist deployer in place today. Deployment is highly contingent and remains a long way off. The framework for the near term is Parson's World Commission to inspect research, though that Commission could plausibly evolve into one that would direct deployment. On the other hand, waiting until the cusp of deployment to put in place the deployment governance institution would be too late. I don't fear technical lock-in with respect to SAI research, but I do more nearly fear *institutional* lock-in with respect to divided SAI deployment. Once separate national SAI programs are underway, I expect it would be much more difficult to derail them in favor of a single global program. More specifically, since the sort of high-altitude, high-payload aircraft fleet required to implement SAI does not yet exist and needs therefore to be developed, the key temporal fulcrum is actually the commencement of the development of the first generation of deployment aircraft. If that happens in national silos, it may prove hard to avoid national SAI programs. Once funding materializes to develop aircraft, it is essential that such funding be multilateral rather than national.

While legitimacy demands that such a deployment organization represent every state in the world, cohesion and effectiveness requires that at minimum it include every state that could plausibly undertake unilateral geoengineering. If a small state declines a seat at the table because it seeks faster or slower action on SAI, that dents aspirations for universal legitimacy, inflicting an injury on the project, but hardly a fatal one. However, if a large state decides to proceed on its own rather than act in concert, that is an existential threat to the global monopoly. The scope of a deployment organization needs to be structured with that in mind. Some observers imagine that as a matter of climate justice, any

SAI operation should be forced to set aside substantial funds either to compensate parties that may be negatively impacted either by an SAI program or by climate change itself. While such side-payment regimes may play well in Chapter 18 which considers ethics, in this governance chapter, it should be noted that they would reduce the likelihood of successfully lashing unruly superpowers into a single global monopolist deployment scheme.

## Implications for Global Order

Isolationists and ardent nationalists will have gotten queasy several pages ago as we contemplated the scope of the global governance that would be required to implement SAI in the fashion considered here. In what is, in my view, the best-case SAI scenario, we have a global deployment organization directing and monitoring a huge climate intervention all over the planet for decades that may stretch to a century. One prays (perhaps naively) that it would act in pursuit of the public good but may well make mistakes like any other institution. While it will be intended for humanity as a whole to gain, there may well be regional losers as well. States will lobby fervently for their individual interests, but even in an idealized democratic process, some will get the short end of various sticks. Nonetheless, for all of this to work, states would have to be willing to subsume some of their sovereign interests to a global collective.

If that sounds like either a fairy tale or a nightmare, it may in time prove that the governance structures required to enforce deep decarbonization or massive, long-term CDR would be even more intrusive on national sovereignty and certain forms of personal liberty. It is simply not yet clear that the free-rider problems associated with mitigation or carbon removal can be left to voluntary national contributions. In all events, your presumed right to turn your acre of forest into pastureland or to drive the biggest SUV you can afford or fly to Bali for a vacation may need to be curtailed in the context of some global framework necessary to solve the biggest collective action problems humanity has ever faced. We are only at the beginning of the global governance evolution required to pull any of this off. But the climate as we know it and therefore our sustaining environment hangs in the balance. However we manage the climate problem, we will need somehow to accommodate empowered international institutions and a lot of Big Brother.

# 18 ETHICS

## Ethics of Climate Change

In respect of climate change and our portfolio of possible responses to it, humanity confronts daunting and awesome decisions. Our choices will be shaped by a great deal of science, economics, and policy, all of which have been at the core of this book. But they will also be informed by ethics, what *should* we do rather than merely what *can* we do. And unfortunately, the ethical terrain here is awful – "a Perfect Moral Storm"[1] in the words of Stephen Gardiner, one of SAI's chief ethical critics.

Almost everything about climate change is unfair. To reformulate and thereby confound an old axiom of karmic payback, in the climate arena, what goes around comes around – to someone else. It is largely the wealthy within societies who enjoy the benefits of large carbon footprints, but the poor who suffer the most immediate consequences of climate change. The Global North has advanced via the economic development that industrialization and then the knowledge economy have enabled, while the Global South will disproportionately bear the brunt of heat stress, food insecurity, and desertification. The past and present have profited from the unmitigated right to dump our carbon and methane refuse into the atmosphere, but the future will foot the bill. None of that seems just, but unfairness is unfortunately intrinsic to the climate problem and the incentives to behave well are very weak.

In Gardiner's analysis, this Perfect Moral Storm results from several structural aspects of the climate problem. There is firstly a ruinous dispersal of cause and effect.[2] With air or water pollution, the cause and effect are generally easy to link. The flue beside a paper mill belches acrid smoke, and the people downwind both smell the sulfur and suffer the health effects of breathing it. An industrial chemical discharge drains into a river, and the fish downstream die. While some of the impacts of such pollution can be discerned far from the emission source, the intensity of effects is usually positively correlated to proximity, such that the region of the emission source has the greatest interest in abating it. On the other hand, the GHGs that affect climate become very well mixed into the atmosphere and affect conditions equally in places that are immediately adjacent to the emission source and halfway around the world. The impacts are also well dispersed not only spatially but temporally and will be experienced not only by the next generation but by the next millennium.[3]

Although by no means unique to climate change, there is also at work here a fragmentation of agency.[4] With our smokestack example, it is clear who the polluter is and at least usually clear who has the authority to regulate, tax, or impede the polluter. In the case of climate, some environmentalists seek to pin responsibility for the emissions on the fossil fuel industry, but nearly all of us are its customers, so pointing that finger seems hypocritical in a discussion of ethics. Nor is it clear who has agency to solve this problem. With the abandonment of the more prescriptive Kyoto Protocol, it is now under Paris the province of each of the nearly 200 sovereign nations on Earth to elect (or not) to address these issues within its borders.

Which is to say that we further suffer here from an institutional inadequacy.[5] It may prove that the UNFCCC in furtherance of the Paris Agreement will evolve into the institution the world needs in order to marshal effective mitigation and perhaps even CDR as well, but it is certainly not that yet. Nor has any state constructed, within its borders, the regulations, economic incentives, monitoring capabilities, and reporting frameworks necessary to get to net zero. Most of the required institution building is beyond the horizon of our headlights rather than in the rearview mirror.

However, the most vexing aspects of the moral storm are intergenerational. Climate change is a severely lagged phenomenon.[6] Its back-loaded impacts dissociate cause and effect and undermine the motivation to act. By the time it is bad enough to be widely perceived as an urgent priority, we will already be committed to much worse. Agents that are spatially separated can negotiate, but ones that are temporally separated cannot.[7] Democratic processes do not serve us here. In any vote about climate actions, the tally will always be: Present-1; Future-0. As the benefits of emissions accrue mostly to the present while the costs are exported to the future, the temptation to behave in ways that the future will perceive as morally corrupt will be overwhelming, and iterative.[8] Each generation will mature into power only to realize that it can extract no retribution from the past, but can reluctantly screw the future in its turn. To assuage its conscience, each generation can in fact find clever ways to justify such decisions, since money spent to address the problems of tomorrow's poor can instead be spent to ameliorate the plight of today's poor, and by the logic of discounting, the interests of today's poor count more than those of tomorrow's poor. It's perfect, an endless generational scheme for passing the buck along with the torch.

Nonetheless, the concept of discounting is itself controversial in this context. As noted in Chapter 5, the idea is imported from the world of finance and recognizes that a dollar today is worth more than a dollar a year or a decade from now, due both to opportunity costs and to differing levels of certainty. It is less clear that the opportunity cost concept ports neatly from finance to climate policy, but the certainty differential clearly does. We simply know much more about the present than we do about the future, and can therefore make better decisions about how to allocate current resources than we can about future resources. However, if we haul that concept into the arena of intergenerational climate ethics, it means that we should value happiness in the near term more highly than happiness in the long term, and therefore the happiness of this generation more than that of the next generation. Can we justify that? Can we really deem that the interests of people in the future count less than do ours today?

One avenue by which perhaps to justify such a conclusion would be to recognize that tomorrow's poor are likely to be more affluent than today's poor and therefore less needful of our help. This raises the admittedly fraught question of whether we can actually justify to our grandchildren the environmental damage we are bequeathing them by continuing to sustain high economic growth. In other words, if we leave them hotter but richer, is that a square intergenerational deal? (As I said, this is awful terrain.)

## Notions of Justice

Against this dismal ethical backdrop, it is essential to ask ourselves how we find a way out of the trap such that we may be perceived by our descendants with something like gratitude rather than moral censure. Now that we can no longer claim ignorance as to the science (though a few still do ...), how can we escape a fate in which our great grandchildren perceive us the way the descendants of former Klansmen may view their forbearers?

Presumably that starts with unearthing principles that we can consider to be ethical bedrocks and proceeding from there. In the climate arena, the three most common justice framings are distributive, reparative, and procedural. Among these, distributive justice is usually front and center, as this pertains to the equitable distribution of: the benefits afforded by the activities that lead to emissions; the costs of remediating those emissions; and the damages that will accrue from climate change. The ethical problem here of course is that the wealthy and the living get the benefits of our GHG-rich economy, whereas the poor and the unborn will experience an unjustifiably high share of the costs and risks of climate change. While the method of enforcing a more ethical distribution continues to prove hard to devise, *conceiving* a more equitable distribution is pretty straightforward. The wealthy within societies and the developed world as a whole should be called upon to shoulder a larger share of the burdens necessary to reduce emissions and adapt to a warmer world. And they need to do so sooner than the rest of the world. As the largest wealthy society, it is hard to defend an ethical position that the US should be permitted to be a foot-dragger rather than a leader in combating climate change.

A related but distinct ethical lens is reparative justice, which would adopt a backward-looking orientation and elicit compensation for past harms, meaning that those who most contributed to the accumulation of the climate problem have the greatest obligation to repair it. This is yet again straightforward in concept, but complicated in the climate arena by the slow accumulation of harms. The industrial revolution in England was both midwifed by and the midwife of the emergence of the widespread adoption of coal power. Does that give the UK some differentiated climate debt that it owes to future generations? The US long ago surpassed the UK in emissions per capita and, along with Australia, Saudi Arabia, and Kazakhstan, now leads the world's major emitters in this dubious category.[9] Are my children somehow responsible for this legacy? What about Gulf petro-states, whose economies were built by enabling the world to foul its atmosphere? Does a girl born today in Abu Dhabi inherit some sort of original sin which she is obligated in her life to redeem? That girl might someday join my own children in saying "we can't possibly be held responsible for misdeeds committed before we were born. It can't be ethically sound that some people in the world are born into a status of climate debtors, owing the world for carbon they didn't consume." And yet a representative of the world's developing nations might respond that what those fortunate children of the developed world inherit is a standard of living that was created by those prior emissions, and that such a gilded patrimony should come at a price.

In addition to fairness as to who gets what, it also matters who is making the decisions and whose voices are being heard – issues that fall under the rubric of procedural justice. Under the "all affected" principle, all those who will be impacted by a decision should have a right to participate in making it. Since climate affects everyone, that would suggest a universal right to some form of participation in the process as well as transparency in the outcomes. Prior to the establishment of the UNFCCC, greenhouse gas emissions were not the subject of international law. It has only been via the UNFCCC process that greenhouse gases have been formally recognized as a common concern for all of humanity and that therefore Country A should have any interest in Country B's emissions. As noted, Paris does not yet include any mechanism whereby the outside world can enforce its emissions preferences upon any state, but the Global Stocktake exercise that is just now ramping up does give the global community a right to assess and interrogate the emissions of other countries. That is a critical early step in evolving to a view that your emissions are my business and vice versa, which is essential to achieving participatory justice in the climate arena.

The IPCC has also made notable strides in ensuring that the voices of all nations are heard in the climate process. As one would expect from a forum that grew out of other UN bodies, a scan of the nationalities of the hundreds of authors contributing to the forthcoming Sixth Assessment Report makes clear that while developed countries with well-funded universities perhaps get an outsized voice, the entire world including the less developed nations of the Global South is clearly participating. While poorer nations are well represented, whether poor people are is much tougher to say. The authors of the Report are selected from the global scientific elite, so how well a professor speaks for people living in slums is unclear.

Even if everyone is represented at the table, the process by which decisions are made can also be more just or less so. Emissions decisions are still made at a national level, which would seem procedurally unjust since their impact is global. The UNFCCC like most UN bodies seeks to make decisions by consensus, which is highly inclusive but gives small states outsized clout. What would constitute just procedures by which to make decisions either about emissions or about climate intervention in all its forms are matters on which the world is at a very immature state of evolution. Nonetheless, effective and inclusive solutions to the climate problem will require that humanity drive out some legitimate answers to those questions.

We already have some starting points. The Oxford Principles reviewed in the preceding chapter were promulgated in respect of geo-engineering specifically, but they include ethical judgments that seem valid in the climate regime more generally. A duty to act in the common interest with public inclusion in the decision making and transparency about process and results, all that seems not only ethically sound but rather incontrovertible. To these we might add a duty to manage risks via the precautionary principle. There is a great deal about the science of climate that is well established. Nonetheless, it is equally true that we are steering into uncharted waters and confronting enormous unpredictability in respect of issues such as climate sensitivity and tipping points. Given that, the precautionary principle would suggest that we minimize risks and take precautions where we reasonably can. Wherever possible, we should look before we leap and research before we act. The fact that we can't accurately anticipate the magnitude of warming we are selecting for our grandchildren does not justify deferring all decisions until the answers are known. It would instead mandate taking a more conservative emissions approach until we are reasonably certain we are not making the world utterly inhospitable for our descendants, as well as responsibly researching the likely impacts of climate interventions before we undertake them.

The context in which such discussions take place relates to the idea of a fixed carbon budget for the world. According to the IPCC, in order to have a high likelihood of limiting climate change to no more than

$2°C$ above the preindustrial baseline, mankind had a cumulative budget of just below 1,200 additional Gt of $CO_2e$ (all greenhouse gases, expressed in $CO_2$ equivalents) that it could emit between 2018 and the net zero year.[10] However, just since 2018, we have emitted roughly 7 percent of that budget, meaning we only have ~1,100 Gt remaining or 26 years of further emissions at our current rate. As soon as we conceive the emissions problem as one wherein there is a finite budget, ethical issues arise. It seems straightforward that each human should have a right to an equal share of that budget. Peter Singer has estimated that to stabilize emissions at current levels, we would need to limit per capita emissions of carbon to one metric tonne per year (note: we have switched units here, from gigatonnes to tonnes, and from $CO_2e$ to simply carbon).[11] Americans average more nearly five. Citizens of Europe, Japan, and Australia are in the range of two to four. Though climbing rapidly, the Chinese are at 0.8, whereas carbon-thrifty Indians are at 0.3.[12] If Americans emit five times their allotted share, they are consuming the emissions allocation of several people in Pakistan or Malawi. One might, in the first instance, say that the Americans can't ethically justify that, or in the second instance, that they should at least compensate their counterparts in the Global South for their carbon gluttony. That would saddle the developed world with the burden of cleaning up the mess it is continuing to make and force it to comply with the "polluter pays" principle.

And yet, if we further seek to consider arguments that nations (if not necessarily individuals) are indeed responsible for the past, the matter becomes yet more vexing. One could argue that the US has been over-spending its fair carbon budget for all of the past century and therefore has none left. It has used it up long ago. It has no remaining allowable positive emissions, but rather, should immediately flip to negative emissions, sucking previously emitted carbon out of the atmosphere in order to make room in the carbon budget for the Indonesians of tomorrow, for whom there is currently insufficient headroom to allow them to emit their fair share and develop their economies.

Will that happen? No. But is that an ethically tenable position? It would seem to be . . .

## Ethics of Climate Intervention

While all of the ethical questions that arise with respect to climate change also map onto geoengineering, climate interventions also evince particular ethical challenges, the most salient of which (as we have previously noted) is the prospective crowding out of mitigation ambition, or "moral hazard." The idea is that mitigation will prove hard, expensive, and slow, which will naturally and quite rationally cause people to seek excuses not to do it. The easiest excuse is to argue that climate change is not in fact real, anthropogenic, or dangerous, or to imagine solving these problems is someone else's responsibility. But, if we get past all that, there is then the fear that people will hear about adaptation and/or climate intervention in any of its forms and decide that we can mitigate less, or later, because those other solutions will bail us out. The idea is that if there are various possible candidates for "Plan B," humanity will reduce its ambition with respect to Plan A.

Using an analytical framework applied by Daniel Edward Callies to other reservations about SAI,[13] this moral hazard claim is comprised of both an empirical and a normative claim. The empirical claim is that people would in fact react in that way, that knowledge about other possibilities will weaken the incentive to reduce emissions. As we will discuss in Chapter 19, it is not yet clear – particularly with respect to SAI – that this prediction is accurate.

Nonetheless, there is also herein a normative claim that if people reduced their emissions ambition because they believed there were other strategies by which to respond, such a substitution would necessarily be ethically unjustifiable. In my view, this part of the claim fails. I urge the world to mitigate more and faster – all good climate pathways start with that. And I am straining to ensure that this book does not misrepresent geoengineering as a perfect and pain-free "solution" to climate change, such that any substitution choices for which readers hereafter advocate are well informed, warts and all. However, would it be ethically wrong for people to choose a little less mitigation and a little more – say – DACCS? I don't see that, particularly if that decision is soundly considered and the substitution is undertaken by the same temporal cohort such that it does not involve any generational buck-passing. The world will struggle mightily with the climate debt we are racking up and it will have little choice but to avail itself of an "all of the above" portfolio of solutions. The last 20 percent or so of our emissions from sectors like steel, cement manufacturing, rice farming, and aviation will prove very expensive to eliminate. I can certainly imagine that in respect of those, it may prove cheaper to offset them with flue gas capture or DACCS than to eliminate them. I don't see it as our place today to make moral judgments about how others in the future choose to optimize that portfolio.

However, someone making the moral hazard argument might respond that the salient concern is not one of constraining the future, but of channeling the efforts of the present. The fear is that publications such as this book will create more widespread knowledge about a prospective climate intervention toolbox, which may provide thought-less, or worse yet, cynical excuses to further defer mitigation *this year*, irresponsibly passing more burden to the future. Expressed in those terms, I am entirely sympathetic to this concern. I worry that this book may be received in just that way (mostly by people who don't actually read it), despite my best efforts to the contrary. But what is the right response to that concern? It can't be, as the moral hazard argument usually implies, that we seek to conceal knowledge from people or enforce ignorance upon them. The geoengineering toolbox does exist, at least in the form of a list of promising early stage R&D projects. I am pretty convinced that later in this century the world will eagerly want to employ some of those tools. Despite our concern that the world may misunderstand the best use of these climate interventions, the ethical response can't possibly be to seek to hide them and bequeath to our descendants the "gift of ignorance." In a chapter wherein our quest is to discern an ethical true north, our burden must be to ensure that people gain a full and unvarnished understanding of geoengineering rather than to blind them. To do the latter would be to commit the sin of paternalism (an oddly gendered insult, but the term that is used none-theless), whereby one seeks to make decisions for other people presum-ably in their best interest but without their knowledge or consent. The risk that moral hazard leads to bad decisions is real, but the ethical response mustn't be to rob other people of their agency.

Another common ethical objection to climate intervention is simply that it smacks of hubris. SAI in particular is described as an arrogant technofix with a high risk of unintended consequences.[14, 15, 16] The view would be that the global climate system is so exquisitely complex that we can't possibly expect to master it. All we are likely to do is screw it up and profane God's magnificent handiwork in the process. It is not merely the interests of mankind that must be served here, but those of animals, ecosystems, and the biosphere, none of whom of course have any representatives at the decision-making table. It is, indeed, a sort of arrogance that tempts us down this path, with the likely consequence that we will get burned and destroy the planet in the process.

I think all of that is an accurate description – of climate change. Some might seek to make an omission/commission distinction here, but, in my view, we are way past that point. While one could argue that emissions in the last century were an act of omission, those in this century are an act of fully cognizant commission, just as geoengineering would be. It is possible that some cures would prove worse than the disease, but that can't be asserted now. That would be like having halted the recent frantic global search for a COVID vaccine because some vaccine alternatives might have proven worse than COVID itself. That was/is entirely possible, but it is an empirical question that will be illuminated via research. The hope with pandemics and climate both is that some interventions can be found that improve the situation.

The plea that is implicit in the hubris argument is that we ought not to fiddle with the climate and mess with Mother Nature, but as events have unfolded over the last century, this has evolved into a false choice. There is no longer a viable "no climate change" option. The choices now are between a lot of climate change or merely some, and between climate change with geoengineering or without. Like it or not, we opted for hubris a long time ago.

Some critics also argue that climate intervention, and more particularly SAI, shirks responsibility for our emissions, and passes on to future generations a massive climate debt[17] that they may be unable to repay. This situation would arise if humanity emits its way to 3°C of forcing, but masks 2°C of that via SAI. An unwitting step towards such future climate liability would be for the world to place outsized faith in overshoot and claw back emission scenarios such as the P4 pathway presented in the SR15 report (see Chapter 2).[18] This would represent an unverified climate gamble rather than a secure strategy.[19] One tranche of this climate debt could be the obligation inherited by future generations continue to fund an ongoing SAI program for fear of triggering a rapid temperature snap-back ("termination shock"). SAI is relatively cheap, so the financial obligation involved may not be a very heavy lift, but ethicists sensibly ask whether it is justifiable to place the future in such a dilemma.

An even greater obligation could be that since prior generations had spent the entire finite climate budget noted above, future generations should be able to afford no emissions. In fact, to return the world to an acceptable climate, they may be obligated to fund massive *negative* emissions for decades or centuries, and at least with currently envisioned technologies, that would be onerously expensive. We would bequeath to the future limited flexibility and awesome obligations while reserving the benefits of cheap energy and rampant emissions for ourselves, offending distributive and procedural justice at minimum.

All that would seem unethical indeed, but would result from continuing high emissions, not from climate intervention research. If we don't quickly and responsibly abate our emissions, we will enforce climate dilemmas upon the future whether we develop geoengineering tools or not. In fact, if we put the future in such a position, I expect it would be grateful to also inherit prospective interventions by which to rescue themselves from the fate we have shipped to them. The near-term harm that could result from climate intervention capability development derives not from the research, but rather from how it is portrayed. If geoengineering is presented as a "get out of jail free" card, then mitigation deterrence likely will ensue. I worry that the SR15 has done exactly that by promising that we could claw back temperature overshoots later in this century via an impractical minuet with trees.

As regards how climate intervention might actually be used in the future, the capacity for evil lies not in the tools, but in the hands in which the tools are placed, which would make geoengineering like artificial intelligence, recombinant DNA, and lots of other emergent technology. Its misuse is a prospective danger but by no means an inevitability, or a reason to halt research and development.

An argument for, rather than against, the morality of SAI has been made by Josh Horton and David Keith of Harvard. They note that if climate change does indeed (as is widely predicted) have asymmetrical impacts which fall most heavily upon the world's poorest people and its poorest countries, and if SAI proves effective in ameliorating the harmful impacts of climate change (as yet unproven), then it is the poor who will benefit most asymmetrically from SAI.[20] They argue that the Global North has an ethical *obligation* (rather than merely a justification) to robustly research SAI and thereby be prepared should the need arise.[21]

Prominent among the critics of this view is Colorado College climate ethicist Marion Hourdequin, who notes the unfortunate irony embedded in the fact that research purportedly intended primarily to benefit the poor is being carried out by "those whose lived experience intersects relatively little with these burdens"[22] (though such an observation would appear to apply equally to Dr. Hourdequin). More substantively, she observes that the Horton/Keith rationale ignores procedural and recognitional justice.[23] She also calls out this ethical imperative as too self-serving a rationalization, coming as it did from a group already committed to researching solar geoengineering.[24] Her arguments have proven influential. Irrespective of whether the impacts of geoengineering would be asymmetrical or merely symmetrical in the Global South, it would be ethically unjustifiable to make any substantial decisions about climate interventions without the informed consent of such countries, and yet those countries are at a disadvantage in respect of the resources necessary to develop such informed views.[25] Stepping into the breach of this chicken/egg problem is a truly remarkable institution in the ethics and governance landscape of SAI, The Solar Radiation Management Governance Initiative (SRMGI). This UK-based charity hosts conferences and funds research grants intended to build knowledge of and governance capacity for SAI among developing countries. For example, SRMGI recently launched the world's first international SRM research fund for scientists from developing countries and emerging economies. They have also run 17 outreach meetings in 14 different countries, including Bangladesh, Brazil, China, Ethiopia, India, Jamaica, Kenya, Pakistan, the Philippines, Senegal, South Africa, and Thailand.[26]

## Making Climate Ethics Personal

Climate change and the prospect of addressing it via all the tools at our disposal are among the biggest issues confronting the world. They affect every person and every living thing today, tomorrow, and for millennia hereafter. The fate of the world, at least as we know it, really does seem to hang in the balance. And yet in the ethical arena, it is the smallest questions with which I most strenuously wrestle, and with which we are all called to grapple. What contribution to the solution are we personally called to make? What do the climate gods demand of us as individuals?

To call a spade a spade, I too am affiliated with fancy universities and have a "lived experience that intersects relatively little" with that of the global poor. I am an American, with a carbon footprint well above the already excessive national average. I spent most of my career as a commercial aviation executive, facilitating cheap jet travel for international salespeople, boozy vacationers, and imported consumer electronics alike. I perceived no ethical dilemmas in that, despite the fact that mine was among the most carbon-intensive industries in the world. Was I wrong to pursue that career? Did I toil in an evil industry?

I have traveled the world extensively and may soon do so again (COVID permitting) to promote this book. After "flight shaming" has emerged as a concept, can I justify that? We *must* reduce global emissions, all the way to zero, as quickly as possible. I have no coherent ethical argument as to why I should have a greater right to warm the planet than my counterpart in Bolivia, or for that matter a Bolivian born 50 years from now. And yet, that is what I am doing, and what I have always done. Am I a carbon sinner? Are you?

I teed up these questions in the penultimate meeting of my geoengineering course at Yale. I forewarned my students that in this session I would not instruct them, but instead we would for two hours grapple with these questions as peers, feeling our way in a common darkness. It reminded me of a Unitarian church service, wherein we contemplated ethical questions in communion but without the expectation of a common answer. A spiritual exploration. As preparation before class, I had each of them calculate not only their own thrifty student carbon footprints, but also those of their parents as proxies for whom these 21-year-olds might evolve to become. As it proved out, the class-average carbon footprints of their parental proxies exceeded the American average, and my own well exceeded the average of their parents.

After exploring the broad ethical landscape that has occupied the bulk of this chapter, I focused in on these final questions. What are we called to do *personally* to solve the climate problem? What sacrifices are we prepared to make?

I braced myself for accusatory fingers pointing out my bad prior and current habits, my American excesses: how I had spent the prior spring in Europe and did the once weekly 2.5-hour commute from Cambridge to New Haven mostly by car rather than by train. How my shameful diet still included beef and sushi, and how the square footage and energy inefficiency of my primary residence was beyond justification. I was ready to spend the drive back to Cambridge contemplating the moral challenge that would be presented by the long list of personal sacrifices that my students would enumerate that they had undertaken. How could I justify failing to thereafter join them in that carbon thrift? I was as ready as I could be.

I managed the class to a crescendo and then popped the question. "What personal sacrifices are each of you prepared to undertake to solve the climate problem?" The astonishing answer was – they shrugged. These were brilliant, climate-woke juniors and seniors all of whom had competed to get into this class at what is purported to be a bastion of liberalism. And yet, they had no answer. The question did not appear even to have previously occurred to them.

I say they had "no answer," but of course they were far from silent. These kids were high school valedictorians with sterling SAT scores all of whom had surmounted the withering Yale admissions process. They fairly burst with well-crafted and hyper-articulate answers – about what *others* should do. And how they would compel others to do those things: lobby their congressmen; vote out Trump; force Yale to divest from fossil fuel investments; join climate marches; cheer on Greta Thunberg; excoriate Exxon.

But no one was skipping the trip home at the end of the week for Thanksgiving, not even the student from Alaska. No one was forgoing the summer internship in Asia because it would take too long to get there and back by boat. Those that were vegans made that decision on bases other than climate. Even the most committed climate activist had been to a conference in South Korea the prior week and was shortly headed to another in Chile. No one had turned down the heat in their dorm to save fuel. Nada.

I drove home in a different state of shock than the one for which I had prepared. I don't know why I had expected my students to have made sacrifices that I myself had not, but I somehow did. My own personal lifetime score on climate actions was something like 1,000 to zero. All my decisions about my own carbon emissions were made on other bases: "do I have the desire, the time, the money to do this thing?" But not "what is the carbon impact?" This perspective along with the means to afford it had led me to a high emitting lifestyle. By that point, there was little I could do about the 1,000, but I couldn't stand the zero. I decided on that drive that given its outsized carbon footprint, I would give up beef. I don't particularly miss it actually. The least tasty part of a bacon cheeseburger on a toasted English muffin with lettuce and tomato and a dash of Tabasco is the little brown hockey puck at the center of it. More to the point though, I have now put *one* pathetic little point on the board. A paltry gesture, I know. Merely symbolic. But the scoreboard no longer reads zero.

I asked a handful of my climate colleagues at Harvard the following day the same question. Same nada. Are we all screaming climate hypocrites? What are we waiting for? I think part of it is no one can stand the sucker's share. I am willing to make sacrifices if we all make sacrifices. I am willing to curtail my lifestyle if the collective action context in which I do so leads to a collective good. But the utility of say air travel is so great relative to its cost that I am not willing to give that up for the mere purpose of virtue signaling. That may make me morally small. I would struggle to defend that choice at the Pearly Gates.

But I would be in a very long queue of people with the same problem.

My biggest learning from my own course at Yale was that few people have yet internalized the personal sacrifice that climate ethics would seem to demand of us. Which means a solution is a long way off indeed. I hope our great-grandchildren will be very understanding of us.

# 19 PUBLIC PERCEPTION

The societal changes that will be required to address the climate crisis are huge. They will impact nearly every aspect of the economy and our lifestyles – where we live, how we travel, what we eat, what we buy, how prosperous we will be, how we will govern the planet, how we will reconceive our ethical responsibilities to one another and future generations – more or less everything. The menu of options from which we may choose in each of these respects will be informed by the realities of science and economics and technology, but also by public perception. Policies driving changes as profound as those that will be required are unlikely to obtain or endure if they fail to garner widespread public support by diverse populations of citizens all over the world. This is obviously true in democracies, where unconvinced voters can "toss the rascals out," but even in autocracies such as China and Russia, the governments are very mindful of and attuned to the attitudes of the public. Public perception will not only shape the options on the table, but also the speed with which we can embrace them. A world mistrustful of climate science or fearful of prospective interventions will be far more reluctant to act quickly and boldly than one in which citizens are marching in the streets demanding solutions. If this is true in respect of collective action challenges such as mitigation or CDR, it is even more so in respect of SAI, where approximately the whole world's permission is required for legitimate deployment. The relevant "public" here is the broadest possible definition – essentially everyone, around the world. Climate solutions of the magnitude required can't reasonably be imposed on the world by elites. They will necessitate widespread, grassroots global support. So, what does the "person on the street" think about climate change, mitigation, adaptation, and most importantly for our purpose, climate intervention? Let's see what we can find.

## Public Views on Climate Change

On climate change, the first thing to note is that opinions are changing rapidly and there is increasingly widespread agreement that warming is real and constitutes a grave threat. With the world's most prominent climate denier no longer in the White House, an optimist can imagine that this may soon constitute something like global consensus. The World Risk Poll,[1] released in 2019 by the Lloyd's Register Foundation and Gallup Poll, surveyed over 150,000 people in 142 countries revealing that nearly 70 percent perceived climate to be either a "very" or "somewhat" serious threat, versus just 13 percent who were unconcerned and 18 percent who expressed no opinion. Distinct regional dichotomies exist, with roughly 90 percent of southern and northern/western Europeans deeply concerned, as are 85 percent of Latin American and Caribbean citizens.[2] Even at the other end of the scale, no fewer than 60 percent of East Asians and North Africans express the same views.[3] A different recent survey of 20 geographically diverse countries by Pew Research[4] found that majorities in all but one state viewed climate change as a very serious problem (the outlier was the Czech Republic at 49 percent). A similar survey a year earlier found that in 26 countries, a median of 68 percent viewed climate change as a major threat and 20 percent as a minor threat, with merely 9 percent seeing it as not a threat. These majorities have coalesced over time. In the early part of the decade, barely 50 percent of respondents viewed climate as a serious problem, but by the decade's end, it was over two-thirds.[5, 6]

This, in part, simply means the world is paying attention and starting to get the message. Over the last decade, the science has gotten clearer and the compounding impacts of climate-accentuated disasters such as heat waves, droughts, wildfires, storms, and floods have gotten harder to ignore. More than a handful of surveys over the past decade of either scientific literature[7] or climate scientists[8] directly have separately concluded that between 90 percent and 100 percent of sources concur with the view that human activity is warming the planet to a dangerous degree. In fact, there are enough such surveys producing sufficiently similar results to enable the compilation of a synthesis report titled "Consensus on Consensus"[9] which more or less said "there is unanimity on the finding that there is near unanimity" among scientists on the climate story (see Figure 19.1). A recent report went further yet, announcing that a literature search of 11,602 climate-related articles published in peer-reviewed journals during the first seven months of 2019 revealed virtually 100 percent agreement on the reality of human-induced warming.[10] This study has since been convincingly criticized for assuming concurrence in many instances where none was explicitly stated,[11] so a more accurate portrayal would be to say that all the reviewed articles either concurred or abstained, with no explicit contrary opinions. In all events, it is clear that among actual climate scientists, the naysayers have virtually disappeared. I for instance have never met one.

Nonetheless, the high degree of scientific consensus is poorly understood by the general public, so much so that the term "consensus gap" has been coined[12] to describe the wide gulf between the roughly 97 percent agreement among scientists and the public perception that there remains a raging debate between large cohorts on each side. A recent study revealed that only 12 percent of Americans are aware that more than 90 percent of scientists are in accord with respect to the basic climate story.[13] However, whereas scientists are in fact not substantially divided on these questions, the public is, with Pew finding that barely more than half of global respondents identified a human fingerprint in the observed warming, and less than 50 percent in a third of the countries surveyed.[14]

Perceptions of the threat of climate change turn out to be highly positively correlated with education, such that among people with 16 years of education (essentially, college graduates), 54 percent perceive climate as a very serious threat versus just 9 percent who report it to be not a threat at all. Among people with 0–8 years of education on the other hand, the numbers are 30 percent and 17 percent respectively.[15] However, this correlation does not map cleanly onto regions. Well-educated Southern and Western Europe are very climate concerned, but so too are less schooled Latin America and Southern Africa.[16] Northern America along with Australia and New Zealand are highly educated but mid-tier on the climate concern scale.[17] South Korea, Japan, and Taiwan all report higher levels of climate concern than the Anglophone countries on either side of the Pacific,[18] while Chinese surveys indicate that a stunning 94 percent of citizens believe that climate change is already happening.[19] Eastern Europeans are much

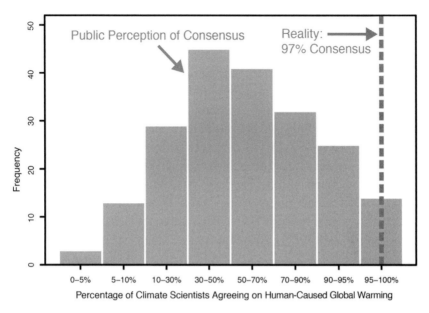

**Figure 19.1** Perception vs. reality regarding scientific consensus. *Source*: Skeptical Science, licensed under Creative Commons CC BY-SA 3.0[20]

more climate skeptical than their Western counterparts,[21] and the remainder of Africa, Asia, and the Middle East are yet less concerned.

The 20 countries with the highest level of respondents who see climate change as "not a threat at all" is a compendium of very lowly developed and educated countries such as Ethiopia, Uzbekistan, Iraq, Egypt, Myanmar, and the Dominican Republic.[22] Sitting smack in the middle of this list is one utterly bizarre outlier – the United States, home to the world's most active and ardent climate denial infrastructure (more on that shortly). This helps explain why the US appears to be the most polarized country on climate issues. A Pew study probing right/ left dichotomies in this arena reported that 86 percent of self-identified left-leaning respondents consider climate change to be a "very serious problem" versus just 22 percent of right leaners – a whopping 64 percent left/right differential.[23] Next on that spectrum were Australia and Canada with 43 percent/38 percent differentials respectively. Sweden, the UK, the Netherlands, and Germany have differentials clustered near 30 percent, whereas Spain, South Korea, and Brazil were below 15 percent. France came in at just 6 percent (i.e., virtually identical views on this issue across the political spectrum). While the US in particular and the Anglosphere more generally seem to be deeply riven on climate, that is not necessarily true elsewhere in the world.

That said, even in the US, we seem to be grinding towards grudging agreement on the fundamental story. The sixth iteration of a periodic national climate attitude survey[24] was recently completed and shows that large majorities of Americans now hold "green" opinions on several key issues. Fully 81 percent believe that temperature has been rising over the last 100 years and 63 percent are "highly certain" in that conclusion, versus just 45 percent in 1997.[25] This increasing certainty may result from the elevated percentage claiming at least a moderate amount of knowledge about global warming, which rose from 42 percent to 75 percent over the period.[26] Eighty-two percent attribute the warming at least partly to human actions. The survey data presented from Pew Research (Figure 19.2) and the Yale Program on Climate Change Communication (Figure 19.3) show similar convergence towards widespread agreement since 2008.

---

### Increased support for prioritizing policies on the environment, climate change since 2011

*% US adults who say protecting the environment/dealing with global climate change should be a top priority for the President and Congress:*

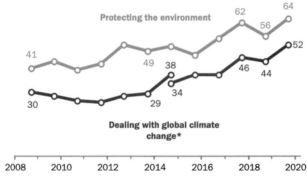

*In 2014 and earlier, respondents were asked about dealing with "global warming." In 2015 half the sample was asked about either "global warming" or "global climate change"; 34% called "global climate change" a top priority while 38% said this about "global warming." Source: Survey of U.S. adults conducted Jan. 8-13, 2020.
"As Economic Concerns Recede, Environmental Protection Rises on the Public's Policy Agenda"

**PEW RESEARCH CENTER**

---

**Figure 19.2** Increased support for climate policies. *Source*: Pew Research Center[27]

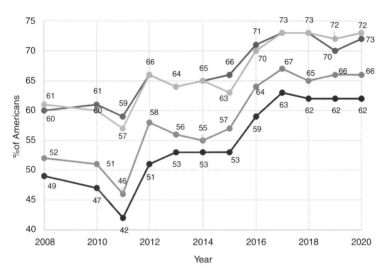

Figure 19.3 Risk perceptions of Americans about climate change over time. *Data source*: Yale Program on Climate Change Communication[28,29,30]

Perhaps even more remarkable than these substantial national majorities is that even among relatively climate-skeptical US states, majorities have coalesced on most of these issues. On the question of whether global warming has been happening, 88 percent of respondents in Massachusetts (the highest state) agreed, but an even more surprising 71 percent in Utah (the lowest) did as well.[31] Scores for whether warming will continue in the future were perhaps 5–10 percent lower, but all the New England states were still above 80 percent; all but six states were above 70 percent; and all states were above 60 percent.[32] On the crucial question of whether the past warming has been caused by humans, no state was below 70 percent in the affirmative and a few were above 90 percent.[33] As to whether this will be a serious problem for the US and separately for the world, concurrence in all states was above 60 percent and in some above 90 percent.[34] Even on the question of whether the US government should do more to address climate change, bare majorities of 53 percent in the mountain west were supportive as were more than 80 percent in some New England states.[35]

While in general the red state/blue state (i.e., Republican versus Democratic) dichotomy predicts attitudes on climate reasonably well, significant exceptions are South Carolina, Florida, Louisiana, and Texas, all of which show more climate-receptivity than their politics on other issues would imply, owing presumably to their long, low-lying hurricane-exposed coastlines. Pew Research indicates that those living within 25 miles of the coast are substantially more climate concerned than are other Americans.[36] If a consensus for much stronger climate action ultimately emerges in the US, it may well be due to these Southeastern seaboard states becoming strange bedfellows with climate-woke New Englanders and Californians.

As for *what* the government should do (see Figure 19.4), the most popular idea seems to be planting trees (more on this below). Enforcing better carbon behavior requirements on corporations is also very popular, be those emissions limitations for utilities, fuel efficiency standards for cars, or energy efficiency requirements for appliances and buildings.[37] Tax credits for good carbon behavior such as switching to electric vehicles or installing solar panels are even more popular.[38] Prioritizing the development of alternative energy sources is also widely favored. On the other hand, punitive measures for carbon-harmful behavior such as consumption taxes on electricity or gasoline are viewed very dimly,[39] particularly if the obligations fall directly on individuals rather than on corporations or governments. The unifying themes seem to be that we like positive incentives (rewards) rather than negative ones (penalties), and we would prefer that the obligations fall on someone else, particularly as we seem easily misled as to who foots the bill if corporate taxes or costs are increased (of course, we do via higher prices charged to consumers).

## The Climate Denial Industry

Americans appear to be migrating towards a consensus view on climate issues despite the determined and persistent efforts of a small but well-funded "denial machine" to sow continuing doubt on matters that science has long since put to rest. This movement is the latest incarnation of what is an unfortunately extensive heritage of American commercial interests using public relations campaigns to confuse and dupe the public on scientific matters. These tactics had their infamous birth in the early 1950s after the revelation by the medical profession that smoking was damaging to health.[41] Several major tobacco companies

Americans see too little federal action on climate
change, back range of policies to reduce its effects

*% of US adults who say:*

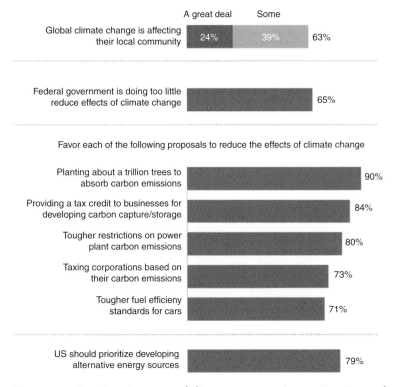

Figure 19.4 Americans' support of climate measures. *Source:* Pew Research
Center.[40] Note: Respondents who gave other responses or did not give an answer
are not shown. Survey conducted April 29–May 5, 2020.

converged on the public relations firm of Hill & Knowlton to devise
a counter-offensive. In a tactically brilliant insight that nonetheless led
to millions of unnecessary deaths, the firm's president John W. Hill
advised that simply denying the medical research would smack too
much of self-interest and would quickly lose credibility.[42] Instead, he
advised his clients to demonstrate their concern for the health of their
customers by publicly demanding and funding *more* science. Thus, the
Tobacco Industry Research Committee was born with a mission to
produce and/or cause others to produce a blizzard of reports that
would muddy the waters.[43] The aim was not to disprove the medical

research but simply to create the appearance of a legitimate and unsettled scientific controversy that would of course require yet more research and therefore time to resolve. Doubt and uncertainty became the "product" that was marketed by the industry in what proved to be a very successful effort to obscure the truth for several decades and allow credulous smokers to continue their deadly habit. This intentional campaign of deceit ultimately cost the tobacco industry billions of dollars in class action suits,[44] but the public relations model of manufacturing an apparent scientific controversy where none exists has proven regrettably durable.

As was ably dissected by Naomi Oreskes and Eric M. Conway in their book and subsequent documentary film "Merchants of Doubt,"[45] this tactic was rolled forward – in many cases by the same groups and "scientists for hire" – from tobacco to acid rain, DDT, the ozone hole, and more recently, climate change. Corporations fighting against science in their own names was deemed to be too transparently self-serving, so they instead lavishly funded front groups to serve as an alternate academia.[46] Thus, organizations such as the George C. Marshall Institute[47] and the Global Climate Coalition,[48] followed more contemporaneously by the American Enterprise Institute and the Heritage Foundation,[49] produce a steady stream of reports, press releases, and critiques that seek to cast doubt on emerging or even well-established science. The Heartland Institute, for instance, produces and periodically updates a Nongovernmental International Panel on Climate Change or "NIPCC" report that mimics but contradicts reports produced by the IPCC. A recent iteration seeks to demonstrate that fossil fuels are a nearly unalloyed benefit to the world whose only downside is the prospect of oil spills.[50] This full-throated endorsement of fossil fuel use is a bit of a "tell" as to the source of their funding, which is widely perceived to be the fossil fuel industry.[51] Nonetheless, the report lays out an assertive and extensively cited argument that fossil fuel use is essential for civilization; that climate change is uncertain but might prove to be beneficial for society; and that increased atmospheric $CO_2$ concentrations will be good for plants and agriculture.

The product follows two tactics. It pursues questions that are not in dispute (such as whether fossil fuels are useful) and endorses conclusions that fly in the face of all the established science ("there is absolutely no observational evidence that provides any compelling support for the contention there is something unusual, unnatural, or unprecedented about Earth's current warmth").[52] The tip-off that this is not sincere intellectual inquiry is that these views are generally presented to the media or in public statements rather than to the science community or in peer-reviewed journals. If these are valid arguments, why not present them in scientific forums? Instead of self-publishing, why not submit to the academic press and peer-review?

The answer of course is that influencing science is not the real target. The target is to cause non-scientists to believe that scientists are still arguing over even the most basic points of climate science and to keep the controversy alive. In fact, a 2008 study concluded that 92 percent of the "environmentally skeptical" literature produced in the US was wholly or partly affiliated with self-proclaimed conservative think tanks rather than mainstream academia.[53] The fact that reputable journals decline to publish such thoroughly debunked arguments is often touted as evidence of a "global warming conspiracy" intolerant of dissent that might threaten its continued flow of grant money. Deniers funded by commercial interests often masquerade as mere skeptics, contemporary Galileos unjustly shunned by the scientific establishment for daring to challenge the conventional wisdom. Unable to publish in the most prestigious journals, they find more fertile soil in the fact-free zones on the far-right perimeter of the Internet where they fit nicely alongside other conspiracy theories. In 2012, Donald Trump claimed that "The concept of global warming was created by and for the Chinese in order to make US manufacturing uncompetitive"[54] – a theme to which he returned several times as President.

With all this well-funded "Astroturf" (as opposed to "grass roots") denialism brewing on the right, it is little wonder that the US is so polarized on climate like so many other things. It is the most prominent source of both legitimate climate science and illegitimate denialist nonsense. Nonetheless, as was the case with tobacco, it appears that the professional effort to manufacture climate controversy and obscure real science has delayed but not derailed an accurate public understanding of the climate issue, either in the US or elsewhere. The truth seems to be unavoidably seeping through, and the world is developing a consensus that climate change is real, man-made, and coming. An appetite to sacrifice for this purpose remains rare, but first things first.

## Public Views on Climate Intervention

If we pivot from public perception of climate to views on geoengineering, by far the most common reaction to the term is, geo-what? This is a set of prospective climate interventions of which the general public has "exceptionally low prior knowledge,"[55] as confirmed by various surveys in the UK, US, Canada, Germany, Japan, Korea, and Australia.[56] In fact, respondents who report high familiarity might do so out of confusion, mistaking it to pertain to artificial rainmaking or civil engineering.[57] The need to reduce (or at least get someone else to reduce) emissions has become apparent to most people, and mid-century net zero emission pledges are the current climate fad sweeping the world. They will likely prove tougher to implement than they now appear, but formulating and articulating such an ambition is an absolutely wonderful start. Public officials and many common folk are also increasingly aware of the need for adaptation, particularly to sea level rise, which seems to have caught on in the public imagination. Nevertheless, the idea that a combination of aggressive mitigation and prescient adaptation will not be wholly equal to the climate task is news to almost everyone. There simply isn't much "public perception" yet of climate intervention.

Where familiarity does exist, it is much more likely to pertain to CDR than to SRM. Air travel is among the most carbon-wasteful activities in which ordinary citizens engage, and after Greta Thunberg's courageous and well-publicized sail across the Atlantic to address the UN in 2019,[58] "flight shaming" made a cameo appearance in the court of public opinion. In response, airlines stepped up their marketing of voluntary "carbon offsets," whereby passengers can pay additional fees to have their flight emissions partially or wholly offset via supporting healthy forests or enhancing soils. These offsets are often of dubious efficacy and equivalency and have been compared to the medieval church practice of selling indulgences[59] that assuaged the consciences of wealthy transgressors but likely did little to elevate their status in the eyes of God. Nonetheless, the marketing of such carbon indulgences has boosted the public view that carbon sins can be countervailed via the planting of trees.

This intervention has received an enormous further boost in popularity following the creation by the World Economic Forum of the Trillion Tree Initiative, which was announced at Davos early in

2020.[60] This was the culmination of a few decades of inflating tree-planting aspiration initially instigated by an off-hand comment by Nobel Peace Prize recipient Wangari Maathai that we need to "plant a billion trees."[61] By 2019, a high-profile article published by *Science*[62] asserted that a reforestation campaign 1,000 times larger could offset roughly ten years of anthropogenic carbon emissions.[63] Within half a year, the champagne set at Davos was enthralled and the Trillion Tree Initiative was announced with fanfare and funding provided by, among others, Salesforce CEO Marc Benioff. The underlying science in the 2019 article came under immediate and intense criticism for (in the view of its critics) inflating by five times the amount of carbon such an initiative would sequester and underestimating the environmental effects of converting so much non-forested land to forests.[64] Detractors pointed out that we are still losing rather than gaining forest cover and that energy spent planting new forests would be much better channeled into preserving existing ones from further destruction.[65] However, the public loved it (see Figure 19.4) and a climate star was born. Even the American President who had labeled climate change a Chinese hoax was charmed and signed onto the plan. On Earth Day 2020 as the First Lady planted a maple tree on the South Lawn of the White House, the President enthused "We're . . . honoring our country's heritage of conservation through the One Trillion Tree Initiative, which is a very big deal!"[66] Setting aside the debatable climate efficacy of all this, the societal cost of commandeering and setting aside a further 20 percent of the world's forestable land during an era in which world population is projected to grow by almost 50 percent with a presumably commensurate increase in land-use requirements seems unlikely to prove sustainable. Nonetheless, trees as a geoengineering solution currently occupy a larger share of public attention than is likely warranted.

Moving from the exaggerated to the ridiculous, another geoengineering-related idea that occupies an excessive share of public regard is the "chemtrailing" conspiracy theory which holds that the military industrial complex is secretly spraying toxic chemicals over the US and perhaps globally with goals ranging from weather modification to eugenics to mind control[67, 68] for purposes and on behalf of forces unclear. These conspiracists point to the condensation trails that form behind jet aircraft (for the same nucleation reasons explored in our discussion of marine cloud brightening) and imagine that these are in fact chemical trails being dumped in the wake of jets. Among other chapters of my checkered past, I was once the Chief Operating Officer of a large global cargo airline that did enormous amounts of contract flying for the US military. If the government were chemtrailing the country or world, my airline would likely have been in the thick of it. We were not (but then, that's just what I *would* say, right?) Anyway, there is no sound evidence of the existence of actual chemtrailing.

Despite the fact that this is dismissed as a baseless conspiracy theory by the overwhelming majority of scientists,[69] a study of geoengineering discourse on social media reveals that roughly 10 percent of Americans believe chemtrailing to be "completely true," with another 20–30 percent regarding it as somewhat true.[70] Moreover, "chemtrail" mentions outweighed more factual posts about climate intervention by a ratio of roughly 4 to 1.[71] On the one hand, it is easy to dismiss chemtrail conspiracists as utter kooks, but if something like one-third of Americans put some stock in this theory and it is the primary focus of geoengineering discussion on social media, then those facts can't be ignored. As became robustly clear on January 6, 2021, fake news can have real-world consequences. One hope for this book is that it will help move the needle a little bit towards fact-based consideration of climate intervention.

Returning once again to the topic of moral hazard, there is survey evidence that the perceptual expectation inherent in this narrative may be false and that knowledge of some possible "Plan Bs" does not necessarily reduce the willpower of the public to sacrifice for "Plan A." In Germany, a prominent study that probed the empirical basis for the moral hazard behavioral prediction in respect of SRM found more nearly the opposite: the more people knew about SAI in particular, the more they favored aggressive mitigation ("Reverse Moral Hazard").[72] The conclusion was that people see SAI as a threat rather than a palliative, and believe that if scientists and policy makers are considering so extreme an intervention, perhaps the climate problem is worse than was previously perceived. A related study considered public attitudes in Germany towards three possible climate interventions: afforestation, carbon capture and sequestration, and SAI.[73] Not surprisingly, it reaffirmed that everyone loves trees, and that CCS is unobjectionable in spite of its high cost. SAI on the other hand was widely rejected. Interestingly, the more information that was provided in respect of each option, the less enthusiastic respondents were about all of them, though their relative ranking remained unchanged.[74]

This preference order also corresponded to the extent to which respondents had prior knowledge of these interventions. Over 60 percent had heard of afforestation as a climate intervention, whereas a bare majority had heard of CCS. Barely a quarter had heard of stratospheric aerosols. This study is now several years old, so general knowledge of these technologies has likely increased, but it also demonstrated that more knowledge does not necessarily lead to more acceptance.

How generally these German attitudes map onto the world is incompletely known, but other literature certainly points to national and regional differences in perceptions. While the developed world may be deeply concerned about moral hazard, the Global South is at least as focused on "moral responsibility," whereby the developed world takes ownership of the climate problem of which it was the primary causal agent and in some way discharges a debt to the South.[75] One idea is a linkage whereby the South withholds its permission to commence SAI deployment until the North pays whatever toll is deemed fair. This of course fails to account properly for the relative power differentials between the two factions and neglects the likelihood that it is more likely to be the South begging the North for climate interventions rather than the North begging for permission to deploy. However, the fact that this may not be a prescient prediction of future international dynamics does not reduce its validity as a description of perceptions in the Global South today.

A separate study found distinct differences in public opinion between the US, Canada, Western Europe, and China. Chinese respondents, for whom the low cost of SAI relative to mitigation proved to be a more salient characteristic, were therefore more favorably inclined towards this intervention than were Europeans and Canadians, for whom tampering with nature seemed more problematic.[76] This aligns with a separate study[77] that found non-OECD country respondents in such countries as China, India, and the Philippines more concerned about climate change than OECD respondents from Japan, South Korea, and Australia, and therefore more open to the prospect of SAI.

Recent survey data in respect of attitudes towards various CDR technologies in the US and the UK revealed several salient trends. All geoengineering options were seen less favorably than emissions reduction because they failed to address the "root causes" of climate change,[78] though it was not clear that respondents were confronted with the potential costs of mitigation. However, opinions of CDR benefited if it was presented side-by-side with SRM, since the former was then seen as the "least worst" option. Respondents were very skeptical of solutions that seemed to "tamper with nature,"[79] such that forestation solutions were received far better than any sort of sequestration, including BECCS.[80] Sequestration was closely associated with "industrial wastes" and irresponsible "dumping."[81] While I would vigorously debate the accuracy of some of these perceptions, they provide valuable insights into the challenges that will ensue as climate intervention seeps into the public consciousness.

A study of US attitudes towards SAI yet again confirmed low familiarity with the technology, but much more openness to research and even prospective deployment than has been evident elsewhere.[82] Democrats and climate voters were more supportive than Republicans and non-climate voters. The young, who naturally see themselves as having to live with the consequences of climate change, are more intrigued with SAI than are the aged. Contrary to both predictions and studies in the UK,[83] there was no substantial gender differential. Not surprisingly, respondents who highly valued the speed and low cost of SAI were more receptive to it, whereas those who were more off put by the risks of implementation were less so. Even those with substantial concerns about moral hazard were nonetheless open to nuanced arguments about the need for research.

Despite the note of optimism that one could perhaps derive from this study that geoengineering may be finding a bit of mainstream acceptance, I have the same problem with this study that I have with all of them, which is that I don't believe them. We are trying to survey the opinions of people on a topic on which few of them actually *have* opinions, and the opinions they *do* have are quite immature, arguably fairly characterized as "pseudo opinions."[84] These studies must first explain what climate intervention is before they can query people's opinions about it, and they are then soliciting those opinions in circumstances very different from those in which these opinions would become relevant. If people are unaware of geoengineering, they are also highly likely to imagine that we are on a path whereby we can preserve the existing climate. They will therefore be comparing climate intervention to the wrong counterfactual. If large-scale geoengineering ever becomes relevant, it will be because we have dramatically and irretrievably changed the climate, in which case we will be choosing between engineered-world and runaway-climate-world. If you ask people whether they want the current climate or Frankenclimate, they will of course leap at the former. But Frankenclimate versus runaway climate? Much tougher call.

In considering this, I am often reminded of the fact that the early lifeboats left the *Titanic* only partially full. As the tall proud ship was still floating level on the sea and the prospect of a rescue ship seemed plausible, when confronted with the choice of a dinky little lifeboat or the ship itself, many people opted for the ship. John Jacob Astor is reported to have remarked, "We are safer on board the ship than in that little boat." They of course could not quite wrap their heads around the fact that less than two hours later, instead of looking down from the main deck at the bobbing little lifeboats, they would be staring up from the sea with just their heads above the waves. By then those lifeboats would have looked huge, like the only salient things left in the world. Their frame of reference would have been turned upside down, likely causing them to wish they had made very different choices hours earlier.

I think asking randomized survey respondents today how they feel about climate engineering is like asking that first passenger if they want to hop into the lifeboat. It is just too difficult now to envision how the perhaps vastly changed circumstances in the future will inform people's choices. They simply can't know what their preferences will be. I don't mean to suggest that those preferences don't matter. They do – vitally. We can't legitimately engage in climate intervention without widespread public support. But if the climate ends up where I suspect it will, people's perceptions of their interests and risks will be very different in 2050 or 2100 than they are today.

# Section VI

# THE PATH FORWARD

# 20 THE PATH FORWARD FOR CARBON REMOVAL

In this last section of the book, we will look forward and consider the next steps on both sides of the climate intervention toolbox. Mitigation remains the top climate priority, and adaptation is also necessary and urgent. But we will also need climate intervention, and we therefore need as quickly as possible to turn what are now really mostly untested prospects into realities on the ground. Starting on the CDR side of the box, the ultimatum is to stomp on the accelerator. There appear to be tools here that can work, but we need to race down the learning and cost curves and scale up these technologies vastly faster than our current pace. Fortunately, there is some momentum here. The US Department of Energy has recently established two grant programs with funding of $36 million to accelerate research and development of direct air capture technologies.[1, 2]

## The National Academies Report

In 2019, the National Academies of Science, Engineering, and Medicine published a landmark report titled "Negative Emissions Technologies and Reliable Sequestration: A Research Agenda."[3] A twin report on the research agenda for SRM was published in March 2021. The Negative Emissions Technologies (NETs) Report considered most of the salient ideas in the CDR side of our toolbox, although it declared oceanic interventions such as iron fertilization and ocean alkalinization (liming) beyond its scope but separately worthy of research. Nonetheless, the report remains the world's best current source on the path forward here.

After genuflecting before the 1.5/2°C climate targets and acknowledging that mitigation is the first priority, it then reminds readers that NETs are necessary not only after the achievement of net zero emissions, but well beforehand in order to make net zero possible in the first place, or at least possible sooner. As previously noted, this is because some recalcitrant emissions from sectors like aviation and agriculture will prove cheaper to offset with NETs than to actually eliminate. While the report focused only on NETs that appear able to achieve removals at a cost below $100 per metric tonne of $CO_2$, some estimates of the costs to eliminate the most stubborn emissions range up to $1,000 per tonne. Therefore, NETs should be viewed as one element of an integrated portfolio of climate solutions rather than a standalone piece. Figure 20.1 illustrates how NETs would fit into this portfolio both before and after net zero, which interestingly is illustrated to be reached in 2090, rendering my 2080 scenario in Chapter 9 relatively optimistic.

Pursuant to its statement of task, the committee focused on six major technical approaches to $CO_2$ removal and sequestration:

- Coastal blue carbon (tidal or salt-water wetlands)
- Terrestrial carbon removal and sequestration (trees and soils)
- Bioenergy with carbon capture and sequestration (energy from biomass)
- Direct air capture (DAC)
- Carbon mineralization (accelerated weathering either at the surface or underground)
- Geologic sequestration (underground storage of carbon captured from flues or direct air)

The report notes that coastal blue carbon is promising in theory, but that the high developmental pressures on coastal lands combined with sea level rise that may substantially alter or relocate coastlines render the capacity of this approach (~0.1 Gt/yr) too small to contribute substantially to a solution.

On the other hand, both of the terrestrial approaches (better soils management plus afforestation/reforestation/prevention of deforestation) and bioenergy (burning some of the foregoing) could mature to safe and affordable capacities aggregating to ~10 Gt of $CO_2$ annually.[4]

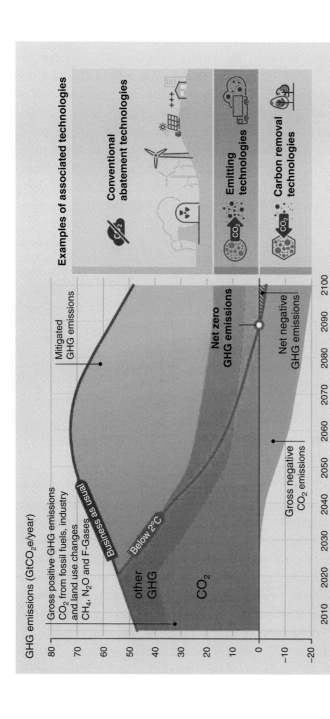

**Figure 20.1** Scenario of the role of negative emissions technologies in reaching net zero emissions. *Source:* UNEP, The Emissions Gap Report 2017[5]

Relative to current emissions in the range of 50 Gt/yr expressed in $CO_2$ equivalents, this is a substantial chunk. Moreover, Figure 20.1 illustrates removal targets of 10 Gt by 2050 and 20 by 2100, so this would appear promising. However, the report immediately notes the land competition arising from the forest-based approaches and the dismal prior record of adoption shortfalls by farmers and landowners in the soils sector, observing that these could reduce actual achieved capacities by a factor of two or more. Their capacity calculations ignore direct air capture because it was assessed as costing from \$100–\$600 per tonne, rendering it unaffordable. The capacity of carbon mineralization is simply unknown.

As catalogued in Table 20.1, the factors that inhibit the scale up of this NETs portfolio include:

- The land constraint for terrestrial approaches
- Other environmental impacts such as water constraints, reduced biodiversity, and mine wastes
- Energy requirements, particularly for DAC and carbon mineralization
- High costs for DAC, carbon mineralization, and to a lesser degree, BECCS
- Practical constraints to scaling all NETs by a factor of >10 percent per year for decades
- Resistance to change
- Monitoring and verification gaps
- Absence of adequate governance
- Insufficient scientific/technical understanding

Given these obstacles, the report recommends an ambitious, wide-ranging, and well-funded research program to address not only knowledge gaps but also the practical considerations related to scaling such as cost impediments and funding gaps. In respect of the terrestrial and bioenergy approaches, priorities would be to find ways to soften the land constraint by reducing food waste and finding crops that more efficiently sequester carbon in the soil. To approach the theoretical potentials for these interventions, revolutionary breakthroughs would be needed in agricultural productivity and dietary changes. Further development and widespread adoption of plant-based meat substitutes or lab-grown meat would be game changers. Improvements in the efficiency of both producing and combusting bioenergy would substantially enhance its cost competitiveness and speed its substitution for fossil fuels.

Table 20.1 Cost, limiting factors, and impact potential of NETs. The National Academies' estimated cost per tonne of $CO_2$ ranges are L (Low): 0–20, M (Medium): 20–100, H (High): => 100. *Source*: The National Academies of Sciences, Engineering, and Medicine 2018[6]

| Technology | Estimated cost | Potential rate of $CO_2$ removal under \$100/t$CO_2$ at current technology readiness levels, Gt$CO_2$/yr | Limiting factors |
|---|---|---|---|
| BECCS | M | 3.5–5.2 | • Availability of biomass<br>• Cost<br>• Practical barriers<br>• Fundamental understanding |
| Agricultural soils | L to M | 3 | • Limited rates of carbon uptake<br>• Practical barriers |
| Forest management | L | 1.5 | • Demand for wood<br>• Practical barriers |
| Afforestation/ reforestation | L | 1 | • Land<br>• Practical barriers |
| Coastal blue carbon | L | 0.13 | • Land<br>• Scientific/technical understanding |
| Direct air capture | H | 0 | • Expensive<br>• Practical barriers |
| Carbon mineralization | M to H | Unknown | • Fundamental understanding |
| Total | | 9.13–10.83 | |

Direct air capture is limited primarily by cost, so huge break-throughs are needed if these are to become competitive and affordable. Since we are merely at the beginning of DAC development, those are certainly possible – after all, solar and wind power costs have declined by 70–90 percent in the last decade.[7] But such cost plunges are by no means guaranteed and are only achievable if we start a rapid process of learning by doing. Solar and wind benefited not only from enormous global incentives and subsidies, but also by the fortunate happenstance that they produce something for which the world has an almost limitless appetite – electricity. Demand for carbon is comparably tiny, so government largesse will be required to take up yet more of the funding requirement. And to ensure we don't skip over the scaling challenge here, meeting the 2100 annual NET goal of 20 Gt/yr entirely from DAC would require 20,000 facilities were they on the ~1 million tonne-per-year scale consistent with the Carbon Engineering vision. This is roughly 1.5 times the number of gas-fired power plants built globally in the twentieth century.[8] If the small modular ~1,000 tonne/yr designs favored by Climeworks and Global Thermostat prove to be the winning formula,[9, 10] we would need 1,000 times that number of units. Could we build more large-scale CCS facilities in this century as we built gas-fired power plants in the last? Sure, but this would be quite an achievement.

Carbon mineralization is at an even earlier stage of development, with the fundamental science still to be explored.[11] There is limited understanding of the kinetics of $CO_2$ uptake for surface applications, and no inventory of appropriate geologic formations where it might successfully be injected underground. Neither is there an inventory of existing and easily accessible supplies of reactive but unreacted rock, nor an understanding of how to manage tailings piles such that they effectively take up $CO_2$.[12] We lack clarity as to what negative feedbacks may arise from widely distributing crushed reactive minerals in agricultural soils or in the seas.

Both DAC and carbon mineralization would consume huge quantities of energy, which must derive from non-emitting sources if we are to avoid exacerbating the problem we are actually trying to solve. Further cost reductions of that energy supply are therefore essential in getting these NETs down the cost curve.

In order to be carbon negative, DAC and BECCS both rely upon a fleet of global underground storage sites, few of which are currently in operation. No global inventory of potential sites yet exists,[13] and our understanding of how to ensure that these sequestrations remain permanent is also immature, in part because it will be somewhat site specific.

To accomplish all the above, the report recommends a research budget of over $9 billion, with $8 billion of that spent in the initial ten years and the remainder over the succeeding decade. Over a third of that budget would be devoted to the terrestrial approaches, mostly forest management and BECCS. The largest budgetary expenditure in that category would be for the development of high carbon input crop phenotypes that would more efficiently vacuum up $CO_2$ from the air than would existing varieties. Another large tranche would be devoted to refining high-efficiency biomass power technologies to increase the energy yield and decrease the greenhouse gas emissions from such operations. Refining the supply and logistics chain such that waste biomass can be efficiently moved to market would be another significant funding priority, as would refining the technology by which biomass might be converted to biochar for soil supplements.

The next largest budgetary category (nearly a quarter) would be targeted at direct air capture, with almost half of this subset being devoted to standing up demonstration projects to accelerate learning by doing. Another quarter of the whole pie would be aimed at research into appropriate sequestration sites, with major focuses including site selection, assessment of seismic risk, development of monitoring and verification techniques, and studies into the secondary trapping of fugitive gases from compromised sites.

Given its small capacity, a surprisingly large tranche of the remaining funds is proposed for the establishment of experimental coastal sites to better study the fixing of blue carbon. On the flip side, carbon mineralization seems at this juncture to be a sufficiently remote prospect that very little of the budget is devoted to it, with expenditures there simply directed towards fundamental science rather than development and engineering. While ocean alkalinization in the high seas was excluded from what is a nationally focused report, I would speculate that a research program for it too would focus initially on basic science rather than the logistics of implementation.

## Time versus Money

In summary, the 2019 National Academies report laid out a detailed and comprehensive blueprint for a $9 billion research agenda for negative emissions technologies most of which was intended to be complete by 2030. Of course, the report was issued under the Trump administration, which didn't believe there was a serious problem to be solved. Naturally, virtually none of this has been funded or implemented.

Nonetheless, to return our gaze to our climate North Star, we need to reach global net zero emissions as fast as possible in order to stop filling the bathtub. Our primary tool by which to do that must be emissions reductions, but that will not happen as quickly as people hope and will prove costly, particularly if we attempt (as we should) to accelerate the pace. If we want decarbonization to be cheap, we should wait until the technology by which to do so matures, diffuses, and solves the problem in a painless fashion. If instead we want to set ambitious net zero and temperature limit goals irrespective of technological readiness, then we need to bring our wallets. We need further to be prepared to make lifestyle sacrifices, not only in the developed world, where such sacrifices mean something akin to less butter, but in the developing world as well, where they may delay a generation's elevation out of poverty and thereby constitute deeply painful sacrifices. However, the climate doesn't care about our welfare – it only cares about the bathtub water level, and so long as it is rising, the planet will warm.

Finding someone to pay for what is really a waste disposal mission will be much easier if the costs come down, but the "learning by doing" cycle is moving rather slowly here. The three prominent (but tiny) companies in this space are all roughly a decade old and are still in the demonstration phase mode. It remains unclear which of the competing capture processes will ultimately prove to be the most feasible, not only from a cost standpoint, but as well in terms of energy, land, chemical, water, and heat requirements. Were this destined to be a small industry, these might prove marginal considerations, but as the CCS/DACCS industry must rival in size the current fossil fuel industry, these could in fact create massive new headaches as we address the climate problem.

Until there is a significant cost for emitting carbon and other greenhouse gases, there will be little interest in capturing and storing much of it. Most of the two dozen or so large capture and storage operations in existence or under construction today are exceptional projects where some use case for the carbon (usually EOR) came together with tax credits and other governmental largesse to create a marginal business case that few are rushing to replicate. We are capturing on the order of 0.1 percent of the carbon we currently emit, and in order to reach our 2050 climate targets, we would need to be scaling this technology at 100 times the rate we are now doing.[14]

In the time it has taken me to draft this manuscript, one of the world's largest carbon capture facilities, the Petra Nova complex in Texas, has been mothballed.[15] NRG which operates the facility announced in May 2020 that the pandemic had driven oil prices down to a point where the higher cost tertiary recovery[16] facilitated by EOR no longer made economic sense. The adjacent coal-fired power plant from which the facility harvested its $CO_2$ is still operating,[17] but the added cost of capturing, purifying, and transporting the $CO_2$ into the EOR market no longer justified itself despite the fact that $1 billion capital cost[18] was already sunk. NRG is maintaining a brave public face about the prospect of restarting the operation if and when higher oil prices ensue, but as world oil demand cools, it is not clear if such price conditions will return. Even if they do, Petra Nova is a very high-profile cautionary tale for others seeking to finance the installation of similar facilities elsewhere. Until carbon emission prices are high and perceived to be durable, financing and therefore developing capture operations will prove very challenging. This is not yet analogous to the market for solar and wind power generation 20 or 30 years ago, where there was high demand for the power if it could be made cheaply enough. There remains almost no demand for the $CO_2$, and until governments around the world manufacture that demand via carbon taxes or their equivalents, an industry that is essential to our decarbonization pathway remains more or less stillborn.

And yet the world has little appreciation of that. Just this morning I noted in the *Financial Times* an article under the headline "Environment groups question UK's carbon capture push."[19] In response to Boris Johnson's pledge to devote £1 billion to develop four CCS schemes in Britain by 2030, campaigners at Global Watch and Friends of the Earth Scotland claimed that reliance on CCS to decarbonize the energy system was "not a solution" to global warming. They asserted that the intended funds should be redirected to other climate priorities since CCS would not deliver meaningful results before 2030, would require massive scaling at "scarcely credible" rates, and is currently characterized by high costs. Guilty on all counts, but these are reasons to stomp the accelerator rather than pump the brakes.

In digging into the underlying report that was the source of this media storm, it is clear that the disconnect derives from two points. First, the campaigners do not understand (in my humble opinion) the degree to which achieving net zero in a timely fashion requires CCS, back to the misunderstanding that many had around the Paris Agreement.

However, there is also a second, more nuanced point that is not so easily dismissed. The environmental groups seem eager to ensure that CCS is not utilized by the fossil fuel industry as a stratagem by which to preserve the role of fossil fuels in the world energy system, and, unfortunately for the image of CCS, there is a substantial history of exactly this. The whole "clean coal" gambit in the US and elsewhere can be seen via some mix of two very different lenses. Charitably viewed, it was an ultimately failed but earnest attempt to determine whether both the technology and economics of coal with CCS would rehabilitate this least climate friendly fuel into a carbon-neutral alternative somewhat like bioenergy in reverse, first taking carbon from geologic stores but then returning it there. More cynically, it can be seen as a deliberate smoke screen by which to thwart environmental regulation and attract government largesse for an "experiment" whose outcome was clear from the start. In all events, coal with CCS has proven uneconomical, as the Petra Nova suspension demonstrates. Nonetheless, much of the carbon capture and storage technology that exists today derived from these and other attempts by fossil fuel companies to preserve their market position. This is particularly true of Equinor, the Norwegian State oil and gas company that nonetheless developed the world's first large $CO_2$ storage site under the North Sea.[20]

The relationship of the CCS industry (to the extent there is such a thing) with EOR is equally fraught. The vast majority of the world's existing and planned CCS capacity is devoted to EOR[21] – a carbon-neutral process at best. Carbon Engineering's world-leading DACCS plant under construction in Texas is similarly intended to serve the EOR market. One can view all this either as merely ironic or diabolical, but carbon removal technologies require developmental funding. Governments are providing too little of it, and clever would-be climate engineers have found ways to instead get the funding from the industry that they ultimately hope to bury. That may seem ethically ambiguous, but for an industry that needs to scale at 100 times the rate at which it is doing so, I for one am grateful that such a marriage of convenience is proving possible. Though environmentalists are right to perceive mixed motives in the nascent carbon removal industry, it would be a grave mistake to turn away from it for fear that it is nothing but a fossil fuel funded ruse.

Meaningful carbon taxes will prove hard to implement, particularly in democracies and states used to subsidizing rather than elevating fuel costs. It is only in 2021 that the EU's decades-old Emissions Trading System finally produced carbon prices that have begun to shape behavior.[22] Before the pandemic, the benchmark carbon price dawdled around €20, but it has recently zoomed into the 50s and may head higher still. At these levels, they will by no means eliminate $CO_2$ emissions, but they are starting to challenge the economics of the most marginal projects and sources. They are also intensifying calls for carbon border adjustments at the EU perimeter, since products produced elsewhere are not similarly saddled with carbon taxes. This is the maiden voyage of substantial carbon pricing in one of the world's major economic blocs and how willing Europeans will be to endure these carbon prices remains to be seen. Outside carbon conscientious Europe, research and development grants, efficiency standards, and other stealth taxes and expenditures through the tax code are more likely to be the vanguard funding required to inch down the learning and cost curve in respect of carbon removal. But unlike renewable energy, there is almost no underlying demand for carbon removal. Until governments start substantially taxing carbon emissions and/or purchasing large-scale carbon removal, meaningful scaling will not occur. We must find a way through this maze – rapidly.

# 21 THE PATH FORWARD FOR SOLAR RADIATION MANAGEMENT

While the world's carbon capture capability seems ready to shed its diapers and begin to scamper around the floor if we would just show it a little love, our readiness for large-scale SRM remains positively embryonic. Setting aside small-scale surface-level interventions such as white roofs or oceanic bubbles and focusing instead on aerial planetary-scale interventions such as cloud modifications, stratospheric aerosol injection, or space-based solar deflection, we are very nearly nowhere. It is not yet clear that cloud modifications will ever prove effective. Whether we can wield the sledgehammer of SAI with sufficient precision and deftness to avoid catastrophic physical risks remains almost entirely unknown, and it is nearly impossible to see how the governance challenges related to such a climate intervention could be legitimately overcome in a way that would be both equitable and acceptable in the global political theater. Some more futuristic proposals such as deploying space-based assets between the Sun and the Earth to deflect incoming sunlight are so far beyond our current capabilities that they are unlikely to be relevant to the climate problems we will face in this century. Nonetheless, a thousand mile journey begins with a single step, and our immediate challenge with respect to any form of SRM is to simply get started in a *serious* way. And by "started," I certainly don't mean deployment, but rather research, mostly of a scientific variety. We need to know a lot more about what techniques would work and how. We need to know what our realistic options are.

For all of its potential importance in managing our way out of the climate corner into which we are painting ourselves, the world's aggregate SRM research effort is tiny.

## Status of SRM Research

The US and other large countries need to start devoting hundreds of millions (rather than handfuls of millions) of dollars a year to researching geoengineering in all its forms, in part because unlike carbon capture where there are at least some private market revenue streams that can help fund the technological development, there are none in the case of SRM. Simply put, SRM will be funded by the public sector or not at all. Currently universities and private foundations are taking the lead in backing research efforts in North America, but these efforts have only begun to expose the potential of SRM. If the world is to get serious about these technologies, governments and particularly the US government must make significant financial contributions to the research sector. The US National Science Foundation has allocated roughly $2.5 million over several years to fund the work of a handful of university scientists as well as several workshops on such subjects as the possible agricultural impacts of SRM.[1] The US National Oceanic and Atmospheric Administration has a $4 million program[2] for understanding the stratosphere that includes explicit mention of geoengineering but is a much broader effort and it is still unclear how these funds will benefit geoengineering research. The Department of Energy has designated several million dollars for research into aerosol, clouds, and thermodynamic processes, but little of that is specifically targeted towards geoengineering. For the US government which has long prided itself on pioneering technological innovation, that's about it. The Harvard Solar Geoengineering Research Program is small but better funded nonetheless than any targeted Federal program.[3] In fact, during the decade from 2008 through 2018, the entire North American research budget for SRM was $26 million, of which more than 70 percent came from private funding.[4] Europe spent $22 million, virtually all of it government funding.[5] Asian governments spent a mere $4 million, and the rest of the world spent very nearly nothing.[6]

In recent years, China had perhaps the largest and best funded national program on SRM with roughly 40 active PhD and master's students researching the full range of possible interventions including SAI, cloud modifications, surface albedo changes, and glacial preservation.[7] It was equally involved in governance initiatives and international outreach, positioning itself as a prospective representative for the developing world in international decision making. Nonetheless, after hosting a prestigious global climate modeling meeting in late 2019, the program was substantially scaled back. Its residual funding will shortly be exhausted and no new funding has yet been approved insofar as I can determine. China's attention seems in part to have been diverted to the "Sky River" cloud seeding project in Tibet,[8] which is not "climate intervention" as I would define it, but is often lumped together with it. Whether China's rainmaking efforts will surpass the dismal history of similar prior endeavors remains to be seen. Universities in the UK, Russia, and Germany figure prominently in this field, and Canada punches above its weight given the prominence of native Canadian scholars such as David Keith, Edward Parson, and Douglas Graham MacMartin. Still, the current research format is small potatoes relative to what is likely to be required and the spin-up time for an entire field of research can take many years.

A 2009 experiment, led by Russian researcher Yu Izrael,[9] which tested how solar radiation passes through aerosol layers is the only SAI field test to date. Most of the field data being used to guide the theoretical work surrounding SAI derives from measurements snatched from opportunistic natural experiments such as volcanoes or from somewhat antiquated experiments in the 1990s and early 2000s when researchers were attempting to understand the effects of supersonic aircraft and solid rocket motors on the stratosphere.[10, 11] Fortunately, the research community was able to glean valuable information about behavior and evolution of stratospheric aerosols during these experiments, but SAI would require a much more robust and verified understanding of the dynamical and aerosol properties that would ultimately determine the success of the method.

## The National Academy Research Agenda

In the US at least, there is cause for optimism that change may be coming. In 2019, the National Academy of Sciences, Engineering, and Medicine commenced a study titled "Developing a Research Agenda and Research Governance Approaches for Climate Intervention Strategies that Reflect Sunlight to Cool Earth." The study was issued in March 2021 and builds directly upon a National Academy 2015 report that evaluated the cost and performance of such strategies. The new report is the solar geoengineering counterpart to the CDR research agenda report that was the core of Chapter 20. The report pulls some punches, but makes one thing clear. The time has come for a comprehensive and well-funded federal push to research SRM.

Like virtually all climate intervention reports, it starts by reiterating that there is no substitute for rapid and complete mitigation and that adaptation and CDR must also be pursued vigorously. However, it argues that among our portfolio of climate solutions there may well be a role for managing sunlight. It calls for a national solar geoengineering research program that would focus on all three facets of the SRM trinity: marine cloud brightening, cirrus cloud thinning, and stratospheric aerosol injection. Though important, it suggests that this should be a "minor part of the overall US research portfolio related to climate change,"[12] and "should not shift the focus from other important global change research."[13] With respect to SRM, the focus should be on "advancing understanding of options for responding to climate-change risks and developing policy-relevant knowledge,"[14] with the caveat that it should not advance a path to deployment.

The research agenda is framed as a means to enable future policy makers to come to informed decisions about such interventions and proposes extensive international cooperation rather than national silos. "A transdisciplinary domestic research program, established in coordination with other countries, can help build the foundation of scientific insights and information that will help decision makers and stakeholders faced with choices about possible future implementation of solar geoengineering."[15] Faced with such decisions, "evidence either in favor or disfavor of SG [solar geoengineering] deployment could have profound value. Such knowledge could be time-critical for policy makers especially if there were intense public or political pressure for a dramatic climate action, or if SG were deployed in the absence of broad international cooperation and safeguards."[16]

While proposing to accelerate the pace of research, the report also calls for robust governance of that research as well as American support for the development of international governance mechanisms:

> A research governance program should include the following elements: a research code of conduct, a public registry for research, regular program assessment and review processes, permitting systems for outdoor experiments, guidance on intellectual property, inclusive public and stakeholder engagement processes, mechanisms for advancing international information

sharing and collaboration (within research teams, among national scientific agencies), and establishment of an expert committee to advance discussions about international governance needs and strategies.[17]

This is all very sensible and modest, with a tone sounding much more multilaterally Bidenesque than unilaterally Trumpian.

The report proposes research in three broad categories: context and goals; social dimensions; and technical dimensions. The first would seek to clarify the goals for solar geoengineering research, devising strategies for decision making in the context of uncertainty, and the capacity for all countries to engage meaningfully on this issue. The social science bucket would explore public perception, governance, justice, ethics, and equity considerations.

The technical basket would focus on the science and engineering issues – to my mind at least, the heart of the matter at this juncture. While the social science aspects need to advance in tandem, the fundamental question with any form of solar geoengineering remains: is there anything in this side of our toolbox that looks like it would be a good climate intervention? Is anything here going to work? Unlike CDR, where the questions are more nearly how to do it well and cheaply, the questions here remain whether we should do solar geoengineering at all.

The National Academy report subdivides that question into five subsets, each of which apply to the three major focus areas of SAI, MCB, and CCT. The first subset focuses on atmospheric processes, in that each of these possible interventions entails deploying substances in the atmosphere to induce changes that would deflect sunlight. Nonetheless, our understanding of the microphysical processes in the atmosphere remains too rudimentary to accurately predict how our proposed interventions would actually work, both at the molecular level and at a planetary scale. These questions remain the subject of exquisite computer simulations that are run on supercomputers all over the world and then compared with other model runs to refine their accuracy. We also have real-world data from volcanic eruptions, jet plumes, and ship tracks to inform the models. Nonetheless, until we start actually experimenting with our intended aerosols in the real atmosphere, it will remain somewhat mysterious as to how well our models predict real conditions.

The second subset focuses on the climate response. If we did implement these atmospheric interventions, would the climate respond as we intended? How much deployment would be required to cool the Earth by say 1°C, and would the second degree of cooling require the same deployed mass as the first? What regional heterogeneity should we expect and to what degree can that be predicted? The third subset would seek to illuminate what *other* impacts might derive from such interventions. How would the hydrological cycle be affected and where? How would agriculture and natural ecosystems respond to slightly less direct sunlight but more diffuse sunlight? How might each form of solar geoengineering affect human health? Beyond the known unknowns, what unknown unknowns might leap out of Pandora's Toolbox should we open it, and to what degree can those uncertainties be reduced in the absence of full-scale deployment?

The fourth subset focuses on monitoring and attribution. How might we design an observational system that could help us (i) detect unexpected deployment from covert or unilateral actors; (ii) provide the observations needed to tailor, adjust, or terminate deployment; and (iii) understand the broader global effects of deployment? Moreover, how might we distinguish impacts of solar geoengineering from those of climate change or non-anthropogenically induced environmental variations?

The final subset of this technical basket probes my own little corner of these endeavors, the technology development and assessment. For SAI, that returns us to the question of how to get the gunk up in the sky efficiently and cheaply. In fact, the report issues instructions that appear to be directed specifically at me and my team of Boeing alumni, which is to complete a report that we have undertaken on whether deployment can be reasonably and cheaply done at an altitude of 25 km rather than 20 km. For MCB, the primary question is how to produce salt of an appropriate size distribution that can be lofted into boundary layer clouds and serve as nuclei. For CCT, the atmospheric science is too rudimentary to focus yet on deployment technologies. We still need to clarify whether it is feasible at all.

## Field Tests

In respect of the most sensitive issue on the table, which is field experiments, particularly related to SAI, the report endeavors to touch this third rail, but with a ten-foot pole:

Limited outdoor experimentation could help advance the study of certain atmospheric processes that are critical for understanding solar geoengineering. Such activities, however, are controversial, with significant likelihood for public concerns and objections. If subject to appropriate governance and oversight, outdoor experimentation could feasibly be pursued in a balanced manner that is sufficient in scale to acquire critical observations not available by other means, but small enough in scale to limit impacts.[18]

More specifically, the report states that:

Deliberate outdoor experiments that involve releasing substances into the atmosphere should be considered only when they can provide critical observations not already available and not likely to become available through laboratory studies, modeling, and experiments of opportunity (e.g., observing volcanic eruptions, rocket plumes, or ship tracks). All outdoor experiments involving the release of substances into the atmosphere should be subject to ... governance ... including a permitting system and impact assessment. In addition, any outdoor substance releases should be limited to a quantity of material at least two orders of magnitude smaller than the quantity that could cause detectable changes in global mean temperature or adverse environmental effects.[19]

While this text describes stringent limitations on field experiments, its purpose is in fact to carve out a safe space for them.

In addition to such limitations on any single experiment, the report also proposes an aggregate global annual cap that is one order of magnitude below the detectability limit. This would require a global registry and clearinghouse for all perturbative experiments, perhaps operating under the auspices of the UN or the World Meteorological Organization. The clearinghouse would also opine on the need for and value of any such field experiments, and would ensure that the data derived from them was openly shared. Membership in and subjugation under such an organization would be voluntary, but as the US is among the countries often most resistant to such multilateralism, the fact that the US National Academy is calling for such steps is notable.

The report proposes as well to bolster the legitimacy and public acceptance of such research by stressing the need for transparency and inclusion. "The program should establish robust mechanisms for inputs from civil society and other key stakeholders in the design of the research program, as well as promote their engagement in relevant program components. Key stakeholders include climate-vulnerable communities and underrepresented groups, including from indigenous populations and the Global South."[20]

"The program and its outcomes should be regularly reviewed and assessed by a diverse, inclusive panel of experts and stakeholders (including consultation with international counterparts) to determine whether continued research is justified and, if so, how goals and priorities should be updated."[21]

It further proposes that "'Exit ramps' (i.e., criteria and protocols for terminating research programs or areas) should be an explicit part of the program, with mechanisms to terminate a research activity, for example, if it is deemed to pose unacceptable physical, social, geopolitical, or environmental risks or if research indicates clearly that a particular SG technique is not likely to work."[22]

In terms of an organizational framework, the authors observe that "SG research and research governance efforts to date have been ad hoc and dispersed. There would be significant value in pursuing more active integration across key research areas – such as modeling, observations, process studies, social and economic studies, and scenario designs – to ensure that research being conducted informs and is informed by other research as efficiently as possible. The United States does not currently have a coordinated federal approach to SG research. Building an effective, transdisciplinary research program will require coordination across multiple agencies, national laboratories, and cooperative institutes. The US Global Change Research Program (USGCRP), charged with coordinating federal global change research across the federal science agencies, is the most logical entity for orchestrating an SG research program."[23]

As regards the budget for the program, the report states "A reasonable initial investment for this program is within a range of $100–200 million total over 5 years. A program of this size would be sufficient to advance all the research topics identified, but represent a small fraction of the national budget for climate-change research."[24] A program of this size would also represent a downpour in the desert –

more funding over five years in one country than has been devoted to solar geoengineering globally since the field was first conceived. A US program of this magnitude would also undoubtedly spur other nations to substantially step up their efforts, in part to keep up but equally to engage in the sort of international cooperation that this report forthrightly invites. Nonetheless, this is a small sum in comparison to the $9 billion over 10 years proposed in respect of CDR in the twin 2019 report.

## My Own Path Forward

Pivoting from a national/global research agenda to a personal one (sorry if that seems a bit anticlimactic), there is no end in sight as regards the narrow row that I intend to continue to hoe in trying to illuminate the practicalities of SAI implementation. As noted in Chapter 15, I focused initially on the nuts and bolts of deployment for impact: how much material, how many planes, how much money. This has proven very helpful in clarifying such questions as: what kinds of actors would be capable of climate-altering deployment; whether it could be done covertly; and how cheap is "cheap." However, since full-on deployment is presumably some decades away (if ever), I have more recently turned my attention to practicalities of the sorts of field experiments that (despite all the valid reservations noted above) I believe will be necessary to properly evaluate the efficacy, optimization, and risks of SAI. Before we would ever need a deployment aircraft fleet, we would need a research aircraft fleet – that's the more temporally proximate aeronautical need for SAI.

With that in mind, I collaborated yet again over the last year with my merry band of fellow Boeing alumni at VPE Aerospace Consulting in St Louis to produce a paper presenting two conceptual designs for prospective SAI research aircraft. The paper was published as a part of the January 2021 SciTech conference of the American Institute of Aeronautics and Astronautics, the same conduit that published our deployment aircraft paper a year earlier.

The paper presents preliminary information on two research aircraft: a miniature version of the SAIL-01 deployment aircraft called the SAI Researcher or "SAIR-01"; and a huge, long-dwell solar-powered airship called the stratospheric aerosol research airship, or "SARA-01." The SAIR is simply a scaled down version of the SAIL that could carry a payload less than a tenth the size of its big sister, so one tonne versus nearly 14 tonnes. This would mean that single injections from the SAIR would fit well below the threshold defined by the recent National Academy report. SAIR has even more excess wing area and thrust than SAIL and can therefore cruise a bit higher, 22 km rather than 20. SAIR would have a maximum gross take-off weight less than half that of a Gulfstream G650 business jet, but a wing span similar to that of a much larger narrowbody airliner such as a Boeing 737-800 (see Figure 21.1). It could fly in one of two modes. In Deployment Mode, it could carry its one tonne payload to 22 km and cruise there for up to three hours, slowly dispersing its load and creating an aerosol plume. A second SAIR flying in Monitoring Mode would carry no aerosol payload but instead 360 kg of instrumentation and much more fuel, such that it could cruise at altitude for more than five hours, traversing the plume many times and taking measurements. Such an aircraft would be very useful not only for the sort of perturbative experiments described here, but for non-perturbative ones (therefore in Monitoring Mode only) that would measure either background atmospheric conditions to probe our understanding of climate processes and conditions unrelated to SAI, or to measure "found" plumes from such sources as volcanoes rather than "caused" perturbations. In addition to its other functions, SAIR would serve as a proof of concept for the much larger SAIL design.

SARA on the other hand would be a huge solar-powered ultra-long-duration superpressure airship that could cruise between 18 and 23

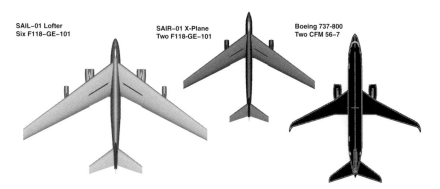

Figure 21.1 Size comparisons among SAIL, SAIR, and the Boeing 737-800.[25] Image courtesy of Donald A. Bingaman and Christian Rice, VPE Aerospace Consulting

km for up to six months, taking "far field" (rather than "near field") measurements of both background atmospheric conditions and the evolution of deployed aerosol. It would use helium as the lifting gas needed to carry a payload of instrumentation only and would have no perturbative capability. Four gimballed electric motors would propel it such that it could either station-keep or traverse the globe at a speed of 25 meters per second as its mission required. SARA is huge, roughly 2.5 times the length of a Goodyear blimp. It could operate anywhere between 50°N and 50°S on the shortest day of the year, and could venture further poleward in the summer hemisphere as the days lengthen. These limitations ensure that its fore-mounted solar photovoltaic "horse blanket" would get sufficient direct sunlight to keep it powered, enabling it to make long-term passive observations that would not be possible with SAIR. Both craft would be somewhat cutting edge (the SARA more so than the SAIR), but upon our preliminary review, we believe they would be feasible and economically viable. The full paper can be found on the AIAA's website at: https://doi .org/10.2514/6.2021-1681

What we have not yet established is whether the world's scientists actually need such aircraft. You could note that we therefore have the cart before the horse, but we chose first to try to define what sorts of research craft we thought we could build (and it's fun to dream about

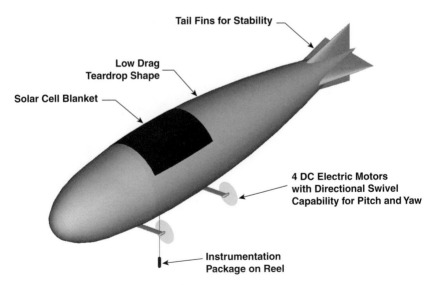

**Figure 21.2** SARA-01 diagram.[26] Image courtesy of: Donald A. Bingaman and Christian Rice, VPE Aerospace Consulting

cool new aircraft). Among my next tasks upon shipping this manuscript to my publisher will be to perform a gaps analysis that seeks to clarify what high-altitude field research requirements the world may have over the next several decades both for climate generally and for climate intervention specifically, and to compare those to the capabilities of the world's high-altitude research aircraft fleet. That fleet consists today of exactly seven American aircraft. An eighth non-US prospect, a Russian M-55 80s-era spy plane dubbed the Geophysica, seems permanently out of service. Among the seven American planes, only half are generally operational on any given day. All are managed by NASA, and five of the seven are roughly as old as I am (so really flippin' old!). These consist of two 50s-era ER-2s (the civilianized version of the U-2 spy plane in which Gary Powers was shot down), three 60s-era WB-57 spy planes, and two 90s-era Global Hawk drones. The Global Hawks are mostly purposed to defense missions, so the scientific community is reliant upon the five ancient spy planes, which in the aggregate fly well fewer than 1,000 hours per year. That's less than 200 hours per aircraft, one four-hour mission a week. This low utilization is partly reflective of demand but also of the creaking maintenance condition of these aircraft and the long intervals that are required between flights.

The question for the gaps analysis then is whether this tiny and aged fleet will be capable of handling the much increased volume of flying that would be necessary to accommodate the field experiments that may be required by both American and foreign researchers. A related but even more acute question is how much longer these museum pieces will remain in service. My intuition is that new research fleets will be required and would necessitate the better part of a decade to develop, but I am getting ahead of myself. I need to complete the analysis.

As noted earlier, we are also engaged in a separate study to answer the question of whether SAI deployment would be feasible, economical, and safe at an altitude of 25 km rather than 20. As higher deployment would increase radiative forcing efficiency, the scientific community is hopeful that the answer is "yes." We are therefore reviewing five diverse concepts (both transonic and supersonic) to see how this might be done. There is a ceiling in the sky beyond which traditional aircraft cannot sustain level flight and at 25 km we are very near it, but were there sufficient will, there undoubtedly would be a way, and aircraft are not the only possible lofting platforms.

Also in my research queue with other sets of collaborators are studies on the mechanisms by which rogue, covert SAI deployments might be detected by the uninvolved world, and what the national security implications may be (from an American perspective) of the emergence of SAI technologies around the world. More similarly practical projects are lined up behind these. Rather oddly, I seem to have discovered more than a lifetime of compelling research topics to pursue at a time when I have considerably less than a lifetime in which to complete them. Onward and upward.

## A Sea Change

The 2019 National Academy CDR report called for huge forward steps on that side of our toolbox but has thus far had little impact on policy or funding. However, it was planted in the infertile soil of the Trump administration. Within a week of taking office, Biden issued an extremely ambitious Executive Order on Tackling Climate Change at Home and Abroad.[27] It is difficult to imagine how it could be more starkly different than that of the position of the Trump Administration. It's first sentence flatly asserts that the US and the world face a profound climate crisis, and goes on to declare that "we must listen to science and meet the moment."[28] It promises to put the climate crisis at the center of US foreign policy and national security, and aspires to reach global net zero emissions by mid-century.[29] Biden promises to host a "Leaders' Climate Summit"[30] aimed at raising climate ambition while appointing a Special Presidential Envoy on Climate, a new high-level position promptly filled by former Democratic presidential nominee John Kerry. Rather than abandoning the Paris Agreement, the Order pledges that the US will develop its first-cycle nationally determined contribution and will submit it before the Leaders' Summit,[31] making clear that Biden is willing to put his own feet to the fire in this arena. Various agencies are given 90- and 120-day timelines to devise detailed plans on how to achieve all this.[32]

Climate intervention is mentioned nowhere in the Order, nor are research priorities articulated for climate more generally. Nonetheless, after a four-year absence from the climate arena, it is clear that "America is back,"[33] at least for the next four years. As of this writing, it is too soon to know how the American body politic will react to the 2021 National Academy report and whether the proposed funding will materialize. Nonetheless, my "spidey senses" are tingling. The confluence of the clear road map provided by National Academies report, the 180 degree pirouette in climate engagement from the Biden administration, accelerating momentum in the rest of the world, and the novel inclusion of climate intervention in the impending IPCC AR6 report all seem to comprise a sea change for this field. It seems that solar geoengineering may well now crawl out of the shadows in which it used to lurk to become a substantial field of exploration. For intensive scholarship (though decidedly *not* deployment), perhaps the rains have come.

# EPILOGUE

It has been over a year since I wrote the first line of the prologue of this book. The process of writing it has slotted almost perfectly into what would otherwise have been a COVID hole in my life, but it has proven to be a wonderful quarantine companion. I have simply hunkered down, researched, and written.

Geographically, I have migrated ever Westward, from London on day one back to Long Island for an isolated but glorious summer and ultimately to the Palm Springs area of California, where I am tapping out the epilogue in the shadow of a steep stone mountain. The life I had intended for the last year at Yale and Harvard has been obliterated, but it appears that by the autumn term, I will be able to resume my commute between the New Haven Green and Harvard Square. So what have I learned this year?

I wish I could say that the pandemic has demonstrated that humanity can do great things when the need arises, but that seems only half right. Yes, the vaccine development process that is rescuing us was completed with stunning speed, for which big pharma deserves big credit. On the other hand, we have mostly fumbled through shutdowns and mask mandates as if in the dark. American states that seemed to take the situation very seriously fared no better than those that didn't. European countries led by technocrats did no better than the COVID-careless US. Instead, what I really have learned is that we are much more vulnerable to worldwide disruptions than we seemed to believe, and that we lack the sort of capable, empowered institutions that are required to respond effectively to global-scale crises. Moreover, preparedness is essential.

Many epidemiologists had warned that despite all the medical advances of the past century, the world remained susceptible to just the sort of pandemic which overwhelmed us, but few people or countries properly heeded their warning. In the case of climate change however, we can clearly see what is coming. While certain catastrophic impacts such as fires and floods will arrive as sudden crises, the implacable larger climate change story will unfold in agonizingly slow motion. We will have no excuse to exclaim "How could we have known?"

The paleoclimatological record assures us that Earth's climate is much more variable and fragile than recent human history would cause one to believe, and it is equally clear that high atmospheric $CO_2$ levels are closely correlated with higher surface temperatures. As we take atmospheric $CO_2$ concentrations to double their preindustrial levels and beyond, we should expect enormous changes to ensue. In the words of the late Columbia University climate scientist Wally Broecker "The climate system is an angry beast, and we are poking it with sticks."

I encounter no one these days who is unaware that climate is an issue, but what seems to be a surprise to most is the amount of inertia that is in the climate system. The general belief seems to be that once we stop emitting, the problem is solved and the climate is saved. They are therefore both surprised and horrified to learn that for centuries thereafter, the seas will keep rising, the heat waves will keep coming, and the ecosystems will keep dying. They imagine that net zero is the end rather than merely the end of the beginning.

I came to my second career as an academic and author because I became convinced that the world has committed to a lot more climate change than it realizes, and that it will need tools it does not yet possess to deal with that. Moreover, on the CDR side of the box, I believe we will need to start deploying some of those tools at massive scales before they are inexpensive, which will mean they will require substantial economic sacrifice. And on the SRM side, I worry that some heavily climate-damaged state or alliance of states may become tempted to deploy cheap SAI before we fully understand its potential unintended consequences and before we have in place a global governance system that could confer upon it legitimacy. Given all that, the sooner we start down the path of exploring these tools and their ramifications, the better.

I should clarify that I have no financial aspirations for these endeavors, either in the field of climate engineering, or for this book.

I have no intention of starting a company to perfect cheap CDR or build geoengineering's air force, and any proceeds that derive from this book will be used to fund student research into this field. I intend to donate funds to the cause of geoengineering rather than profit from it.

Climate engineering remains mostly unknown even to climate-informed people. I hope my writings and teaching will change that a little, but what will have vastly wider impact is the IPCC's Sixth Assessment Report (the AR6) which should be issued more or less contemporaneously with this volume. For the first time, the AR6 will assess the state of knowledge on the full range of prospective climate engineering approaches, which I expect will send a lot of people scrambling to understand what the heck they are talking about. The AR6 will be geoengineering's debutante ball, though I don't expect the IPCC to slather it in make-up. It will likely be a "warts and all" portrayal, exactly as is needed.

I wish we were on a path that would not require climate engineering, but that's not the case. I also wish my skills and background would allow me to make a meaningful contribution on the CDR side of the toolbox, where the greater and more immediate need is. But they don't. So I expect to spend the bulk of my time hereafter toiling in the other side of the box, trying to illuminate that path forward on scary, risky SAI.

This gives rise to the perfectly fair question of whether it is in some way self-contradictory to help facilitate an option for which I hope the world will have no need. Perhaps. But my perspective on this takes me back to my 18th birthday when I aged out of scouting, laid my Eagle pin in the drawer, and newly met the minimum age requirement to join the local volunteer fire department. For the following 15 or so years – as long as my parents still occupied my childhood home – whenever I was there on vacations or summer breaks and the siren blew, I hopped into my Plandome Fire Department coveralls, sprinted to the car, sped to the firehouse, and tried to make the first engine. It was a quiet little bedroom community with few buildings larger than a single-family home and most call-outs were laughers (capsized backyard grills or smoking kitchen ovens).

From first-hand experience, I can tell you no volunteer fire fighter sits at home hoping for fire. You hope for beer and Monday Night Football in your flip-flops, followed by sound sleep until your morning alarm beeps. But if the siren blows and you round the corner on the back of an engine only to see flames coming out of half the windows, you lumber across the front lawn towards the inferno as best you can in your cumbersome gear and rue your failure to pay closer attention during your training. Nonetheless, you better be carrying a hose or some other effective tool that can stabilize the situation. In their very worst moments, your neighbors are relying upon you.

So, am I troubled by the paradox of building tools I hope are never used? No. Not a bit.

# ACRONYMS

| | |
|---|---|
| °C | degrees Celsius |
| °F | degrees Fahrenheit |
| A320 | Airbus 320 |
| AFOLU | agriculture, forestry, and other land use |
| AIAA | American Institute of Aeronautics and Astronautics |
| AR5 | Fifth Assessment Report |
| AR6 | Sixth Assessment Report |
| B737 | Boeing 737 |
| BECCS | bioenergy with carbon capture and sequestration |
| $CaCO_3$ | calcium carbonate |
| CBD | Convention on Biological Diversity |
| CCS | carbon capture and sequestration |
| CCT | cirrus cloud thinning |
| CDR | carbon dioxide removal |
| CE | carbon engineering |
| CEO | chief executive officer |
| CFC | chlorofluorocarbon |
| $CH_4$ | methane |
| CIA | Central Intelligence Agency |
| ClO | chlorine monoxide |
| $CO_2$ | carbon dioxide |
| $CO_2e$ | carbon dioxide equivalent |
| COP | Conference of Parties |
| DAC | direct air capture |

| | |
|---|---|
| DACCS | direct air carbon capture and sequestration |
| DDT | dichlorodiphenyltrichloroethane |
| DNA | deoxyribonucleic acid |
| EIA | Energy Information Administration |
| ENMOD | Environmental Modification Convention (or Convention on the Prohibition of Military or Any Other Hostile Use of Environmental Modifications Techniques) |
| EOR | enhanced oil recovery |
| EU | European Union |
| EV | electric vehicle |
| FAR | First Assessment Report |
| FEMA | Federal Emergency Management Agency |
| GCCSI | Global Carbon Capture and Storage Institute |
| GDP | gross domestic product |
| GE | General Electric |
| GGR | greenhouse gas removal |
| GHG | greenhouse gas |
| GJ | gigajoule |
| GM | General Motors |
| GMO | genetically modified organism |
| Gt | gigatonne |
| GtC | gigatonne of carbon |
| GWP | global warming potential |
| GW | gigawatt |
| $H_2O$ | water |
| $H_2SO_4$ | sulfuric acid |
| HALE | high-altitude long-endurance |
| IEA | International Energy Agency |
| IPCC | Intergovernmental Panel on Climate Change |
| ITCZ | Intertropical Convergence Zone |
| km | kilometers |
| $km^2$ | square kilometers |
| $L_1$ | Lagrangrian equilibrium point |
| LED | light-emitting diode |
| LIDAR | light detection and ranging |
| LNG | liquefied natural gas |
| LUCF | land use change and forestry |
| m | meters |
| MCB | marine cloud brightening |

| | |
|---|---|
| MIT | Massachusetts Institute of Technology |
| Mtpa | metric tonnes per annum |
| $N_2O$ | nitrous oxide |
| NASA | National Aeronautics and Space Administration |
| NDC | nationally determined contribution |
| NET | negative emissions technology |
| NIPCC | Nongovernmental International Panel on Climate Change |
| NM | nautical mile |
| NOx | oxides of nitrogen |
| NZEY | net-zero emissions year |
| $O_2$ | oxygen |
| $O_3$ | ozone |
| OECD | Organization for Economic Co-operation and Development |
| ppb | parts per billion |
| ppm | parts per million |
| ppt | parts per trillion |
| PV | photovoltaic |
| R&D | research and development |
| SAI | stratospheric aerosol injection |
| SAIL | stratospheric aerosol injection lofter |
| SAIR | stratospheric aerosol injection researcher |
| SARA | stratospheric aerosol research airship |
| SCoPEx | Stratospheric Controlled Perturbation Experiment |
| SG | solar geoengineering |
| $SO_2$ | sulfur dioxide |
| SPICE | stratospheric particle injection for climate engineering |
| SR15 | Special Report on Global Warming of 1.5°C |
| SRM | solar radiation management |
| SRMGI | Solar Radiation Management Governance Initiative |
| SSP | shared socioeconomic pathway |
| TACCC | transparency, accuracy, consistency, comparability, completeness |
| TWh | terawatt-hours |
| UK | United Kingdom |
| UN | United Nations |
| UNEP | United Nations Environment Programme |
| UNFCCC | United Nations Framework Convention on Climate Change |

| | |
|---|---|
| US | United States |
| USGCRP | United States Global Change Research Program |
| UV | ultraviolet |
| $W/m^2$ | watts per square meter |
| WHO | World Health Organization |

# APPENDIX: DETAIL IN RESPECT OF FIGURES 9.4–9.8

## Figure 9.4 and Figure 9.5

The data for the annual anthropogenic carbon dioxide emissions from fossil fuels and cement production from 1960 to 2019 were obtained from the Global Carbon Project database.[1] The COVID-stricken world economy saw the global fossil $CO_2$ emissions drop by 6.4 percent in 2020 from 2019 levels.[2] The projection for $CO_2$ emissions beyond 2022 is based on scenarios developed by McKinsey and Bloomberg. McKinsey's reference case in their latest Global Energy Perspective sees the emissions peak in 2023 and fall down by 25 percent in 2050[3] whereas a similar scenario in Bloomberg's New Energy Outlook sees the emissions peak in 2027 and then drop by 0.7 percent every year until 2050.[4] Our scenario, which is an equally weighted blend of these two scenarios, sees the fossil-based $CO_2$ emissions peak in 2027 followed by a steady decline until 2050 to a figure ~20 percent less than the 2019 levels (see Figures 9.4 and 9.5 below).

The projections beyond 2050 are then based on the four 1.5° C-consistent mitigation pathways put forward by the IPCC in its 2018 special report on "Global Warming of 1.5°C."[5] The P1 pathway outlines a low energy development scenario made possible by rather rapid decarbonization of energy supply without compromising with living standards. Pathways P2, P3, and P4 are based on the shared socioeconomic pathways (SSPs) SSP1 (sustainability), SSP2 (middle of the road) and SSP5 (fossil-fueled development), each illustrative pathway outlining

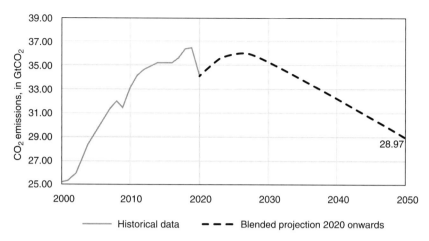

**Figure 9.4** Blended McKinsey and Bloomberg projection of $CO_2$ emissions from fossil fuels and industry until 2050

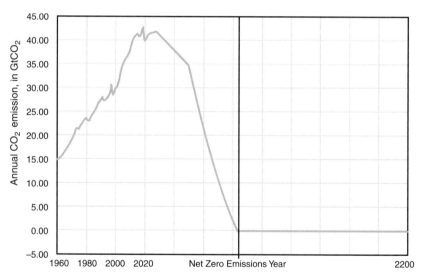

**Figure 9.5** Annual $CO_2$ emission scenario through 2200. Note that the curve is taken to be zero after Net Zero Emissions Year

global net $CO_2$ emissions for different levels of socioeconomic development. While the four IPCC pathways begin in present time and then achieve carbon neutrality between 2050 and 2060, we blended the four emissions trajectories to reach an equally-weighted blended emissions pathway to guide our emissions beyond 2050 on a decadal scale. This imposition of the blended curve resulted in us achieving net-zero $CO_2$

emissions in 2084. The global net $CO_2$ emissions have been kept constant at zero Gt per year beyond our net-zero year.

The data on historical $CO_2$ emissions associated with land-use change (LUC) for the period from 1960 to 2019 were obtained from the Global Carbon Project database.[6] The projections for emissions from land-use change show a wide range of possibilities, with several sources indicating LUC-related emissions could go up in the future while certain scenarios requiring strict adherence to nationally determined contributions demonstrating possible reductions in LUC-related $CO_2$ emissions.[7, 8, 9] Due to this uncertainty in projections, for the period from 2020 until 2050, the $CO_2$ emissions from LUC have been held constant at the average for 2010–2019 levels at 1.6 GtC/yr (1 GtC = 3.67 $GtCO_2$).[10] For simplification of projection, beyond 2050, the LUC-related $CO_2$ emissions have been assumed to follow the same trajectory as the blended IPCC curve created for fossil-related $CO_2$ emissions. Thus, the LUC-related $CO_2$ emissions also reach net-zero in 2084.

## Figure 9.6

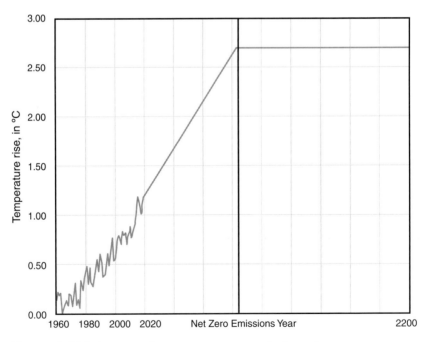

Figure 9.6 Global mean surface temperature scenario through 2200

### Scenario for Atmospheric Concentration of Carbon Dioxide

The data on the atmospheric concentration of $CO_2$ from 1960 to 2020 were obtained from the Global Monitoring Laboratory database maintained by the National Oceanic and Atmospheric Administration.[11] To calculate the atmospheric concentration of $CO_2$ beyond 2020, a constant annual airborne fraction – the fraction of anthropogenic $CO_2$ emissions which remains in the atmosphere after natural sinks have absorbed some of it – of 45 percent has been assumed.[12] While we understand that the climate-carbon cycle feedback might affect the airborne fraction of $CO_2$ in the future particularly in response to declining emissions levels, we have simplified our model by holding the fraction constant given the near-constant figures for airborne fraction of anthropogenic $CO_2$ over the last several decades.[13] Using this fraction and the fact that 2.13 Gt of carbon[14] (7.81 $GtCO_2$) is required for an increase of atmospheric concentration by 1 part per million, the atmospheric concentration was then calculated until the net-zero year. The atmospheric concentration of $CO_2$ has been assumed to drop at the rate of 1 ppm/yr after the net-zero year.[15, 16]

For the sake of illustrating a simple net-zero scenario that does not rely upon carbon removals, the concentrations of other greenhouse gases were assumed to follow the same trajectory as that of $CO_2$ concentration. This is a more optimistic assumption than is incorporated in Figure 9.1 which is sourced from the IPCC SR15 report. We are not claiming any factual basis for such reductions in other greenhouse gases. The annual reductions were calculated by translating the concentration of $CO_2$ to a GHGs only concentration-equivalent of $CO_2$ using a fixed ratio. The ratio of $CO_2$-eq concentration to $CO_2$ concentration was obtained by averaging the ratios of concentrations of $CO_2$-eq to $CO_2$ between 2020 and 2080 under IPCC's RCP4.5 scenario.[17] The RCP4.5 scenario was chosen because it most closely resembles our projections of $CO_2$ concentration.

### Scenario for Global Mean Surface Temperature

The data on the historical global surface temperature from 1960 to 2020 were obtained from NASA's Goddard Institute for Space Studies (see Figure 9.6).[18] The annual mean temperatures were used to arrive at an average anomaly of 1.18°C above the 1880 levels. For projecting the temperature rise beyond 2020, the temperature level in the year before our net-zero year (2083) was calculated and the temperatures were assumed to rise linearly from 2021 until 2083.

First, the radiative forcing due to the greenhouse gases was calculated for the year 2083 using:[19]

$$F = \frac{F_{2X}}{\ln(2)} \ln\left(\frac{C}{C_0}\right)$$

where $F$ is the radiative forcing, $F_{2X}$ is the forcing due to doubling of $CO_2$ in the atmosphere ($3.74$ $Wm^{-2}$),[20] $C$ is the atmospheric $CO_2$ concentration and $C_0$ is the preindustrial $CO_2$ concentration ($278$ ppm).[21] The $CO_2$-equation concentration was used to obtain the total radiative forcing due to all greenhouse gases. The total radiative forcing in 2083 was then calculated by adding the negative forcing due to aerosols to the radiative forcing obtained using the equation above. The negative forcing due to aerosols was obtained to be $-0.226$ W/m² by averaging the negative forcing due to aerosols between 2080 and 2090 under the RCP4.5 scenario. The total radiative forcing thus calculated was then multiplied by a climate sensitivity parameter of $0.7$ K/(W/m²) to get the temperature above the preindustrial levels in 2083. The transient climate sensitivity parameter was selected as a reasonable middle value in the range referenced in the IPCC's AR5 report.[22] The global mean surface temperature in the net-zero year was obtained to be $2.69°C$ above the preindustrial level, or $2.11°C$ above the 1986–2005 period (within the RCP4.5 range of 1.4 to 3.1 above 1986–2005 period).[23]

To emphasize on the warming from $CO_2$ beyond net-zero, the forcings due to non-$CO_2$ greenhouse gases and aerosols have been held constant at 2083 levels (the year before net-zero). The cooling from the reduction in atmospheric $CO_2$ is balanced by the warming due to slower ocean heat uptake,[24] resulting in almost flat temperature levels beyond net-zero emissions until 2200. Both the aerosol and non-$CO_2$ greenhouse gases emissions will have significantly reduced by 2083 under this projection. Thus, reducing the emissions to zero and letting the respective radiative forcings change naturally will have a rather small effect, but some effect, nonetheless. Reducing the aerosols to zero will see an initial bump in the temperature as the negative forcing falls down followed by a convergence with the zero-$CO_2$ curve due to their short-lived nature.[25] A similar zeroing of the non-$CO_2$ greenhouse gases will result in an initial

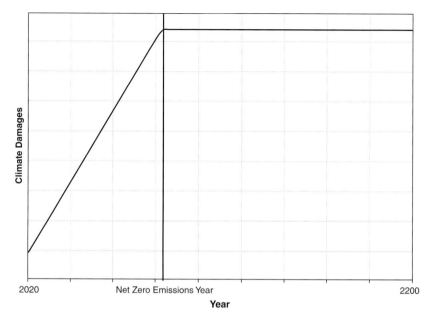

**Figure 9.7** Representation of climate damages after Net Zero

decline in temperature followed by stabilization of temperatures as methane and nitrous oxides, with atmospheric lifetimes of ~12 years and ~120 years respectively, are removed from the atmosphere.[26]

## Figure 9.7

Figure 9.7 is simply a graphical representation of the concept that continuing elevated temperatures will cause continuing physical climate damages. The curve is identical to that in Figure 9.6, but the scale on the y axis has been removed to signal that this is not a data-derived figure. It is meant to represent physical damages rather than the economic impact of those damages.

## Figure 9.8

The data on the historical global mean sea level rise from 1960 (see Figure 9.8 below) until 2018 was obtained from the Frederikse et al. paper "The causes of sea level rise since 1900."[27] Another 6.1 mm was added to the global mean sea level in 2019.[28] The sea level rise between

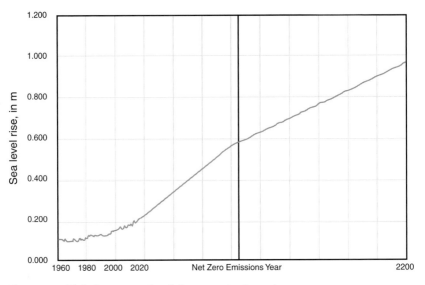

**Figure 9.8** Global mean sea level rise scenario through 2200

2019 and the net-zero year was then calculated by first extrapolating the sea level rise data under RCP4.5[29] for 2084 and then assuming a linear sea level rise between 2019 and 2084. The RCP4.5 scenario was chosen because of its resemblance with our temperature projection and near similarity between the RCP4.5 and RCP6.0 scenarios.

For the projections beyond the net-zero year, the findings of a 2019 paper by Nauels et al. were used.[30] The paper presents a scenario where the emissions are reduced to zero in 2030 and the committed sea level rise because of the emissions until 2030 are then calculated. They estimate a sea level rise commitment of 104.6 cm by 2300 above the 1986–2005 baseline under such constraints. We used this zero-emissions commitment figure from Nauels et al. to arrive at a global mean sea level rise of 0.964 m above preindustrial levels by 2200. But because our scenario experiences a ~2.7°C warming above preindustrial levels versus 1.5°C limit that the Nauels et al. paper stays under, this figure of 0.964 m of sea level rise is likely a rather conservative figure. Furthermore, more recent findings about contributors to sea level rise such as marine ice-cliff instability and isostatic rebound were not considered in our models due to uncertainty about the magnitude of their respective contributions. However, factoring these mechanisms in could result in a global sea level rise that is several tenths of a meter higher than our figure by 2200.[31, 32]

# NOTES

## 1 Where Do We Stand on Climate Change?

1. NASA Global Climate Change, "Global Surface Temperature | NASA Global Climate Change," Climate Change: Vital Signs of the Planet, https://climate.nasa .gov/vital-signs/global-temperature.

2. "Climate Change: Global Temperature | NOAA Climate.Gov," www.climate.gov/ news-features/understanding-climate/climate-change-global-temperature.

3. Max Roser, Hannah Ritchie, and Esteban Ortiz-Ospina, "World Population Growth," *Our World in Data,* https://ourworldindata.org/world-population-growth.

4. "7. Is the Current Level of Atmospheric $CO_2$ Concentration Unprecedented in Earth's History? Answer | Royal Society," https://royalsociety.org/topics-policy/ projects/climate-change-evidence-causes/question-7/.

5. Intergovernmental Panel on Climate Change, World Meteorological Organization, and United Nations Environment Programme, *Climate Change: The 1990 and 1992 IPCC Assessments: IPCC First Assessment Report Overview and Policymaker Summaries and 1992 IPCC Supplement.* (Geneva: WMO : UNEP, 1992).

6. IPCC, "IPCC Press Release: IPCC Launches Complete Synthesis Report," March 2015, www.ipcc.ch/site/assets/uploads/2018/04/150318_SYR_final_ publication_pr.pdf; IPCC, "IPCC Press Release: 831 Experts Selected for the Fifth Assessment Report," June 2010, www.ipcc.ch/site/assets/uploads/2018/04/pr-23june2010.pdf.

7. R. K. Pachauri, Leo Mayer, and Intergovernmental Panel on Climate Change, eds., *Climate Change 2014: Synthesis Report* (Geneva, Switzerland: Intergovernmental Panel on Climate Change, 2015).

8. Rebecca Lindsey, "Did Global Warming Stop in 1998?," NOAA Climate.gov, September 2018, www.climate.gov/news-features/climate-qa/did-global-warming-stop-1998.

9. Pachauri, Mayer, and Intergovernmental Panel on Climate Change, *Climate Change 2014.*

10. "IPCC Science Report: Climate Change Unequivocal, Human Influence at Least 95% Certain," Climate Action – European Commission, https://ec.europa.eu/clima/ news/articles/news_2013092701_en.

11. "Energy, Environment and Climate | Royal Society," https://royalsociety.org/topics-policy/energy-environment-climate/topic/.

12. Tom Phillips, "China Ratifies Paris Climate Change Agreement Ahead of G20," *The Guardian*, September 3, 2016, sec. World news, www.theguardian.com/world/2016/sep/03/china-ratifies-paris-climate-change-agreement.

13. "Climate Science for Australia's Future: A Report by the National Climate Science Advisory Committee" (Department of the Environment and Energy, July 2019), www.industry.gov.au/sites/default/files/2019-12/climate-science-for-australias-future-2019.pdf.

14. Svante Arrhenius, "On the Influence of Carbonic Acid in the Air upon the Temperature of the Ground," *Philosophical Magazine and Journal of Science* 41, no. 5 (1896): 237–76.

15. Jules G. Charney et al., "Carbon Dioxide and Climate: A Scientific Assessment" (National Academy of Sciences, 1979), https://www.bnl.gov/envsci/schwartz/charney_report1979.pdf.

16. Intergovernmental Panel on Climate Change, World Meteorological Organization, and United Nations Environment Programme, *Climate Change 2014*.

17. IPCC, "AR5 Climate Change 2013: The Physical Science Basis – IPCC," 2013, https://www.ipcc.ch/report/ar5/wg1/; IPCC, "Global Warming of 1.5°C: An IPCC Special Report on the Impacts of Global Warming of 1.5°C above Pre-Industrial Levels and Related Global Greenhouse Gas Emission Pathways, in the Context of Strengthening the Global Response to the Threat of Climate Change, Sustainable Development, and Efforts to Eradicate Poverty" (IPCC, 2018), www.ipcc.ch/sr15/.

18. NOAA, "Global Monitoring Laboratory – Carbon Cycle Greenhouse Gases," 2020, www.esrl.noaa.gov/gmd/ccgg/trends/gl_trend.html.

19. NASA, "Carbon Dioxide Concentration | NASA Global Climate Change," Climate Change: Vital Signs of the Planet, 2020, https://climate.nasa.gov/vital-signs/carbon-dioxide; NOAA, "Global Monitoring Laboratory – Carbon Cycle Greenhouse Gases."

20. NOAA, "Global Monitoring Laboratory – Carbon Cycle Greenhouse Gases."

21. Jessica E. Tierney et al., "Glacial Cooling and Climate Sensitivity Revisited," *Nature* 584, no. 7822 (August 2020): 569–73, https://doi.org/10.1038/s41586-020-2617-x.

22. Gerald A. Meehl et al., "Context for Interpreting Equilibrium Climate Sensitivity and Transient Climate Response from the CMIP6 Earth System Models," *Science Advances* 6, no. 26 (June 1, 2020): eaba1981, https://doi.org/10.1126/sciadv.aba1981.

23. S. C. Sherwood et al., "An Assessment of Earth's Climate Sensitivity Using Multiple Lines of Evidence," *Reviews of Geophysics* 58, no. 4 (2020): e2019RG000678, https://doi.org/10.1029/2019RG000678.

## 2 Climate Science 101

1. NOAA, "NOAA National Centers for Environmental Information, State of the Climate: Global Climate Report for Annual 2019," 2020, www.ncdc.noaa.gov/sotc/global/201913.

2. Coquiltam Weather and Climate, "ATSC 201(2): Electromagnetic Radiation From the Sun to the Earth," Coquitlam Weather and Climate, https://coquitlamwx.wordpress.com/tag/inverse-square-law/.

3. NASA Science Mission Directorate, "Solar System Exploration – Sun," NASA Solar System Exploration, 2019, https://solarsystem.nasa.gov/solar-system/sun/in-depth.

4. NASA Science Mission Directorate, "Solar System Exploration – Earth," NASA Solar System Exploration, 2019, https://solarsystem.nasa.gov/planets/earth/in-depth.

5. UCAR (University Corporation for Atmospheric Research), "Calculating Planetary Energy Balance and Temperature," 2015, https://scied.ucar.edu/planetary-energy-balance-temperature-calculate.

6. ACS, "Predicted Planetary Temperatures," American Chemical Society, www.acs.org/content/acs/en/climatescience/energybalance/predictedplanetarytemperatures.html.

7. C. Donald Ahrens and Robert Henson, *Essentials of Meteorology: An Invitation to the Atmosphere* (Cengage Learning, 2016).

8. Ibid.

9. Kevin E. Trenberth, John T. Fasullo, and Jeffrey Kiehl, "Earth's Global Energy Budget," *Bulletin of the American Meteorological Society* 90, no. 3 (March 1, 2009): 311–24, https://doi.org/10.1175/2008BAMS2634.1.

10. C. D. Keeling, S. C. Piper, R. B. Bacastow, M. Wahlen, T. P. Whorf, M. Heimann, and H. A. Meijer, Exchanges of atmospheric $CO_2$ and $^{13}CO_2$ with the terrestrial biosphere and oceans from 1978 to 2000. I. Global aspects, SIO Reference Series, No. 01–06, Scripps Institution of Oceanography, San Diego, 88 pages, 2001.

11. GCP, "Global Carbon Project, Carbon Budget and Trends 2019" (Global Carbon Project (GCP), December 4, 2019), www.globalcarbonproject.org/carbonbudget.

12. Intergovernmental Panel on Climate Change, "Climate Change 2014: Mitigation of Climate Change: Working Group III Contribution to the Fifth Assessment Report of the Intergovernmental Panel on Climate Change" (New York, NY: Cambridge University Press, 2014).

13. Lelde Timma, Elina Dace, and Marie Trydeman Knudsen, "Temporal Aspects in Emission Accounting – Case Study of Agriculture Sector," *Energies* 13, no. 4 (January 2020): 800, https://doi.org/10.3390/en13040800.

14. Gunnar Myhre and Drew Shindell, "Anthropogenic and Natural Radiative Forcing," in *Climate Change 2013: The Physical Science Basis. Contribution of Working Group I to the Fifth Assessment Report of the Intergovernmental Panel on Climate Change* (Cambridge, UK and New York, NY, USA: Cambridge University Press, 2013), www.ipcc.ch/site/assets/uploads/2018/02/WG1AR5_Chapter08_FINAL.pdf.

15. NOAA US Department of Commerce, "Global Monitoring Laboratory – Carbon Cycle Greenhouse Gases," www.esrl.noaa.gov/gmd/ccgg/.

16. US Department of Commerce.

17. Ibid.

18. NOAA US Department of Commerce, "NOAA Global Monitoring Laboratory – Halocarbons and Other Atmospheric Trace Species," www.esrl.noaa.gov/gmd/hats/data.html.

19. US Department of Commerce.

20. "AGAGE Data and Figures | Advanced Global Atmospheric Gases Experiment," 2021, http://agage.mit.edu/data/agage-data.

21. David Archer et al., "Atmospheric Lifetime of Fossil Fuel Carbon Dioxide," *Annual Review of Earth and Planetary Sciences* 37, no. 1 (May 2009): 117–34, https://doi.org/10.1146/annurev.earth.031208.100206; David Archer and Stefan Rahmstorf, *The Climate Crisis: An Introductory Guide to Climate Change* (Cambridge University Press, 2009).

22. Greg Kopp and Judith L. Lean, "A New, Lower Value of Total Solar Irradiance: Evidence and Climate Significance," *Geophysical Research Letters* 38, no. 1 (2011), https://doi.org/10.1029/2010GL045777.

23. F. Steinhilber, J. Beer, and C. Fröhlich, "Total Solar Irradiance during the Holocene," *Geophysical Research Letters* 36, no. 19 (2009), https://doi.org/10.1029/2009GL040142.
24. Ahrens and Henson, *Essentials of Meteorology.*
25. NOAA, "NOAA National Data Buoy Center – What Is Air Pressure," 2016, www.ndbc.noaa.gov/educate/pressure.shtml.
26. Ahrens and Henson, *Essentials of Meteorology.*
27. Frederick K. Lutgens, Edward J. Tarbuck, and Redina Herman, *The Atmosphere: An Introduction to Meteorology,* 14th edition (Pearson, 2018).
28. Ahrens and Henson, *Essentials of Meteorology.*
29. Ibid.
30. Lutgens, Tarbuck, and Herman, *The Atmosphere: An Introduction to Meteorology.*
31. Ahrens and Henson, *Essentials of Meteorology*; Lutgens, Tarbuck, and Herman, *The Atmosphere: An Introduction to Meteorology.*
32. Lutgens, Tarbuck, and Herman, *The Atmosphere: An Introduction to Meteorology.*
33. Jean Jouzel, Valerie Masson-Delmotte, O. Cattani, Gabrielle Dreyfus, S. Falourd, Georg Hoffmann, B. Minster, et al. "Orbital and Millennial Antarctic Climate Variability over the Past 800,000 Years." *Science* (New York, NY) 317 (September 1, 2007): 793–96. https://doi.org/10.1126/science.1141038.
34. NASA, "Milankovitch (Orbital) Cycles and Their Role in Earth's Climate," Climate Change: Vital Signs of the Planet, https://climate.nasa.gov/news/2948/milankovitch-orbital-cycles-and-their-role-in-earths-climate.
35. Carolyn W. Snyder, "Evolution of Global Temperature over the Past Two Million Years," *Nature* 538, no. 7624 (October 2016): 226–28, https://doi.org/10.1038/nature19798.
36. NASA Earth Observatory. "How Is Today's Warming Different from the Past?" Text.Article. NASA Earth Observatory, June 3, 2010. https://earthobservatory.nasa.gov/features/GlobalWarming/page3.php.
37. Michael E. Mann et al., "Proxy-Based Reconstructions of Hemispheric and Global Surface Temperature Variations over the Past Two Millennia," *Proceedings of the National Academy of Sciences* 105, no. 36 (September 9, 2008): 13252–57, https://doi.org/10.1073/pnas.0805721105.
38. Jeremy S. Hoffman et al., "Regional and Global Sea-Surface Temperatures during the Last Interglaciation," *Science* 355, no. 6322 (January 20, 2017): 276–79, https://doi.org/10.1126/science.aai8464.
39. "State of the Climate: Global Climate Report for Annual 2019" (NOAA National Centers for Environmental Information, 2020), www.ncdc.noaa.gov/sotc/global/201913; NASA Space Science Data Coordinated Archive, "Earth Fact Sheet," NASA Space Science Data Coordinated Archive, https://nssdc.gsfc.nasa.gov/planetary/factsheet/earthfact.html.
40. "State of the Climate: Global Climate Report for Annual 2019."
41. NOAA, "The Global Conveyor Belt – Currents," NOAA National Ocean Service Education, https://oceanservice.noaa.gov/education/tutorial_currents/05conveyor2.html.
42. Krzysztof Zawierucha and Daniel H. Shain, "Disappearing Kilimanjaro Snow – Are We the Last Generation to Explore Equatorial Glacier Biodiversity?," *Ecology and Evolution* 9, no. 15 (2019): 8911–18, https://doi.org/10.1002/ece3.5327.
43. "Sea Ice," NASA Earth Observatory, September 16, 2016, https://earthobservatory.nasa.gov/features/SeaIce.

44. NASA Global Climate Change, "Arctic Sea Ice Minimum | NASA Global Climate Change," Climate Change: Vital Signs of the Planet, https://climate.nasa.gov/vital-signs/arctic-sea-ice.

45. Tom Prater, "Interactive: When Will the Arctic See Its First Ice-Free Summer?," https://interactive.carbonbrief.org/when-will-the-arctic-see-its-first-ice-free-summer/.

46. Dirk Notz and Simip Community, "Arctic Sea Ice in CMIP6," *Geophysical Research Letters* 47, no. 10 (2020): e2019GL086749, https://doi.org/10.1029/2019GL086749.

47. Juan Siliezar, "Study Says Antarctic Ice Sheet Melt to Lift Sea Level Higher than Thought," *Harvard Gazette* (blog), https://news.harvard.edu/gazette/story/2021/04/study-says-antarctic-ice-sheet-melt-to-lift-sea-level-higher-than-thought/.

48. Robert Mulvaney et al., "Recent Antarctic Peninsula Warming Relative to Holocene Climate and Ice-Shelf History," *Nature* 489, no. 7414 (September 2012): 141–44, https://doi.org/10.1038/nature11391.

49. Chao Li et al., "The Transient versus the Equilibrium Response of Sea Ice to Global Warming," *Journal of Climate* 26, no. 15 (August 1, 2013): 5624–36, https://doi.org/10.1175/JCLI-D-12-00492.1.

50. Igor V. Polyakov et al., "Weakening of Cold Halocline Layer Exposes Sea Ice to Oceanic Heat in the Eastern Arctic Ocean," *Journal of Climate* 33, no. 18 (August 20, 2020): 8107–23, https://doi.org/10.1175/JCLI-D-19-0976.1.

51. Mark Pagani et al., "The Role of Carbon Dioxide During the Onset of Antarctic Glaciation," *Science* 334, no. 6060 (December 2, 2011): 1261–64, https://doi.org/10.1126/science.1203909; Helen K. Coxall et al., "Rapid Stepwise Onset of Antarctic Glaciation and Deeper Calcite Compensation in the Pacific Ocean," *Nature* 433 (January 1, 2005): 53–57, https://doi.org/10.1038/nature03135.

## 3 What's So Bad about Climate Change?

1. United Nations Environment Programme. *The Emissions Gap Report 2019*, 2019.

2. IPCC, *Climate Change 2014: Synthesis Report. Contribution of Working Groups I, II and III to the Fifth Assessment Report of the Intergovernmental Panel on Climate Change* [Core Writing Team, R. K. Pachauri and L. A. Meyer (eds.)]. (2014), 63.

3. Matthew C. Fitzpatrick and Robert R. Dunn, "Contemporary Climatic Analogs for 540 North American Urban Areas in the Late 21st Century," *Nature Communications* 10, no. 1 (February 12, 2019): 614, https://doi.org/10.1038/s41467-019-08540-3.

4. NOAA, "NOAA National Centers for Environmental Information, State of the Climate: Global Climate Report for Annual 2019," 2020, www.ncdc.noaa.gov/sotc/global/201913.

5. R. K. Pachauri, Leo Mayer, and Intergovernmental Panel on Climate Change, eds., *Climate Change 2014: Synthesis Report. Contribution of Working Groups I, II and III to the Fifth Assessment Report of the Intergovernmental Panel on Climate Change* (Geneva, Switzerland: Intergovernmental Panel on Climate Change, 2015).

6. Matthew C. Fitzpatrick and Robert R. Dunn, "Contemporary Climatic Analogs for 540 North American Urban Areas in the Late 21st Century," *Nature Communications* 10, no. 1 (February 12, 2019): 614, https://doi.org/10.1038/s41467-019-08540-3.

7. Jeremy S. Pal and Elfatih A. B. Eltahir, "Future Temperature in Southwest Asia Projected to Exceed a Threshold for Human Adaptability," *Nature Climate Change* 6, no. 2 (February 2016): 197–200, https://doi.org/10.1038/nclimate2833.

8. Thomas Schneider von Deimling et al., "How Cold Was the Last Glacial Maximum?," *Geophysical Research Letters* 33, no. 14 (2006), https://doi.org/10.1029/2006GL026484.

9. The Editors of Encyclopedia Britannica. "Laurentide Ice Sheet | Ice Sheet, North America." Encyclopedia Britannica. www.britannica.com/place/Laurentide-Ice-Sheet.

10. McKinsey Global Institute, "Climate Risk and Response: Physical Hazards and Socioeconomic Impacts," January 2020, www.mckinsey.com/~/media/mckinsey/business%20functions/sustainability/our%20insights/climate%20risk%20and%20response%20physical%20hazards%20and%20socioeconomic%20impacts/mgi-climate-risk-and-response-full-report-vf.pdf.

11. Michael Oppenheimer et al., "Sea Level Rise and Implications for Low-Lying Islands, Coasts and Communities," in *IPCC Special Report on the Ocean and Cryosphere in a Changing Climate*, 2019, www.ipcc.ch/site/assets/uploads/sites/3/2019/12/SROCC_FullReport_FINAL.pdf.

12. IPCC, *Climate Change 2014: Synthesis Report. Contribution of Working Groups I, II and III to the Fifth Assessment Report of the Intergovernmental Panel on Climate Change* [Core Writing Team, R. K. Pachauri and L. A. Meyer (eds.)]. (2014).

13. H.-O. Pörtner et al., "IPCC Special Report on the Ocean and Cryosphere in a Changing Climate," 2019, www.ipcc.ch/srocc/.

14. William D. Nordhaus, *The Climate Casino: Risk, Uncertainty, and Economics for a Warming World* (Yale University Press, 2013).

15. Barbara Neumann et al., "Future Coastal Population Growth and Exposure to Sea-Level Rise and Coastal Flooding – A Global Assessment," *PLOS One* 10, no. 3 (March 11, 2015): e0118571, https://doi.org/10.1371/journal.pone.0118571.

16. Thomas Kutty Abraham and Arys Aditya, "Why Indonesia Is Shifting Its Capital From Jakarta," *Bloomberg.Com*, August 24, 2019, www.bloomberg.com/news/articles/2019-08-24/why-indonesia-is-shifting-its-capital-from-jakarta-quicktake.

17. Norman Miller, "A New Island of Hope Rising from the Indian Ocean," www.bbc.com/travel/story/20200909-a-new-island-of-hope-rising-from-the-indian-ocean.

18. Pierre-Louis, Kendra, "How to Rebound After a Disaster: Move, Don't Rebuild, Research Suggests." *The New York Times*, sec. Climate, www.nytimes.com/2019/08/22/climate/sea-level-managed-retreat.html.

19. Lisa Fu, "Insurers Rethink Property Coverage as Seas Rise." Content. PERE (blog), www.perenews.com/insurers-rethink-property-coverage-as-seas-rise/.

20. Greg Holland and Cindy L. Bruyère, "Recent Intense Hurricane Response to Global Climate Change." *Climate Dynamics* 42, no. 3 (February 1, 2014): 617–27. https://doi.org/10.1007/s00382-013-1713-0.

21. IPCC, "Global Warming of 1.5°C: An IPCC Special Report on the Impacts of Global Warming of 1.5°C above Pre-Industrial Levels and Related Global Greenhouse Gas Emission Pathways, in the Context of Strengthening the Global Response to the Threat of Climate Change, Sustainable Development, and Efforts to Eradicate Poverty" (IPCC, 2018), www.ipcc.ch/sr15/.

22. Benjamin I. Cook, Toby R. Ault, and Jason E. Smerdon, "Unprecedented 21st Century Drought Risk in the American Southwest and Central Plains," *Science Advances* 1, no. 1 (February 1, 2015): e1400082, https://doi.org/10.1126/sciadv.1400082.

23. K. E. Trenberth, "Changes in Precipitation with Climate Change." *Climate Research* 47, no. 1–2 (2011): 123–38.

24. Im Eun-Soon, Jeremy S. Pal, and Elfatih A. B. Eltahir, "Deadly Heat Waves Projected in the Densely Populated Agricultural Regions of South Asia," *Science Advances* 3, no. 8 (August 1, 2017): e1603322, https://doi.org/10.1126/sciadv.1603322.

25. Colin Raymond, Tom Matthews, and Radley M. Horton, "The Emergence of Heat and Humidity Too Severe for Human Tolerance," *Science Advances* 6, no. 19 (May 1, 2020): eaaw1838, https://doi.org/10.1126/sciadv.aaw1838.

26. Pal, E.-S. Im, and A. B. Eltahir, "Deadly Heat Waves Projected in the Densely Populated Agricultural Regions of South Asia," *Science Advances* 3, 2017.

27. Jeremy S. Pal and Elfatih A. B. Eltahir, "Future Temperature in Southwest Asia Projected to Exceed a Threshold for Human Adaptability," *Nature Climate Change* 6, no. 2 (February 2016): 197–200, https://doi.org/10.1038/nclimate2833.

28. "Population Density (People per Sq. Km of Land Area) | Data," 2021, https://data.worldbank.org/indicator/EN.POP.DNST.

29. "The Ganges River Basin | GRID-Arendal," www.grida.no/resources/6685.

30. "Monsoons | UCAR Center for Science Education," https://scied.ucar.edu/learning-zone/storms/monsoons.

31. Kim Stanley Robinson, *The Ministry for the Future* (Orbit Books, 2020).

32. Paolo D'Odorico, Abinash Bhattachan, Kyle F. Davis, Sujith Ravi, and Christiane W. Runyan. "Global Desertification: Drivers and Feedbacks." *35th Year Anniversary Issue* 51 (January 1, 2013): 326–44. https://doi.org/10.1016/j.advwatres.2012.01.013.

33. California Department of Forestry and Fire Protection, "Top 20 Largest California Wildfires," n.d., www.fire.ca.gov/media/4jandlhh/top20_acres.pdf.

34. IPCC, *Climate Change 2014: Synthesis Report. Contribution of Working Groups I, II and III to the Fifth Assessment Report of the Intergovernmental Panel on Climate Change* [Core Writing Team, R.K. Pachauri and L .A. Meyer (eds.)]. (2014), 13.

35. McKinsey Global Institute, "Climate Risk and Response: Physical Hazards and Socioeconomic Impacts," Report, 2020.

36. IPCC, *Climate Change 2014*.

37. IPCC, *Climate Change 2014*.

38. Giovanni Strona and Corey J. A. Bradshaw, "Co-Extinctions Annihilate Planetary Life during Extreme Environmental Change," *Scientific Reports* 8, no. 1 (November 13, 2018): 16724, https://doi.org/10.1038/s41598-018-35068-1; Anthony D. Barnosky et al., "Has the Earth's Sixth Mass Extinction Already Arrived?," *Nature* 471, no. 7336 (March 2011): 51–57, https://doi.org/10.1038/nature09678; Gerardo Ceballos, Paul R. Ehrlich, and Rodolfo Dirzo, "Biological Annihilation via the Ongoing Sixth Mass Extinction Signaled by Vertebrate Population Losses and Declines," *Proceedings of the National Academy of Sciences* 114, no.30 (July 25, 2017): E6089–96, https://doi.org/10.1073/pnas.1704949114.

39. McKinsey Global Institute, "Climate Risk and Response: Physical Hazards and Socioeconomic Impacts."

40. Laura E. Erban, Steven M. Gorelick, and Howard A. Zebker, "Groundwater Extraction, Land Subsidence, and Sea-Level Rise in the Mekong Delta, Vietnam," *Environmental Research Letters* 9, no. 8 (August 2014): 084010, https://doi.org/10.1088/1748-9326/9/8/084010.

41. "Sinking Land and Rising Seas: The Dual Crises Facing Coastal Communities," Environment, March 8, 2021, www.nationalgeographic.com/environment/article/sinking-land-rising-seas-dual-crises-facing-coastal-communities.

42. Tapan B. Pathak et al., "Climate Change Trends and Impacts on California Agriculture: A Detailed Review," *Agronomy* 8, no. 3 (March 2018): 25, https://doi.org/10.3390/agronomy8030025.

43. McKinsey Global Institute, "Climate Risk and Response: Physical Hazards and Socioeconomic Impacts."

44. Mamta Patel Nagaraja, "Climate Variability | Science Mission Directorate." NASA.gov, September 11, 2020. https://science.nasa.gov/earth-science/oceanography/ocean-earth-system/climate-variability.

45. Ibid.

46. David J. R. Thornalley, Delia W. Oppo, Pablo Ortega, Jon I. Robson, Chris M. Brierley, Renee Davis, Ian R. Hall, et al. "Anomalously Weak Labrador Sea Convection and Atlantic Overturning during the Past 150 Years." *Nature* 556, no. 7700 (April 2018): 227–30. https://doi.org/10.1038/s41586-018-0007-4.

47. Hu Yang, Gerrit Lohmann, Wei Wei, Mihai Dima, Monica Ionita, and Jiping Liu. "Intensification and Poleward Shift of Subtropical Western Boundary Currents in a Warming Climate." *Journal of Geophysical Research: Oceans* 121, no. 7 (2016): 4928–45. https://doi.org/10.1002/2015JC011513.

48. McKinsey Global Institute, "Climate Risk and Response: Physical Hazards and Socioeconomic Impacts."

49. World Bank, "Population, Total | Data," World Bank Open Data, 2020, https://data.worldbank.org/indicator/SP.POP.TOTL.

50. UNSC, "United Nations Security Council, 8451st Meeting, UN Doc S/PV.8451," January 25, 2019, https://undocs.org/en/S/PV.8451.

51. USGCRP, "Fourth National Climate Assessment," 2018, https://nca2018.globalchange.govhttps://nca2018.globalchange.gov/chapter/16.

52. United Nations, "The Climate Crisis – A Race We Can Win," United Nations (United Nations), www.un.org/en/un75/climate-crisis-race-we-can-win.

53. IPCC, *Climate Change 2014: Synthesis Report. Contribution of Working Groups I, II and III to the Fifth Assessment Report of the Intergovernmental Panel on Climate Change* [Core Writing Team, R. K. Pachauri and L. A. Meyer (eds.)]. (2014), 15.

54. Ibid., 15–16.

55. McKinsey Global Institute, "Climate Risk and Response: Physical Hazards and Socioeconomic Impacts."

56. Ibid.

# 4 Climate Negotiations

1. CFCs were widely used until the 1980s or so, but are far from the only ozone-depleting substance. Hydrochlorofluorocarbons (HCFCs), a less ozone-damaging substitute for CFCs, are still in the process of being phased out, while the use of other damaging halocarbons including tetrachloromethane, methyl bromide, and hydro-bromofluorocarbons is also controlled by the Montreal Protocol.

2. Mario J. Molina and F. S. Rowland, "Stratospheric Sink for Chlorofluoromethanes: Chlorine Atom-Catalysed Destruction of Ozone," *Nature* 249, no. 5460 (June 1974): 810–12, https://doi.org/10.1038/249810a0.

3. "Quotation of DuPont Chairman Irving S. Shapiro," *Chemical Week*, July 16, 1975.

4. Sara Blumberg, "Warm Air Helped Make 2017 Ozone Hole Smallest Since 1988," Text, NASA, November 2, 2017, www.nasa.gov/feature/goddard/2017/warm-air-helped-make-2017-ozone-hole-smallest-since-1988.

5. "A Greener Bush," *The Economist*, February 13, 2003, www.economist.com/leaders/2003/02/13/a-greener-bush.

6. "What Is the Kyoto Protocol? | UNFCCC," https://unfccc.int/kyoto_protocol.
7. Robert Stowe (Executive Director, Harvard Environmental Economics Program), in an email exchange with the author, February, 2021.
8. Richard Schmalensee, "Greenhouse Policy Architectures and Institutions" (MIT Joint Program on the Science and Policy of Global Change, 1996), https://dspace.mit.edu/bitstream/handle/1721.1/50226/37336496.pdf;sequence=1.
9. "Brazil | Climate Action Tracker," https://climateactiontracker.org/climate-target-update-tracker/brazil/.
10. "Australia | Climate Action Tracker," https://climateactiontracker.org/countries/australia/.
11. "Home | Climate Action Tracker," https://climateactiontracker.org/.

## 5  Climate Economics

1. Kenji Yamaji et al., "A Study on Economic Measures for $CO_2$ Reduction in Japan," *Energy Policy* 21, no. 2 (February 1, 1993): 123–32, https://doi.org/10.1016/0301-4215(93)90134-2.
2. Paul R. Ehrlich and John P. Holdren, "Impact of Population Growth," *Science* 171, no. 3977 (March 26, 1971): 1212–17, https://doi.org/10.1126/science.171.3977.1212.
3. William D. Nordhaus, *The Climate Casino: Risk, Uncertainty, and Economics for a Warming World* (Yale University Press, 2013).
4. United Nations Population Division, "World Population Prospects," 2019, https://population.un.org/wpp/.
5. Oliver Morton, *The Planet Remade: How Geoengineering Could Change the World* (Princeton University Press, 2015).
6. IEA, "World Energy Outlook 2019," November 2019, www.iea.org/reports/world-energy-outlook-2019.
7. "EIA Projects Global Energy-Related $CO_2$ Emissions Will Increase through 2050 – Today in Energy – U.S. Energy Information Administration (EIA)," www.eia.gov/todayinenergy/detail.php?id=41493.
8. William D. Nordhaus, *The Climate Casino: Risk, Uncertainty, and Economics for a Warming World* (Yale University Press, 2013).
9. Ibid.
10. "GDP per Capita (Current US$) – China | Data," https://data.worldbank.org/indicator/NY.GDP.PCAP.CD?locations=CN.
11. Food and Agriculture Organization of the United Nations, *The State of Food Security and Nutrition In the World: Safeguarding Against Economic Slowdowns and Downturns*, 2019, www.fao.org/3/ca5162en/ca5162en.pdf.
12. William D. Nordhaus, *The Climate Casino: Risk, Uncertainty, and Economics for a Warming World* (Yale University Press, 2013).
13. Ted Halstead, "The Economic and Business Case for Bipartisan Climate Policy," www.congress.gov/116/meeting/house/109473/witnesses/HHRG-116-WM00-Wstate-HalsteadT-20190515.pdf.
14. Ibid.
15. William D. Nordhaus, *The Climate Casino: Risk, Uncertainty, and Economics for a Warming World* (Yale University Press, 2013).
16. Ibid.
17. "Climate Change and Health," www.who.int/news-room/fact-sheets/detail/climate-change-and-health.

18. William D. Nordhaus, *The Climate Casino: Risk, Uncertainty, and Economics for a Warming World.*

19. William D. Nordhaus.

20. Barbara Neumann et al., "Future Coastal Population Growth and Exposure to Sea-Level Rise and Coastal Flooding – A Global Assessment," *PLOS One* 10, no. 3 (March 11, 2015): e0118571, https://doi.org/10.1371/journal.pone.0118571.

21. William D. Nordhaus, *The Climate Casino: Risk, Uncertainty, and Economics for a Warming World* (Yale University Press, 2013).

22. Ibid.

23. James P. Kossin et al., "Global Increase in Major Tropical Cyclone Exceedance Probability over the Past Four Decades," *Proceedings of the National Academy of Sciences* 117, no. 22 (June 2, 2020): 11975–80, https://doi.org/10.1073/pnas.1920849117.

24. William D. Nordhaus, *The Climate Casino: Risk, Uncertainty, and Economics for a Warming World* (Yale University Press, 2013).

25. Ibid.

26. Ibid.

27. *The Oxford Handbook of Climate Change and Society* (Oxford University Press, 2011), https://doi.org/10.1093/oxfordhb/9780199566600.001.0001.

28. William Nordhaus, "Economics of the Disintegration of the Greenland Ice Sheet," *Proceedings of the National Academy of Sciences* 116, no. 25 (June 18, 2019): 12261–69, https://doi.org/10.1073/pnas.1814990116.

29. Rowan T. Sutton, "ESD Ideas: A Simple Proposal to Improve the Contribution of IPCC WGI to the Assessment and Communication of Climate Change Risks," *Earth System Dynamics* 9, no. 4 (October 4, 2018): 1155–58, https://doi.org/10.5194/esd-9-1155-2018.

30. "Climate Economics Nobel May Do More Harm Than Good," *Gernot Wagner/Economist and Author* (blog), https://gwagner.com/afp-nordhaus-nobel/.

## 6 The Energy Transition

1. R. K. Pachauri, Leo Mayer, and Intergovernmental Panel on Climate Change, eds., *Climate Change 2014: Synthesis Report* (Geneva, Switzerland: Intergovernmental Panel on Climate Change, 2015).

2. Bradley E. Layton, "A Comparison of Energy Densities of Prevalent Energy Sources in Units of Joules Per Cubic Meter," *International Journal of Green Energy* 5, no. 6 (December 4, 2008): 438–55, https://doi.org/10.1080/15435070802498036.

3. "BP Takes $17.5 Billion Write-Down, Expects Oil Price to Stay Low – WSJ," www.wsj.com/articles/bp-takes-17-5-billion-write-down-expects-oil-price-to-stay-low-11592211169.

4. "Hubbert's Peak Prediction vs. Actual Oil Production in the United States," Our World in Data, https://ourworldindata.org/grapher/hubberts-peak-vs-actual-oil-production-in-the-united-states.

5. BP, "Statistical Review of World Energy," bp global, www.bp.com/en/global/corporate/energy-economics/statistical-review-of-world-energy.html.

6. "BP Energy Charting Tool," BP, www.bp.com/en/global/corporate/energy-economics/energy-charting-tool-desktop.html.

7. BP, "Statistical Review of World Energy."

8. Ibid.

9. Environmental Health and Engineering, Inc., "Emissions of hazardous air pollutants from coal-fired power plants," March 2011, www.lung.org/getmedia/25962184-d2fc-42f8-b5a3-8ece3257fbab/emissions-of-hazardous-air.pdf.

10. NASA's GMS, "GMS: Carbon and Climate Briefing – November 12, 2015," November 12, 2015, https://svs.gsfc.nasa.gov/12044.

11. Vaclav Smil, "World History and Energy," in *Encyclopedia of Energy* (Elsevier, 2004), 549–61, https://doi.org/10.1016/B0-12-176480-X/00025-5.

12. Dennis Anderson, "Energy and Economic Prosperity," in *World Energy Assessment: Energy and the Challenge of Sustainability* (UNDP, 2000), 394–411.

13. John P. DeLong and Oskar Burger, "Socio-Economic Instability and the Scaling of Energy Use with Population Size," *PLOS One* 10, no. 6 (June 19, 2015): e0130547, https://doi.org/10.1371/journal.pone.0130547.

14. "Norwegian EV policy," https://elbil.no/english/norwegian-ev-policy/.

15. International Council on Clean Transportation, "Update on the Global Transition to Electric Vehicles through 2019," July 2020, https://theicct.org/sites/default/files/publications/update-global-EV-stats-sept2020-EN.pdf.

16. "Governor Newsom Announces California Will Phase Out Gasoline-Powered Cars and Drastically Reduce Demand for Fossil Fuel in California's Fight Against Climate Change," California Governor, September 23, 2020, www.gov.ca.gov/2020/09/23/governor-newsom-announces-california-will-phase-out-gasoline-powered-cars-drastically-reduce-demand-for-fossil-fuel-in-californias-fight-against-climate-change/.

17. Jack Ewing, "Volvo Plans to Sell Only Electric Cars by 2030," *The New York Times*, March 2, 2021, sec. Business, www.nytimes.com/2021/03/02/business/volvo-electric-cars.html.

18. Neal E. Boudette and Coral Davenport, "G.M. Will Sell Only Zero-Emission Vehicles by 2035," *The New York Times*, January 28, 2021, sec. Business, www.nytimes.com/2021/01/28/business/gm-zero-emission-vehicles.html.

19. "Insider," www.insider.com/.

20. Florian Knobloch et al., "Net Emission Reductions from Electric Cars and Heat Pumps in 59 World Regions over Time," *Nature Sustainability* 3, no. 6 (June 2020): 437–47, https://doi.org/10.1038/s41893-020-0488-7.

21. "Frequently Asked Questions (FAQs) – U.S. Energy Information Administration (EIA)," www.eia.gov/tools/faqs/faq.php.

22. "Fuel Economy," www.fueleconomy.gov/feg/PowerSearch.do?action=noform&path=1&year1=1984&year2=2021&vtype=Electric&pageno=1&rowLimit=50.

23. Hiroko Tabuchi and Brad Plumer, "How Green Are Electric Vehicles?," *The New York Times*, sec. Climate, www.nytimes.com/2021/03/02/climate/electric-vehicles-environment.html.

24. "Gasoline vs Electric – Who Wins on Lifetime Global Warming Emissions? We Found Out," Union of Concerned Scientists, November 12, 2015, https://blog.ucsusa.org/rachael-nealer/gasoline-vs-electric-global-warming-emissions-953.

25. "Natural Gas," Center for Climate and Energy Solutions, July 1, 2020, www.c2es.org/content/natural-gas/.

26. "Natural Gas Is a Much 'Dirtier' Energy Source, Carbon-Wise, than We Thought," Science, February 19, 2020, www.nationalgeographic.com/science/article/super-potent-methane-in-atmosphere-oil-gas-drilling-ice-cores.

27. Vaclav Smil, "'Too Cheap to Meter' Nuclear Power Revisited – IEEE Spectrum," IEEE Spectrum: Technology, Engineering, and Science News, https://spectrum.ieee.org/energy/nuclear/too-cheap-to-meter-nuclear-power-revisited.

28. BP, "Statistical Review of World Energy."

29. IEA, "World Energy Outlook 2019," November 2019, www.iea.org/reports/world-energy-outlook-2019.
30. BP, "Statistical Review of World Energy."
31. M. J. (Mariska) de Wild-Scholten, "Energy Payback Time and Carbon Footprint of Commercial Photovoltaic Systems," *Solar Energy Materials and Solar Cells*, Thin-film Photovoltaic Solar Cells, 119 (December 1, 2013): 296–305, https://doi.org/10.1016/j.solmat.2013.08.037.
32. BP, "Statistical Review of World Energy."
33. "2019 Wind Energy Data and Technology Trends," Energy.gov, www.energy.gov/eere/wind/2019-wind-energy-data-technology-trends.
34. Lazard, "Lazard's Levelized Cost of Energy Analysis – Version 13.0," 2019, www.lazard.com/media/451086/lazards-levelized-cost-of-energy-version-130-vf.pdf.
35. Emilio F. Moran et al., "Sustainable Hydropower in the 21st Century," *Proceedings of the National Academy of Sciences* 115, no. 47 (November 20, 2018): 11891–98, https://doi.org/10.1073/pnas.1809426115.
36. BP, "Statistical Review of World Energy."
37. Hannah Ritchie and Max Roser, "Renewable Energy," *Our World in Data*, December 17, 2017, https://ourworldindata.org/renewable-energy.
38. IRENA, "Renewable Energy Highlights," July 1, 2020, www.irena.org/-/media/Files/IRENA/Agency/Publication/2020/Jul/Renewable_energy_highlights_July_2020.pdf.
39. "Fossil Fuels Have Made up at Least 80% of U.S. Fuel Mix since 1900 – Today in Energy – U.S. Energy Information Administration (EIA)," www.eia.gov/todayinenergy/detail.php?id=21912.
40. "Energy Mix," Our World in Data, https://ourworldindata.org/energy-mix.
41. Hannah Ritchie and Max Roser, "Fossil Fuels," *Our World in Data*, October 2, 2017, https://ourworldindata.org/fossil-fuels.
42. "Levelized Cost of Energy and Levelized Cost of Storage 2019," Lazard.com, 2020, www.lazard.com/perspective/levelized-cost-of-energy-and-levelized-cost-of-storage-2019/.
43. "Why Is China Placing A Global Bet On Coal?," NPR.org, www.npr.org/2019/04/29/716347646/why-is-china-placing-a-global-bet-on-coal.
44. *Fox Business – Murray Energy CEO: Lack of Coal Will Leave People Freezing in the Dark*, 2017, www.youtube.com/watch?v=THt1hPR2LWw.
45. "Plan for Climate Change and Environmental Justice | Joe Biden," Joe Biden for President: Official Campaign Website, https://joebiden.com/climate-plan/.
46. "The Biden Plan to Build a Modern, Sustainable Infrastructure and an Equitable Clean Energy Future," Joe Biden for President: Official Campaign Website, 2021, https://joebiden.com/clean-energy/.
47. "Plan for Climate Change and Environmental Justice | Joe Biden."
48. "The Biden Plan to Build a Modern, Sustainable Infrastructure and an Equitable Clean Energy Future."
49. David Roberts, "Why Wind and Solar Power Are Such a Challenge for Energy Grids," Vox, June 19, 2015, www.vox.com/2015/6/19/8808545/wind-solar-grid-integration.
50. Roberts.
51. US Energy Information Administration, "Electricity Generation, Capacity, and Sales in the United States," www.eia.gov/energyexplained/electricity/electricity-in-the-us-generation-capacity-and-sales.php.
52. US Department of Energy, "Global Energy Storage Database | Energy Storage Systems," 2020, www.sandia.gov/ess-ssl/global-energy-storage-database-home/.

53. David Roberts, "Is 100% Renewable Energy Realistic? Here's What We Know," Vox, www.vox.com/energy-and-environment/2017/4/7/15159034/100-renewable-energy-studies.

54. Ibid.

55. Ibid., 100.

56. "Electric Power Monthly – U.S. Energy Information Administration (EIA)," www.eia.gov/electricity/monthly/epm_table_grapher.php.

57. Ibid.

58. Ibid.

59. David Roberts, "We Need Lots More Power Lines. Why Are We so Bad at Planning Them?," Vox, June 9, 2016, www.vox.com/2016/6/9/11881556/power-lines-bad-planning.

# 7 Other Mitigation

1. UN Environment, "About Montreal Protocol," Ozonaction, October 29, 2018, www.unenvironment.org/ozonaction/who-we-are/about-montreal-protocol.

2. United Nations Environment Programme, "Emissions Gap Report 2020," UNEP – UN Environment Programme, December 2020, www.unep.org/emissions-gap-report-2020.

3. "| Greenhouse Gas (GHG) Emissions | Climate Watch," www.climatewatchdata.org/ghg-emissions?breakBy=sector&end_year=2018&sectors=agriculture%2Cenergy%2Cindustrial-processes%2Cland-use-change-and-forestry%2Ctotal-including-lucf%2Cwaste&start_year=1990.

4. United Nations Environment Programme, "Emissions Gap Report 2019," 2019, https://wedocs.unep.org/bitstream/handle/20.500.11822/30797/EGR2019.pdf?sequence=1&isAllowed=y.

5. Hiroko Tabuchi and Jonah M. Kessel, "It's a Vast, Invisible Climate Menace. We Made It Visible," *The New York Times*, December 12, 2019, sec. Climate, www.nytimes.com/interactive/2019/12/12/climate/texas-methane-super-emitters.html.

6. "Biomass Explained – U.S. Energy Information Administration (EIA)," www.eia.gov/energyexplained/biomass/.

7. Intergovernmental Panel on Climate Change, "Annex II: Metrics and Methodology," *Climate Change 2014: Mitigation of Climate Change: Working Group III Contribution to the IPCC Fifth Assessment Report of the Intergovernmental Panel on Climate Change* (Cambridge: Cambridge University Press, 2014), https://doi.org/10.1017/CBO9781107415416.024.

8. Helmut Haberl, "Net Land-Atmosphere Flows of Biogenic Carbon Related to Bioenergy: Towards an Understanding of Systemic Feedbacks," *Global Change Biology. Bioenergy* 5, no. 4 (July 2013): 351–57, https://doi.org/10.1111/gcbb.12071.

9. Timothy D Searchinger, "Biofuels and the Need for Additional Carbon," *Environmental Research Letters* 5, no. 2 (April 2010): 024007, https://doi.org/10.1088/1748-9326/5/2/024007.

10. Francesco Cherubini et al., "$CO_2$ Emissions from Biomass Combustion for Bioenergy: Atmospheric Decay and Contribution to Global Warming," *GCB Bioenergy* 3, no. 5 (2011): 413–26, https://doi.org/10.1111/j.1757-1707.2011.01102.x.

11. "Global Methane and Nitrous Oxide Emissions from Terrestrial Ecosystems Due to Multiple Environmental Changes – Tian – 2015 – Ecosystem Health and

Sustainability – Wiley Online Library," https://esajournals.onlinelibrary.wiley.com/doi/10.1890/EHS14-0015.1.

12. Intergovernmental Panel on Climate Change, "Agriculture, Forestry and Other Land Use (AFOLU)," *Climate Change 2014 Mitigation of Climate Change: Working Group III Contribution to the Fifth Assessment Report of the Intergovernmental Panel on Climate Change* (Cambridge: Cambridge University Press, 2014), https://doi.org/10.1017/CBO9781107415416.017.

13. Ibid.

14. Ibid.

15. Ibid.

16. Ibid.

17. Vaclav Smil, "Eating Meat: Evolution, Patterns, and Consequences," *Population and Development Review* 28, no. 4 (2002): 599–639.

18. "Food and Agriculture Organization of the United Nations," www.fao.org/home/en/.

19. Food and Agriculture Organization of the United Nations, "Global Livestock Environmental Assessment Model," www.fao.org/gleam/en/.

20. Intergovernmental Panel on Climate Change, "Agriculture, Forestry and Other Land Use (AFOLU)."

21. IPCC, "AR5 Climate Change 2013: The Physical Science Basis," 2013, www.ipcc.ch/report/ar5/wg1/.

22. G. Myhre, D. Shindell, F.-M. Bréon, W. Collins, J. Fuglestvedt, J. Huang, D. Koch, J.-F. Lamarque, D. Lee, B. Mendoza, T. Nakajima, A. Robock, G. Stephens, T. Takemura, and H. Zhang, "Anthropogenic and Natural Radiative Forcing," in *Climate Change 2013: The Physical Science Basis. Contribution of Working Group I to the Fifth Assessment Report of the Intergovernmental Panel on Climate Change* (IPCC, 2013), www.ipcc.ch/site/assets/uploads/2018/02/WG1AR5_Chapter08_FINAL.pdf.

23. Pete Smith et al., "Agriculture," in *Climate Change 2007: Mitigation. Contribution of Working Group III to the Fourth Assessment Report of the Intergovernmental Panel on Climate Change* (Cambridge: Cambridge University Press, 2007), www.ipcc.ch/site/assets/uploads/2018/02/ar4-wg3-chapter8-1.pdf.

24. Neville Millar, Julie E. Doll, and G. Philip Robertson, "Management of Nitrogen Fertilizer to Reduce Nitrous Oxide ($N_2O$) Emissions from Field Crops," www.canr.msu.edu/uploads/resources/pdfs/management_of_nitrogen_fertiler_(e3152).pdf.

25. Rodney T. Venterea et al., "Challenges and Opportunities for Mitigating Nitrous Oxide Emissions from Fertilized Cropping Systems," *Frontiers in Ecology and the Environment* 10, no. 10 (2012): 562–70, https://doi.org/10.1890/120062.

26. Thomas A. M. Pugh et al., "Role of Forest Regrowth in Global Carbon Sink Dynamics," *Proceedings of the National Academy of Sciences* 116, no. 10 (March 5, 2019): 4382–87, https://doi.org/10.1073/pnas.1810512116.

27. Intergovernmental Panel on Climate Change, "Agriculture, Forestry and Other Land Use (AFOLU)."

28. Ibid.

29. Ibid.

30. Intergovernmental Panel on Climate Change, "Industry," in *Climate Change 2014 Mitigation of Climate Change: Working Group III Contribution to the Fifth Assessment Report of the Intergovernmental Panel on Climate Change* (Cambridge: Cambridge University Press, 2014), https://doi.org/10.1017/CBO9781107415416.016.

31. Ibid.

32. "Ipcc_wg3_ar5_chapter10.Pdf."
33. "Ipcc_wg3_ar5_chapter10.Pdf."
34. "Ipcc_wg3_ar5_chapter10.Pdf."
35. "Explained: Cement vs. Concrete – Their Differences, and Opportunities for Sustainability," MIT News, 2020, http://news.mit.edu/2020/explained-cement-vs-concrete-understanding-differences-and-sustainability-opportunities-0403.
36. World Resources Institute, "CAIT Climate Data Explorer: Country Greenhouse Gas Emissions," 2019, http://cait.wri.org/.
37. "Trends in Global $CO_2$-Emissions. 2016 Report," n.d., 86.
38. "Q&A: Why Cement Emissions Matter for Climate Change," Carbon Brief, September 13, 2018, www.carbonbrief.org/qa-why-cement-emissions-matter-for-climate-change.
39. Intergovernmental Panel on Climate Change, "Waste Management," in *Climate Change 2007: Mitigation. Contribution of Working Group III to the Fourth Assessment Report of the Intergovernmental Panel on Climate Change.* (Cambridge: Cambridge University Press, 2007), https://doi.org/10.1017/CBO9780511546013.014.
40. Silpa Kaza et al., *What a Waste 2.0: A Global Snapshot of Solid Waste Management to 2050*, Urban Development (Washington, DC: World Bank, 2018), https://openknowledge.worldbank.org/handle/10986/30317.

# 8  Adaptation

1. Scott Barrett, *Environment and Statecraft: The Strategy of Environmental Treaty-Making* (Oxford University Press, 2003).
2. "Chapter 3 : Desertification – Special Report on Climate Change and Land," www.ipcc.ch/srccl/chapter/chapter-3/.
3. CDC, "Climate Change and Public Health – Disease Vectors," www.cdc.gov/climateandhealth/effects/vectors.htm.
4. "Adapt Now: A Global Call for Leadership on Climate Resilience" (Global Commission on Adaptation, 2019), https://gca.org/global-commission-on-adaptation/report.
5. Ibid.
6. Ibid.
7. Ibid.
8. Ibid.
9. Ibid.
10. Ibid.
11. "The Coral Assisted Evolution Project," n.d., http://coralassistedevolution.com/.
12. "Adapt Now: A Global Call for Leadership on Climate Resilience."
13. Ibid.
14. Ibid.
15. Ibid.
16. Ibid.
17. United Nations Office for Disaster Risk Reduction, "Sendai Framework for Disaster Risk Reduction 2015–2030," 2015, www.undrr.org/publication/sendai-framework-disaster-risk-reduction-2015-2030.
18. National Oceanic and Atmospheric Administration, "National Coastal Population Report," 2020, https://aamboceanservice.blob.core.windows.net/oceanservice-prod/facts/coastal-population-report.pdf.

19. Matti Kummu et al., "Over the Hills and Further Away from Coast: Global Geospatial Patterns of Human and Environment over the 20th–21st Centuries," *Environmental Research Letters* 11, no. 3 (March 2016): 034010, https://doi.org/10.1088/1748-9326/11/3/034010.

20. "Sea Level Rise Projection Map – Amsterdam," Earth.Org – Past | Present | Future, https://earth.org/data_visualization/sea-level-rise-by-2100-amsterdam/.

21. Intergovernmental Panel on Climate Change, "Sea Level Change," in *Climate Change 2013: The Physical Science Basis. Contribution of Working Group I to the Fifth Assessment Report of the Intergovernmental Panel on Climate Change*, www.ipcc.ch/site/assets/uploads/2018/02/WG1AR5_Chapter13_FINAL.pdf.

22. The Center for Climate Integrity, "High Tide Tax: The Price to Protect Coastal Communities from Rising Seas," www.climatecosts2040.org/files/Climate Costs2040_Report-v5.pdf.

23. "Sea Walls | Climate Technology Centre and Network," www.ctc-n.org/technologies/sea-walls.

24. Ibid.

25. Ibid.

26. Peter J. Baxter, "The East Coast Big Flood, 31 January–1 February 1953: A Summary of the Human Disaster," *Philosophical Transactions. Series A, Mathematical, Physical, and Engineering Sciences* 363, no. 1831 (June 15, 2005): 1293–1312, https://doi.org/10.1098/rsta.2005.1569.

27. Herman Gerritsen, "What Happened in 1953? The Big Flood in the Netherlands in Retrospect," *Philosophical Transactions. Series A, Mathematical, Physical, and Engineering Sciences* 363, no. 1831 (June 15, 2005): 1271–91, https://doi.org/10.1098/rsta.2005.1568.

28. Baxter, "The East Coast Big Flood."

29. "Seven Wonders: Engineering Feats," ArcGIS StoryMaps, 2020, https://storymaps.arcgis.com/stories/adc39e21a48645daad302f14e8bb4923.

30. Rolf Kranz, *Deutsch: Oosterschelde-Sperrwerk, Seeseite Bei Ebbe*, June 16, 2019, Own work, https://commons.wikimedia.org/wiki/File:Oosterschelde-Sperrwerk.jpg.

31. "The Thames Barrier," GOV.UK, www.gov.uk/guidance/the-thames-barrier.

32. Unsplash, "Photo by John Cameron on Unsplash," 2021, https://unsplash.com/photos/lmYIAQb6q1w.

33. Chico Harlan and Stefano Pitrelli, "How Venice's Plan to Protect Itself from Flooding Became a Disaster in Itself," *Washington Post*, www.washingtonpost.com/world/europe/how-venices-plan-to-protect-itself-from-flooding-became-a-disaster-in-itself/2019/11/19/7e1fe494-09a8-11ea-8054-289aef6e38a3_story.html.

34. Hilary Whiteman CNN, "Staten Island Seawall: Designing for Climate Change," CNN, www.cnn.com/style/article/staten-island-seawall-climate-crisis-design/index.html.

35. "Miami-Dade Back Bay Coastal Storm Risk Management Feasibility Study,", www.saj.usace.army.mil/MiamiDadeBackBayCSRMFeasibilityStudy/.

36. "US Army Corps of Engineers Charleston Peninsula Sea Wall," Coastal Conservation League, www.coastalconservationleague.org/projects/charleston-peninsula-coastal-flood-risk-management-study-by-the-us-army-corps-of-engineers/.

37. Associated Press, "Will a Giant Sea Wall Save Indonesia's Capital From Sinking?," https://thediplomat.com/2019/07/will-a-giant-sea-wall-save-indonesias-capital-from-sinking/.

38. "Tokyo, Ho Chi Minh City, Shanghai and New York at Risk of Rising Seas, Study Says," *The Japan Times*, www.japantimes.co.jp/news/2020/02/28/asia-pacific/science-health-asia-pacific/climate-change-tokyo/.

39. John Carey, "Core Concept: Managed Retreat Increasingly Seen as Necessary in Response to Climate Change's Fury," *Proceedings of the National Academy of Sciences* 117, no. 24 (June 16, 2020): 13182–85, https://doi.org/10.1073/pnas.2008198117.

40. Ibid.

41. Ibid.

42. Ibid.

43. A. R. Siders, "Managed Retreat in the United States," *One Earth* 1, no. 2 (October 2019): 216–25, https://doi.org/10.1016/j.oneear.2019.09.008.

44. Ibid.

# 9 Our Descendants Will Demand Climate Intervention

1. "FACT SHEET: President Biden Sets 2030 Greenhouse Gas Pollution Reduction Target Aimed at Creating Good-Paying Union Jobs and Securing U.S. Leadership on Clean Energy Technologies," The White House, April 22, 2021, www.whitehouse.gov/briefing-room/statements-releases/2021/04/22/fact-sheet-president-biden-sets-2030-greenhouse-gas-pollution-reduction-target-aimed-at-creating-good-paying-union-jobs-and-securing-u-s-leadership-on-clean-energy-technologies/.

2. Somini Sengupta, "Biden's Climate Summit Sets Up a Bigger Test of American Power," *The New York Times*, April 23, 2021, sec. Climate, www.nytimes.com/2021/04/23/climate/biden-climate-summit.html.

3. "Each Country's Share of $CO_2$ Emissions | Union of Concerned Scientists," www.ucsusa.org/resources/each-countrys-share-co2-emissions.

4. Jude Clemente, "Coal Isn't Dead. China Proves It," Forbes, www.forbes.com/sites/judeclemente/2019/01/23/coal-is-not-dead-china-proves-it/.

5. "Why Is China Placing A Global Bet On Coal?," NPR.org, www.npr.org/2019/04/29/716347646/why-is-china-placing-a-global-bet-on-coal.

6. Sengupta, "Biden's Climate Summit Sets Up a Bigger Test of American Power."

7. United Nations Environment Programme, *The Emissions Gap Report 2020*, 2020, www.unep.org/emissions-gap-report-2020.

8. Ibid.

9. Tim McDonnell, "There's a Fundamental Problem with How Rich Countries Are Paying for Climate Damages," Quartz, https://qz.com/2000418/rich-countries-need-to-cut-the-strings-off-climate-finance/.

10. Intergovernmental Panel on Climate Change, "Global Warming of 1.5°C. An IPCC Special Report on the Impacts of Global Warming of 1.5°C above Pre-industrial Levels and Related Global Greenhouse Gas Emission Pathways, in the Context of Strengthening the Global Response to the Threat of Climate Change, Sustainable Development, and Efforts to Eradicate Poverty," 2018.

11. "Summary for Policymakers – Global Warming of 1.5 °C," www.ipcc.ch/sr15/chapter/spm/.

12. United Nations Environment Programme, *The Emissions Gap Report 2019*, 2019.

13. "Global Energy Review 2021 – Analysis," IEA, www.iea.org/reports/global-energy-review-2021.

14. "Global Energy Review 2021 – Analysis."

15. UNEP, *The Emissions Gap Report 2020*.

16. UNEP, *The Emissions Gap Report 2019*.

17. International Energy Agency, "World Energy Outlook 2020," www.iea.org/reports/world-energy-outlook-2020.
18. Ibid.
19. UNEP, *The Emissions Gap Report 2020*.
20. bp, "Energy Outlook: 2020 Edition," www.bp.com/content/dam/bp/business-sites/en/global/corporate/pdfs/energy-economics/energy-outlook/bp-energy-outlook-2020.pdf.
21. Equinor, "Energy Perspectives 2020: Long-term Macro and Market Outlook," 2020.
22. Ibid
23. Ibid.
24. "The Sustainable Development Agenda," *United Nations Sustainable Development Goals*, 2020, www.un.org/sustainabledevelopment/development-agenda/.
25. Equinor, "Energy Perspectives 2020," 2020.
26. Ibid.
27. IPCC, "Global Warming of 1.5°C," 2018.
28. Bloomberg New Energy Finance, "New Energy Outlook 2020," 2020.
29. McKinsey & Company, "Global Energy Perspective 2021," January 2021, www.mckinsey.com/~/media/McKinsey/Industries/Oil%20and%20Gas/Our%20Insights/Global%20Energy%20Perspective%202021/Global-Energy-Perspective-2021-final.pdf.
30. McKinsey & Company.
31. UNEP, *The Emissions Gap Report 2020*.
32. Ibid.
33. Ibid.
34. Ibid.
35. Ibid.
36. Ibid.
37. IPCC, "Climate Change 2014: Synthesis Report. Contribution of Working Groups I, II and III to the Fifth Assessment Report of the Intergovernmental Panel on Climate Change" (IPCC, Geneva, Switzerland, 2014), www.ipcc.ch/site/assets/uploads/2018/05/SYR_AR5_FINAL_full_wcover.pdf.
38. "Data Supplement to the Global Carbon Budget 2020," ICOS, www.icos-cp.eu/science-and-impact/global-carbon-budget/2020.
39. "Global Energy Perspective 2021: Energy Landscape | McKinsey," www.mckinsey.com/industries/oil-and-gas/our-insights/global-energy-perspective-2021.
40. "New Energy Outlook 2020 | BNEF," *BloombergNEF* (blog), https://about.bnef.com/new-energy-outlook/.
41. "Data Supplement to the Global Carbon Budget 2020," ICOS, www.icos-cp.eu/science-and-impact/global-carbon-budget/2020.
42. Susan Solomon et al., "Irreversible Climate Change Due to Carbon Dioxide Emissions," *Proceedings of the National Academy of Sciences* 106, no. 6 (February 10, 2009): 1704–9, https://doi.org/10.1073/pnas.0812721106.
43. David Archer, "Fate of Fossil Fuel $CO_2$ in Geologic Time," *Journal of Geophysical Research* 110 (2005), https://doi.org/10.1029/2004JC002625.
44. Solomon et al., "Irreversible Climate Change Due to Carbon Dioxide Emissions."
45. Solomon et al.
46. Andrew H. MacDougall et al., "Is There Warming in the Pipeline? A Multi-Model Analysis of the Zero Emissions Commitment from $CO_2$," *Biogeosciences* 17, no. 11 (June 15, 2020): 2987–3016, https://doi.org/10.5194/bg-17-2987-2020.

47. Solomon et al., "Irreversible Climate Change Due to Carbon Dioxide Emissions."
48. NOAA US Department of Commerce, "Global Monitoring Laboratory – Carbon Cycle Greenhouse Gases," https://gml.noaa.gov/ccgg/trends/.
49. Anders Levermann et al., "The Multimillennial Sea-Level Commitment of Global Warming," *Proceedings of the National Academy of Sciences* 110, no. 34 (August 20, 2013): 13745–50, https://doi.org/10.1073/pnas.1219414110.
50. Thomas Frederikse et al., "The Causes of Sea-Level Rise since 1900," *Nature* 584, no. 7821 (August 2020): 393–97, https://doi.org/10.1038/s41586-020-2591-3.
51. MacDougall et al., "Is There Warming in the Pipeline?"
52. Gerald A. Meehl et al., "Context for Interpreting Equilibrium Climate Sensitivity and Transient Climate Response from the CMIP6 Earth System Models," *Science Advances* 6, no. 26 (June 1, 2020): eaba1981, https://doi.org/10.1126/sciadv.aba1981.
53. Thorsten Mauritsen and Robert Pincus, "Committed Warming Inferred from Observations," *Nature Climate Change* 7, no. 9 (September 2017): 652–55, https://doi.org/10.1038/nclimate3357.
54. MacDougall et al., "Is There Warming in the Pipeline?"
55. Mauritsen and Pincus, "Committed Warming Inferred from Observations."
56. "Autumn 1942 (Age 68)," International Churchill Society, March 12, 2015, https://winstonchurchill.org/the-life-of-churchill/war-leader/1940-1942/autumn-1942-age-68/.

# 10  Natural Climate Solutions

1. OAR US EPA, "Climate Change Indicators: Greenhouse Gases," Reports and Assessments, US EPA, December 16, 2015, www.epa.gov/climate-indicators/greenhouse-gases.
2. J. E. Lovelock, "Gaia as Seen through the Atmosphere," *Atmospheric Environment* (1967) 6, no. 8 (August 1, 1972): 579–80, https://doi.org/10.1016/0004-6981(72)90076-5.
3. Intergovernmental Panel on Climate Change and Ottmar Edenhofer, eds., *Climate Change 2014: Mitigation of Climate Change: Working Group III Contribution to the Fifth Assessment Report of the Intergovernmental Panel on Climate Change* (New York, NY: Cambridge University Press, 2014).
4. "4 Charts Explain Greenhouse Gas Emissions by Countries and Sectors," World Resources Institute, February 6, 2020, www.wri.org/blog/2020/02/greenhouse-gas-emissions-by-country-sector.
5. US EPA, 2015.
6. Kenneth L Denman et al., "Couplings Between Changes in the Climate System and Biogeochemistry," in *Climate Change 2007: The Physical Science Bais. Contribution of Working Group I to the Fourth Assessment Report of the Intergovernmental Panel on Climate Change* (Cambridge and New York, NY: Cambridge University Press, 2007), www.ipcc.ch/site/assets/uploads/2018/02/ar4-wg1-chapter7-1.pdf.
7. US EPA, 2015.
8. "Trees Help Tackle Climate Change – European Environment Agency," SOER 2010 Key fact (Deprecated), www.eea.europa.eu/articles/forests-health-and-climate-change/key-facts/trees-help-tackle-climate-change.
9. Monica Crippa et al., "Fossil $CO_2$ and GHG Emissions of All World Countries: 2019 Report," Website (Publications Office of the European Union, September 26,

2019), http://op.europa.eu/en/publication-detail/-/publication/9d09ccd1-eodd-11e9-9c4e-01aa75ed71a1/language-en.

10. "Forests and Climate Change," www.fao.org/3/ac836e/AC836E03.htm.

11. Josep G. Canadell et al., "Saturation of the Terrestrial Carbon Sink," in *Terrestrial Ecosystems in a Changing World*, ed. Josep G. Canadell, Diane E. Pataki, and Louis F. Pitelka, Global Change – The IGBP Series (Berlin, Heidelberg: Springer Berlin Heidelberg, 2007), 59–78, https://doi.org/10.1007/978-3-540-32730-1_6.

12. *The State of the World's Forests 2020* (FAO and UNEP, 2020), https://doi.org/10.4060/ca8642en.

13. "It's Not Your Imagination. More Trees than Ever Are Standing Dead in Colorado Forests," *The Denver Post* (blog), February 15, 2017, www.denverpost.com/2017/02/15/dead-trees-colorado-forests/.

14. Sabine Fuss et al., "Negative Emissions – Part 2: Costs, Potentials and Side Effects," *Environmental Research Letters* 13, no. 6 (May 2018): 063002, https://doi.org/10.1088/1748-9326/aabf9f.

15. R. A. Houghton, Brett Byers, and Alexander A. Nassikas, "A Role for Tropical Forests in Stabilizing Atmospheric CO2," *Nature Climate Change* 5, no. 12 (December 2015): 1022–23, https://doi.org/10.1038/nclimate2869.

16. "Global Carbon Project (GCP)" (Global Carbon Project (GCP)), www.globalcarbonproject.org/.

17. United Nations Environment Programme, *The Emissions Gap Report 2019*, 2019.

18. Fuss et al., "Negative Emissions – Part 2."

19. Ibid.

20. International Panel on Climate Change, "Capture of $CO_2$," *IPCC Special Report on Carbon Dioxide Capture and Storage*, www.ipcc.ch/site/assets/uploads/2018/03/srccs_chapter3-1.pdf.

21. James J. Dooley, "Estimating the Supply and Demand for Deep Geologic $CO_2$ Storage Capacity over the Course of the 21st Century: A Meta-Analysis of the Literature," *Energy Procedia*, GHGT-11 Proceedings of the 11th International Conference on Greenhouse Gas Control Technologies, 18–22 November 2012, Kyoto, Japan, 37 (January 1, 2013): 5141–50, https://doi.org/10.1016/j.egypro.2013.06.429.

22. Energy Sector Planning and Analysis, "A Review of the $CO_2$ Pipeline Infrastructure in the U.S.," *U.S. Department of Energy National Energy Technology Laboratory*, https://doi.org/10.2172/1487233.

23. Hanqin Tian et al., "A Comprehensive Quantification of Global Nitrous Oxide Sources and Sinks," *Nature* 586, no. 7828 (October 2020): 248–56, https://doi.org/10.1038/s41586-020-2780-0.

24. Donald M Johnson and Sammy Sadaka, "Biomass Combustion," *University of Arkansas Division of Agriculture*, n.d., 6.

25. Duncan Brack, "Woody Biomass for Power and Heat: Impacts on the Global Climate," *Chatham House*, 2017, www.chathamhouse.org/publication/woody-biomass-power-and-heat-impacts-global-climate.

26. Fuss et al., "Negative Emissions – Part 2."

27. Mathilde Fajardy et al., "The Economics of Bioenergy with Carbon Capture and Storage (BECCS) Deployment in a 1.5°C or 2°C World," *Joint Program Report Series Report 345*, 2020, https://globalchange.mit.edu/publication/17489.

28. Fuss et al., "Negative Emissions – Part 2."

29. "Carbon Sequestration in Dryland Soils," 2020, www.fao.org/3/y5738e/y5738e05.htm.

30. Fuss et al., "Negative Emissions – Part 2."

31. "What Is Regenerative Agriculture?," *Regeneration International* (blog), February 24, 2017, https://regenerationinternational.org/2017/02/24/what-is-regenerative-agriculture/.

32. Jonathan Sanderman, Tomislav Hengl, and Gregory J. Fiske, "Soil Carbon Debt of 12,000 Years of Human Land Use," *Proceedings of the National Academy of Sciences* 114, no. 36 (September 5, 2017): 9575–80, https://doi.org/10.1073/pnas.1706103114.

33. Rodale Institute.

34. Fuss et al., "Negative Emissions – Part 2."

35. Dominic Woolf et al., "Sustainable Biochar to Mitigate Global Climate Change," *Nature Communications* 1 (August 10, 2010): 1, https://doi.org/10.1038/ncomms1053.

36. Dane Dickinson et al., "Cost-Benefit Analysis of Using Biochar to Improve Cereals Agriculture," *GCB Bioenergy* 7, no. 4 (2015): 850–64, https://doi.org/10.1111/gcbb.12180.

37. Fuss et al., "Negative Emissions – Part 2."

38. Ibid.

39. Holly Jean Buck, *After Geoengineering: Climate Tragedy, Repair, and Restoration* (Verso Books, 2019).

40. Ibid..

41. Fuss et al., "Negative Emissions – Part 2."

42. Buck, 2019.

43. Fuss et al., "Negative Emissions – Part 2."

44. Lyla L. Taylor et al., "Enhanced Weathering Strategies for Stabilizing Climate and Averting Ocean Acidification," *Nature Climate Change* 6, no. 4 (April 2016): 402–6, https://doi.org/10.1038/nclimate2882.

45. Miriam Ferrer González and Tatiana Ilyina, "Impacts of Artificial Ocean Alkalinization on the Carbon Cycle and Climate in Earth System Simulations," *Geophysical Research Letters* 43, no. 12 (2016): 6493–6502, https://doi.org/10.1002/2016GL068576.

46. Phil Renforth and Gideon Henderson, "Assessing Ocean Alkalinity for Carbon Sequestration," *Reviews of Geophysics* 55, no. 3 (2017): 636–74, https://doi.org/10.1002/2016RG000533.

47. Renforth and Henderson.

48. Aaron L. Strong, John J. Cullen, and Sallie W. Chisholm, "Ocean Fertilization: Science, Policy, and Commerce," *Oceanography* 22, no. 3 (2009): 236–61.

49. David Biello, "Pacific Ocean Hacker Speaks Out," *Scientific American*, 2012, www.scientificamerican.com/article/questions-and-answers-with-rogue-geoengineer-carbon-entrepreneur-russ-george/.

50. "World's Biggest Geoengineering Experiment 'violates' UN Rules," *The Guardian*, October 15, 2012, www.theguardian.com/environment/2012/oct/15/pacific-iron-fertilisation-geoengineering.

51. O. Aumont and L. Bopp, "Globalizing Results from Ocean in Situ Iron Fertilization Studies," *Global Biogeochemical Cycles* 20, no. 2 (2006), https://doi.org/10.1029/2005GB002591.

# 11 Carbon Capture and Sequestration

1. Global Energy Observatory et al., "Global Power Plant Database" (Resource Watch and Google Earth Engine, 2018), https://datasets.wri.org/dataset/global powerplantdatabase.

2. Sabine Fuss et al., "Negative Emissions – Part 2: Costs, Potentials and Side Effects," *Environmental Research Letters* 13, no. 6 (May 2018): 063002, https://doi.org/10.1088/1748-9326/aabf9f.

3. Mathilde Fajardy et al., "The Economics of Bioenergy with Carbon Capture and Storage (BECCS) Deployment in a 1.5°C or 2°C World," Joint Program Report Series Report 345, 2020, https://globalchange.mit.edu/publication/17489.

4. DOEFE (USDOE Office of Fossil Energy (FE) (United States)), "Report of the Interagency Task Force on Carbon Capture and Storage," August 1, 2010, https://doi.org/10.2172/985209.

5. University of California Berkeley. "New Technique to Capture Carbon Dioxide Could Greatly Reduce Power Plant Greenhouse Gases: Tetraamine-modified MOFs Remove 90% of $CO_2$ More Efficiently and Cheaply," *ScienceDaily*, www.sciencedaily.com/releases/2020/07/200723143729.htm.

6. International Energy Agency, "Putting $CO_2$ to Use: Creating Value from Emissions," September 2019, https://webstore.iea.org/download/direct/2830?fileName=Putting_CO2_to_Use.pdf.

7. IHS Markit, "Chemical Economics Handbook," IHS Markit, https://ihsmarkit.com/products/carbon-dioxide-chemical-economics-handbook.html.

8. Fossil Energy Research Benefits, "Enhanced Oil Recovery – Fact Card," www.energy.gov/sites/prod/files/eor_factcard.pdf.

9. IEA, "Putting $CO_2$ to Use – IEA Technology Report," 2019, www.iea.org/reports/putting-co2-to-use.

10. IEA; European Commission and Directorate-General for Research and Innovation, *Novel Carbon Capture and Utilisation Technologies*, 2018.

11. European Commission and Directorate-General for Research and Innovation, *Novel Carbon Capture and Utilisation Technologies*; Global CCS Institute, "The Global Status of CCS: 2019" (Australia, 2019), www.globalccsinstitute.com/.

12. Clifford Krauss, "Blamed for Climate Change, Oil Companies Invest in Carbon Removal (Published 2019)," *The New York Times*, April 7, 2019, sec. Business, www.nytimes.com/2019/04/07/business/energy-environment/climate-change-carbon-engineering.html.

13. Global CCS Institute, "Global Status Of CCS 2020," 2020, www.globalccsinstitute.com/wp-content/uploads/2021/03/Global-Status-of-CCS-Report-English.pdf.

14. Oliver Morton, *The Planet Remade: How Geoengineering Could Change the World* (Granta Books, 2016).

15. Global CCS Institute, "Global Status Of CCS 2020."

16. United Nations Environment Programme, "Emissions Gap Report 2020," UNEP – UN Environment Programme, December 2020, www.unep.org/emissions-gap-report-2020.

17. Global CCS Institute, "Global Status Of CCS 2020."

18. Ibid.

19. Lee Beck and Lucy Temple-Smith, "Is CCS Expensive: Decarbonisation Costs in the Net-Zero Context" (Global CCS Institute, May 2020), www.globalccsinstitute.com/wp-content/uploads/2020/05/Cost_Brief_Final_May_2020.pdf.

20. Global CCS Institute, "Global Status Of CCS 2020."

21. Ibid.

22. Ibid.

23. Global CCS Institute, "The Global Status of CCS: 2019."

24. United Nations Environment Programme, "Emissions Gap Report 2020."

25. J. G. J. Olivier, and J. A. H. W. Peters, "Trends in Global $CO_2$ and Total Greenhouse Gas Emissions: 2019 Report," revised May 2020.

26. Sara Budinis et al., "An Assessment of CCS Costs, Barriers and Potential," *Energy Strategy Reviews* 22 (November 1, 2018): 61–81, https://doi.org/10.1016/j.esr .2018.08.003.
27. Edward S. Rubin, John E. Davison, and Howard J. Herzog, "The Cost of $CO_2$ Capture and Storage," *International Journal of Greenhouse Gas Control* 40 (September 2015): 378–400, https://doi.org/10.1016/j.ijggc.2015.05.018.
28. "GDP (Current US$) | Data," https://data.worldbank.org/indicator/NY.GDP .MKTP.CD.
29. "IBISWorld – Industry Market Research, Reports, and Statistics," www.ibisworld .com/default.aspx.
30. Martin C. Hänsel et al., "Climate Economics Support for the UN Climate Targets," *Nature Climate Change* 10, no. 8 (August 2020): 781–89, https://doi.org/10.1038/ s41558-020-0833-x.
31. "Gasoline and Diesel Fuel Update – U.S. Energy Information Administration (EIA)," www.eia.gov/petroleum/gasdiesel/index.php.
32. Lee Beck and Lucy Temple-Smith, "Is CCS Expensive: Decarbonisation Costs in the Net-Zero Context."
33. Global CCS Institute, "Global Status Of CCS 2020."
34. Lee Beck and Lucy Temple-Smith, "Is CCS Expensive: Decarbonisation Costs in the Net-Zero Context."
35. Global CCS Institute, "Global Status Of CCS 2020."
36. Lee Beck and Lucy Temple-Smith, "Is CCS Expensive: Decarbonisation Costs in the Net-Zero Context."
37. Ibid.
38. Global CCS Institute, "Global Status Of CCS 2020."
39. Ibid.
40. Ibid.
41. Ibid.
42. "Climate Watch," www.climatewatchdata.org/ghg-emissions.
43. Ibid.
44. Ibid.
45. Global CCS Institute, "Global Status Of CCS 2020."
46. National Petroleum Council, "Meeting the Dual Challenge: A Roadmap to At-Scale Deployment of Carbon Capture, Use, And Storage. Appendix C – CCUS Project Summaries," December 2019, https://dualchallenge.npc.org/documents/CCUS-Appendix_C-111820.pdf?a=1614413372.
47. National Petroleum Council.
48. Global CCS Institute, "Global Status Of CCS 2020."
49. Ibid.
50. Ibid.
51. Ibid.
52. Ibid.
53. Ibid.
54. Ibid.
55. Ibid.
56. Ibid.
57. Ibid.
58. Ibid.
59. Ibid.
60. Ibid.
61. "IEA Energy Atlashttp://energyatlas.iea.org/.

62. Global CCS Institute, "Global Status Of CCS 2020."
63. World Bank Group, "State and Trends of Carbon Pricing 2020," 2020, https://open knowledge.worldbank.org/bitstream/handle/10986/33809/9781464815867.pdf.
64. "Carbon Price Viewer," *Ember* (blog), https://ember-climate.org/data/carbon-price-viewer/.
65. "EU Emissions Trading System (EU ETS)," Text, Climate Action – European Commission, November 23, 2016, https://ec.europa.eu/clima/policies/ets_en.
66. Global CCS Institute, "Global Status of CCS 2020."
67. Ibid.
68. "California's $CO_2$ Reduction Program Opens Doors to CCS," Clean Air Task Force, November 10, 2018, www.catf.us/2018/11/californias-co2-reduction-program/.

## 12 Direct Air Carbon Capture and Sequestration

1. SAPEA, "Novel Carbon Capture and Utilisation Technologies: Research and Climate Aspects" (Berlin: Science Advice for Policy by European Academies (SAPEA), 2018), http://doi.org/10.26356/carboncapture.
2. "The Swiss Company Hoping to Capture 1% of Global $CO_2$ Emissions by 2025," Carbon Brief, June 22, 2017, www.carbonbrief.org/swiss-company-hoping-capture-1-global-co2-emissions-2025.
3. John Bruce (of Carbon Engineering), in personal communications with the author.
4. NOAA, "Climate Change: Atmospheric Carbon Dioxide," 2020, www.climate.gov/news-features/understanding-climate/climate-change-atmospheric-carbon-dioxide.
5. NOAA, "Global Monitoring Laboratory – Carbon Cycle Greenhouse Gases," 2020, www.esrl.noaa.gov/gmd/ccgg/trends/gl_trend.html.
6. "Comparing $CO_2$ Emissions to $CO_2$ Levels," https://skepticalscience.com//print.php?r=45.
7. GCP, "Global Carbon Project, Carbon Budget and Trends 2019" (Global Carbon Project (GCP), December 4, 2019), www.globalcarbonproject.org/carbonbudget.
8. David W. Keith et al., "A Process for Capturing $CO_2$ from the Atmosphere," *Joule* 2, no. 8 (August 15, 2018): 1573–94, https://doi.org/10.1016/j.joule.2018.05.006.
9. "Climeworks," www.climeworks.com/.
10. "Breaking the Record for the Largest Ever Investment into Direct Air Capture," https://climeworks.com/news/recent-investment-in-climeworks-has-been-boosted-from.
11. 1 CHF = 1.1 USD.
12. "Climeworks: Where the World Is Saved?," Red Bull, www.redbull.com/mk-mk/theredbulletin/climeworks-co2-filtering-interview.
13. Howard Herzog, "Direct Air Capture," in *Negative Emissions Technologies*, ed. Niall Mac Dowell and Mai Bui (Royal Society of Chemistry, n.d.).
14. Howard Herzog.
15. "Direct Air Capture Technology," Carbon Engineering, https://carbonengineering.com/our-technology/.
16. Cathy Bussewitz, "Insider Q&A: Occidental Wants to Be Tesla of Carbon Capture," *AP News*, April 23, 2021, https://apnews.com/article/environment-climate-change-b2ac9969bf69154ff2a6cd45f33295ad.
17. David W. Keith et al., "A Process for Capturing $CO_2$ from the Atmosphere," *Joule* 2, no. 8 (August 15, 2018): 1573–94, https://doi.org/10.1016/j.joule.2018.05.006.
18. Howard Herzog, "Direct Air Capture."
19. Ibid.

20. Bloomberg NEF, "New Energy Outlook 2019," 2019, https://about.bnef.com/new-energy-outlook/.
21. "Markets," *Global Thermostat* (blog), https://globalthermostat.com/our-markets/.

## 13 Solar Radiation Management Alternatives

1. "Global Cool Cities Alliance," Global Cool Cities Alliance, https://globalcoolcities.org/. Hashem Akbari, Surabi Menon, and Arthur Rosenfeld, "Global Cooling: Increasing World-Wide Urban Albedos to Offset CO2," *Climatic Change* 94, no. 3 (June 1, 2009): 275–86, https://doi.org/10.1007/s10584-008-9515-9.
2. "Global Cool Cities Alliance," Global Cool Cities Alliance, https://globalcoolcities.org/.
3. Ibid.
4. Center for International Earth Science Information Network – CIESIN – Columbia University, CUNY Institute for Demographic Research – CIDR, International Food Policy Research Institute – IFPRI, The World Bank, and Centro Internacional de Agricultura Tropical – CIAT, "Global Rural-Urban Mapping Project, Version 1 (GRUMPv1)," 2017, https://sedac.ciesin.columbia.edu/data/collection/grump-v1.
5. The Royal Society, "Geoengineering the Climate: Science, Governance and Uncertainty," Policy Document (The Royal Society, September 2009).
6. The Royal Society.
7. Russell Seitz, "Bright Water: Hydrosols, Water Conservation and Climate Change," *Climatic Change* 105, no. 3 (April 1, 2011): 365–81, https://doi.org/10.1007/s10584-010-9965-8.
8. Alan Buis and Steve Cole, "NASA Looks at Soot's Role in 1800s Glacier Retreat," Climate Change: Vital Signs of the Planet, https://climate.nasa.gov/news/979/nasa-looks-at-soots-role-in-1800s-glacier-retreat.
9. Alan Buis and Steve Cole.
10. David G Vaughan et al., "Observations: Cryosphere," in *Climate Change 2013: The Physical Science Basis. Contribution of Working Group I to the Fifth Assessment Report of the Intergovernmental Panel on Climate* Change, 2013.
11. Vaughan et al., "Observations: Cryosphere," 2013.
12. Stef Lhermitte et al., "Damage Accelerates Ice Shelf Instability and Mass Loss in Amundsen Sea Embayment," *Proceedings of the National Academy of Sciences* 117, no. 40 (October 6, 2020): 24735–41, https://doi.org/10.1073/pnas.1912890117.
13. John C. Moore et al., "Geoengineer Polar Glaciers to Slow Sea-Level Rise," *Nature* 555, no. 7696 (March 2018): 303–5, https://doi.org/10.1038/d41586-018-03036-4.
14. Ibid.
15. Ibid.
16. Vaughan et al., "Observations: Cryosphere," 2013.
17. Ibid.
18. "Arctic Ice Project," Arctic Ice Project, www.arcticiceproject.org.
19. "Current Geoengineering Proposals for the Polar Regions," *Geoengineering Monitor*, December 19, 2019, www.geoengineeringmonitor.org/2019/12/current-geoengineering-proposals-for-the-polar-regions/.
20. Ibid.
21. National Academies of Sciences, Engineering, and Medicine, *Reflecting Sunlight: Recommendations for Solar Geoengineering Research and Research Governance* (The National Academies Press, 2021), https://doi.org/10.17226/25762.
22. Seymour M. Hersh Special to The New York Times, "Rainmaking Is Used As Weapon by U.S. (Published 1972)," *The New York Times*, July 3, 1972, sec.

Archives, www.nytimes.com/1972/07/03/archives/rainmaking-is-used-as-weapon-by-us-cloudseeding-in-indochina-is.html.

23. Eyal Freud et al., "Cloud Microphysical Background for the Israel-4 Cloud Seeding Experiment," *Atmospheric Research* 158–159 (May 1, 2015): 122–38, https://doi.org/10.1016/j.atmosres.2015.02.007.

24. "How Beijing Used Rockets to Keep Opening Ceremony Dry," *The Independent*, August 11, 2008, www.independent.co.uk/sport/olympics/how-beijing-used-rockets-to-keep-opening-ceremony-dry-890294.html.

25. S. Twomey, "Pollution and the Planetary Albedo," *Atmospheric Environment* (1967) 8, no. 12 (December 1, 1974): 1251–56, https://doi.org/10.1016/0004-6981(74)90004-3.

26. Stephen Salter, "Figure 2. A Practical Demonstration of the Twomey Effect with 4 Mm And …, " ResearchGate, www.researchgate.net/figure/A-practical-demonstration-of-the-Twomey-effect-with-4-mm-and-40-micron-glass-balls_fig2_258843270.

27. NASA Earth Observatory, "Ship Tracks off North America," Text.Article (NASA Earth Observatory, January 20, 2013), https://earthobservatory.nasa.gov/images/80203/ship-tracks-off-north-america.

28. J. Latham and M. H. Smith, "Effect on Global Warming of Wind-Dependent Aerosol Generation at the Ocean Surface," *Nature; London* 347, no. 6291 (September 27, 1990): 372–73, http://dx.doi.org.ezp-prod1.hul.harvard.edu/10.1038/347374a0.

29. Kenneth L Denman et al., "Couplings Between Changes in the Climate System and Biogeochemistry," n.d., 90.

30. Ibid.

31. Stephen H. Salter, Thomas Stevenson, and Andreas Tsiamis, "Chapter 6: Engineering Ideas for Brighter Clouds," in *Geoengineering of the Climate System*, 2014, 131–61, https://doi.org/10.1039/9781782621225-00131.

32. Michael Mautner and Kelly Parks, "Space-Based Control of the Climate" (Engineering, Construction, and Operations in Space II, ASCE, 1990), 1159–68, https://cedb.asce.org/CEDBsearch/record.jsp?dockey=0065641.

33. David Keith et al., "Reflections on a Meeting about Space-Based Solar Geoengineering," 2020, https://geoengineering.environment.harvard.edu/blog/reflections-meeting-about-space-based-solar-geoengineering.

34. Lagrangian points are equilibrium points because at that spot, the gravitational forces of the Sun and Earth balance the centrifugal force felt by the object in orbit (such as a satellite or sunshield).

35. Keith et al.

36. Ibid.

## 14 Stratospheric Aerosol Injection

1. Gunnar Myhre et al., "Aerosols and Their Relation to Global Climate and Climate Sensitivity," www.nature.com/scitable/knowledge/library/aerosols-and-their-relation-to-global-climate-102215345/.

2. S. A. Carn et al., "A Decade of Global Volcanic $SO_2$ Emissions Measured from Space," *Scientific Reports* 7, no. 1 (March 9, 2017): 44095, https://doi.org/10.1038/srep44095.

3. Christiane Textor et al., "Emissions from Volcanoes," in *Emissions of Atmospheric Trace Compounds*, ed. Claire Granier, Paulo Artaxo, and Claire E. Reeves, vol. 18, Advances in Global Change Research (Dordrecht: Springer Netherlands, 2004), 269–303, https://doi.org/10.1007/978-1-4020-2167-1_7.

4. Douglas G. MacMartin and Ben Kravitz, "The Engineering of Climate Engineering," *Annual Review of Control, Robotics, and Autonomous Systems* 2, no. 1 (2019): 445–67, https://doi.org/10.1146/annurev-control-053018-023725.
5. "Remembering Mount Pinatubo 25 Years Ago: Mitigating a Crisis," www.usgs.gov/news/remembering-mount-pinatubo-25-years-ago-mitigating-crisis.
6. Ibid.
7. Chris Newhall et al., "The Cataclysmic 1991 Eruption of Mount Pinatubo, Philippines, Fact Sheet 113–97," https://pubs.usgs.gov/fs/1997/fs113-97/.
8. Charles R. Trepte, Robert E. Veiga, and M. Patrick McCormick, "The Poleward Dispersal of Mount Pinatubo Volcanic Aerosol," *Journal of Geophysical Research: Atmospheres* 98, no. D10 (1993): 18563–73, https://doi.org/10.1029/93JD01362.
9. Trepte et al., "The Poleward Dispersal of Mount Pinatubo, " 1993.
10. Ellsworth G. Dutton and John R. Christy, "Solar Radiative Forcing at Selected Locations and Evidence for Global Lower Tropospheric Cooling Following the Eruptions of El Chichón and Pinatubo," *Geophysical Research Letters* 19, no. 23 (1992): 2313–16, https://doi.org/10.1029/92GL02495.
11. Alan Robock et al., "Southern Hemisphere Atmospheric Circulation Effects of the 1991 Mount Pinatubo Eruption," *Geophysical Research Letters* 34, no. 23 (2007), https://doi.org/10.1029/2007GL031403.
12. Tom Simkin, and Richard S. Fiske, *Krakatau, 1883 – The Volcanic Eruption and Its Effects* (Washington, DC: Smithsonian Institution Press, 1983).
13. Henry Stommel and Elizabeth Stommel, "The Year without a Summer," *Scientific American* 240, no. 6 (1979): 176–87.
14. Chaochao Gao et al., "Climatic Aftermath of the 1815 Tambora Eruption in China," *Journal of Meteorological Research* 31, no. 1 (February 1, 2017): 28–38, https://doi.org/10.1007/s13351-017-6091-9.
15. Clive Oppenheimer, "Climatic, Environmental and Human Consequences of the Largest Known Historic Eruption: Tambora Volcano (Indonesia) 1815," *Progress in Physical Geography: Earth and Environment* 27, no. 2 (June 1, 2003): 230–59, https://doi.org/10.1191/0309133303pp379ra.
16. William J. Broad, "A Volcanic Eruption That Reverberates 200 Years Later (Published 2015)," *The New York Times*, August 2015, sec. Science, www.nytimes.com/2015/08/25/science/mount-tambora-volcano-eruption-1815.html.
17. Rosanne D'Arrigo et al., "The Anomalous Winter of 1783–1784: Was the Laki Eruption or an Analog of the 2009–2010 Winter to Blame?," *Geophysical Research Letters* 38, no. 5 (2011), https://doi.org/10.1029/2011GL046696.
18. J. B. Witter and S. Self, "The Kuwae (Vanuatu) Eruption of AD 1452: Potential Magnitude and Volatile Release," *Bulletin of Volcanology* 69, no. 3 (January 1, 2007): 301–18, https://doi.org/10.1007/s00445-006-0075-4.
19. Neil Prince, *Children of Ash and Elm: A History of the Vikings* (Basic Books: 2020).
20. U.S. Geological Survey, "Mineral Commodity Summaries 2020," https://doi.org/10.3133/mcs2020.
21. Ibid.
22. "How to Get a Satellite to Geostationary Orbit," The Planetary Society, www.planetary.org/articles/20140116-how-to-get-a-satellite-to-gto.
23. Peter Davidson et al., "Lifting Options for Stratospheric Aerosol Geoengineering: Advantages of Tethered Balloon Systems," 2012, 38.
24. Wake Smith, "The Cost of Stratospheric Aerosol Injection through 2100," *Environmental Research Letters* 15, no. 11 (October 21, 2020): 114004, https://doi.org/10.1088/1748-9326/aba7e7.
25. United Nations Environment Programme, *The Emissions Gap Report 2019*, 2019.

## 15 SAI Deployment

1. "Dreamscapes of Modernity: Sociotechnical Imaginaries and the Fabrication of Power," www.hks.harvard.edu/publications/dreamscapes-modernity-sociotechnical-imaginaries-and-fabrication-power.
2. Dian J. Seidel and William J. Randel, "Variability and Trends in the Global Tropopause Estimated from Radiosonde Data," *Journal of Geophysical Research: Atmospheres* 111, no. D21 (2006), https://doi.org/10.1029/2006JD007363.
3. Dian J. Seidel et al., "Climatological Characteristics of the Tropical Tropopause as Revealed by Radiosondes," *Journal of Geophysical Research: Atmospheres* 106, no. D8 (2001): 7857–78, https://doi.org/10.1029/2000JD900837.
4. Simone Tilmes et al., "Sensitivity of Aerosol Distribution and Climate Response to Stratospheric SO2 Injection Locations," *Journal of Geophysical Research: Atmospheres* 122, no. 23 (2017): 12591–615, https://doi.org/10.1002/2017JD026888.
5. Douglas G. MacMartin et al., "The Climate Response to Stratospheric Aerosol Geoengineering Can Be Tailored Using Multiple Injection Locations," *Journal of Geophysical Research: Atmospheres* 122, no. 23 (2017): 12574–590, https://doi.org/10.1002/2017JD026868.
6. M. M. Holland and C. M. Bitz, "Polar Amplification of Climate Change in Coupled Models," *Climate Dynamics* 21, no. 3 (September 1, 2003): 221–32, https://doi.org/10.1007/s00382-003-0332-6.
7. Ben Kravitz et al., "First Simulations of Designing Stratospheric Sulfate Aerosol Geoengineering to Meet Multiple Simultaneous Climate Objectives," *Journal of Geophysical Research: Atmospheres* 122, no. 23 (2017): 12616–634, https://doi.org/10.1002/2017JD026874.
8. "U.S. Standard Atmosphere," www.engineeringtoolbox.com/standard-atmosphere-d_604.html.
9. David W. Keith, "Photophoretic Levitation of Engineered Aerosols for Geoengineering," *Proceedings of the National Academy of Sciences of the United States of America* 107, no. 38 (September 21, 2010): 16428–31, https://doi.org/10.1073/pnas.1009519107.
10. Jeffrey R. Pierce et al., "Efficient Formation of Stratospheric Aerosol for Climate Engineering by Emission of Condensible Vapor from Aircraft," *Geophysical Research Letters* 37, no. 18 (2010), https://doi.org/10.1029/2010GL043975.
11. "World Economic Outlook (October 2020) – GDP, Current Prices," www.imf.org/external/datamapper/NGDPD@WEO.

## 16 Governance of Carbon Removal

1. Marie-Valentine Florin, Paul Rouse, Anna-Maria Hubert, Matthias Honegger, and Jesse Reynolds. "International Governance Issues on Climate Engineering Information for Policymakers," 2020. https://doi.org/10.5075/EPFL-IRGC-277726.
2. The Royal Society. "Geoengineering the Climate: Science, Governance and Uncertainty." Policy Document. The Royal Society, September 2009.
3. Steve Rayner, Clare Heyward, Tim Kruger, Nick Pidgeon, Catherine Redgwell, and Julian Savulescu. "The Oxford Principles." *Climatic Change* 121, no. 3 (January 1, 2013): 499–512. https://doi.org/10.1007/s10584-012-0675-2.
4. Steve Rayner, Catherine Redgwell, Julian Savulescu, Nick Pidgeon, and Tim Kruger. "Brief Memorandum to the House of Commons Science and Technology Committee

Enquiry into The Regulation of Geoengineering." House of Commons Science and Technology Committee,

5. John Shepherd et al., *Geoengineering the Climate: Science, Governance and Uncertainty* (London: The Royal Society, 2009), https://royalsociety.org/~/media/royal_society_content/policy/publications/2009/8693.pdf.

6. Paris Agreement (Dec. 13, 2015), *in* UNFCCC, COP Report No. 21, Addenum, at 21, U.N. Doc. FCCC/CP/2015/10/Add, 1 (Jan. 29, 2016) [hereinafter Paris Agreement].

7. Jennifer Huang, "A Brief Guide to the Paris Agreement and Rulebook." Center for Climate and Energy Solutions, June 2019.

8. M. J. Mace, C. L. Fyson, M. Schaeffer, and W. L. Hare, "Governing Large-scale Carbon Dioxide Removal: Are We Ready?" Carnegie Climate Geoengineering Governance Initiative (C2G2), November 2018, New York, US.

9. Ross W. Gorte, "U.S. Tree Planting for Carbon Sequestration." Congressional Research Service, May 4, 2009.

10. Global CCS Institute, "Global Status of CCS 2020," n.d., www.globalccsinstitute.com/wp-content/uploads/2020/12/Global-Status-of-CCS-Report-2020_FINAL_December11.pdf.

11. Duncan P. McLaren et al., "Beyond 'Net-Zero': A Case for Separate Targets for Emissions Reduction and Negative Emissions," *Frontiers in Climate* 1 (2019), https://doi.org/10.3389/fclim.2019.00004.

12. Claire L. Fyson et al., "Fair-Share Carbon Dioxide Removal Increases Major Emitter Responsibility," *Nature Climate Change* 10, no. 9 (September 2020): 836–41, https://doi.org/10.1038/s41558-020-0857-2.

13. Ibid.

## 17 Governance of SRM and SAI

1. *The Cartagena Protocol on Biosafety*, Convention on Biological Diversity, http://bch.cbd.int/protocol/; Protocol text in English, http://bch.cbd.int/protocol/text/.

2. United Nations. "About the Secretariat | UNFCCC." United Nations Climate Change, https://unfccc.int/about-us/about-the-secretariat.

3. IPCC Press Office. "IPCC Statement: Clarifying the Role of the IPCC in the Context of 1.5°C – IPCC." The Intergovernmental Panel on Climate Change, September 21, 2017. www.ipcc.ch/2017/09/21/ipcc-statement-clarifying-the-role-of-the-ipcc-in-the-context-of-1-50c/.

4. "Convention on the Prohibition of Military or Any Other Hostile Use of Environmental Modification Techniques" New York, 10 December 1976, United Nations, *Treaty Series*, vol. 1108, p. 151, https://treaties.un.org/Pages/ViewDetails.aspx?src=IND&mtdsg_no=XXVI-1&chapter=26&clang=_en.

5. Ibid.

6. Conference of the Parties to the Convention on Biological Diversity, "Decision Adopted by the Conference of the Parties to the Convention on Biological Diversity at its Tenth Meeting: X/33. Biodiversity and Climate Change," October 2010, https://www.cbd.int/doc/decisions/cop-10/cop-10-dec-33-en.pdf.

7. ETC Group. "The Geoengineering Moratorium under the UN Convention on Biological Diversity" www.etcgroup.org (10 November 2010): www.etcgroup.org/sites/www.etcgroup.org/files/publication/pdf_file/ETCMoratorium_note101110.pdf.

8. Conference of the Parties to the Convention on Biological Diversity, "Decision Adopted by the Conference of the Parties to the Convention on Biological

Diversity at its Tenth Meeting: X/33. Biodiversity and Climate Change," October 2010, https://www.cbd.int/doc/decisions/cop-10/cop-10-dec-33-en.pdf.

9. Conference of the Parties to the Convention on Biological Diversity, "Decision Adopted by the Conference of the Parties to the Convention on Biological Diversity: XIII/14. Climate-Related Geoengineering," December 2016, www.cbd .int/doc/decisions/cop-13/cop-13-dec-14-en.pdf.

10. US House of Representatives Committee on Science and Technology One Hundred Eleventh Congress (2009). Hearing: Geoengineering: Parts I, II and III, Assessing the Implications of Large Scale Climate Intervention. Washington DC: US House of Representatives, 111–62, 75, 88. http://gpo.gov/fdsys/pkg/chrg-111hhrg53007/pdf/ chrg111hhrg53007.pdf.

11. Kelsi Bracmort, R. K. Lattanzio, and E. C. Barbour (2010) Geoengineering: Governance and Technology Policy. Washington, DC: Congressional Research Service.

12. US House of Representatives Committee on Science and Technology One Hundred Eleventh Congress (2009). Hearing: Geoengineering: Parts I, II and III, Assessing the Implications of Large Scale Climate Intervention. Washington, DC: US House of Representatives, 111–62, 75, 88. http://gpo.gov/fdsys/pkg/chrg-111hhrg53007/pdf/ chrg111hhrg53007.pdf.

13. Daniel Bodansky, "May We Engineer the Climate?" *Climatic Change* 33, no. 3 (July 1996): 309–21. https://doi.org/10.1007/BF00142579.

14. Yu. A Izrael, V. M. Zakharov, N. N. Petrov, A. G. Ryaboshapko, V. N. Ivanov, A. V. Savchenko, Yu. V. Andreev, Yu. A. Puzov, B. G. Danelyan, and V. P. Kulyapin. "Field Experiment on Studying Solar Radiation Passing through Aerosol Layers." *Russian Meteorology and Hydrology* 34, no. 5 (May 2009): 265–73. https://doi.org/ 10.3103/S106837390905001X.

15. Jack Stilgoe *Experiment Earth: Responsible Innovation in Geoengineering.* (Routledge, 2016).

16. Lynn M. Russell et al., "Eastern Pacific Emitted Aerosol Cloud Experiment," *Bulletin of the American Meteorological Society* 94, no. 5 (May 1, 2013): 709–29, https://doi.org/10.1175/BAMS-D-12-00015.1.

17. Reef Trust Partnership, "Annual Work Plan 2020–2021," www.barrierreef.org/ uploads/RTP-Annual-Work-Plan-2020-2021-FINAL.pdf.

18. Keutsch Research Group. "SCoPEx." Harvard University, 2020. https://projects.iq .harvard.edu/keutschgroup/scopex.

19. Keutsch Research Group. "SCoPEx." Harvard University, 2020. https://projects.iq .harvard.edu/keutschgroup/scopex.

20. Keutsch Research Group. "SCoPEx." Harvard University, 2020. https://projects.iq .harvard.edu/keutschgroup/scopex.

21. Steven R. H. Barrett, Rex E. Britter, and Ian A. Waitz. "Global Mortality Attributable to Aircraft Cruise Emissions." *Environmental Science & Technology* 44, no. 19 (October 1, 2010): 7736–42. https://doi.org/10.1021/ es101325r.

22. "Keutsch Group at Harvard – SCoPEx," www.keutschgroup.com/scopex.

23. "News and Updates," *SCoPEx Advisory Committee* (blog), https://scopexac.com/ news-and-updates/.

24. Christina Henriksen, "Open Letter to SCoPEx Advisory Committee," https:// static1.squarespace.com/static/5dfb35a66f00d54ab0729b75/t/603e2167a9c0b96ff b027c8d/1614684519754/Letter+to+Scopex+Advisory+Committee+24+February .pdf.

25. Edward A. Parson, "Starting the Dialogue on Climate Engineering Governance: A World Commission," 2017. www.cigionline.org/publications/starting-dialogue-climate-engineering-governance-world-commission.

26. Ralph Bodle, Sebastian Oberthür, Lena Donat, Gesa Homann, Stephan Sina, and Elizabeth Tedsen. "Options and Proposals for the International Governance of Geoengineering." *Climate Change, Umweltbundesamt / Federal Environment Agency (Germany)* 14/2014.

27. D. G. Victor, "On the Regulation of Geoengineering." *Oxford Review of Economic Policy* 24, no. 2 (June 1, 2008): 322–36. https://doi.org/10.1093/oxrep/grn018.

28. Ibid.

29. Gernot Wagner and Martin L. Weitzman. "Climate Shock: The Economic Consequences of a Hotter Planet." *Population and Development Review* 41, no. 4 (2015): 730–31. https://doi.org/10.1111/j.1728-4457.2015.00100.x.

30. Wake Smith, "The Cost of Stratospheric Aerosol Injection through 2100." *Environmental Research Letters* 15, no. 11 (October 2020): 114004. https://doi.org/10.1088/1748-9326/aba7e7.

31. Sébastien Philippe, "Monitoring and Verifying the Deployment of Solar Geoengineering." In *Governance of the Deployment of Solar Geoengineering*, 71–74. Harvard Project on Climate Agreements, 2019.

32. Wake Smith, "The Cost of Stratospheric Aerosol Injection through 2100."

33. Wake Smith and Gernot Wagner. "Stratospheric Aerosol Injection Tactics and Costs in the First 15 Years of Deployment." *Environmental Research Letters* 13, no. 12 (November 22, 2018): 124001. https://doi.org/10.1088/1748-9326/aae98d.

34. Wake Smith, "The Cost of Stratospheric Aerosol Injection through 2100."

35. Joshua Horton, "Evaluating Solar Geoengineering Deployment Scenarios." In *Governance of the Deployment of Solar Geoengineering*, 37–39. Harvard Project on Climate Agreements, 2019.

36. Edward A. Parson, "Climate Engineering in Global Climate Governance: Implications for Participation and Linkage," *Transnational Environmental Law* 3, no. 1 (2014): 89–110. https://doi.org/10.1017/S2047102513000496.

37. James Rodger Fleming, "Weather as a Weapon: The Troubling History of Geoengineering so Far," September 23, 2010. www.slate.com/id/2268232/.

38. Chad Briggs, "Is Geoengineering a National Security Risk?" *Geoengineering Our Climate Working Paper and Opinion Article Series*, 2013.

39. Peter Irvine, Kerry Emanuel, Jie He, Larry W. Horowitz, Gabriel Vecchi, and David Keith, "Halving Warming with Idealized Solar Geoengineering Moderates Key Climate Hazards." *Nature Climate Change*, March 11, 2019. https://doi.org/10.1038/s41558-019-0398-8.

40. Mike Hulme, *Can Science Fix Climate Change? A Case Against Climate Engineering*. New Human Frontiers Series (Cambridge: Polity Press, 2014).

41. A. Robock, M. Bunzl, B. Kravitz, and G. L. Stenchikov. "A Test for Geoengineering?" *Science* 327, no. 5965 (January 29, 2010): 530–31. https://doi.org/10.1126/science.1186237.

42. Wake Smith and Gernot Wagner. "Stratospheric Aerosol Injection Tactics and Costs in the First 15 Years of Deployment."

43. D. Jamieson, "Ethics and Intentional Climate Change." *Climatic Change* 33, no. 3 (July 1996): 323–36.

44. Mike Hulme, *Can Science Fix Climate Change?*.

45. Jack Stilgoe, *Experiment Earth: Responsible Innovation in Geoengineering*. Routledge, 2016.

46. Clive Hamilton, *Earthmasters: The Dawn of the Age of Climate Engineering* (New Haven: Yale University Press, 2013).
47. Mike Hulme, *Can Science Fix Climate Change?*
48. Daniel Edward Callies, "The Slippery Slope Argument against Geoengineering Research." *Journal of Applied Philosophy* 36, no. 4 (2019): 675–87.
49. Rob Bellamy and Peter Healey, "'Slippery Slope' or 'Uphill Struggle'? Broadening out Expert Scenarios of Climate Engineering Research and Development." *Environmental Science & Policy* 83 (May 2018): 1–10. https://doi.org/10.1016/j.envsci.2018.01.021.
50. W. Brian Arthur, "Competing Technologies, Increasing Returns, and Lock-In by Historical Events." *The Economic Journal* 99, no. 394 (1989): 116–31. https://doi.org/10.2307/2234208.
51. Stan Liebowitz and Stephen Margolis. "Path Dependence, Lock-In, and History." *Journal of Law, Economics and Organization* 11 (February 1, 1995): 205–26. https://doi.org/10.2139/ssrn.1706450.
52. Jack Stilgoe, *Experiment Earth*.
53. Edward Parson and David Keith. "End the Deadlock on Governance of Geoengineering Research." *Science* 339 (2013): 1278–79. https://doi.org/10.1126/science.1232527.
54. Wake Smith, "The Cost of Stratospheric Aerosol Injection through 2100."
55. Jesse L. Reynolds, *The Governance of Solar Geoengineering: Managing Climate Change in the Anthropocene* (Cambridge: Cambridge University Press, 2019). doi:10.1017/9781316676790.
56. Jesse L. Reynolds, *The Governance of Solar Geoengineering*.
57. "Convention on the Prohibition of Military or Any Other Hostile Use of Environmental Modification Techniques." New York, 10 December 1976, United Nations, *Treaty Series* , vol. 1108, p. 151, https://treaties.un.org/Pages/ViewDetails.aspx?src=IND&mtdsg_no=XXVI-1&chapter=26&clang=_en.
58. Jesse L. Reynolds, *The Governance of Solar Geoengineering*.

## 18 Ethics

1. Stephen Mark Gardiner, ed. *Climate Ethics: Essential Readings* (Oxford and New York: Oxford University Press, 2010).
2. Ibid.
3. Ibid.
4. Ibid.
5. Ibid.
6. Ibid.
7. Ibid.
8. Ibid.
9. Union of Concerned Scientists. "Each Country's Share of $CO_2$ Emissions," 2020. www.ucsusa.org/resources/each-countrys-share-co2-emissions.
10. J. Rogelj, D. Shindell, K. Jiang, S. Fifita, P. Forster, V. Ginzburg, C. Handa, H. Kheshgi, S. Kobayashi, E. Kriegler, L. Mundaca, R. Séférian, and M. V. Vilariño, "2018: Mitigation Pathways Compatible with 1.5°C in the Context of Sustainable Development," in *Global Warming of 1.5°C. An IPCC Special Report on the Impacts of Global Warming of 1.5°C above Pre-industrial Levels and Related Global Greenhouse Gas Emission Pathways, in The Context of Strengthening the Global Response to the Threat of Climate Change, Sustainable Development, and Efforts to Eradicate Poverty* [V. Masson-Delmotte, P. Zhai, H.-O. Pörtner,

D. Roberts, J. Skea, P. R. Shukla, A. Pirani, W. Moufouma-Okia, C. Péan, R. Pidcock, S. Connors, J. B. R. Matthews, Y. Chen, X. Zhou, M. I. Gomis, E. Lonnoy, T. Maycock, M. Tignor, and T. Waterfield (eds.)]. 2018.

11. Peter Singer, 2008. "One Atmosphere," *The Global Justice Reader*, ed. Thom Brooks. Oxford: Blackwell Publishing. 667–688. First published in Peter Singer, *One World: The Ethics of Globalization*, 2nd ed. New Haven: Yale University Press, 2002.

12. Ibid.

13. Daniel Edward Callies, *Climate Engineering: A Normative Perspective* (Lexington Books, 2019).

14. D. Jamieson, "Ethics and Intentional Climate Change." *Climatic Change* 33, no. 3 (July 1996): 323–36.

15. Dane Scott, "Insurance Policy or Technological Fix: The Ethical Implications of Framing Solar Radiation Management." In *Engineering the Climate: The Ethics of Solar Radiation Management*, edited by Christopher J. Preston, 151–68 (Lexington, 2012).

16. C. J. Preston, A. Borgmann, H. J. Buck, W. Carr, F. Clingerman, M. Galarraga, B. Hale, et al. *Engineering the Climate: The Ethics of Solar Radiation Management* (Lexington Books, 2012), https://books.google.com/books?id=__7FdtVobcAC.

17. Shinichiro Asayama and Mike Hulme. "Engineering Climate Debt: Temperature Overshoot and Peak-Shaving as Risky Subprime Mortgage Lending." *Climate Policy*, June 14, 2019, 1–10. https://doi.org/10.1080/14693062.2019.1623165.

18. Ibid.

19. Ibid.

20. Joshua Horton and David Keith. "Solar Geoengineering and Obligations to the Global Poor." In *Climate Justice and Geoengineering: Ethics and Policy in the Atmospheric Anthropocene*, edited by Christopher J. Preston (London: Rowman & Littlefield, 2016). www.rowmaninternational.com/books/climate-justice-and-geoengineering.

21. Ibid.

22. Marion Hourdequin, "Climate Change, Climate Engineering, and the 'Global Poor': What Does Justice Require?," *Ethics, Policy & Environment* 21, no. 3 (September 2, 2018): 270–88, https://doi.org/10.1080/21550085.2018.1562525.

23. Hourdequin, Marion. "Climate Change, Climate Engineering, and the 'Global Poor': What Does Justice Require?" *Ethics, Policy & Environment* (January 8, 2019): 1–19. https://doi.org/10.1080/21550085.2018.1562525.

24. Ibid.

25. Ibid.

26. SRMGI. "Our Work – SRMGI." *Solar Radiation Management Governance Initiative* (blog), 2020. www.srmgi.org/about/our-work/.

# 19 Public Perception

1. Lloyd's Register Foundation, "The Lloyd's Register Foundation World Risk Poll 2019," https://wrp.lrfoundation.org.uk/LRF_WorldRiskReport_Book.pdf.

2. Ibid.

3. Ibid.

4. Pew Research Center, "Science and Scientists Held in High Esteem Across Global Publics," September 2020.

5. Pew Research Center, "Climate Change Still Seen as the Top Global Threat, but Cyberattacks a Rising Concern," February 2019.

6. Pew Research Center, "Science and Scientists," 2020.
7. John Cook et al., "Consensus on Consensus: A Synthesis of Consensus Estimates on Human-Caused Global Warming," *Environmental Research Letters* 11, no. 4 (April 2016): 048002, https://doi.org/10.1088/1748-9326/11/4/048002.
8. John Cook et al., "Quantifying the Consensus on Anthropogenic Global Warming in the Scientific Literature," *Environmental Research Letters* 8, no. 2 (June 1, 2013): 024024, https://doi.org/10.1088/1748-9326/8/2/024024.
9. Cook et al., "Consensus on Consensus."
10. James Powell, "Scientists Reach 100% Consensus on Anthropogenic Global Warming," *Bulletin of Science, Technology & Society* 37, no. 4 (December 1, 2017): 183–84, https://doi.org/10.1177/0270467619886266.
11. "James Powell Is Wrong about the 99.99% AGW Consensus," Skeptical Science, https://skepticalscience.com/Powell.html.
12. John Cook, "Understanding and Countering Misinformation about Climate Change," *Handbook of Research on Deception, Fake News, and Misinformation Online*: Advances in Media, Entertainment, and the Arts (IGI Global, 2019), https://doi.org/10.4018/978-1-5225-8535-0.
13. Ibid.
14. Pew Research Center, "Science and Scientists," 2020.
15. Lloyd's Register Foundation, "World Risk Poll 2019."
16. Ibid.
17. Ibid.
18. Pew Research Center, "Science and Scientists," 2020.
19. China Center for Climate Change Communication, "Climate Change in the Chinese Mind Survey Report 2017," November, 2017.
20. "The Consensus Gap," Skeptical Science, https://skepticalscience.com/graphics.php?g=78.
21. Pew Research Center, "Science and Scientists," 2020.
22. Lloyd's Register Foundation, "World Risk Poll 2019."
23. Pew Research Center, "Science and Scientists," 2020.
24. Jared McDonald, Bo MacInnis, and Jon A. Krosnick, "Climate Insights 2020 | Opinion in the States: Surveying American Public Opinion on Climate Change and the Environment," 2020.
25. Jon A. Krosnick, Allyson L. Holbrook, and Penny S. Visser, "The Impact of the Fall 1997 Debate about Global Warming on American Public Opinion," *Public Understanding of Science* 9, no. 3 (July 2000): 239–60, https://doi.org/10.1088/0963-6625/9/3/303.
26. "Climate Insights," Resources for the Future, www.rff.org/publications/data-tools/climate-insights/.
27. "How Americans See Climate Change and the Environment in 7 Charts," *Pew Research Center* (blog), www.pewresearch.org/fact-tank/2020/04/21/how-americans-see-climate-change-and-the-environment-in-7-charts/.
28. "Explore Climate Change in the American Mind," *Yale Program on Climate Change Communication* (blog), http://climatecommunication.yale.edu/visualizations-data/americans-climate-views/.
29. Matthew T. Ballew et al., "Climate Change in the American Mind: Data, Tools, and Trends," *Environment: Science and Policy for Sustainable Development* 61, no. 3 (May 4, 2019): 4–18, https://doi.org/10.1080/00139157.2019.1589300.
30. Anthony Leiserowitz, "Climate Change in the American Mind: National Survey Data on Public Opinion (2008–2018)," February 14, 2020, https://doi.org/10.17605/OSF.IO/JW79P.

31. McDonald, MacInnis, and Krosnick, "Surveying American Public Opinion on Climate Change and the Environment."
32. Ibid.
33. Ibid.
34. Ibid.
35. Ibid.
36. Pew Research Center, "Two-Thirds of Americans Think Government Should Do More on Climate," June, 2020.
37. McDonald, MacInnis, and Krosnick, "Surveying American Public Opinion on Climate Change and the Environment."
38. Ibid.
39. Ibid.
40. Pew Research Center, "Two-Thirds of Americans Think Government Should Do More on Climate," *Pew Research Center Science & Society* (blog), June 23, 2020, www.pewresearch.org/science/2020/06/23/two-thirds-of-americans-think-government-should-do-more-on-climate/.
41. Allan M. Brandt, "Inventing Conflicts of Interest: A History of Tobacco Industry Tactics," *American Journal of Public Health* 102, no. 1 (January 2012): 63–71, https://doi.org/10.2105/AJPH.2011.300292.
42. Ibid.
43. Ibid.
44. "Master Settlement Agreement," Truth Initiative, https://truthinitiative.org/who-we-are/our-history/master-settlement-agreement.
45. Naomi Oreskes and Erik M. Conway, *Merchants of Doubt: How a Handful of Scientists Obscured the Truth on Issues from Tobacco Smoke to Global Warming* (New York: Bloomsbury, 2011).
46. Riley E. Dunlap and Aaron M. McCright, "Organized Climate Change Denial," *The Oxford Handbook of Climate Change and Society*, August 18, 2011, https://doi.org/10.1093/oxfordhb/9780199566600.003.0010.
47. Ibid.
48. "Industry Ignored Its Scientists on Climate – The New York Times," www.nytimes.com/2009/04/24/science/earth/24deny.html.
49. Dunlap and McCright, "Organized Climate Change Denial."
50. Nongovernmental International Panel on Climate Change, "Climate Change Reconsidered II: Fossil Fuels," http://climatechangereconsidered.org/wp-content/uploads/2019/01/Full-Book.pdf.
51. Tik Root, Lisa Friedman, and Hiroko Tabuchi, "Following the Money That Undermines Climate Science (Published 2019)," *The New York Times*, July 10, 2019, sec. Climate, www.nytimes.com/2019/07/10/climate/nyt-climate-newsletter-cei.html.
52. Ibid.
53. Peter J. Jacques, Riley E. Dunlap, and Mark Freeman, "The Organisation of Denial: Conservative Think Tanks and Environmental Scepticism," *Environmental Politics* 17, no. 3 (June 1, 2008): 349–85, https://doi.org/10.1080/09644010802055576.
54. "Opinion | Temperatures Rise, and We're Cooked – The New York Times," www.nytimes.com/2016/09/11/opinion/sunday/temperatures-rise-and-were-cooked.html.
55. Emily Cox, Elspeth Spence, and Nick Pidgeon, "Public Perceptions of Carbon Dioxide Removal in the United States and the United Kingdom," *Nature Climate Change* 10, no. 8 (August 2020): 744–49, https://doi.org/10.1038/s41558-020-0823-z.

56. Elizabeth T. Burns et al., "What Do People Think When They Think about Solar Geoengineering? A Review of Empirical Social Science Literature, and Prospects for Future Research," *Earth's Future* 4, no. 11 (2016): 536–42, https://doi.org/10.1002/2016EF000461.

57. Masahiro Sugiyama et al., "Public Attitudes to Climate Engineering Research and Field Experiments: Preliminary Results of a Web Survey on Students' Perception in Six Asia-Pacific Countries," *Policy Alternatives Research Institute Working Paper Series*, no. 24 (2016): 39.

58. "Greta Thunberg: Climate Change Activist Sets Sail from Plymouth," *BBC News*, August 14, 2019, sec. Devon, www.bbc.com/news/uk-england-devon-49330423.

59. Camilla Cavendish, "Carbon Offset Gold Rush Is Distracting Us from Climate Change," November 22, 2019, www.ft.com/content/e2000050-0c7f-11ea-bb52-34c8d9dc6d84.

60. "One Trillion Trees – Uniting the World to Save Forests and Climate," World Economic Forum, www.weforum.org/agenda/2020/01/one-trillion-trees-world-economic-forum-launches-plan-to-help-nature-and-the-climate/.

61. "Plant a Billion New Trees, Says Nobel Laureate," the Guardian, November 8, 2006, www.theguardian.com/environment/2006/nov/08/kenya.climatechange.

62. Jean-Francois Bastin et al., "The Global Tree Restoration Potential," *Science* 365, no. 6448 (July 5, 2019): 76–79, https://doi.org/10.1126/science.aax0848.

63. "Planting 1.2 Trillion Trees Could Cancel Out a Decade of $CO_2$ Emissions, Scientists Find," Yale E360, https://e360.yale.edu/digest/planting-1-2-trillion-trees-could-cancel-out-a-decade-of-co2-emissions-scientists-find.

64. "Planting 1 Trillion Trees Might Not Actually Be a Good Idea – The Verge," www.theverge.com/2020/1/31/21115862/davos-1-trillion-trees-controversy-world-economic-forum-campaign.

65. Wayne S. Walker et al., "The Role of Forest Conversion, Degradation, and Disturbance in the Carbon Dynamics of Amazon Indigenous Territories and Protected Areas," *Proceedings of the National Academy of Sciences* 117, no. 6 (February 11, 2020): 3015–25, https://doi.org/10.1073/pnas.1913321117.

66. "Trump Administration Furthers Commitment to One Trillion Trees Initiative," October 13, 2020, www.doi.gov/pressreleases/trump-administration-furthers-commitment-one-trillion-trees-initiative.

67. "'Chemtrail' Conspiracy Theorists: The People Who Think Governments Control the Weather," *BBC News*, January 31, 2018, sec. BBC Trending, www.bbc.com/news/blogs-trending-42195511.

68. Dustin Tingley and Gernot Wagner, "Solar Geoengineering and the Chemtrails Conspiracy on Social Media," *Palgrave Communications* 3, no. 1 (October 31, 2017): 1–7, https://doi.org/10.1057/s41599-017-0014-3.

69. Christine Shearer et al., "Quantifying Expert Consensus against the Existence of a Secret, Large-Scale Atmospheric Spraying Program," *Environmental Research Letters* 11, no. 8 (August 2016): 084011, https://doi.org/10.1088/1748-9326/11/8/084011.

70. Tingley and Wagner, "Solar Geoengineering and the Chemtrails Conspiracy on Social Media."

71. Ibid.

72. Christine Merk, Gert Pönitzsch, and Katrin Rehdanz, "Knowledge about Aerosol Injection Does Not Reduce Individual Mitigation Efforts," *Environmental Research Letters* 11, no. 5 (May 1, 2016): 054009, https://doi.org/10.1088/1748-9326/11/5/054009.

73. Carola Braun et al., "Public Perception of Climate Engineering and Carbon Capture and Storage in Germany: Survey Evidence," *Climate Policy* 18, no. 4 (April 21, 2018): 471–84, https://doi.org/10.1080/14693062.2017.1304888.

74. Ibid.
75. David E. Winickoff, Jane A. Flegal, and Asfawossen Asrat, "Engaging the Global South on Climate Engineering Research," *Nature Climate Change* 5, no. 7 (July 2015): 627–34, https://doi.org/10.1038/nclimate2632.
76. Vivianne H. M. Visschers et al., "Beliefs and Values Explain International Differences in Perception of Solar Radiation Management: Insights from a Cross-Country Survey," *Climatic Change* 142, no. 3–4 (June 2017): 531–44, https://doi.org/10.1007/s10584-017-1970-8.
77. Sugiyama et al., "Public Attitudes to Climate Engineering Research and Field Experiments: Preliminary Results of a Web Survey on Students' Perception in Six Asia-Pacific Countries."
78. Cox, Spence, and Pidgeon, "Public Perceptions of Carbon Dioxide Removal in the United States and the United Kingdom."
79. Kimberly S. Wolske et al., "Public Support for Carbon Dioxide Removal Strategies: The Role of Tampering with Nature Perceptions," *Climatic Change* 152, no. 3 (March 1, 2019): 345–61, https://doi.org/10.1007/s10584-019-02375-z.
80. Ibid.
81. Cox, Spence, and Pidgeon, "Public Perceptions of Carbon Dioxide Removal in the United States and the United Kingdom."
82. Aseem Mahajan, Dustin Tingley, and Gernot Wagner, "Fast, Cheap, and Imperfect? US Public Opinion about Solar Geoengineering," *Environmental Politics* 28, no. 3 (April 16, 2019): 523–43, https://doi.org/10.1080/09644016.2018.1479101.
83. Adam Corner and Nick Pidgeon, "Like Artificial Trees? The Effect of Framing by Natural Analogy on Public Perceptions of Geoengineering," *Climatic Change* 130, no. 3 (June 2015): 425–38, https://doi.org/10.1007/s10584-014-1148-6.
84. Cox, Spence, and Pidgeon, "Public Perceptions of Carbon Dioxide Removal in the United States and the United Kingdom."

## 20. The Path Forward for Carbon Removal

1. "Department of Energy Invests $72 Million in Carbon Capture Technologies," Energy.gov, www.energy.gov/articles/department-energy-invests-72-million-carbon-capture-technologies.
2. "U.S. Department of Energy Announces $15 Million in Funding Opportunities for Direct Air Capture Technologies," Energy.gov, www.energy.gov/fe/articles/us-department-energy-announces-15-million-funding-opportunities-direct-air-capture-0.
3. National Academies of Sciences, Engineering, and Medicine, *Negative Emissions Technologies and Reliable Sequestration: A Research Agenda* (Washington, DC: The National Academies Press, 2019), https://doi.org/10.17226/25259.
4. National Academies of Sciences, Engineering, and Medicine, *Negative Emissions Technologies and Reliable Sequestration: A Research Agenda.*
5. United Nations Environment Programme, "The Emissions Gap Report 2017," November 2017, https://wedocs.unep.org/bitstream/handle/20.500.11822/22070/EGR_2017.pdf.
6. Ibid.
7. Energy Innovation: Policy and Technology, "Renewable Energy Prices Hit Record Lows: How Can Utilities Benefit From Unstoppable Solar And Wind?," Forbes, www.forbes.com/sites/energyinnovation/2020/01/21/renewable-energy-prices-hit-record-lows-how-can-utilities-benefit-from-unstoppable-solar-and-wind/.

8. Giulia Realmonte et al., "An Inter-Model Assessment of the Role of Direct Air Capture in Deep Mitigation Pathways," *Nature Communications* 10, no. 1 (July 22, 2019): 3277, https://doi.org/10.1038/s41467-019-10842-5.
9. Ibid.
10. "Global Thermostat Seeks Additional Partnerships to Scale up Technology," *Global Thermostat* (blog), August 15, 2019, https://globalthermostat.com/2019/08/global-thermostat-seeks-additional-partnerships-to-scale-up-technology/.
11. National Academies of Sciences, Engineering, and Medicine, *Negative Emissions Technologies and Reliable Sequestration: A Research Agenda*.
12. Ibid.
13. Ibid.
14. Global CCS Institute, "Global Status of CCS 2020," www.globalccsinstitute.com/wp-content/uploads/2020/12/Global-Status-of-CCS-Report-2020_FINAL_December11.pdf.
15. Institute for Energy Economics and Financial Analysis, "Petra Nova Mothballing Post-Mortem: Closure of Texas Carbon Capture Plant is a Warming Sign," https://ieefa.org/wp-content/uploads/2020/08/Petra-Nova-Mothballing-Post-Mortem_August-2020.pdf.
16. "Petra Nova Mothballing."
17. "Petra Nova Carbon Capture Project Stalls with Cheap Oil," *Energy and Policy Institute* (blog), August 6, 2020, www.energyandpolicy.org/petra-nova/.
18. "Petra Nova Is One of Two Carbon Capture and Sequestration Power Plants in the World – Today in Energy – U.S. Energy Information Administration (EIA)," www.eia.gov/todayinenergy/detail.php?id=33552.
19. Nathalie Thomas, "Environment Groups Question UK's Carbon Capture Push," January 11, 2021, www.ft.com/content/c92f62ce-451b-4727-8bf9-6ce5429d38d7.
20. "Carbon Capture and Storage in Equinor – Equinor.Com," www.equinor.com/en/what-we-do/carbon-capture-and-storage.html.
21. "Driving $CO_2$ Emissions to Zero (and beyond) with Carbon Capture, Use, and Storage | McKinsey," www.mckinsey.com/business-functions/sustainability/our-insights/driving-co2-emissions-to-zero-and-beyond-with-carbon-capture-use-and-storage.
22. Sam Meredith, "Why the World's Largest Carbon Market Is Experiencing a Boom like Never Before," CNBC, May 18, 2021, www.cnbc.com/2021/05/18/why-europes-carbon-market-is-experiencing-a-boom-like-never-before.html.

## 21. The Path Forward for Solar Radiation Management

1. "NSF Award Search: Advanced Search," www.nsf.gov/awardsearch/advancedSearch.jsp.
2. "U.S. Geoengineering Research Gets a Lift with $4 Million from Congress | Science | AAAS," www.sciencemag.org/news/2020/01/us-geoengineering-research-gets-lift-4-million-congress.
3. Ella Necheles et al., "Funding for Solar Geoengineering from 2008 to 2018," https://geoengineering.environment.harvard.edu/blog/funding-solar-geoengineering.
4. Ibid.
5. Ibid.
6. Ibid.
7. John C. Moore (Chief Scientist, GCESS, Beijing Normal University and Research Professor at University of Lapland), in personal communication with the author, March 2021.

8. "China Plans Rapid Expansion of 'Weather Modification' Efforts," *The Guardian*, December 3, 2020, www.theguardian.com/world/2020/dec/03/china-vows-to-boost-weather-modification-capabilities.

9. Yu. A. Izrael et al., "Field Experiment on Studying Solar Radiation Passing through Aerosol Layers," *Russian Meteorology and Hydrology* 34, no. 5 (May 1, 2009): 265–73, https://doi.org/10.3103/S106837390905001X.

10. Jonathan Proctor et al., "Estimating Global Agricultural Effects of Geoengineering Using Volcanic Eruptions," *Nature* 560, no. 7719 (August 2018): 480–83, https://doi.org/10.1038/s41586-018-0417-3.

11. Justin McClellan, David W. Keith, and Jay Apt, "Cost Analysis of Stratospheric Albedo Modification Delivery Systems," *Environmental Research Letters* 7, no. 3 (August 2012): 034019, https://doi.org/10.1088/1748-9326/7/3/034019.

12. National Academies of Sciences, Engineering, and Medicine, "Consensus Study Report Highlights Reflecting Sunlight: Recommendations for Solar Geoengineering Research and Research Governance," March 2021, www.nap.edu/resource/25762/Reflecting%20Sunlight%204-Pager.pdf.

13. Ibid.

14. Ibid.

15. Ibid.

16. National Academies of Sciences, Engineering, and Medicine, *Reflecting Sunlight: Recommendations for Solar Geoengineering Research and Research Governance* (The National Academies Press, 2021), https://doi.org/10.17226/25762.

17. National Academies of Sciences, Engineering, and Medicine, "Consensus Study Report Highlights Reflecting Sunlight: Recommendations for Solar Geoengineering Research and Research Governance."

18. Ibid.

19. National Academies of Sciences, Engineering, and Medicine, *Reflecting Sunlight*.

20. National Academies of Sciences, Engineering, and Medicine, "Consensus Study Report."

21. Ibid.

22. Ibid.

23. Ibid.

24. Ibid

25. Don C. Bingaman et al., "Stratospheric Aerosol Research Experiments and Aircraft for Solar Geoengineering," in *AIAA Scitech 2021 Forum*, AIAA SciTech Forum (American Institute of Aeronautics and Astronautics, 2021), https://doi.org/10.2514/6.2021-1681.

26. Ibid.

27. "Executive Order on Tackling the Climate Crisis at Home and Abroad," The White House, January 27, 2021, www.whitehouse.gov/briefing-room/presidential-actions/2021/01/27/executive-order-on-tackling-the-climate-crisis-at-home-and-abroad/.

28. Ibid.

29. Ibid.

30. Ibid.

31. Ibid.

32. Ibid.

33. "Biden Tells the World 'America Is Back.' The World Isn't so Sure. – The Washington Post," www.washingtonpost.com/politics/biden-us-global-doubts/2021/02/27/3fe52862-781d-11eb-8115-9ad5e9c02117_story.html.

## Appendix: Detail in Respect of Figures 9.4–9.8

1. "Data Supplement to the Global Carbon Budget 2020," ICOS, www.icos-cp.eu/science-and-impact/global-carbon-budget/2020.
2. Jeff Tollefson, "COVID Curbed Carbon Emissions in 2020 – but Not by Much," *Nature* 589, no. 7842 (January 15, 2021): https://doi.org/10.1038/d41586-021-00090-3.
3. "Global Energy Perspective 2021: Energy Landscape | McKinsey," www.mckinsey.com/industries/oil-and-gas/our-insights/global-energy-perspective-2021.
4. "New Energy Outlook 2020 | BNEF," *BloombergNEF* (blog), https://about.bnef.com/new-energy-outlook/.
5. IPCC, "Global Warming of 1.5°C. An IPCC Special Report on the Impacts of Global Warming of 1.5°C above Pre-Industrial Levels and Related Global Greenhouse Gas Emission Pathways, in the Context of Strengthening the Global Response to the Threat of Climate Change, Sustainable Development, and Efforts to Eradicate Poverty," 2018, www.ipcc.ch/site/assets/uploads/sites/2/2019/06/SR15_Full_Report_Low_Res.pdf.
6. "Data Supplement to the Global Carbon Budget 2020."
7. Alexander Popp et al., "Land-Use Futures in the Shared Socio-Economic Pathways," *Global Environmental Change* 42 (January 1, 2017): 331–45, https://doi.org/10.1016/j.gloenvcha.2016.10.002.
8. McKinsey & Company, "Agriculture and Climate Change: Reducing Emissions through Improved Farming Practices," April 2020.
9. Duncan Brack, "Forests and Climate Change," 2019, www.un.org/esa/forests/wp-content/uploads/2019/03/UNFF14-BkgdStudy-SDG13-March2019.pdf.
10. Pierre Friedlingstein et al., "Global Carbon Budget 2020," *Earth System Science Data* 12, no. 4 (December 11, 2020): 3269–3340, https://doi.org/10.5194/essd-12-3269-2020.
11. NOAA US Department of Commerce, "Global Monitoring Laboratory – Carbon Cycle Greenhouse Gases," https://gml.noaa.gov/ccgg/trends/.
12. Mikkel Bennedsen, Eric Hillebrand, and Siem Jan Koopman, "Trend Analysis of the Airborne Fraction and Sink Rate of Anthropogenically Released CO&lt;Sub&gt;2&lt;/Sub&gt;," *Biogeosciences* 16, no. 18 (September 26, 2019): 3651–63, https://doi.org/10.5194/bg-16-3651-2019.
13. Ibid.
14. "Conversion Tables," https://cdiac.ess-dive.lbl.gov/pns/convert.html.
15. Bill Hare and Malte Meinshausen, "How Much Warming Are We Committed to and How Much Can Be Avoided?," *Climatic Change* 75, no. 1–2 (June 2, 2006): 111–49, https://doi.org/10.1007/s10584-005-9027-9.
16. Susan Solomon et al., "Irreversible Climate Change Due to Carbon Dioxide Emissions," *Proceedings of the National Academy of Sciences* 106, no. 6 (February 10, 2009): 1704–9, https://doi.org/10.1073/pnas.0812721106.
17. "RCP Database," https://tntcat.iiasa.ac.at/RcpDb/dsd?Action=htmlpage&page=download.
18. NASA Global Climate Change, "Global Surface Temperature | NASA Global Climate Change," Climate Change: Vital Signs of the Planet, https://climate.nasa.gov/vital-signs/global-temperature.
19. Richard J. Millar et al., "A Modified Impulse-Response Representation of the Global near-Surface Air Temperature and Atmospheric Concentration Response to Carbon Dioxide Emissions," *Atmospheric Chemistry and Physics* 17, no. 11 (June 16, 2017): 7213–28, https://doi.org/10.5194/acp-17-7213-2017.

20. Ibid.

21. "Atmospheric Greenhouse Gas Concentrations – European Environment Agency," Indicator Assessment, www.eea.europa.eu/data-and-maps/indicators/atmospheric-greenhouse-gas-concentrations/atmospheric-greenhouse-gas-concentrations-assessment-1.

22. "AR5 Climate Change 2013: The Physical Science Basis – IPCC," www.ipcc.ch/report/ar5/wg1/.

23. "Topic 2: Future Changes, Risks and Impacts," IPCC 5th Assessment Synthesis Report, 2021, http://ar5-syr.ipcc.ch/topic_futurechanges.php.

24. Andrew H. MacDougall et al., "Is There Warming in the Pipeline? A Multi-Model Analysis of the Zero Emissions Commitment from $CO_2$," *Biogeosciences* 17, no. 11 (June 15, 2020): 2987–3016, https://doi.org/10.5194/bg-17-2987-2020.

25. H. Damon Matthews and Kirsten Zickfeld, "Climate Response to Zeroed Emissions of Greenhouse Gases and Aerosols," *Nature Climate Change* 2, no. 5 (May 2012): 338–41, https://doi.org/10.1038/nclimate1424.

26. Ibid.

27. Thomas Frederikse et al., "The Causes of Sea-Level Rise since 1900," *Nature* 584, no. 7821 (August 2020): 393–97, https://doi.org/10.1038/s41586-020-2591-3.

28. Rebecca Lindsey, "Climate Change: Global Sea Level," January 25, 2021, www.climate.gov/news-features/understanding-climate/climate-change-global-sea-level.

29. IPCC 2019, "IPCC Special Report on the Ocean and Cryosphere in a Changing Climate," n.d., www.ipcc.ch/site/assets/uploads/sites/3/2019/12/SROCC_Full Report_FINAL.pdf.

30. Alexander Nauels et al., "Attributing Long-Term Sea-Level Rise to Paris Agreement Emission Pledges," *Proceedings of the National Academy of Sciences* 116, no. 47 (November 19, 2019): 23487–92, https://doi.org/10.1073/pnas.1907461116.

31. Tamsin L. Edwards et al., "Projected Land Ice Contributions to Twenty-First-Century Sea Level Rise," *Nature* 593, no. 7857 (May 2021): 74–82, https://doi.org/10.1038/s41586-021-03302-y.

32. Robert M. DeConto et al., "The Paris Climate Agreement and Future Sea-Level Rise from Antarctica," *Nature* 593, no. 7857 (May 2021): 83–89, https://doi.org/10.1038/s41586-021-03427-0.

# INDEX